The Porter Sargent Handbook Series

GUIDE TO PRIVATE
SPECIAL EDUCATION

PUBLISHER'S STATEMENT

Esteemed educational and social critic Porter Sargent established *The Handbook of Private Schools* in 1914, with the aim "to present a comprehensive and composite view of the private school situation as it is today. No attempt has been made at completeness. The effort on the contrary has been to include only the best, drawing the line somewhat above the average."

Today, **The Porter Sargent Handbook Series** continues its founder's mission: to serve parents, educators and others concerned with the independent and critical evaluation of primary and secondary educational options, leading to a suitable choice for each student.

The Handbook of Private Schools, Guide to Summer Programs (1924) and *Guide to Private Special Education* (2011) provide the tools for objective comparison of programs in their respective fields.

GUIDE TO PRIVATE
SPECIAL EDUCATION

A DESCRIPTIVE SURVEY OF
SPECIAL-NEEDS SCHOOLS
AND PROGRAMS

SECOND EDITION
2013/14

PORTER SARGENT HANDBOOKS
A Division of Carnegie Communications

2 LAN Drive, Suite 100
Westford, Massachusetts 01886
Tel: 978-842-2812   Fax: 978-692-2304
info@portersargent.com   www.portersargent.com

ISBN 978-0-87558-175-0
ISSN 2166-1499

3 9547 00376 3617

All information as reported to Porter Sargent Handbooks as of October 12, 2012. Programs and organizations should be contacted for updated information.

Cost: US$32.00 plus shipping and handling. Additional copies are available from booksellers, or from Porter Sargent Handbooks, 2 LAN Dr., Ste. 100, Westford, MA 01886. Tel: 978-692-9708. Fax: 978-692-2304. info@portersargent.com. www.portersargent.com.

TABLE OF CONTENTS

This index assists the reader in quickly identifying appropriate programs by grouping special-needs conditions into broader categories. The reader can then advance to the geographically organized editorial listings to learn more about potentially suitable programs.

ADHD

Blindness/Visual Impairment

Deaf-Blindness

Deafness

Hearing Impairment

Emotional Disturbances

(includes Anorexia Nervosa, Anxiety Disorders, Bulimia, Conduct Disorder, Mood Disorder, Obsessive/Compulsive Disorder, Oppositional Defiant Disorder, Posttraumatic Stress Disorder, Prader-Willi Syndrome, Psychosis, Schizophrenia, School Phobia, Sex Offender, Sexually Abused)

Intellectual Disabilities

(includes Down Syndrome)

Learning Disabilities

(includes Auditory Processing Disorders, Dyscalculia, Dysgraphia, Dyslexia, Dyspraxia, Nonverbal LD)

Multiple Disabilities

Orthopedic/Neurological Impairments

(includes Apraxia, Arthritis, Cerebral Palsy, Cleft Lip/Cleft Palate, Infantile Paralysis, Multiple Sclerosis, Muscular Dystrophy, Neurofibromatosis, Spina Bifida)

Pervasive Developmental Disorders

(includes Asperger's Syndrome, Autism)

Speech/Language Impairments
  (includes Aphasia)
Substance Abuse
Traumatic Brain Injury
Other Health Impairments
  (includes Cardiac Disorders, Cystic Fibrosis, Diabetes, Epilepsy, Hemophilia, Leukemia, Sickle Cell Anemia, and Tourette's Syndrome)

PROGRAM LISTINGS *(listed alphabetically by program name within each state)*

GUIDE TO PRIVATE SPECIAL EDUCATION

Senior Editor   Daniel P. McKeever

Production Manager   Leslie A. Weston

PORTER SARGENT HANDBOOKS
A division of Carnegie Communications

President & CEO   Joseph F. Moore

Executive Vice President,
Operations   Meghan Dalesandro

PREFACE

This Second Edition of the *Guide to Private Special Education* continues the tradition of *The Directory for Exceptional Children*. Published over a span of more than 50 years, the 16 editions of the *Directory* covered a broad spectrum of programs for children and young adults with developmental, emotional, physical and medical disabilities. The *Guide* continues Porter Sargent Handbooks' long tradition of serving the special-needs community. Many educational programs that formerly appeared in the *Directory* have been included in this new reference.

As it now focuses upon special-education schools, the biennial *Guide* nicely complements the other two Porter Sargent Handbooks: *The Handbook of Private Schools* and the *Guide to Summer Programs*. All three of our titles deal primarily with private programs for elementary and secondary students.

Programs in the *Guide* serve boys and girls with a wide range of special needs. With education being the focus, various learning differences are now the most common of the special needs addressed. Programs for students with emotional, developmental and physical special needs are also well represented, however.

As part of this title's natural evolution, the Second Edition of the *Guide* concentrates specifically on educational programs. Those familiar with the *Directory* and the First Edition of the *Guide* will note this continuing shift in emphasis from clinical and hospital programs to school settings. As a consequence of this changing approach, programs that consist entirely of early intervention and diagnostic services have been removed from the *Guide*. Many of the remaining programs that deal with very young populations, however, do provide these services. Provided they also offer educational programming, these facilities are suitable for listing and thus appear in the Second Edition.

In order to present as many facts as possible in a concise format, it has been necessary to abbreviate statistical information that appears throughout the *Guide*. In all cases, we have attempted to use simple and straightforward abbreviations. The Key to Abbreviations, which begins on page 23, assists the reader in gaining familiarization with these abbreviations. In the Key, the reader will also find our abbreviations for the special-needs conditions represented in the listings.

Detailed information describing each program is presented at no cost or obligation to the facilities. Statistics are printed as supplied in response to our questionnaire, enabling smooth and rapid processing of data. From an aggregate of information, aspects that impartially and objectively depict programs and services are selected for the *Guide*'s objective paragraph descriptions. These paragraph descriptions, like the remainder of the free editorial listings, are composed by the Porter Sargent Handbooks staff. The short descriptions are not intended to be promotional or advertising pieces for the programs; as a result, factual information is the focus.

Although we strive for maximum information in each editorial listing, length and content of entries are solely dependent on the material elicited from each program. The quality of a facility, therefore, should not be measured by the length of its listing.

Associations and Organizations, a section that follows the editorial listings, presents entities dedicated to special-needs children and their families. Included here are organizations relating to accreditation, advocacy, special-needs professionals and recreation.

Parents should view this book as a preliminary source for appropriate programs for their children's special needs. Finding the right environment for each student is an individual search, and inclusion in the *Guide* does not constitute an endorsement. It is vitally important to gather as much firsthand information as possible before a decision is made. Visit the facilities and talk with administrators and staff. The more thorough your research, the more likely you are to choose the proper setting for the young person's growth and development.

We hope that this *Guide* will enjoy popularity and wide usage, and that it may prove helpful to those concerned with special-needs children. Our readership's comments on facilities listed in this volume and notification of those closed, omitted or newly established will be invaluable in ensuring that forthcoming editions may continue to present the most complete and accurate data on educational programs for special-needs children, adolescents and young adults.

In closing, we wish to thank the many program administrators who updated their listings by completing our questionnaire. Their responses to our queries for new information have enabled our editors to present the most accurate and up-to-date possible data on each program.

HOW TO READ THE PROGRAM LISTINGS

The information presented in the Guide *is arranged in a standardized format to facilitate ready comparison of programs. In searching for programs to fulfill special needs, one should first consult the Program Emphasis Index, by state, city and special needs addressed.*

The Guide *is organized alphabetically by state. The listing of programs within a state is arranged alphabetically by program name.*

1.   **PORTER SARGENT SCHOOL**

Bdg and Day — Coed Ages 12-18

2. Westford, MA 01886. 2 LAN Dr, Ste 100.
   Tel: 978-692-9708. TTY: 978-692-0000. Fax: 978-692-2304.
   www.portersargent.com E-mail: info@portersargent.com.
3. **Bill Covaleski**, BA, MA, Head. **Garrett Oliver**, BA, MEd, Prin.
   David Yarrington, Adm.
4. **Conditions: Primary**—ED Mood. **Sec**—ADHD Dlx LD. **IQ 80 and up. Not accepted**—SO.
5. **Gen Acad. Underachiever.** Gr 7-12. **AP classes** (Calc). **Feat**—Creative_ Writing Fr Span Stats Comp_Sci Studio_Art Drama Music. **Avg SAT:** CR 520. M 535. W 510. ESL. SAT/ACT prep. Interscholastic sports. **Expected outcome:** Return to local school (Avg stay: 12-18 mos).
6. **Therapy:** Hear Lang Music Phys Speech. **Psychotherapy:** Fam Group. **Counseling:** Educ.
7 **Adm:** Appl fee: $50. Appl due: Rolling. On-campus interview.
8. **Enr:** 106. (Cap: 125). Bdg 50. Day 56. B 45. G 61. **Prof staff:** 30 (Full 20, Part 10). **Fac:** 24 (Full 16, Part 8). Spec ed 10. Lay 14.
9. **Tui '12-'13:** $42,950-45,000/sch yr (+$2500). Day Rate $30,750-37,500/sch yr (+$1650). **Aid:** School 9 ($102,000). State 15 (100% of tui). **Summer prgm:** Day. Tui Day $2500. 5 wks.
10. Endow $2,000,000. Plant value $13,500,000. Acres 5. Bldgs 2 (100% ADA). Dorms 2. Class rms 21. Lib 8500 vols. Sci labs 3. Art studios 1. Gyms 1. Fields 4. Courts 2. Pools 1. Comp labs 1. Laptop prgm Gr 9-12.
11. **Est 1914.** Nonprofit. **Spons:** National Association for Special-Needs Children.
12.   PSS serves adolescents with emotional and related learning problems. Prescriptive treatment plans are designed for each student and are incorporated into the total therapeutic educational process. Small classes and one-on-one tutorials facilitate academic development. The school's goal is to prepare each student for reentry into the educational mainstream as soon as he or she is capable.
     Counseling and family support services are integral to the program.

1. FACILITY NAME and TYPE. Gender and age range of individuals accepted are provided here.

2. CITY or TOWN; STATE; ZIP CODE; STREET/MAILING ADDRESS; TELEPHONE, TTY and FAX NUMBERS; and E-MAIL and WEBSITE ADDRESSES. If a program has locations at more than one site, the additional location address(es) will be at the end of this section.

3. DIRECTOR(S) OF PROGRAM. One or two head administrators may be listed, depending upon who is directly responsible for facility leadership. Academic degrees and relevant licenses held by the director(s) are often noted. The director of admissions or intake (or the administrator who fills this role) immediately follows, unless the head administrator serves in this capacity.

4. CONDITIONS ACCEPTED. Special needs of primary concern for treatment or diagnosis appear first, followed by SECONDARY CONDITIONS. The INTELLIGENCE QUOTIENT RANGE of children eligible for acceptance is often given. NOT ACCEPTED indicates that the facility does not admit individuals with the condition(s) cited.

For a complete Key to Abbreviations, see page 23.

5. ACADEMIC ORIENTATION, GRADES OFFERED, CURRICULUM, SPECIAL PROGRAMS, STANDARDIZED TEST SCORES and EXPECTED OUTCOME. For programs with an educational or vocational component, the basic curriculum is described as college preparatory, general academic or vocational. If a program is ungraded, a notation appears; otherwise, the facility's grade range is listed. AP CLASSES indicates regularly offered Advanced Placement courses. Available in the upper high school grades, courses listed here follow the curriculum formulated by the College Board and prepare students for standardized Advanced Placement examinations. Other noteworthy academic courses and vocational offerings follow.

Secondary school listings may include average critical reading, math and writing Scholastic Aptitude Test (SAT) scores, in addition to ACT assessment results. In some cases, combined critical reading/math or critical reading/math/writing scores (designated by "CR/M" or "CR/M/W") are relayed. Also, some listings include mid-50th percentile SAT and ACT scores instead of (or in addition to) straight averages.

Schools that that offer interscholastic sports are so noted. Outcome information comes next. If most boys and girls remain at the facility until graduation, GRADUATION is the designated outcome. Programs that instead aim to return the student to a mainstream academic setting may provide AVERAGE LENGTH OF STAY information; if so, a time estimate follows.

6. THERAPY, PSYCHOTHERAPY and COUNSELING OFFERINGS are cited where applicable. See the Glossary and Key to Abbreviations for further details.

7. ADMISSIONS. The school's application fee appears first, followed by the annual application due month (or ROLLING or YEAR-ROUND if applications are considered throughout the year). Facilities requiring in-person application interviews are so designated by ON-CAMPUS INTERVIEW.

8. ENROLLMENT and STAFF. The total number of students enrolled during the current academic year is reported with the following breakdowns: number of boarders, number of day pupils, number of boys and number of girls.

   Staff figures may include PROFESSIONAL STAFF (and full- and part-time breakdowns) and TEACHING FACULTY. In addition to full- and part-time faculty breakdowns, listings frequently include the numbers of SPECIAL EDUCATION and LAY instructors.

9. TUITION, FINANCIAL ASSISTANCE and SUMMER SESSION. When both boarding and day divisions are maintained, both rates are given, unless the program failed to provide this data.

   Rate ranges (e.g., $30,750-37,500/sch yr) show the fee span from the lowest to the highest grade, age range or level of care. The facility's estimate of extra expenses incurred by the average student follows in parentheses.

   In some instances, sliding-scale rates are reported, indicating that a fee schedule is based on each family's ability to pay. Clinical rates are generally given per session or per hour.

   Availability of FINANCIAL AID follows rates. When the facility supplies the number of financial aid recipients and the total monetary value of the awards, this information is detailed. STATE AID indicates that the program is licensed to receive state funding for special-needs students. Where available, the number of students covered by state aid is included, and a parenthetical reference typically indicates that 100% of tuition expenses (and, in many cases, transportation costs) are paid by the state.

   SUMMER PROGRAM. The type and orientation are given for facilities operating distinct summer sessions. This information does not appear in the listings of year-round programs.

10. PLANT EVALUATION and ENDOWMENT. Following the dollar values of the endowment and the physical plant is a brief listing of the school's facilities. When the school has supplied this data, listings parenthetically indicate the percentage of school buildings that meet the standards set in the wake of the Americans with Disabilities Act. Schools that require students to rent or purchase laptop computers for class work are designated by LAPTOP PRGM and the grade range associated with this one-to-one program.

11. ESTABLISHMENT and ORGANIZATIONAL STRUCTURE. The date of establishment, the organizational nature, the religious affiliation and the sponsoring organization follow.

12. PARAGRAPH DESCRIPTION. Additional information about programs, unique aspects, limitations and other features not adaptable to abbreviated presentation is compiled by our editors on the basis of information provided by the facility.

GLOSSARY

adaptive physical education: Provided for students who are cannot take part in a mainstream physical education program. Participation in this program is often mandated by the student's Individualized Education Program (see description below).

aqua therapy: Performed in a warm-water pool, this form of physical therapy benefits those recovering from orthopedic injuries and the like. Particularly useful for patients who are unable to tolerate weight-bearing exercises.

art therapy: A form of psychotherapy that uses the creative process of art making to improve and enhance the physical, mental and emotional well-being of the client.

attentional disorder: A developmental disorder typically characterized by developmentally inappropriate levels of inattention, overactivity and impulsiveness. Symptoms—which are neurologically based and are not due to gross neurological impairment, sensory impairment, language or motor impairment, mental retardation or emotional disturbance—arise in early childhood and tend to be chronic.

auditory processing: The process by which one's brain interprets sounds around him or her. Those with disorders in this area have difficulty processing or interpreting incoming aural information.

behavioral disorder: See **emotional disturbance.**

chemotherapy: Treatment of a disease with drugs or chemical agents that are selectively toxic to the disease's causative agent.

clinic: Often affiliated with a hospital, medical center or university, this facility provides diagnostic and treatment services on a short-term, outpatient basis.

dance therapy: Also referred to as movement therapy, this form of psychotherapy uses movement as a means of improving the client's social, cognitive and physical integration skills.

early intervention program: Applying to children of kindergarten age or younger, this program treats children who either have a handicapping condition or are at risk of developing one. Early intervention seeks to lessen the effects of the client's condition(s), and it can be used to remediate an existing developmental problem or to prevent a condition from occurring.

educational counseling: A means of improving the student's academic performance, often by identifying obstacles the pupil faces and devising ways to overcome these obstacles.

emotional disturbance: Also referred to as behavioral disorder, this condition causes notable impairments in academic, social or occupational functioning (or a combination of these elements). Evident in childhood when a student exhibits a repetitive and persistent pattern of behavior that significantly disrupts other pupils, emotional disturbance may involve aggressive behavior toward others; bullying, threats or other intimidating behavior; physical abuse of others; willful destruction of property; lack of empathy; the absence of guilt or remorse when such feelings are appropriate; or a tendency to blame others for one's own misdeeds.

equine therapy: Also called equine-assisted therapy, this form of psychotherapy employs horses to promote emotional growth. By working with a horse, patients explore their feelings, behaviors, boundaries and, in cases of chemical addiction, impediments to recovery.

fine motor: Small-muscle movements in the fingers that are coordinated with the eyes.

genetic counseling: Conducted with expectant mothers or expectant couples, this process involves the evaluation of family history and medical records, the scheduling of genetic tests, an evaluation of these test results, and a consultation with the parents in light of their test findings.

gross motor: Movements of the large muscles of the body.

hydrotherapy: Bathing in hot or cold water (often alternately) as a form of relief for various physical ailments.

hypnotherapy: Exercises that put the client into a deep state of relaxation and an altered state of consciousness, also known as a trance. Therapy performed during this state of awareness often helps patients alter their bodily functions or psychological responses.

Individualized Education Plan [or Program] (IEP): According to guidelines devised by the United States Department of Education, each public school child who receives special education and related services must have an IEP, which is a personalized document that is jointly created by parents, teachers, school administrators, relevant service providers and, when appropriate, the student him- or herself. The IEP sets forth an educational strategy intended to improve educational results for the special-needs child.

intermediate care facility: A healthcare setting for individuals with disabilities or nonacute illnesses who require less intensive care than that provided at a hospital or a skilled nursing facility.

learning disability: A neurological disorder that does not indicate a lack of intelligence, this lifelong condition results from a difference in the way a person's brain operates. Those with learning disabilities may have difficulty reading, writing, spelling, reasoning, recalling or organizing information (or some combination thereof) if forced to figure things out by themselves or if taught by conventional methods. While there is no cure for learning disabilities, professional support and intervention can help individuals with learning disabilities experience success in school and, subsequently, in a career.

massage therapy: A system of stroking, pressing and kneading designed to relieve pain or to relax, stimulate or tone the body. Although primarily beneficial to muscles just beneath the skin, it may also affect deeper layers of muscle.

milieu therapy: Often provided in a hospital setting, this treatment attempts to put the patient in an environment conducive to his or her emotional and interpersonal needs. Patients and staff together form the community; the milieu offers structure, safety and mutual support, and it encourages active participation through an open flow of communication and feedback.

movement therapy: See **dance therapy.**

music therapy: Utilizes music to address the physical, emotional, cognitive and social needs of the client. Typical treatment goals are stress management, pain reduction, memory enhancement, physical rehabilitation and communication improvement.

nonprofit: Refers to private institutions that are legally categorized as Section 501(c)(3) organizations.

nutritional counseling: Consultation with a nutritionist designed to improve general health through an improved diet.

occupational therapy: Treatment intended to foster a greater level of independence in the client's life. Services may include one or more of the following: customized treatment programs designed to improve one's ability to perform daily activities, home or job site evaluations that are followed by adaptation recommendations, performance skills assessments and treatment, adaptive equipment recommendations and usage training, or guidance to family members and caregivers.

on-the-job training: A structured, supervised training method that seeks to broaden employee skills and increase productivity.

outpatient: Typically provided in a clinical setting, these hourly or otherwise short-term treatment or evaluation sessions differ in length from traditional day programs.

partial hospitalization: Programming for patients who require intensive care to remain in their communities, but do not require 24-hour supervision.

perceptual motor: The system of nerve pathways that processes incoming sensory information, organizes it, interprets it and then responds to it.

physical therapy: Treatment that seeks to restore function, improve mobility, relieve pain, and prevent or limit permanent physical disabilities in patients who have sustained injuries or who are suffering from a disease.

play therapy: This structured, theoretically based treatment utilizes the normal communicative and learning processes of children to remedy emotional or social skills deficits. While treatment can take many different forms, play therapy differs from traditional play in that a therapist works with the child to resolve his or her problems.

postgraduate: Typically a year in duration, "PG" offers course work to high school graduates who wish to bolster their academic credentials, improve their readiness for college, or both.

preschool: For reasons of standardization, "PS" in the statistical portion of the editorial listings refers to any schooling prior to five-year-old kindergarten (for example, nursery, transitional kindergarten or prekindergarten), regardless of how the institution itself refers to such programming.

recreational therapy: Also referred to as therapeutic recreation, this seeks to restore, remediate or rehabilitate the patient to improve functioning and independence, as well as to reduce or eliminate the effects of illness or disability. Therapists employ treatment, educational and recreational services to help individuals with illnesses or special needs develop and utilize their leisure pursuits to improve their health, functional abilities, level of independence and quality of life.

rehabilitation: Services for individuals who have sustained severe injury, a trauma, a stroke, an infection, a tumor, surgery or a progressive disease. Treatment typically centers on physical therapy, occupational therapy, and the treatment of pain and inflammation.

sensory integration: Disorders in this area result in unusual—generally, but not always, overreactive—responses to touch or movement.

sheltered workshop: A supportive working environment in which individuals with physical or mental special needs acquire job skills and vocational experience.

sliding-scale fee range: The reduced fees that some facilities charge to low-income clients. Sliding-scale fees are typically calculated based upon the family's annual income.

special education: School programming designed for special-needs children.

supported employment: Competitive work in integrated work settings for clients with severe special needs. These individuals have not typically engaged in previous remunerative employment, and they usually are in need of ongoing support services (such as job coaches, transportation, assistive technology, specialized job training or close supervision) to perform a job.

TTY (teletypewriter): A telephone-like device than enables deaf or hearing- or speech-impaired individuals to converse through typed communication with others who have a similar device.

tutoring: One-on-one or small-group instruction for students requiring extra assistance in a subject.

ungraded: School programs that group students by age, not by the grades utilized in the traditional 12-grade American system.

vocational: Training or counseling relating to a special skill that the client intends to pursue as a trade.

KEY TO ABBREVIATIONS
CONDITIONS ACCEPTED

ADHD	Attention Deficit Hyperactivity Disorder	**ID**	Intellectual Disabilities
AN	Anorexia Nervosa	**IP**	Infantile Paralysis
Anx	Anxiety Disorders	**LD**	Learning Disabilities
Ap	Aphasia	**Lk**	Leukemia
APD	Auditory Processing Disorders	**MD**	Muscular Dystrophy
Apr	Apraxia	**Mood**	Mood Disorder
Ar	Arthritis	**MS**	Multiple Sclerosis
As	Asthma	**Multi**	Multiple Disabilities
Asp	Asperger's Syndrome	**Nf**	Neurofibromatosis
Au	Autism	**NLD**	Nonverbal Learning Disabilities
Bu	Bulimia	**OCD**	Obsessive–Compulsive Disorder
B/VI	Blindness/Visual Impairment	**ODD**	Oppositional Defiant Disorder
C	Cardiac Disorder	**ON**	Orthopedic/Neurological Impairments
CD	Conduct Disorder	**PDD**	Pervasive Developmental Disorder
CF	Cystic Fibrosis		
CLP	Cleft Lip/Cleft Palate	**Psy**	Psychosis
CP	Cerebral Palsy	**PTSD**	Posttraumatic Stress Disorder
D	Deafness	**PW**	Prader–Willi Syndrome
D-B	Deaf-Blindness	**S**	Speech Impairments
Db	Diabetes	**SA**	Sexually Abused
Dc	Dyscalculia	**SB**	Spina Bifida
Dg	Dysgraphia	**SC**	Sickle Cell Anemia
Dx	Dyslexia	**SO**	Sex Offender
Dpx	Dyspraxia	**SP**	School Phobia
DS	Down Syndrome	**Subst**	Substance Abuse
ED	Emotional Disturbances	**Sz**	Schizophrenia
Ep	Epilepsy	**TBI**	Traumatic Brain Injury
Hemo	Hemophilia	**TS**	Tourette's Syndrome
HI	Hearing Impairment		

GENERAL ABBREVIATIONS

Commonly accepted abbreviations do not appear on this list. For further clarification, refer to How to Read the Program Listings.

Acad	Academic
Actg	Acting
Adm	Admissions, Director of Admission(s)
AP	Advanced Placement
Appl	Application

Cap	Capacity
Clin	Clinical
Chair	Chairperson
Chrm	Chairman
Comp	Comparative, Computer
Coord	Coordinate, Coordinator
CR	Critical Reading (SAT Score)
CR/M	Critical Reading/Math (Combined SAT Score)
CR/M/W	Critical Reading/Math/Writing (Combined SAT Score)
Crse	Course
Dev	Development, Developmental
Ec, Econ	Economics
Elem	Elementary (Preschool–Grade 8)
Endow	Endowment
Enr	Enrollment
Enrich	Enrichment
Environ	Environmental
Head	Head of School, Headmaster, Headmistress
Hort	Horticulture
Indiv	Individual
IQ	Intelligence Quotient
Japan	Japanese
Journ	Journalism
M	Math (SAT Score)
Neuro	Neurological
Occup	Occupational
On-Job	On-the-Job
PG	Postgraduate
Prgm	Program
PS	Preschool
Rem	Remedial
Sec	Secondary (Grades 9–PG)
Sem	Semester
Shelt	Sheltered
Spec	Special
Stud	Studies
Ther	Therapy, Therapeutic
Trng	Training
TTY	Teletypwriter Number
W	Writing (SAT Score)

DEGREES AND PROFESSIONAL TITLES

ACSW	Academy of Certified Social Workers
AuD	Doctor of Audiology
BA	Bachelor of Arts
BBA	Bachelor of Business Administration
BD	Bachelor of Divinity
BEd	Bachelor of Education
BFA	Bachelor of Fine Arts
BS	Bachelor of Science
BSN	Bachelor of Science in Nursing
BSOT	Bachelor of Science in Occupational Therapy
BSPT	Bachelor of Science in Physical Therapy
BSW	Bachelor of Social Work
CB	Bachelor of Surgery
CCC	Certificate of Clinical Competence
CSW	Clinical Social Worker
DMD	Doctor of Dental Medicine
DMH	Doctor of Mental Health
DO	Doctor of Osteopathy
DPA	Doctor of Public Administration
DPH	Doctor of Public Health
DSW	Doctor of Social Work
EdD	Doctor of Education
EdS	Educational Specialist
LCSW	Licensed Certified Social Worker
LCSW-C	Licensed Certified Social Worker-Clinical
LCSW-R	Licensed Certified Social Worker-Reimbursement
LICSW	Licensed Independent Clinical Social Worker
LISW	Licensed Independent Social Worker
LMFT	Licensed Marriage and Family Therapist
LMSW	Licensed Master Social Worker
LPT	Licensed Physical Therapist
LSW	Licensed Social Worker
MA	Master of Arts
MAT	Master of Arts in Teaching
MB	Bachelor of Medicine
MBA	Master of Business Administration
MD	Doctor of Medicine
MDiv	Master of Divinity
MEd	Master of Education
MFA	Master of Fine Arts
MHA	Master of Hospital Administration
MHR	Master of Human Relations

MN	Master of Nursing
MPA	Master of Public Administration
MPH	Master of Public Health
MPS	Master in Personnel Service
MS	Master of Science
MSA	Master of Science in Accounting
MSEd	Master of Science in Education
MSN	Master of Science in Nursing
MSP	Master of Science in Planning
MSPC	Master of Science in Professional Communication
MSpecEd	Master in Special Education
MSSA	Master of Science in Social Administration
MSSW	Master of Science in Social Work
MST	Master of Science for Teachers, Master of Science and Technology
MSW	Master of Social Work
OD	Doctor of Optometry
OTR	Registered Occupational Therapist
OTR/L	Registered, Licensed Occupational Therapist
PhD	Doctor of Philosophy
PSW	Psychiatric Social Worker
PsyD	Psychology Doctorate
RN	Registered Nurse
RPT	Registered Physical Therapist
ScD	Doctor of Science
STM	Master of Sacred Theology

FEATURED SCHOOLS

Schools in this section have paid for space to supplement their basic descriptions in the editorial listing section of the book.

If your child is struggling with school...

"*Someone mentioned to me that if I had a creative and bright child, he would thrive at Winston Prep.*

Winston changed his life."

Jenifer Levin, mother of Mak Levin
Winston Prep Class of 2008
Roger Williams University Class of 2012

...we can help.

The
Winston
Preparatory
Schools

NEW YORK
126 W. 17th St.
New York City, NY 10011
646.638.2705 x634

CONNECTICUT
57 West Rocks Road
Norwalk, CT 06851
203.229.0465 x535

www.winstonprep.edu

The mission of The Woodhall School is to provide an opportunity for success to young men of above-average intellectual ability in grades 9-12, who have had difficulties in traditional school environments. The school embraces an individualized approach that allows each student to realize his potential and to take accountability in all areas of his life.

The school's individualized approach includes an interpersonal and intrapersonal component that permeates the four pillars of The Woodhall School: Academics, Athletics, Residential Life and Communications.

The Woodhall School
P. O. Box 550
58 Harrison Lane
Bethlehem, CT 06751
203-266-7788

www.woodhallschool.org
woodhallschool@woodhallschool.org

PROGRAM EMPHASIS
INDEX

USING THE PROGRAM EMPHASIS INDEX

The index that follows assists the reader in quickly identifying appropriate programs by grouping special-needs conditions into broader categories. The reader can then advance to the geographically organized editorial listings to learn more about potentially suitable programs. See the list below for special-needs abbreviations and categorization.

ADHD   Attention Deficit Hyperactivity Disorder

B   Birth

B/VI   Blindness/Visual Impairment

Deaf/Blind   Deaf-Blindness

Deaf   Deafness

Hear   Hearing Impairment

Emot Disturb   Emotional Disturbances
                      includes Anorexia Nervosa, Anxiety Disorders,
                      Bulimia, Conduct Disorder, Mood Disorder, Obsessive/
                      Compulsive Disorder, Oppositional Defiant Disorder,
                      Posttraumatic Stress Disorder, Prader-Willi Syndrome,
                      Psychosis, Schizophrenia, School Phobia, Sex Offender,
                      Sexually Abused

ID   Intellectual Disabilities
                      includes Down Syndrome

LD   Learning Disabilities
                      includes Auditory Processing Disorders, Dyscalculia,
                      Dysgraphia, Dyslexia, Dyspraxia, Nonverbal LD

Multi   Multiple Disabilities

N   Not Accepted—indicates that the program does not accept
                      individuals with condition(s) specified

Ortho/Neuro   Orthological/Neurological Disorders
                      includes Apraxia, Arthritis, Cerebral Palsy, Cleft Lip/
                      Cleft Palate, Infantile Paralysis, Multiple Sclerosis,
                      Muscular Dystrophy, Neurofibromatosis, Spina Bifida

P   Primary—indicates that a category is accepted as a
                          primary condition

PDD   Pervasive Developmental Disorders
                          includes Asperger's Syndrome, Autism

S   Secondary—indicates that a category is accepted as a
                          secondary condition

Speech   Speech Impairments
                          includes Aphasia

Subst   Substance Abuse

TBI   Traumatic Brain Injury

Other   Other Health Impairments
                          includes Cardiac Disorders, Cystic Fibrosis, Diabetes,
                          Epilepsy, Hemophilia, Leukemia, Sickle Cell Anemia,
                          and Tourette's Syndrome

B=Birth   N=Not Accepted   P=Primary   S=Secondary

Program	Town	Girls Bdg	Girls Day	Boys Bdg	Boys Day	ADHD	B/VI	Deaf/Blind	Deaf	Hear	Emot Disturb	ID	LD	Multi	Ortho/Neuro	PDD	Speech	Subst	TBI	Other	Page
ALABAMA																					
PORTA CRAS SCH	Green Pond	6-21		6-21		P						P	P							P	59
HUNTSVILLE ACHIEVE	Huntsville		5-18		5-18				S		P	P	P		P	P	P		P	P	59
ARIZONA																					
ACCEL	Phoenix		5-22		5-22	P	S		S		S	P			P		S		P		61
HOWARD'S GRAY SCH	Scottsdale		9-21		9-21	P					P	S	P		S	P				P	62
NEW WAY ACAD	Scottsdale		5-19		5-19	P					S	S	P				S			P	63
ABBIE TULLER SCH	Tucson		4-14		4-14	P															61
OAK CREEK	West Sedona	13-18		13-18		P							P								63
CALIFORNIA																					
CHARLES ARMSTRONG	Belmont		6-14		6-14	P	S						P						P		68
VIA CTR	Berkeley		5-21		5-21	P			S		P	S	P		P	P	P		P	P	81
PARK CENTURY	Culver City		7-14		7-14	P							P								75
HAWTHORNE ACAD	Hawthorne		9-22		9-22	P					P	P	P	P	S	P	S	P		P	71
BRIDGE SCH	Hillsborough		3-14		3-14		S					S			P		S		S		67
HILLSIDE SCH & LEARN	La Canada		12-18		12-18	P					S	P	P	P					S		72
CLETA HARDER SCH	La Habra		3-22		3-22	P	S				S	S	S	P	P		S		P		71
NEW VISTA SCH	Laguna Hills		11-18		11-18	S	S			S	S	S	P		P		S	S	S	P	74
BENCHMARK YOUNG ADLT	Loma Linda	18-28		18-28		P	N		N		P	N	P							P	66
VISTA HILLS/BARON	Los Angeles		3-22		3-22	P	N		N		P	P	P				P			P	82
WESTVIEW SCH-CA	Los Angeles		11-18		11-18	P					P		P								82
MID-PENINSULA	Menlo Park		14-18		14-18	S	N		N			N	P		N			N			73
ORION ACAD	Moraga		13-19		13-19	S	N		N		P	N						N			75
BIG SPRINGS	Moreno Valley		5-12		5-12	S	N		N				P								66

School	City																					Index
STELLAR ACAD	Newark		6-14	6-14	S			N	N	N	N	N	S				N			79
RASKOB	Oakland		8-14	8-14	S	N	N	N	N	N	N	S	P	S	N			P	N	77
VILLA ESPERANZA	Pasadena		5-22	5-22		S	S	S	S	P	S	P	P						P	81
JEAN WEINGARTEN-ORAL	Redwood City		3-6	3-6			P			S										73
WINGS LEARNING CTR	Redwood City		5-22	5-22	S					P	P		P							83
SACRAMENTO CHILDREN	Sacramento	6-18	5-18	5-18	P		N	N	P	P	P	P	N	P				P	P	78
ASELTINE SCH	San Diego		5-19	5-19	P	N			N	N	P	P	S	N		S		S		65
CHILDRENS WORKSHOP	San Diego		3-12	3-12			P		P	P	P	P	P	P		P		N	P	69
EXCELSIOR ACAD	San Diego		6-19	6-19	P	S			S	S	P	P								70
SPRINGALL ACAD	San Diego		5-21	5-21	P				P	P	P	P	P	S	P			P		79
STERNE SCH	San Francisco		10-18	10-18	P				P	S	P	P		P				P		80
BEACON SCH-CA	San Jose		9-22	9-22	P				P	S	P	P			P			P		65
PINE HILL SCH	San Jose		6-21	6-21	P				P		P	P			P					76
COUNTRY SCH-CA	San Marcos		8-18	8-18	P				S	S	P	P	S		P	S			P	70
RUSSELL BEDE SCH	San Mateo		6-12	6-12	S						P	P	S	S	S			S		78
PRENTICE SCH	Santa Ana		4-18	4-18	S						P	P	S							77
CHARTWELL	Seaside		7-19	7-19	S	N	N			N	P	P		N	N			N		69
HELP GROUP	Sherman Oaks		2¾-22	2¾-22	P			P		P	P	P	P	P	P			P	P	72
BRIDGES ACAD	Studio City		10-18	10-18	P						P	P	S			S				68
PARKHILL	West Hills		8-18	8-18	S				S	S	P	P	S	S	S					76
ORALINGUA SCH-HEARIN	Whittier		5-11	5-11				P												74
COLORADO																				
TEMPLE GRANDIN	Boulder		11-18	11-18	P				S	S		P		P	N			N	S	85
DENVER ACAD	Denver		6-18	6-18	P				N	N	P	P								84
HAVERN SCH	Littleton		5-14	5-14	P	S			N	N						P				84
CONNECTICUT																				

B=Birth   N=Not Accepted   P=Primary   S=Secondary

Program	Town	Girls Bdg	Girls Day	Boys Bdg	Boys Day	ADHD	B/VI	Deaf/Blind	Deaf	Hear	Emot Disturb	ID	LD	Multi	Ortho/Neuro	PDD	Speech	Subst	TBI	Other	Page
CT WOODHALL	Bethlehem			14-18	14-18	P							P								98
EAGLE HILL-GREENWICH	Greenwich	10-16	6-16	10-16	6-16	S							P								87
CEDARHURST SCH	Hamden		12-21		12-21	P					P		P								87
GRACE S WEBB SCH	Hartford		5-21		5-21	S	S		S		P		S		S	P	S		S	P	92
MARVELWOOD	Kent	14-18	14-18	14-18	14-18								P								93
FORMAN	Litchfield	14-18	14-18	14-18	14-18	P							P								89
GROVE SCH	Madison	12-19	12-19	12-19	12-19	P					P	N	S								91
FOUNDATION SCH	Milford		3-21		3-21						P		P								89
ELIZABETH IVES SCH	North Haven		5-21		5-21	S					P	P	S		S		S		S		88
ST THOMAS MORE-CT	Oakdale			13-19									P								95
WATERFORD COUNTRY	Quaker Hill	8-18	8-21	8-18	8-21	P	N		N		P	S	S		S				S		97
EAGLE HILL-SOUTHPORT	Southport		6-14		6-14	P							P								88
VILLA MARIA SCH	Stamford		5-14		5-14	P							P			P					96
HIGH RD SCHS	Wallingford		5-21		5-21	P	S		S		S	P	P		P	P	P	S	P	P	92
GLENHOLME	Washington	10-18	10-18	10-18	10-18	P					P	P	S								90
AM SCH FOR THE DEAF	West Hartford	8-21	3-21	8-21	3-21				P		S	S	S						S		86
BEN BRONZ ACAD	West Hartford		7-18		7-18	S					S	S	P		S						86
INTENSIVE EDUCATION	West Hartford		5-21		5-21	P	P			P	P	P	P	P			P		P		93
OXFORD ACAD	Westbrook			14-20		P							P								94
SETON ACAD	Westport		10-20		10-20	P	N		N	N	P	S	S	S	N	P	S	N	N		96
DELAWARE																					
CENTREVILLE	Centreville		3-14		3-14	P							P								99
PILOT	Wilmington		5-14		5-14	P							P								99
DISTRICT OF COLUMBIA																					

LAB SCH	Washington		6-19		6-19	P							P								101
	FLORIDA																				
LIGHTHOUSE PT ACAD	Coconut Creek		8-18		8-18	P							P								106
VANGUARD-COCONUT	Coconut Grove		6-14		6-14	P							P								109
NOVA SE U-BAUDHUIN	Fort Lauderdale		2-5		2-5		S		S												107
DEPAUL SCH OF NE FL	Jacksonville		6-14		6-14	P							P								104
MORNING STAR-JAX	Jacksonville		5-15		5-15	P	N		N		S	S	P				S		S		106
VANGUARD	Lake Wales	10-18	10-18	10-18	10-18	P	S	N	S	S	N		P		N	S	S	N	S		108
PACE-BRANTLEY HALL	Longwood		6-18		6-18	P	N		N		N	N	P					N			108
ATLANTIS-MIAMI	Miami		5-18		5-18	P					P	S	P		S		S				102
EASTER SEALS S FL	Miami		B-22		B-22	P			P		S	S	P			P	S		S	P	104
KILLIAN OAKS	Miami		3-18		3-18	S							P				S				105
CENTER ACAD	Pinellas Park		10-19		10-19	P	N		N		N	N	P		N			N	N		103
AMERICAN ACAD-PLANT	Plantation		3-18		3-18								P								102
WOODLAND HALL ACAD	Tallahassee		6-20		6-20	P		N	N	S		N	P	P							110
MORNING STAR-TAMPA	Tampa		6-15		6-15	P	N		S	S	N	N	P	S	S	S	P	N	P		107
ATLANTIS-PALM BEACH	West Palm Beach		5-22		5-22	P	N	N	N		S	S	P		N			N	S		103
	GEORGIA																				
MILL SPRINGS ACAD	Alpharetta		6-18		6-18	P	S			S	N	N	P	P	S				N		116
ATLANTA SPEECH-HAMM	Atlanta		2-8		2-8	S			P	P			S								111
ATLANTA SPEECH SCH	Atlanta		5-12		5-12	S							P				S				111
BRANDON HALL	Atlanta		11-19	12-19	11-19	P							P								113
HOWARD SCH	Atlanta		5-18		5-18	P							P								115
SCHENCK	Atlanta		5-12		5-12	S							P								116
BEDFORD SCH	Fairburn		6-16		6-16	P					S		P						S		112
COTTAGE SCH	Roswell		11-18		11-18	P	N	N	N	S	S	S	P	S	N	S	S	S	S		114

B=Birth   N=Not Accepted   P=Primary   S=Secondary

Program	Town	Girls		Boys		ADHD	B/VI	Deaf/Blind	Deaf	Hear	Emot Disturb	ID	LD	Multi	Ortho/Neuro	PDD	Speech	Subst	TBI	Other	Page
		Bdg	Day	Bdg	Day																
GA CHATHAM ACAD	Savannah		6-18		6-18	P	N	N	N				P		N	N	S				113
GABLES ACAD-GA	Stone Mountain	12-18	9-18	12-18	9-18	P					S					P		S	S		114
HAWAII																					
ASSETS	Honolulu		5-18		5-18	P					S		P			P	S	S	S		118
VARIETY SCH OF HI	Honolulu		5-13		5-13	P					S	S	P			P					119
HORIZONS ACAD-MAUI	Kihei		5-20		5-20	P					S	S	P			P	S	S	S		118
ILLINOIS																					
CLARE WOODS ACAD	Bartlett		3-22		3-22	P					P	P	P	S	S	P	S		P	P	122
BREHM PREP	Carbondale	11-21	11-21	11-21	11-21	P					S	N	P					N	S		121
BEACON THERAPEUTIC	Chicago		3-21		3-21	P					P	P	P				P	S	S		120
HOLY TRINITY SCH	Chicago		3-15		3-15				P												124
SONIA SHANKMAN	Chicago	6-20	6-20	6-20	6-20	S					P		S							P	126
JOSEPH ACAD	Des Plaines		5-21		5-21	S			N		P	S	P								125
SUMMIT SCH-IL	Elgin		2-21		2-21	P	N				S	S	P				P				127
ACACIA ACAD	La Grange		6-18		6-18	P					S	S	P				S				120
TRINITY SCH-IL	New Lenox		3-21		3-21	S	S		S		S	P	S				S		S		128
COVE SCH	Northbrook		5-21		5-21	S							P								123
ELIM CHRISTIAN SCH	Palos Heights		3-21		3-21	S	S		S	S	S	P	S	P	P	P	P	N	P		123
TRANSITIONS SCH	Quincy		3-21		3-21	S			S			P			S	P	P		S		127
HOPE SCH	Springfield	5-21	5-21	5-21	5-21	S	S		S			P	P		P	P	S		P		124
JOSEPH P KENNEDY-IL	Tinley Park	6+	6-21	6+	6-21	S					P	P			S	P	S		P	P	125
CHILD'S VOICE SCH	Wood Dale		3-9	3-9	3-9				P	P					S	P	P				121
INDIANA																					
WORTHMORE ACAD	Indianapolis		5-22		5-22	P					S	P	P	P	S	P	S		P	P	129

KANSAS

Facility	City	Ages				Page
MARILLAC	Overland Park	6-17	6-17	6-17	6-17	130
HEARTSPRING	Wichita	5-21	5-21			130

KENTUCKY

Facility	City	Ages				Page
STEWART HOME	Frankfort	6+	6+			133
HINDMAN SETTLEMENT		6-14	6-14			133
DE PAUL SCH	Louisville	6-14	6-14			132
HEUSER HEARING ACAD	Louisville	3-7	3-7			132
SUMMIT ACAD-KY	Louisville	5-14	5-14			134

LOUISIANA

Facility	City	Ages				Page
BRIGHTON SCH	Baton Rouge	5-19	5-19			135

MAINE

Facility	City	Ages				Page
SPURWINK	Portland	7+	5+	7+	5+	136

MARYLAND

Facility	City	Ages				Page
HARBOUR SCH	Annapolis	6-21	6-21			141
CHIMES SCH	Baltimore	6-21	6-21			138
GATEWAY SCH-MD	Baltimore	3-12	3-12			140
MD SCH FOR THE BLIND	Baltimore	7-21	3-21	3-21		144
ST ELIZABETH SCH	Baltimore	6-21	6-21			146
UCP DELREY SCH	Baltimore	2-21	2-21			147
SUMMIT SCH-MD	Edgewater	6-14	6-14			146
LAUREL HALL SCH-MD	Hagerstown	5-20	5-20			143
JEMICY SCH	Owings Mills	6-18	6-18			142
FORBUSH SCH	Reisterstown	11-18	3-21	3-21		139
HANNAH MORE SCH	Reisterstown	11-21	11-21			140
BENEDICTINE SCH	Ridgely	5-21	5-21	5-21		137

B=Birth   N=Not Accepted   P=Primary   S=Secondary

Program	Town	Girls Bdg	Girls Day	Boys Bdg	Boys Day	ADHD	B/VI	Deaf/Blind	Deaf	Hear	Emot Disturb	ID	LD	Multi	Ortho/Neuro	PDD	Speech	Subst	TBI	Other	Page
MD FROST SCH	Rockville		5-21		5-21	S					P		S							P	139
IVYMOUNT SCH	Rockville		4-21		4-21							P	P			P					142
RIDGE SCH-	Rockville	11-18	11-18	11-18	11-18	P						P	P		S						145
CHELSEA	Silver Spring		10-18		10-18	S					N	N	P								137
PATHWAYS SCHS	Silver Spring		11-21		11-21				N		P	S	S			N	S		S		145
ODYSSEY SCH	Stevenson		5-14		5-14	S		N	N		N	N	P	N	N	N	P	N	N		144
MASSACHUSETTS																					
DEARBORN ACAD	Arlington		5-22		5-22	P					P		P								157
CRYSTAL SPRINGS SCH	Assonet	3-22		3-22			S			S				S	S				S		157
STETSON SCH	Barre			9-21		S	N					S	P	S	S				S		171
ARLINGTON SCH	Belmont		12-20		12-20	P	N		N		P	N	P								148
BEVERLY SCH FOR DEAF	Beverly		3-22		3-22				P		S	S	P		P	P	S	S	S		149
ST COLETTA-BRAINTREE	Braintree		3-22		3-22						S	P			S	P	S				170
FRANCISCAN-KENNEDY	Brighton	5-21		5-21		S					S	S	S		P	P	S		P	P	160
IVY STREET SCH	Brookline	13-22	13-22	13-22	13-22	S					P	P			P				P	P	162
FARR ACAD	Cambridge	12-18		12-18		P					P		P							P	159
BOSTON COLLEGE SCH	Chestnut Hill		3-21		3-21		S	P			P	P		P	P	P			P		150
SCHWARTZ CTR DAY SCH	Dartmouth		3-21		3-21		S		S	S		P		P	P	P			P		170
WHITNEY ACAD	East Freetown			10-22		S	N		N		P	P	S								174
RIVERVIEW	East Sandwich	11-23	11-23	11-23	11-23	S					P	S	P				S		S		169
LEARN CTR-DEAF CHILD	Framingham	12-22	3-22	12-22	3-22	S			P			S	P								165
REED ACAD	Framingham			7-14	7-14	P					P	S	P		P	P					168
CARDINAL CUSHING	Hanover	6-22	6-22	6-22	6-22	P	S				S	P	S	P	S	P	S		P		152
EAGLE HILL-MA	Hardwick	13-19	13-19	13-19	13-19	P						P	P								158

School	City	Age	Age	Age																			Page
NEARI SCH	Holyoke			7-22		P					P	P	P				P				P	P	P	167
CORNERSTONES SCH	Ipswich	6-14	7-22	6-14	6-14	P		S			P	S	P				P	S					P	155
DR FRANKLIN PERKINS	Lancaster	5-21	5-18	5-21	5-18	P			N		P	P	P				P	S	N					158
ARCHWAY-MA	Leicester	10-22	10-22			S		N	S									N			N			148
COTTING SCH	Lexington		3-22	3-22	3-22	S		S			P	S		P			P	S		S				156
CARROLL	Lincoln	6-15	6-15	6-15							P													152
WILLIE ROSS SCH	Longmeadow	3-22	3-22	3-22		S	P	P				S	S											174
HILLSIDE	Marlborough		10-15	10-15		P				S		P	P				P							162
FL CHAMBERLAIN SCH	Middleboro	11-20	11-20	11-20	11-20	P					P	P	P				P							160
SE ALTERNATIVE SCH	Middleboro		14-18	14-18		P					P	P	P				P							171
BRANDON SCH & RTC	Natick		7-18	7-18		S			S		P	S	P	P		S	S	S	S					151
WALKER	Needham	3-14	3-14	3-14		P					P		S	P		S	P	S						173
KENNEDY-DONOVAN CTR	New Bedford		3-22	3-22		S		P			S	S	S	P	S	P	S	P	P			P	P	163
VALLEY VIEW	North Brookfield			11-16		P	N	N			P	N	S	N	P	S	N	P	N	N	N	N		172
LIGHTHOUSE SCH	North Chelmsford		11-16			P	N	S			P	P	S	P	P	S	S	N	S	P	P		P	166
CLARKE SCHS-	Northampton						N	P									P							154
LANDMARK SCH	Prides Crossing	13-20	7-20	13-20	7-20	S		S			P		P			S				N		S		163
BOSTON HIGASHI SCH	Randolph	3-22	3-22	3-22	3-22	S		S			S	N	N			P	S							150
MAY CTR-MA	Randolph	3-22	3-22	3-22							S	S				P								166
CHILDREN'S STUDY HOM	Springfield	6-19	6-19	6-19		P					P	P	P				P							153
CORWIN-RUSSELL	Sudbury	11-19	11-19	11-19		P					S	N	S				S							155
WILLOW HILL	Sudbury	11-19	11-19	11-19		P					P	P	P				S				S			175
SWANSEA WOOD SCH	Swansea	12-22	12-22	12-22		P					P	P	P				P				S	S		172
LEAGUE SCH BOSTON	Walpole	3-22	3-22	3-22		S					S	S	S			P	S							164
GUILD FOR HUMAN SERV	Waltham	6-22	6-22	6-22			P				P	P	P	P		P	P							161
BEACON HS	Watertown	14-22	14-22	14-22		P					P	N	S	N	N	S	N	N						149

B=Birth   N=Not Accepted   P=Primary   S=Secondary

Program	Town	Girls Bdg	Girls Day	Boys Bdg	Boys Day	ADHD	B/VI	Deaf/Blind	Deaf	Hear	Emot Disturb	ID	LD	Multi	Ortho/Neuro	PDD	Speech	Subst	TBI	Other	Page
MA PERKINS SCH BLIND	Watertown	5-22	3-22	5-22	3-22	S	P	P	P	S	S	S			S	S	S				168
CLEARWAY SCH	West Newton		11-18		11-18	P					S		P		S	S		S			154
LEARNING PREP SCH	West Newton		7-22		7-22	S					S		P			P	P	S	S		165
GIFFORD SCH	Weston		8-22		8-22	P					P		P						S	P	161
WINCHENDON	Winchendon	14-20	14-20	14-20	14-20	S							P								175
MICHIGAN																					
MONTCALM SCH	Albion	12-18		12-21		P					P					P					177
ETON ACAD	Birmingham		6-19		6-19	P							P								177
MINNESOTA																					
FRASER SCH	Minneapolis	6wks-6	6wks-6		6wks-6	P	P		P		P	P	P		P	P	P		P	P	178
GROVES ACAD	St Louis Park	6-18	6-18		6-18	P				S			P			S	P				178
MISSISSIPPI																					
EDUCATION CTR SCH-MS	Jackson	6-21	6-21		6-21	P					P		P		P	P					180
MISSOURI																					
RAINBOW CTR DAY SCH	Blue Springs	3-21	3-21		3-21	P					S	P	P		S	P	P				183
ST JOSEPH INSTITUTE	Chesterfield	5-15	3-15	5-15	3-15	S			P								P				184
RIVENDALE CTR-AUTISM	Springfield		3-18		3-18	P					S		P	P		P	P		P	P	183
CENTRAL INST-DEAF	St Louis	3-12	3-12		3-12				P	P											181
CHURCHILL-MO	St Louis	8-16	8-16		8-16								P								181
LOGOS	St Louis	11-21	11-21		11-21	P	S				P	S	P		S	S	S		P	P	182
MIRIAM SCH	St Louis	4-14	4-14		4-14	P			S		N	N	P	P							182
MONTANA																					
ELK MTN ACAD	Heron			14-18		P					P							P			185
NEBRASKA																					

School	City	Age	Age	C1	C2	C3	C4	C5	C6	C7	C8	C9	C10	C11	C12	C13	C14	C15	C16	C17	C18	Page
MADONNA SCH	Omaha	5-21	5-21	P			S		P	P	P	P	P	P	P		P			P	P	186
NEVADA																						
NEW HORIZONS ACAD-NV	Las Vegas	5-18	5-18	P		N	N	N	P	N	P	N	P	P	P	N	P		N	P	P	187
NEW HAMPSHIRE																						
SECOND START ALT HS	Concord	14-18	14-18	P					P	P			P									190
DAVENPORT SCH	Jefferson	13-18							P			S	P									188
GRANITE HILL SCH	Newport	11-21	11-21	P					P	S		S	P									188
HAMPSHIRE COUNTRY	Rindge	8-18		S					S	P		P										189
HUNTER SCH	Runney	5-15	5-15	P	N				P	P		S					P	P			P	189
NEW JERSEY																						
ARCHWAY SCHS	Atco	3-21	3-21	S	S	S			S	S	P	S	S	P	P	S		S				192
LORD STIRLING SCH	Basking Ridge	7-20	7-20	S					P	S	S	S	S	N	S	N				S		205
EAST MOUNTAIN SCH	Belle Mead	12-19	12-19						P	S		S	P			P				S		198
GREEN BROOK ACAD	Bound Brook	10-21	10-21	S					P	S		S	S							S		202
BROOKFIELD SCHS	Cherry Hill	5-21	5-21	P			S		P	P		P	P	P						P	P	193
HARBOR SCH-NJ	Eatontown	5-21	5-21	P	S	S			S	P	P	P	P	S	P	S	P		P	P	P	202
LAKEVIEW SCH	Edison	3-21	3-21					S		S		P		P		P	P	P		P	P	204
SR GEORGINE SCH	Ewing	5-21	5-21	P					P	P		P			P	P			S	S		210
BANYAN SCH	Fairfield	6-18	6-18	P			S		N			P	P						S			192
GLENVIEW ACAD	Fairfield	5-12	5-12	P	N	N	N		P			P	P	P	P	S	N	P	S	P	P	201
GRAMON SCH	Fairfield	12-21	12-21	P					P			S	P				S		S	S	P	201
FIRST CHILDREN SCH	Fanwood	3-12	3-12			S		P	P	P	P	P	P	P		P	P	P	P	P	P	199
NEWGRANGE	Hamilton	7-21	7-21									P					S			S	P	207
ALPHA SCH	Jackson	3-21	3-21	P			S		P	P	P	P	P	P	P	S	P	P	S	P	P	191
ST JOSEPH'S-BLIND	Jersey City	5-21	B-21	S				P	S	S		S	S	P	P	S	S	S		S	S	209
LEHMANN SCH	Lakewood	3-21	3-21						S	S		S								P	P	204

B=Birth   N=Not Accepted   P=Primary   S=Secondary

Program	Town	Girls Bdg	Girls Day	Boys Bdg	Boys Day	ADHD	B/VI	Deaf/Blind	Deaf	Hear	Emot Disturb	ID	LD	Multi	Ortho/Neuro	PDD	Speech	Subst	TBI	Other	Page
NJ FELICIAN SCH	Lodi		3-21		3-21						P	P	P								198
CRAIG SCH	Mountain Lakes		8-19		8-19	P					S	P	P								197
ARC KOHLER SCH	Mountainside		3-11		3-11	P	S				S	P	P		S	P					191
SUMMIT SPEECH SCH	New Providence		3-5		3-5				P	P											210
MIDLAND SCH	North Branch		5-21		5-21	P	S		S	S	S	P	P	P	S	P	P		S		206
SEARCH DAY PRGM	Ocean		3-21		3-21											P	P				209
MATHENY MED & ED CTR	Peapack	3-21	3-21	3-21	3-21		S	S		S		S			P		S				206
CAMBRIDGE SCH-NJ	Pennington		5-14		5-14	P					N	N	P				P	N			194
CHANCELLOR ACAD	Pompton Plains		11-18		11-18						P										195
LEWIS SCH & CLINIC	Princeton		5+		5+	P															204
HOLMSTEAD SCH	Ridgewood		13-18		13-18						P		S								203
WINSTON SCH-NJ	Short Hills		8-14		8-14	S							P								211
ROCK BROOK SCH	Skillman		5-14		5-14	P			P			S	P		P		P				208
COMMUNITY SCH-NJ	Teaneck		14-21		14-21	P							P								196
COMMUNITY ELEM-NJ	Teaneck		5-14		5-14	P							P								196
DOROTHY B HERSH HS	Tinton Falls		14-21		14-21	S					S	P	S		S	S	S				197
TITUSVILLE ACAD	Titusville		5-18		5-18	P	N	S	N		P	P	P		P	P	S	P		P	211
FORUM SCH	Waldwick		3-16		3-16	P					P	S	P								200
RUGBY SCH-WOODFIELD	Wall		5-21		5-21	P					P		P		S	P					208
WOODCLIFF ACAD	Wall		8-18		8-18	P					P	S	P		P	P	P	N	P	P	212
MT CARMEL GUILD ACAD	West Orange		5-21		5-21	P					P	S	P			P					207
CALAIS SCH	Whippany		5-21		5-21	P					P		P		S	P					194
COLLIER HS	Wickatunk		11-18		11-18	P	S				P							P			195
GARFIELD PARK ACAD	Willingboro		5-21		5-21	P					P	S	P		P	P	P	P	P	P	200

NEW YORK

School	City	Age	Age															Page
HENRY VISCARDI SCH	Albertson	5-21	3-21								P		S					223
COBB MEMORIAL	Altamont	5-21	5-21						P									217
KILDONAN	Amenia	11-19	7-19					P										226
MAPLEBROOK	Amenia	11-21	11-21	P				P			S		P			S		227
GREEN CHIMNEYS	Brewster	6-17	5-17	P			S	P	S	S	S	P	S					220
CLEAR VIEW SCH	Briarcliff Manor		3-21				S	P	S	S	S						P	216
LAVELLE SCH	Bronx		3-21		P													226
ST JOSEPH'S DEAF	Bronx		3-14	S		N		S	S	S	S	S	S	N				236
BLOCK INST SCH	Brooklyn		3-8	P				P	P	P	P	P	P	P	P	P		213
HEBREW ACAD-SPECIAL	Brooklyn	5+	3-21	S	S	S	P	P	S	P		S	S	N	S			222
HEBREW ACAD-SP CHILD	Brooklyn		5-21	S	N	S	P	P	N	P		P	P	N	P			223
MARY MCDOWELL CTR	Brooklyn		5-17	P						P		S			S			228
P'TACH	Brooklyn		6-18	P	P					P								233
ST FRANCIS-DEAF	Brooklyn		3-14			P												235
BUFFALO HRNG & SPCH	Buffalo		3-5	P	P	P		S	S	P	S	S	P	N	P		P	214
ST MARYS SCH DEAF	Buffalo	5-21	3-21	S	S	P	S	S	S	S	S	P	S	N	S	S		236
LOWELL SCH-NY	Flushing		6-21					S	P	S	P		P		P			227
SCH FOR LANG_COM DEV	Glen Cove		2-21	P	S		S	P	P	P	P	P	P		P	S		238
FAMILY FOUNDATION	Hancock	13-19	13-19	P			S	P	P	P								218
CHILDREN'S SCH-HAWTH	Hawthorne		3-5								P	P	S					215
HAWTHORNE CO DAY	Hawthorne		3-21	P	N	N		P	N	P	S	P	P		S			221
COARC-STARTING PLACE	Hudson		3-5					P		S	S	S	S		S			217
GERSH ACAD	Huntington	5-21	5-21	P				P	P	P	P	P	P		P		P	218
QUEENS CTRS-PROGRESS	Jamaica	3-21	3-21	S	S	S	S	S	S	S	P	S	P	N	P	P		234
SUMMIT SCH-JAMAICA	Jamaica	7-21	7-21	P	N	N	S	S	S	N	S	N	P	N	S	S		239

B=Birth   N=Not Accepted   P=Primary   S=Secondary

Program	Town	Girls Bdg	Girls Day	Boys Bdg	Boys Day	ADHD	B/VI	Deaf/Blind	Deaf	Hear	Emot Disturb	ID	LD	Multi	Ortho/Neuro	PDD	Speech	Subst	TBI	Other	Page
NY ORANGE COUNTY AHRC	Middletown		5-21		5-21	S	S		S		S	P	S		P	P	S		P	P	232
MILL NECK MANOR SCH	Mill Neck		3-21		3-21				P				S		S	S	S				229
KARAFIN SCH	Mount Kisco		13-21		13-21	P					P	Z	P	P		P	P	N		P	225
CLEARY SCH FOR DEAF	Nesconset		3-21		3-21	S	S	P	P	P	S	S	S		S	S	S	S	S		216
HALLEN SCH	New Rochelle		5-21		5-21	P	P				P	S	P						P	P	221
CHURCHILL-NY	New York		5-21		5-21						P	S	P	P							215
PARKSIDE SCH	New York		5-11		5-11	P					P	S	P								232
ROBERT L STEVENSON	New York		13-18		13-18	P					S		P								234
STEPHEN GAYNOR	New York		3-14		3-14	P							P				P				238
WINSTON PREP	New York		11-18		11-18	P							P								242
WESTCHESTER EXCEPT	North Salem		5-21		5-21	S					P	S	S		P				S	P	241
PLEASANTVLLE COTTAGE	Pleasantville	7-15		7-15							P										233
MARYHAVEN CTR-HOPE	Port Jefferson	5-21	5-21	5-21	5-21	S					S	P	S		S	P	S				229
VINCENT SMITH	Port Washington		9-18		9-18	P						P	P								240
HOLY CHILDHOOD	Rochester		5-21		5-21							P			S	P	P				224
NORMAN HOWARD SCH	Rochester		10-21		10-21	P	N		S	S	N	N	P		S	S	S	N	S	P	231
ROCHESTER SCH-DEAF	Rochester	3-21	3-21	3-21	3-21	S	N	S	P	S	S	S	S	S	S	S	S	S		235
CHILD SCH & LEGACY	Roosevelt Island		5-21		5-21	P					P	S	S		S	P	P		S		214
OAK HILL SCH	Scotia		5-14		5-14						P										231
HAGEDORN LITTLE VILL	Seaford		3-12		3-12	P	S		S	S	S	P	P	P	S	P	P		S	P	220
GOW	South Wales		12-18	12-18	12-18	P						P	P								219
ANDERSON CTR-AUTISM	Staatsburg	5-21	5-21	5-21	5-21	S			S		P	S	S		S	P	S		S	S	213
SUMMIT-NYACK	Upper Nyack	14-21	14-21	14-21	14-21	S					P	P	S			P					239
HOUSE-GOOD SHEPHERD	Utica	12-17	6-18	6-17	6-18	P			S		P	S	S		S	P	S		S	P	224

SCHOOL	CITY	AGES		PROGRAM EMPHASIS CODES	PAGE
NY SCH FOR THE DEAF	White Plains	3-21	3-21	S … S … S … S	230
WINDWARD-NY	White Plains	6-15	6-15	P … P … P … P … P	241
NEW INTERDISCIPLINAR	Yaphank	3-5	3-5	S … P … P … P … S … P … P … P … S … P	230
FERNCLIFF MANOR	Yonkers	3-21		S … S … S … S … P … P … S … S … S … P	237
NORTH CAROLINA					
STONE MTN SCH	Black Mountain	11-17		P … P … P … P … N … S	246
JOHN CROSLAND SCH	Charlotte	5-18	5-18	P … P … N … P … S … S	243
MANUS ACADEMY	Charlotte	6-18	6-18	P … S … N … P … S … P … N … S	244
NOBLE ACAD	Greensboro	5-19	5-19	P … S … S … S … S	245
PIEDMONT SCH	High Point	5-14	5-14	P … P … S	245
FLETCHER ACAD	Raleigh	6-20	6-20	P … N … N … N … P … S … N … S	243
OHIO					
LAWRENCE SCH	Broadview Heights	5-18	5-18	P … P … N … Z … N	248
ST RITA SCH-DEAF	Cincinnati	14-21 / 6wks-21	6wks-21	S … P … S … S … S … S … P … P … N	251
SPRINGER SCH & CTR	Cincinnati	6-14	6-14	S … P … P	251
ELEANOR GERSON	Cleveland	11-21	11-21	P … P … P … N … S … S	247
MARBURN	Columbus	6-18	6-18	P … N … P … N … N … S … N	249
JULIE BILLIART SCH	Lyndhurst	5-14	5-14	P … N … N … P … N	248
NICHOLAS SCH	Piqua	5-14	5-14	P … P … P … P … P … P	250
MARY IMMACULATE SCH	Toledo	6-14	6-14	P … S … N … S … N … P	250
ADRIEL SCH	West Liberty	6-18	6-18	P … P … S … P … P	247
OKLAHOMA					
TOWN & COUNTRY SCH	Tulsa	6-18	6-18	P … P … P	253
OREGON					
ACAD AT SISTERS	Bend	13-18		P … P … P	254
BRIDGES ACAD	Bend	13-18		P … P … S … P … P	254

B=Birth   N=Not Accepted   P=Primary   S=Secondary

Program	Town	Girls Bdg	Girls Day	Boys Bdg	Boys Day	ADHD	B/VI	Deaf/Blind	Deaf	Hear	Emot Disturb	ID	LD	Multi	Ortho/Neuro	PDD	Speech	Subst	TBI	Other	Page
OR OPEN MEADOW ALT SCHS	Portland		11-18		11-18	P					P		P								255
THOMAS A EDISON HS	Portland		14-18		14-18	P					S		P							P	255
PENNSYLVANIA																					
MAIN LINE ACAD	Bala Cynwyd		5-21		5-21	P					P	P	P								268
COMMUNITY CO DAY SCH	Erie		6-20		6-20	P	P	P	P	P	P	S	S	P				P	N	P	261
CARSON VALLEY AID	Flourtown	12-18	6-18	9-18	6-18	P	P				P		P								260
WORDSWORTH ACAD	Fort Washington		5-21		5-21	P		N	N	N	P	S	P		S			S	S		277
CAMPHILL SPECIAL SCH	Glenmoore	5-21	5-21	5-21	5-21	S					S	P	S		S	P	S		S		259
CLELIAN HEIGHTS SCH	Greensburg	5-21	5-21	5-21	5-21	S						P			S	S			S		261
QUAKER SCH-HORSHAM	Horsham		5-15		5-15	P	N	N			S	N	P	P	N	P	S	N	N		271
HILLSIDE SCH-PA	Macungie		5-13		5-13	S		N		S	S	N	P			N	S	N	N		266
PHELPS	Malvern	12-18	12-18	12-18	12-18	P							P				S				271
BENCHMARK	Media		6-14		6-14	P							P				S		N		258
JANUS SCH	Mount Joy		6-19		6-19	P						N	P								267
STRATFORD FRIENDS	Newtown Square		5-14		5-14	S							P								274
PATHWAY-PA	Norristown		5-21		5-21	S					S	P	P		P	P	S	N	S	P	269
DE VALLEY FRIENDS	Paoli		11-19		11-19	P							P								263
ROYER-GREAVES SCH	Paoli	5-21	5-21	5-21	5-21	S	P		P	S	S	S	S		S	P		N	S		272
VANGUARD SCH	Paoli		4-21		4-21	S					P	S	S		P	P			P		275
CREFELD	Philadelphia		12-18		12-18	P					P		P								262
DELTA SCH	Philadelphia		5-21		5-21						P	P								P	263
GREEN TREE SCH	Philadelphia		3-21		3-21	S	S				P					P					265
HMS SCH	Philadelphia	2-21	2-21	2-21	2-21				S			S		P	P		S		P		267
MILL CREEK SCH	Philadelphia		12-20		12-20	P					P	S	S			P					268

School	Location	Age Range	Emphasis (P / S / N indicators, columns unlabeled on this page)	Page
PA SCH FOR THE DEAF	Philadelphia	3-21	S · · S S S · · S S S · S S · · S S	270
ST LUCY DAY SCH	Philadelphia	3-14	· P P · S · P · · S S · P · · · P ·	274
BUXMONT ACAD	Pipersville	12-18 / 12-18 / 12-18	P · · P P S P S N · · S S · · · S	259
ACLD TILLOTSON	Pittsburgh	7-21 / 7-21	P S P P S S P S · · S S · P	257
DEPAUL SCH-HEARING	Pittsburgh	3-14 / 3-14	S P · · · · P · · S P · S · P	264
FRIENDSHIP ACAD	Pittsburgh	6-21 / 6-21	P · · · · P · P · · P · · P	264
OAKLAND SCH-PA	Pittsburgh	13-18 / 13-18	P N · N N · N · · · N · · N	268
WESLEY SPECTRUM ACAD	Pittsburgh	9-21 / 9-21	P P · · P P · P · · P · · P	276
W PA SCH FOR BLIND	Pittsburgh	3-21 / 3-21 / 3-21	· P S N P · S S · S P · P P	276
W PA SCH FOR DEAF	Pittsburgh	3-21 / 3-21 / 3-21	P N P · S S · S S · P · N P	277
ST JOSEPH CTR	Pottsville	4-21 / 4-21	P · · P P P · P P · P · N P	273
HILL TOP PREP	Rosemont	10-18 / 10-18	P P · N N P P P · P N · · P	265
ALLIED DEPAUL SCH	Scranton	7-14 / 7-14	P · · · N N · · P · N	257
CONCEPT SCH	Westtown	11-18 / 11-18	S · · · · P P P · S · · P	262
ST ANTHONY SCH PRGMS	Wexford	5-21 / 5-21	S P · S P P N S · S S · P	272
OUR LADY-CONFIDENCE	Willow Grove	4½-21 / 4½-21	S S · · P P N · · P · P P	269
ST KATHERINE DAY	Wynnewood	4½-21 / 4½-21	S S · P P · S S · · S · P	273
RHODE ISLAND				
HARMONY HILL SCH	Chepachet	8-18 / 8-18	P P · · P S P S S · S · · P	279
HAMILTON SCH	Providence	6-14 / 6-14	P P · · S S P · P · · · ·	279
SOUTH CAROLINA				
SANDHILLS SCH	Columbia	6-18 / 6-18	P · · · P · P · · · · · P	283
PINE GROVE	Elgin	5-18 / 5-18 / 5-18	· · · · · · · · · · ·	283
CAMPERDOWN ACAD	Greenville	5-14 / 5-14	P S · P P P · · · P N P N	281
TRIDENT	Mount Pleasant	5-19 / 5-19	P · · · P P · · · · N · P	284
HIDDEN TREASURE	Taylors	5-21 / 5-21	P S S S P P P P · P N P P P	282

B=Birth   N=Not Accepted   P=Primary   S=Secondary

Program	Town	Girls Bdg	Girls Day	Boys Bdg	Boys Day	ADHD	B/VI	Deaf/Blind	Deaf	Hear	Emot Disturb	ID	LD	Multi	Ortho/Neuro	PDD	Speech	Subst	TBI	Other	Page
SC GLENFOREST SCH	West Columbia		6-18		6-18	P	P	N	N	P	S	S	P	P	S		P	S	S	P	282
CHEROKEE CREEK SCH	Westminster			11-15		P					P									P	281
TENNESSEE																					
CURREY INGRAM	Brentwood		5-18		5-18	P							P								287
ADVENT HOME	Calhoun	12-18		12-18		P					P		P								285
KING'S DAUGHTERS	Columbia	7-22	7-30	7-22	7-30	S	N	N		S	S	P	S			P	S		P		287
BENTON HALL ACAD	Franklin		8-19		8-19	P	N	N			P	S			S					P	286
BODINE SCH	Germantown		6-14		6-14	S							P								286
MEMPHIS ORAL SCH	Germantown		2-6		2-6				P	P											288
BEACON SCH-TN	Greeneville	5-18	5-18	5-18	5-18	P					P	P	P		P	P	P		P	P	285
SUSAN GRAY SCH	Nashville		3-5		3-5		P		P			P			P	P			P	P	289
TEXAS																					
KENLEY SCH	Abilene		6-14		6-14	P		N	N	S		N	P		P			N	P	P	295
GATEWAY SCH-TX	Arlington		10-19		10-19	P		N		S			P								293
DALLAS ACAD	Dallas		5-18		5-18	P							P								292
FAIRHILL SCH	Dallas		6-18		6-18	P							P								293
NOTRE DAME SCH-DALL.	Dallas		8-23		8-23							P		P		P					297
SHELTON	Dallas		3-18		3-18	P			S			S	P								299
WINSTON SCH-TX	Dallas		6-19		6-19	P		N					P								301
EL PASO BRIDGES ACAD	El Paso		6-14		6-14	P	N		N		S	S	P		N	P	P	N	S		292
HILL SCH-FT WORTH	Fort Worth		6-18		6-18	P							P								294
KEY SCH	Fort Worth		6-18		6-18	P			S				P				S		P		296
TCU STARPOINT SCH	Fort Worth		6-12		6-12	S							P								300
BRIARWOOD SCH	Houston		5-21		5-21	P							P								290

School	Location	Age Range	Age Range	Page
CTR HEARING & SPEECH	Houston	1½-6	1½-6	290
HOUSTON LEARN ACAD	Houston	14-18	14-18	294
MONARCH SCH	Houston	3-30	3-30	297
PARISH SCH	Houston	1½-11	1½-11	298
WESTVIEW SCH-TX	Houston	2-14	2-14	301
INCLUDING KIDS	Humble	3-18	3-18	295
CRISMAN SCH	Longview	5-14	5-14	291
RIVER CITY CHRISTIAN	San Antonio	5-19	5-19	298
SUNSHINE COTTAGE SCH	San Antonio	3-19	3-19	300
WINSTON SCH-SAN ANT	San Antonio	5-19	5-19	302

UTAH

School	Location	Age Range	Age Range	Page
SORENSON'S RANCH SCH	Koosharem	12-18	12-18	307
LOGAN RIVER ACAD	Logan	13-17	13-17	304
MAPLE LAKE ACAD	Payson	13-18	13-18	305
DISCOVERY ACAD	Provo	13-17	13-17	303
HERITAGE SCH-UT	Provo	12-18	12-18	304
PROVO CANYON	Provo	8-18	8-18	306
CEDAR RIDGE ACAD	Roosevelt	13-18	13-18	303
SEPS LEARN CTR	Salt Lake City	4-18	4-18	306

VERMONT

School	Location	Age Range	Age Range	Page
BENNINGTON SCH	Bennington	8-21	8-21	308
AUSTINE SCH & VT CTR	Brattleboro	3-21	3-21	308
ROCK PT	Burlington	14-18	14-18	309
GREENWOOD	Putney	11-17	11-17	309
SHELDON ACAD	Rutland	6-18	6-18	311
ST JOHNSBURY	St Johnsbury	14-19	14-19	310

Key: B=Birth N=Not Accepted P=Primary S=Secondary

Program	Town	Girls Bdg	Girls Day	Boys Bdg	Boys Day	ADHD	B/VI	Deaf/Blind	Deaf	Hear	Emot Disturb	ID	LD	Multi	Ortho/Neuro	PDD	Speech	Subst	TBI	Other	Page
VIRGINIA																					
OAKWOOD SCH-VA	Annandale		5-14		5-14	P					P		P								317
MORRISON SCH	Bristol		6-18		6-18	P															315
DISCOVERY SCH-VA	Dillwyn	11-17		11-17		P	N	N	N	S	P	N	P	P	N	S	S	P	N	P	313
LITTLE KESWICK	Keswick			10-17		P							P	P	P	P	S	S				314
OAKLAND	Keswick	6-14	6-14	6-14	6-14	S	N	N			S		P	P							316
NEW VISTAS SCH	Lynchburg		5-19		5-19	P	N	N	N	N	S	N	P	P	N	S	S	S	S		316
CHARTERHOUSE SCH	Richmond	11-18	11-18	11-18	11-18	P	N	N	N	N	P	P	P	P				S			312
NEW COMMUNITY	Richmond		11-18	11-18		S							P								315
RIVERSIDE SCH	Richmond		5-14		5-14	S	S	N	N	S	P		P							P	318
DOOLEY SCH	Richmond		5-21		5-21							P	P					N			318
VA HOME-BOYS & GIRLS	Richmond	12-18	12-18	12-18	12-18	S	N	N	S	S	P	P	P	P	S	P	P	P	S		319
BLUE RIDGE AUTISM	Roanoke		2-22		2-22	P							P		S						312
GRAFTON SCH	Winchester	3-21	3-21	3-21	3-21	P	S		S	S	P	P	P		S	P	S		S		314
TIMBER RIDGE SCH	Winchester			10-22	10-22	P					P		S								319
WASHINGTON																					
HAMLIN ROBINSON SCH	Seattle		6-14		6-14	S							P								321
MORNINGSIDE ACAD	Seattle		7-17		7-17	P							P								321
NW SCH HEARING	Seattle		3-14		3-14				P												322
ST CHRISTOPHER ACAD	Seattle		14-19		14-19	P	N	N	N	N		N	P		S	N		N			322
WISCONSIN																					
EAU CLAIRE ACAD	Eau Claire	10-18		10-18		P					P				S				N		324
WALBRIDGE SCH	Madison		5-18		5-18	P					P							P			325
ST COLETTA-MILWAUKEE	Milwaukee		8-16		8-16	P						S	P			P					324
WYALUSING ACAD	Prairie du Chien	10-18		10-18		P					P	S	P		S	P	S	N	S		325

**PROGRAM
LISTINGS**

ALABAMA

HUNTSVILLE ACHIEVEMENT SCHOOL
Day — Coed Ages 5-18

Huntsville, AL 35801. 406½ Governors Dr.
Tel: 256-539-1772. Fax: 256-539-1772.
www.huntsvilleachievement.com
    E-mail: alyssa.lee@huntsvilleachievement.com
Richard Reynolds, BA, MDiv, MEd, EdS, Dir.
    Conditions: Primary—ADHD Anx As Asp Au CD DS Dx ED LD MD Mood ID
    OCD ON PDD PTSD S SP TBI TS. **IQ 60 and up.**
    Gen Acad. Gr K-12.
    Therapy: Hear Music Occup Perceptual-Motor Play Rec Speech Visual.
    Psychotherapy: Art Dance.
    Adm: Appl fee: $25.
    Enr: 45 (Cap: 45). B 30. G 15. **Fac:** 5 (Full-time). Spec ed 3. Lay 2.
    Tui '10-'11: Day $525-625/mo (+$150-490/yr). **Aid:** School.
    Est 1963. Nonprofit.

The school operates 10 months a year and offers a structured program that includes academics and sensorimotor development. Huntsville Achievement's curriculum combines directed studies, project work and service learning. Boys and girls with dyslexia, high-functioning autism, Asperger's syndrome, attentional disorders and other at-risk conditions constitute the student body.

TRI-WIL
PORTA CRAS SCHOOL
Bdg — Coed Ages 6-21

Green Pond, AL 35074. PO Box 77.
Tel: 205-938-7855. Fax: 205-938-3647.
www.triwil.com   E-mail: triwil@triwil.com
James W. Brown, MA, Dir.
    Conditions: Primary—As CD Db ED Mood ID OCD. **Sec**—Anx D Psy PTSD
    PW SP Sz TS. **IQ 70-110.**
    Gen Acad. Underachiever. Gr 1-12. **Expected outcome:** Return to local
    school (Avg length of stay: 6+ mos).
    Therapy: Rec. **Psychotherapy:** Art.
    Enr: 50. B 40. G 10. **Fac:** 2 (Full-time). Spec ed 1. Lay 1.
    Summer prgm: Bdg. Educ. Rec. 6 wks.
    Est 1984. Inc.

Students enrolled at Porta Cras receive individual instruction designed to promote academic success and improve behavioral and social skills. The therapeutic treatment program consists of milieu and recreational therapy, as well as the formulation of individualized treatment plans. The school's experiential education program teaches creativity, teamwork, leadership and effective communication and listening skills. Among the program's challenge opportunities are an Alpine tower, hiking, orienteering, horsemanship and ropes courses.

ARIZONA

ABBIE LOVELAND TULLER SCHOOL
Day — Coed Ages 4-14

Tucson, AZ 85711. 5870 E 14th St.
Tel: 520-747-1142. Fax: 520-747-5236.
www.tullerschool.com   E-mail: nakins@tullerschool.com
Nannette Akins, Head.
  Conditions: Primary—ADHD.
  Gen Acad. Underachiever. Gr PS-8. **Feat**—Span Computers Studio_Art.
  Expected outcome: Graduation.
  Adm: Appl due: Year-round. On-campus interview.
  Enr: 70. **Fac:** 9.
  Tui '12-'13: Day $7900/sch yr (+$150).
  Acres 5. Bldgs 8. Libs 1. Chapels 1.
  Est 1955. Nonprofit. Episcopal.

Enrolling both students who have underachieved in previous settings and accelerated pupils, Tuller School employs an interdisciplinary teaching method that enables boys and girls to progress at an appropriate pace in small groups, on their own or with assistance. Those with attentional problems also stand to benefit from the school's program.

After three years of elementary instruction, the Tuller Method combines group instruction with individual assessment and progress. At the intermediate and junior high levels, work in all classes revolves around a single unit project. Projects help students develop the learning strategies that they will require for high school and college study. Tuller offers diagnostic and remedial assistance as needed.

ACCEL
Day — Coed Ages 5-22

Phoenix, AZ 85051. 10251 N 35th Ave.
Tel: 602-995-7366. Fax: 602-997-2636.
www.accel.org   E-mail: kmcdougal@accel.org
  Nearby locations: 1430 E Baseline Rd, Tempe 85283.
Connie F. Laird, Exec Dir. **Christine Horton,** Educ Dir. **Kim McDougal,** Adm.
  Conditions: Primary—Au CP DS MD ID ON SB TBI. **Sec**—As B/VI C D ED
    Ep OCD S.
  Voc. Ungraded. Culinary. Hort. Man_Arts & Shop. On-Job Trng. **Expected out-
    come:** Graduation.
  Therapy: Aqua Hear Music Occup Phys Rec Speech Visual. **Psychotherapy:**
    Art Dance Equine.
  Adm: Appl due: Rolling.
  Enr: 250. **Fac:** 27 (Full-time). Spec ed 27.
  Summer prgm: Day. Educ. Rec. Ther. 4 wks.
  Est 1980. Nonprofit.

ACCEL provides an individualized curriculum with an appropriate balance of academic, vocational and daily living skills. Intense programming in small classrooms with a low student/staff ratio helps each student to reach his or her potential. Vocational programs are designed to teach students work skills and prepare them socially and emotionally for a productive life.

Both on-site and off-site employment opportunities provide real-life situations intended to develop confidence, responsibility and independence. Therapy services, which include horseback riding and swimming programs, aim to enhance motor development, sensory awareness, language development, and social and emotional growth.

HOWARD S. GRAY SCHOOL

Day — Coed Ages 9-21

Scottsdale, AZ 85251. 7575 E Earll Dr.
Tel: 480-941-7500. Fax: 480-941-7614.
www.bannerhealth.com/howardgray
   E-mail: shari.carlsted@bannerhealth.com
Shari Carlsted, MEd, Prin.
   Conditions: Primary—ADHD Anx Ap Asp Au Db Dc Dg Dx ED LD Mood OCD PDD Psy SP Sz TS. **Sec**—AN Apr Bu C Ep ID ON PTSD. **IQ 80 and up.**
   Gen Acad. Underachiever. Gr 4-12. Hort. **Feat**—Span Study_Skills. **Expected outcome:** Return to local school (Avg length of stay: 18 mos).
   Therapy: Occup Speech. **Counseling:** Educ.
   Adm: Appl due: Year-round. On-campus interview.
   Enr: 35 (Cap: 48). B 24. G 11. **Fac:** 8 (Full-time). Spec ed 7. Lay 1.
   Tui '11-'12: Day $140/day. **Aid:** State 30. **Summer prgm:** Day. Educ. Rec. Ther. Tui Day $110/day. 7 wks.
   Acres 2. Bldgs 100% ADA. Class rms 4. Sci labs 1. Lang labs 1. Studios 1. Fields 1. Courts 1.
   Est 1985. Nonprofit. **Spons:** Banner Health.

Serving families in Metropolitan Phoenix, Howard Gray provides middle school and high school programming for adolescents with autism, Asperger's syndrome, and emotional and learning disabilities. With a curriculum that emphasizes the development of both academic and social skills, the school considers the student's skills, motivation level, learning style and challenges faced when formulating an educational plan. A group-setting approach facilitates life and social skills development. Lessons address career exploration, body language, social cues, goal setting, bullying, manners and etiquette, self-esteem, empathy for others, assertiveness, honesty, conflict resolution and peer pressure. Career exploration and job interview techniques are also part of the program.

Classrooms contain personal computers with Internet access and current academic materials, thereby facilitating individualized instruction. Educational and recreational activities take place in the arts and crafts center, the outdoor sports court, open fields, landscaped patios and, for group discussions, in lounges.

NEW WAY ACADEMY

Day — Coed Ages 5-19

Scottsdale, AZ 85257. 1300 N 77th St.
Tel: 480-946-9112. Fax: 480-946-2657.
www.newwayacademy.org E-mail: samantha@newwayacademy.org
Michael Walker, MEd, Head. **Samantha Hirsch,** Adm.
Conditions: Primary—ADHD Anx APD Db Dg Dx LD SP. **Sec**—Apr Asp Dc ED Mood NLD OCD S. **IQ 80 and up.**
Col Prep. Gen Acad. Gr K-12. **Feat**—Study_Skills. Interscholastic sports. **Expected outcome:** Graduation.
Therapy: Lang Occup Perceptual-Motor Speech. **Psychotherapy:** Art Group Indiv. **Counseling:** Educ Voc.
Adm: Appl fee: $100. Appl due: Year-round. On-campus interview.
Enr: 135. **Fac:** 29 (Full 22, Part 7). Spec ed 29.
Tui '12-'13: Day $19,950/sch yr (+$2500). **Aid:** School 34. State. **Summer prgm:** Day. Educ. Tui Day $1500-2500. 5 wks.
Acres 2. Bldgs 3. Libs 1. Sci labs 1. Art studios 1. Comp labs 2. Laptop prgm Gr 7-12.
Est 1968. Nonprofit.

New Way provides remediation of specific learning disabilities. The academy designs individualized programs for each student, with an emphasis on both academics and social and emotional development. Other integral aspects of the program are Orton-Gillingham dyslexia training, speech therapy and occupational therapy. A one-to-one laptop program serves boys and girls in grades 7-12. The vast majority of pupils go on to earn their high school diplomas, then attend college.

OAK CREEK RANCH SCHOOL

Bdg — Coed Ages 13-18

West Sedona, AZ 86340. PO Box 4329.
Tel: 928-634-5571, 877-554-6277. Fax: 928-634-4915.
www.ocrs.com E-mail: dwick@ocrs.com
David Wick, Jr., BA, JD, Head. **Nadine O'Brien,** BA, MS, Prin.
Conditions: Primary—ADHD Dx LD. **IQ 85 and up.**
Col Prep. Gen Acad. Gr 8-12. **Feat**—Span Comp_Sci Photog. Avg SAT: CR/M 1100. ESL. Interscholastic sports. **Expected outcome:** Graduation.
Adm: Appl due: Rolling.
Enr: 80. **Fac:** 15 (Full-time).
Tui '08-'09: Bdg $36,500/sch yr (+$1000). **Summer prgm:** Bdg. Educ. Rec. Tui Day $4750/4-wk ses. 8 wks.
Acres 17. Dorms 7. Art studios 1. Fields 2. Courts 2. Pools 1. Riding rings 1. Stables 1. Comp labs 3.
Est 1972.

OCRS' academic program is designed for students who have not succeeded in usual school settings. In addition to the regular nine-month program, Oak Creek offers a year-round option. Emphasis is placed on both basic learning skills and college preparation.

Academics address individual needs, and the school maintains a program for pupils with learning disabilities. Activities include camping, fishing, horseback riding, skiing and other sports.

CALIFORNIA

ASELTINE SCHOOL

Day — Coed Ages 5-19

San Diego, CA 92103. 4027 Normal St.
Tel: 619-296-2135. Fax: 619-296-3013.
www.aseltine.org E-mail: info@aseltine.org
Hayden W. Thomas, BA, MS, PhD, Exec Dir. **Carol Patton,** BA, Prgm Dir.
Kim Groulx, Adm.
Conditions: Primary—ADHD AN Anx Asp CD ED HI LD ODD. **Sec**—Bu Db
Dc Dg Dpx Dx Ep Mood Multi OCD Psy PTSD PW S SA SO SP Subst Sz
TS. **IQ 90 and up. Not accepted**—B/VI D D-B ID MR NLD ON TBI.
Gen Acad. Voc. Gr 3-12. Culinary. Hort. Man_Arts & Shop. On-Job Trng.
Support_Employ. **Feat**—Computers Fine_Arts. Interscholastic sports.
Expected outcome: Return to local school (Avg length of stay: 1-2 yrs).
Therapy: Lang Occup Speech. **Psychotherapy:** Group Indiv. **Counseling:**
Educ Voc.
Adm: Appl fee: $0. Appl due: Year-round. On-campus interview.
Enr: 40 (Cap: 75). B 37. G 3. **Fac:** 14 (Full 12, Part 2). Spec ed 3. Lay 11.
Tui '11-'12: Day $172/day. **Aid:** State 40. **Summer prgm:** Day. Educ. Rec. Voc.
Tui Day $172/day. 6 wks.
Bldgs 1. Class rms 4. Sci labs 1. Art studios 1. Comp labs 1.
Est 1968. Nonprofit.

Aseltine serves students whose severe learning disabilities or emotional disturbances
prevent their needs from being addressed in traditional school settings. Boys and girls with
behavioral disorders work with staff on problem solving and conflict resolution to gain
better control of their emotions and behaviors. Teachers employ multiple modalities in an
effort to overcome obstacles to learning while accommodating various learning styles. In
addition to instruction in the core subjects, Aseltine's program includes fine arts, sports,
online classes, culinary arts, horticulture and vocational education.

BEACON SCHOOL

Day — Coed Ages 9-22

San Jose, CA 95124. 5670 Camden Ave.
Tel: 408-265-8611. Fax: 408-265-7324.
www.beaconschool.com E-mail: info@beaconschool.com
Teresa Malekzadeh, BA, Exec Dir.
Conditions: Primary—ADHD Asp Au ED ON TBI. **Sec**—AN Anx Apr As CP
Dc Dg Dx Ep ID Mood OCD PTSD PW SP TS. **IQ 50 and up.**
Gen Acad. Voc. Gr 6-PG. Culinary. Man_Arts & Shop. **Feat**—Sci Comput-
ers Studio_Art Drama Woodworking. **Expected outcome:** Return to local
school (Avg length of stay: 1½-3 yrs).
Therapy: Occup Speech. **Psychotherapy:** Group Indiv. **Counseling:** Educ.

Enr: 60. B 42. G 18.
Summer prgm: Day. Educ. Rec. 6 wks.
Est 1970. Inc.

The school prepares adolescents with emotional disorders and other mild disabilities for transition into public school and the workplace by providing special education classes and vocational training. Students receive individualized instruction in the core academic courses, and also explore topics of interest through an elective program. Individual and group counseling sessions cover issues such as social skills, anger management and conflict resolution.

BENCHMARK YOUNG ADULT SCHOOL
Bdg — Coed Ages 18-28

Loma Linda, CA 92354. 25612 Barton Rd, Ste 286.
Tel: 909-307-3973, 800-474-4848. Fax: 909-793-4499.
www.benchmarktransitions.com   E-mail: admissions@benchmarkyas.com
Jayne Selby-Longnecker, MEd, Exec Dir. **Florence Reynolds,** BA, Educ Dir.
Shelley Skaggs, Adm.
Conditions: Primary—ADHD AN Anx Bu CD Dc Dg Dx ED LD Mood OCD PTSD SP TS. **Sec**—Apr As Asp C CP Db Ep Psy Subst TBI. **IQ 75 and up.**
Not accepted—B/VI D DS ID MR.
Col Prep. Gen Acad. Voc. Gr 10-12. Culinary. Man_Arts & Shop. On-Job Trng. **Expected outcome:** Return to local school (Avg length of stay: 12-18 mos).
Psychotherapy: Group Indiv Parent. **Counseling:** Educ.
Enr: 66. B 46. G 20.
Est 1993.

Benchmark offers a community-based program for troubled young adults who require specialized assistance to become healthy, productive and independent. Students typically spend at least 12 months enrolled in the program; some require 18 to 24 months at Benchmark, depending upon individual progress. Clients who are willing to live in a structured environment stand to benefit most from the program. Students live in a supervised apartment with a small group of their peers.

Elements of the program include academic coaching, apartment living, community involvement, daily living skills improvement, emotional growth training, finance and budgeting instruction, work experience, meal planning and preparation training, and vocational education.

Those dealing with drug- or alcohol-related issues must adhere to a program of sobriety. Twelve-Step programming is available.

BIG SPRINGS
EDUCATIONAL THERAPY CENTER AND SCHOOL
Day — Coed Ages 5-12

Moreno Valley, CA 92557. 11650 Perris Blvd.

Tel: 951-488-0404.
www.bigspringscenterandschool.org
E-mail: bigspringscenter@sbcglobal.net
Nearby locations: 24977 Washington Ave, Ste K, Murrieta 92562.
Leslie Huscher, MA, Dir.
Conditions: Primary—Dg Dx LD. **Sec**—ADHD. **IQ 80 and up.**
Gen Acad. Gr K-6. **Feat**—Soc_Stud. **Expected outcome:** Return to local school (Avg length of stay: 2+ yrs).
Therapy: Lang Occup Speech Visual. **Counseling:** Educ.
Adm: Appl due: Year-round.
Enr: 18 (Cap: 20).
Est 1980. Nonprofit.

Big Springs' day school program offers remediation in the basic skill areas to children with learning differences. Individual educational programs utilize multisensory and multidisciplinary techniques to provide reading and math remediation, perceptual-motor and sensorimotor training, occupational therapy, and auditory and visual perceptual skills. The goal is to provide the skills necessary for a return to regular school programs.

The Educational Therapy Center, located on the Big Springs campus, provides individualized therapy at all age levels for those with learning differences.

Big Springs also offers services in Murrieta (951-304-9656).

THE BRIDGE SCHOOL

Day — Coed Ages 3-14

Hillsborough, CA 94010. 545 Eucalyptus Ave.
Tel: 650-696-7295. **Fax:** 650-342-7598.
www.bridgeschool.org
Vicki R. Casella, EdD, Exec Dir. **Mary Hunt-Berg,** Educ Dir.
Conditions: Primary—CP ON. **Sec**—Apr B/VI DS Ep ID S TBI.
Gen Acad. Gr PS-8. **Expected outcome:** Return to local school (Avg length of stay: 4 yrs).
Therapy: Lang Music Occup Speech Visual. **Psychotherapy:** Dance.
Adm: Appl due: Year-round. On-campus interview.
Enr: 13 (Cap: 14). **B** 9. **G** 4. **Fac:** 3 (Full-time). Spec ed 3.
Tui '12-'13: Day $183/day. Clinic $110/hr. **Aid:** School 3 ($150,000). State.
Est 1987. Nonprofit.

The school's educational program serves children with severe speech and physical impairments through the use of augmentative and alternative means of communication and assistive technology applications. An outreach program provides information for parents and professionals interested in these applications. Programming emphasizes communication, recreation, academics, community involvement, self-reliance, independence and lifelong learning.

BRIDGES ACADEMY

Day — Coed Ages 10-18

Studio City, CA 91604. 3921 Laurel Canyon Blvd.
Tel: 818-506-1091. Fax: 818-506-8094.
www.bridges.edu   E-mail: info@bridges.edu
Carl Sabatino, Head. **Doug Lenzini,** Adm.
  Conditions: Primary—ADHD APD Dc Dg Dpx Dx LD NLD. **Sec**—Asp Multi.
  Col Prep. Gr 5-12. **Feat**—Humanities Japan Span Calc Stats Anat & Physiol
    Genetics Cold_War Econ Govt Photog Studio_Art Drama. Interscholastic
    sports. **Expected outcome:** Graduation.
  Adm: Appl fee: $150. Appl due: Year-round. On-campus interview.
  Enr: 130. **Fac:** 37 (Full 33, Part 4).
  Tui '11-'12: Day $31,411/sch yr. **Aid:** School.
  Acres 3. Bldgs 3. Sci labs 1. Art studios 1. Gyms 1. Comp labs 1. Laptop prgm
    Gr 5-12.
  Est 1994. Nonprofit.

Bridges enrolls students classified as either gifted or highly gifted who also have learning differences. The academy addresses the particular needs of this population through small classes and differentiated instruction. In some classes, seminar-style seating is utilized to promote discussion and the exchange of ideas. Technology is an important aspect of the program: Each student must possess a laptop computer for classroom work, research and communication. During the middle school years (grades 5-8), programming combines work in the core disciplines with attention to children's social and emotional needs. Regular progress reports enable parents to track student achievement.

The college preparatory high school (grades 9-12) features honors courses, preparation for Advanced Placement examinations in certain subjects, and electives in the visual and performing arts. Spanish and Japanese constitute the foreign language options during these years. High schoolers accumulate 30 hours of required community service prior to graduation.

CHARLES ARMSTRONG SCHOOL

Day — Coed Ages 6-14

Belmont, CA 94002. 1405 Solana Dr.
Tel: 650-592-7570. Fax: 650-591-3114.
www.charlesarmstrong.org   E-mail: information@charlesarmstrong.org
Claudia Koochek, Head. **Debbie Vielbaum,** Adm.
  Conditions: Primary—Dx LD.
  Gen Acad. Gr 1-8. **Feat**—Lib_Skills Studio_Art Drama Music. **Expected outcome:**
    Return to local school (Avg length of stay: 2-4 yrs).
  Adm: Appl fee: $190. Appl due: Year-round.
  Enr: 249 (Cap: 250). **Fac:** 48.
  Tui '12-'13: Day $32,500/sch yr. **Aid:** School.
  Est 1968. Nonprofit.

CAS conducts an academic program that specializes in serving children with such language-based learning disabilities as dyslexia. Classes are designed to address learning-style differences while helping students develop competence in reading, writing and spelling skills. In addition to academics, the program also emphasizes the development of improved social skills and self-esteem. The school attempts to return the pupil to a traditional public or private school in two to four years.

CHARTWELL SCHOOL

Day — Coed Ages 7-19

Seaside, CA 93955. 2511 Numa Watson Rd.
Tel: 831-394-3468. Fax: 831-394-6809.
www.chartwell.org   E-mail: information@chartwell.org
Douglas Atkins, EdM, Exec Dir. **Nora Lee,** MEd, Head. **Graydon Mitchell,** Adm.
  Conditions: Primary—APD Dc Dg Dpx Dx LD NLD. **Sec**—ADHD Db Ep. **IQ 90 and up. Not accepted**—AN Anx Ap Apr Ar Asp Au B/VI Bu C CD CF CLP CP D D-B DS Hemo HI IP Lk MD Mood MS Nf OCD ODD PDD Psy PTSD PW S SA SB SC SO SP Subst Sz TBI TS.
Col Prep. Gr 2-12. **Expected outcome:** Graduation.
Adm: Appl fee: $85. Appl due: Year-round. On-campus interview.
Enr: 86 (Cap: 100). **Fac:** 16 (Full 14, Part 2).
Tui '12-'13: Day $30,650/sch yr. **Aid:** School 29 ($266,000). **Summer prgm:** Day. Educ. Tui Day $350-2500. 2-4 wks.
Endow $1,090,000. Plant val $15,000,000. Acres 60. Bldgs 5 (100% ADA). Libs 1. Sci labs 1. Theaters 1. Fields 1. Comp labs 1.
Est 1983. Nonprofit.

Chartwell utilizes specialized teaching strategies and small classes to assist students who have been diagnosed with dyslexia and other language-based learning differences. The school teaches boys and girls various skills and strategies to expand their learning capacities, and programming also addresses self-esteem and confidence issues. Teachers take advantage of the environmental benefits of Chartwell's 60-acre campus, which features sustainable design, to help pupils learn more successfully.

CHILDREN'S WORKSHOP

Day — Coed Ages 3-12

San Diego, CA 92108. 4055 Camino del Rio S.
Tel: 619-521-3990. Fax: 619-521-0432.
www.tiee.org/childrens-workshop   E-mail: hwhiteside@tiee.org
Hilary Whiteside, MA, Dir.
  Conditions: Primary—Ap Au ED HI LD ID Multi S TBI.
  Gen Acad. Voc. Ungraded.
  Therapy: Lang Occup Speech. **Psychotherapy:** Indiv.
  Enr: 50 (Cap: 50).
  Spons: The Institute for Effective Education.

Serving the San Diego area, Children's Workshop offers a comprehensive, behaviorally based instructional program. Most students have autism, although those with intellectual disabilities hearing impairments, multiple disabilities, traumatic brain injury and emotional disturbances may enroll. Small class size and regular sensorimotor, speech and language, and social skills training provide an intensive program for the child experiencing learning and behavioral problems. The program is data based, and the academic curriculum uses direct instruction programs whenever possible.

The school enrolls both private-pay students and those referred by their local school districts.

THE COUNTRY SCHOOL

Day — Coed Ages 8-18

San Marcos, CA 92078. 1145 Linda Vista Dr, Ste 105.
Tel: 760-744-4870. Fax: 760-510-6866.
www.teriinc.org   E-mail: shanep@teriinc.org
Shane Hamilton, MS, Prin.
   Conditions: Primary—ADHD Anx Asp Au Db LD Mood Nf OCD ODD PDD S. **Sec**—Apr Ar As CP Dc Dg Dx ED Ep ID ON SP. **IQ 70 and up.**
   Gen Acad. Gr 3-12. **Expected outcome:** Return to local school (Avg length of stay: 2 yrs).
   Therapy: Lang Occup Speech. **Psychotherapy:** Equine.
   Adm: Appl due: Rolling. On-campus interview.
   Enr: 27 (Cap: 36). B 16. G 11. **Fac:** 4 (Full-time). Spec ed 4.
   Summer prgm: Day. Educ. Rec. 4 wks.
   Est 1978. Nonprofit. **Spons:** TERI.

The school provides individualized special education classes for students with learning disabilities. Core academic courses such as reading, math, science and social studies are taught at both remedial and accelerated levels. On-site therapeutic options include speech, language and occupational therapies, as well as therapeutic horseback riding. After acquiring the necessary skills (typically about two years), the student returns to a mainstream educational setting.

EXCELSIOR ACADEMY

Day — Coed Ages 6-19

San Diego, CA 92120. 7202 Princess View Dr.
Tel: 619-583-6762. Fax: 619-583-6764.
www.excelsioracademy.com   E-mail: cchapman@excelsioracademy.com
   Conditions: Primary—ADHD Asp Dc Dg Dx LD. **Sec**—Anx B/VI D Db ED OCD PW SP TS. **IQ 85-130.**
   Col Prep. Gen Acad. Gr 1-12. On-Job Trng. Interscholastic sports. **Expected outcome:** Return to local school (Avg length of stay: 3-4 yrs).
   Therapy: Lang Occup Speech. **Counseling:** Educ.
   Enr: 80. B 65. G 15.
   Est 1988. Nonprofit.

The academy serves students of average to above-average intelligence whose needs fall within the areas of processing, memory, language, attention and socialization. Academic and extracurricular opportunities are available in art, drama, music, technology, intramural and interscholastic athletics, and outdoor education.

HAWTHORNE ACADEMY
Day — Coed Ages 9-22

Hawthorne, CA 90250. 12500 Ramona Ave.
Tel: 310-644-8841. Fax: 310-644-8910.
www.hawthorneacademy.com   E-mail: ray.richard@valleyhs.com
Ray Richard, MA, Exec Dir. **Lisa Kirschenbaum**, Clin Dir.
Conditions: Primary—ADHD AN Anx APD Ar Asp Au C CD CLP CP Db Dc Dg Dpx Dx ED Ep Hemo LD MD ID Lk MS Multi Nf ODD PDD PTSD PW SA SB SC SO SP Subst TS. **Sec**—Ap Bu OCD ON Psy S Sz.
Gen Acad. Underachiever. Gr 4-12. On-Job Trng. Support_Employ. **Feat**—Computers Graphic_Arts Music. Interscholastic sports. **Expected outcome:** Return to local school (Avg length of stay: 2 yrs).
Therapy: Lang Occup Play Speech. **Psychotherapy:** Indiv. **Counseling:** Educ Voc.
Adm: Appl due: Year-round. On-campus interview.
Enr: 100 (Cap: 140). B 80. G 20. **Fac:** 28 (Full 27, Part 1).
Tui '10-'11: Day $130/day. Clinic $75/hr. **Aid:** State.
Bldgs 2. Class rms 11. Art studios 1. Music studios 1. Fields 1. Pools 1. Comp labs 1.
Est 1988. Inc.

The academy's individualized curriculum provides the required courses of study, as well as electives for enrichment and remediation in a variety of areas. Where appropriate, students may enroll concurrently in vocational training programs or participate in classes at public schools. High school diplomas are awarded to students who meet the requirements. Hawthorne offers individual counseling, language and speech, and transition services as they are needed.

HELP FOR BRAIN INJURED CHILDREN
THE CLETA HARDER DEVELOPMENTAL SCHOOL
Day — Coed Ages 3-22

La Habra, CA 90631. 981 N Euclid Ave.
Tel: 562-694-5655. Fax: 562-694-5657.
www.hbic.org   E-mail: jcecil@hbic.org
Conditions: Primary—ADHD Asp Au CP ID Multi ON TBI. **Sec**—As B/VI C D Dx ED Ep IP LD MD PW S SB.
Gen Acad. Voc. Ungraded. On-Job Trng.
Therapy: Lang Occup Phys Speech. **Psychotherapy:** Dance Indiv.
Enr: 50 (Cap: 60). B 39. G 11. **Fac:** 5 (Full-time). Spec ed 2. Lay 3.
Est 1981. Nonprofit.

HBIC provides educational and rehabilitative services for children, adolescents and young adults who have a brain injury or dysfunction. Named for the center's founder, the Cleta Harder Developmental School offers an individualized academic program for the pupil who has the potential to move to a higher level of functioning, but who requires a small, controlled environment to do so. Within a highly structured and disciplined environment, the school maintains an individualized motor development regime and a student-faculty ratio of no greater than 2:1.

THE HELP GROUP

Day — Coed Ages 2¾-22

Sherman Oaks, CA 91401. 13130 Burbank Blvd.
Tel: 818-779-5262, 877-994-3588. Fax: 818-779-5295.
www.thehelpgroup.org
Barbara Firestone, PhD, Pres.
　Conditions: Primary—ADHD AN Anx Ap Apr Asp Au CD Dc Dg DS Dx ED LD Mood ID OCD ODD ON PDD Psy PTSD SP Sz TBI TS. **IQ 50 and up.**
　Col Prep. Gen Acad. Voc. Gr PS-12. On-Job Trng.
　Therapy: Lang Milieu Occup Speech. **Psychotherapy:** Art Fam Group Indiv.
　Counseling: Educ Voc.
　Enr: 1400. **Fac:** 115 (Full 110, Part 5). Spec ed 115.
　Summer prgm: Day. Ther. 6 wks.
　Est 1975. Nonprofit.

Through various educational and therapeutic programs, this organization serves children with special needs related to autism, Asperger's syndrome, learning disabilities, emotional development, mental retardation, and abuse and neglect. Within an individualized environment, schools provide academic programs at the elementary, middle school and secondary levels that are designed to improve the student's socialization and communicational skills.

HILLSIDE SCHOOL AND LEARNING CENTER

Day — Coed Ages 12-18

La Canada, CA 91011. 4331 Oak Grove Dr.
Tel: 818-790-3044. Fax: 818-790-4225.
www.hillsideforsuccess.org　E-mail: frank@hillsidelc.org
Robert A. Frank, BS, MS, Exec Dir.
　Conditions: Primary—ADHD Dc Dg Dx LD. **Sec**—Anx Asp CP ED Mood TBI. IQ 90-125.
　Col Prep. Gen Acad. Voc. Gr 7-12. **Feat**—Span Psych Visual_Arts Drama.
　Expected outcome: Return to local school (Avg length of stay: 1-2 yrs).
　Therapy: Lang Speech. **Psychotherapy:** Fam Group Indiv Parent. **Counseling:** Educ Voc.
　Enr: 72 (Cap: 72). B 47. G 25. **Fac:** 9.
　Summer prgm: Day. Educ. Ther. 6 wks.
　Est 1971. Nonprofit.

The facility specializes in the identification and the treatment of learning disorders as they relate to developmental medicine and environmental factors. The center's primary goal is to foster independence and self-reliance in learning-disabled children and adolescents. Related services are available on an adjunctive basis for students who require intensive one-on-one educational or psychological therapy.

Hillside also provides an outreach program for community schools and services, as well as travel programs for students. A computer system for career and vocational counseling allows students to explore interests in various careers.

JEAN WEINGARTEN PENINSULA ORAL SCHOOL FOR THE DEAF

Day — Coed Ages 3-6

Redwood City, CA 94062. 3518 Jefferson Ave.
Tel: 650-365-7500. TTY: 650-365-7500. Fax: 650-365-7557.
www.deafkidstalk.org/site   E-mail: jwposd@jwposd.org
Kathleen Daniel Sussman, MA, Exec Dir. **Pam Hefner-Musladin,** BA, MA, Prin.
 Conditions: Primary—D. **Sec**—LD S.
 Gen Acad. Underachiever. Gr PS-K.
 Therapy: Hear Lang Occup Speech. **Psychotherapy:** Fam Parent.
 Adm: Appl due: Rolling.
 Enr: 69. B 34. G 35.
 Est 1967. Nonprofit.

JWPOSD offers educational and developmental services to deaf and hearing-impaired children and their families through a program that develops listening and spoken communication skills. The program goal is to prepare children to return to their home schools as soon as possible with academic and communication skills that will allow them to function at grade level with their peers. The school's curriculum emphasizes the development of speech, language and audition through a cognitive approach to learning, with a focus on literacy.

Additional offerings include a parent-infant program, a toddler program, mainstream support services, diagnostic services, a parent education program, and counseling and bilingual services.

MID-PENINSULA HIGH SCHOOL

Day — Coed Ages 14-18

Menlo Park, CA 94025. 1340 Willow Rd.
Tel: 650-321-1991. Fax: 650-321-9921.
www.mid-pen.com   E-mail: info@mid-pen.com
Douglas C. Thompson, PhD, Head. **Andrea Henderson,** Adm.
 Conditions: Primary—Dx ED LD. **Sec**—ADHD Anx Asp Bu Dc Dg Mood OCD SA. **Not accepted**—ID MR Subst.
 Col Prep. Gr 9-12. **Feat**—ASL Span Calc Govt Studio_Art Drama SAT_Prep. Interscholastic sports. **Expected outcome:** Return to local school (Avg length of stay: 1-4 yrs).

Psychotherapy: Parent. **Counseling:** Educ.
Adm: Appl fee: $0. Appl due: Rolling.
Enr: 150 (Cap: 150). B 87. G 63. **Fac:** 22.
Tui '12-'13: Day $27,794/sch yr (+$2250). **Aid:** School. **Summer prgm:** Day.
Educ. 7 wks.
Est 1979. Nonprofit.

MPHS offers a comprehensive program catering to students with a variety of learning needs. The program includes remediation and college preparation for pupils who require a personalized learning environment. Certain Advanced Placement courses are available online. The school encourages parental involvement in the learning process.

NEW VISTA SCHOOL
Day — Coed Ages 11-18

Laguna Hills, CA 92653. 23092 Mill Creek Dr.
Tel: 949-455-1270. Fax: 949-455-1271.
www.newvistaschool.org   E-mail: admin@newvistaschool.org
Nancy A. Donnelly, MEd, Exec Dir.
Conditions: Primary—AN As Asp Au Bu. **Sec**—ADHD Anx B/VI Db Dg Dpx Dx ED Ep HI ID MD Mood MS NLD OCD ODD S TS. **IQ 90-130.**
Gen Acad. Gr 6-12. On-Job Trng. Support_Employ. **Feat**—Govt/Econ Health. **Expected outcome:** Graduation.
Therapy: Lang. **Psychotherapy:** Art Dance Group Indiv. **Counseling:** Educ Voc.
Adm: Appl fee: $75. Appl due: Rolling. On-campus interview.
Enr: 63 (Cap: 65). B 40. G 23. **Fac:** 18 (Full-time). Spec ed 18.
Tui '10-'11: Day $21,500/sch yr (+$780). **Aid:** School. **Summer prgm:** Day.
Educ. 5 wks.
Acres 3. Bldgs 1 (100% ADA). Sci labs 1. Lang labs 1. Art studios 1. Fields 1.
Comp labs 1.
Est 2006. Nonprofit.

NVS provides a progressive middle school and high school program in a structured environment for students with Asperger's syndrome, autism (at a high-functioning level) and language learning disabilities. Appropriate placements stand to benefit from social and transitional skills training. The school assists pupils in becoming more independent and in maximizing academic achievement. Social skills training, community involvement and work on self-advocacy skills are important elements of New Vista's program.

ORALINGUA SCHOOL FOR THE HEARING IMPAIRED
Day — Coed Ages 5-11

Whittier, CA 90602. 7056 S Washington Ave.
Tel: 562-945-8391. Fax: 562-945-0361.
www.oralingua.org   E-mail: info@oralingua.org
  Nearby locations: 1305 Deodar Rd, Escondido 92026.

Elisa J. Roche, Exec Dir.
  Conditions: Primary—D. **IQ 90 and up.**
  Gen Acad. Gr K-6. **Feat**—Sci Soc_Stud.
  Therapy: Hear Lang Occup Speech. **Psychotherapy:** Dance Group Parent.
  Adm: Appl due: Year-round.
  Enr: 52. B 30. G 22.
  Est 1969. Nonprofit.

Oralingua's aural-oral program is based on the belief that a deaf child can learn to function effectively in a hearing environment. Through the development of residual hearing, meaningful language, understandable speech and strong cognitive skills, deaf children follow a state-approved curriculum. Classes are small (the student-teacher ratio is 3:1).

Full parental participation is encouraged. A parent-infant tutorial program for children from birth to age 3 is also conducted.

Oralingua operates a satellite campus in Escondido (760-294-0525).

ORION ACADEMY

Day — Coed Ages 13-19

Moraga, CA 94556. 350 Rheem Blvd.
Tel: 925-377-0789. Fax: 925-377-2028.
www.orionacademy.org   E-mail: office@orionacademy.org
Kathryn Stewart, PhD, Dir.
  Conditions: Primary—APD Asp NLD. **Sec**—ADHD Dc Dg OCD TS. **IQ 110
  and up. Not accepted**—B/VI CD D D-B HI ID MR ODD ON Psy PW SO
  Subst Sz.
  Col Prep. Gr 8-12. **Feat**—Lat Anat & Physiol Botany Forensic_Sci Psych
  Visual_Arts Journ Study_Skills. SAT/ACT prep. Interscholastic sports.
  Expected outcome: Graduation.
  Psychotherapy: Group Indiv. **Counseling:** Educ.
  Adm: Appl fee: $100. Appl due: Jan. On-campus interview.
  Enr: 63 (Cap: 63). B 43. G 20. **Fac:** 14 (Full 8, Part 6). Spec ed 2. Lay 12.
  Tui '12-'13: Day $30,500/sch yr. **Aid:** State. **Summer prgm:** Day. Educ. Rec.
  4 wks.
  Laptop prgm Gr 8-12.
  Est 2000. Nonprofit.

Orion offers adolescents with Asperger's syndrome and nonverbal learning disorder an academically challenging secondary curriculum that integrates social skill development into daily activities. Students develop academic and social skills in preparation for college or employment upon graduation. Seniors fulfill a 30-hour community service requirement.

PARK CENTURY SCHOOL

Day — Coed Ages 7-14

Culver City, CA 90232. 3939 Landmark St.

Tel: 310-840-0500. Fax: 310-840-0590.
www.parkcenturyschool.org   E-mail: parkcentury@parkcenturyschool.org
Genevieve Shain, MA, Co-Dir. **Gail Spindler,** MA, Co-Dir. **Judith Fuller,** Adm.
Conditions: Primary—ADHD Dx LD.
Gen Acad. Gr 2-8. **Feat**—Computers Studio_Art Drama Music. **Expected
outcome:** Graduation.
Therapy: Lang Speech.
Adm: Appl due: Rolling. On-campus interview.
Enr: 62 (Cap: 62). B 42. G 20. **Fac:** 23.
Est 1968. Nonprofit.

Park Century's program integrates academic learning, social skills, family relationships and physical education. Boys and girls receive individual tutoring in reading and math. Small-group instruction in social studies and science parallels that found in local public and private schools. Individualized movement education and perceptual-motor therapy are available as needed, and students may also engage in speech and language therapy for an additional hourly fee. A transitional program utilizes materials from local schools.

PARKHILL SCHOOL

Day — Coed Ages 8-18

West Hills, CA 91307. 7401 Shoup Ave.
Tel: 818-883-3500. Fax: 818-883-1519.
www.parkhillschool.net
Conditions: Primary—Dx ED LD. **Sec**—ADHD Anx Ap As Asp Au Ep ID
Mood OCD ON PTSD SP Sz TS. **IQ 80-115.**
Gen Acad. Voc. Gr 3-12. On-Job Trng. **Feat**—Computers Fine_Arts Perform-ing_Arts. SAT/ACT prep. **Expected outcome:** Return to local school (Avg
length of stay: 2-5 yrs).
Therapy: Speech. **Psychotherapy:** Group Indiv Parent. **Counseling:** Educ.
Enr: 90. B 80. G 10. **Fac:** 19 (Full 9, Part 10). Spec ed 9. Lay 10.
Est 1965. Nonprofit.

Parkhill administers complete diagnostic evaluations to determine the nature of the student's academic or learning problem. Only those of at least potentially average intellectual ability are accepted. One-on-one educational therapy is provided on an adjunctive basis for children who are able to maintain themselves in regular school classes. This process involves the following: intensive specific training in those areas of learning difficulty; an individual supportive therapeutic relationship; and an integration of remedial training into the academic program.

PINE HILL SCHOOL

Day — Coed Ages 6-21

San Jose, CA 95118. 1325 Bouret Dr.
•Tel: 408-269-1526. Fax: 408-979-8219.
www.pinehillschool.com   E-mail: leb@secondstart.org

L. E. Boydston, BBA, MA, MDiv, Exec Dir. **Greg Zieman,** BA, Prin.
Conditions: Primary—ADHD Asp Au Dx ED LD PDD S. **IQ 70 and up.**
Gen Acad. Gr 1-12. On-Job Trng. **Expected outcome:** Return to local school
(Avg length of stay: 1-3 yrs).
Therapy: Lang Speech. **Psychotherapy:** Group Indiv. **Counseling:** Educ Voc.
Enr: 60. B 50. G 10. **Fac:** 20 (Full-time).
Est 1976. Nonprofit.

Pine Hill conducts individualized therapeutic programming for students with learning
handicapped, emotionally disturbances or both. Prescriptive academics, behavioral planning, speech and language therapy, counseling and vocational training are integral parts
of the experiential, language-based program. Pupils incur additional fees for speech and
language therapy.

THE PRENTICE SCHOOL

Day — Coed Ages 4-18

Santa Ana, CA 92705. 18341 Lassen Dr.
Tel: 714-538-4511. Fax: 714-538-0273.
www.prentice.org   E-mail: pdadmin@prentice.org
Carol H. Clark, MA, Exec Dir. **Pam Gordon,** Adm.
   Conditions: Primary—Dg Dx LD. **Sec**—ADHD Ar As Asp CP Db Dc Dpx. **IQ
   90 and up.**
   Col Prep. Gen Acad. Voc. Gr PS-12. **Feat**—Computers Studio_Art Drama
   Music.
   Therapy: Lang Music Phys Play Rec Speech. **Psychotherapy:** Art.
   Adm: Appl fee: $75. Appl due: Year-round. On-campus interview.
   Enr: 195 (Cap: 250). B 125. G 70. **Fac:** 48 (Full 21, Part 27).
   Tui '12-'13: Day $12,000-20,000/sch yr. **Aid:** School. **Summer prgm:** Day.
   Educ. Ther. Tui Day $650. 4 wks.
   Acres 7. Bldgs 9. Class rms 18. Libs 1. Sci labs 2. Auds 1. Art studios 1. Music
   studios 1. Fields 1. Courts 1. Comp labs 1.
   Est 1986. Nonprofit.

Prentice offers individualized elementary programming for students with dyslexia and
language-based learning disabilities. Speech and language therapy, tutoring and workshops
are among the available specialized support services.

RASKOB DAY SCHOOL AND LEARNING INSTITUTE

Day — Coed Ages 8-14

Oakland, CA 94619. 3520 Mountain Blvd.
Tel: 510-436-1275. Fax: 510-436-1106.
www.raskobinstitute.org   E-mail: raskobinstitute@hnu.edu
Edith M. Ben Ari, MS, Exec Dir. **Jessica Baiocchi,** Adm.
   Conditions: Primary—Dc Dx LD. **Sec**—ADHD Asp Dg Dpx NLD. **IQ 90 and
   up. Not accepted**—Au B/VI D D-B DS ED HI ID MR PDD Subst.

Gen Acad. Gr 2-8. **Feat**—Studio_Art Music Study_Skills. **Expected outcome:** Graduation.
Therapy: Occup Speech. **Psychotherapy:** Group Indiv. **Counseling:** Educ.
Adm: Appl fee: $150. Appl due: Year-round. On-campus interview.
Enr: 72 (Cap: 78). B 48. G 24. **Fac:** 9 (Full-time). Spec ed 9.
Tui '12-'13: Day $22,250/sch yr. Clinic $100 (Therapy)/hr. **Aid:** School. State 17.
Summer prgm: Day. Educ. Tui Day $2900-5900. 3-6 wks.
Est 1973. Nonprofit.

The academic program at Raskob utilizes a multisensory approach to educating children with learning differences. The curriculum places emphasis on reading/language arts, mathematics and physical education. Eighth graders perform 20 hours of required community service. The school adheres to a strict enrollment limit.

The Learning Institute provides individual educational therapy and diagnostic neuropsychological assessments for both children and adults.

RUSSELL BEDE SCHOOL

Day — Coed Ages 6-12

San Mateo, CA 94401. 446 Turner Ter.
Tel: 650-579-4400. Fax: 650-579-4402.
www.russellbedeschool.com   E-mail: info@russellbedeschool.com
Bonnie Yamane, Prin.
 Conditions: Primary—APD Asp Dx LD. **Sec**—ADHD AN Anx Ap Apr As Au B/VI Bu C CP Db Dc Dg Ep MS ON PDD S SP TBI. **IQ 75-130.**
 Gen Acad. Gr 1-6. **Feat**—Sci Computers Soc_Stud Drama Music. **Expected outcome:** Return to local school.
 Therapy: Music Occup Perceptual-Motor Speech. **Counseling:** Educ.
 Adm: Appl fee: $100. Appl due: Rolling.
 Enr: 18 (Cap: 18). **Fac:** 9 (Full 3, Part 6).
 Tui '11-'12: Day $22,500/sch yr. **Summer prgm:** Day. Educ. Tui Day $1400. 4 wks.
 Est 1983. Nonprofit.

Typical students at Russell Bede have average to above-average intelligence, but must cope with communication difficulties, specific learning disabilities or an alternative learning style. The school uses an instructional model that focuses on individualized instruction and material for each student, small class sizes, development of self-esteem, development of positive character traits, partnership with parents and daily physical education.

SACRAMENTO CHILDREN'S HOME

Bdg — Coed Ages 6-18; Day — Coed 5-18

Sacramento, CA 95820. 2750 Sutterville Rd.
Tel: 916-452-3981. Fax: 916-454-5031.
www.kidshome.org   E-mail: info@kidshome.org
Roy Alexander, LCSW, CEO. **Lisa Ling,** Educ Dir.

Conditions: Primary—ADHD Anx As Asp Au Dc Dg Dx ED LD Mood OCD Psy PTSD PW SP Sz TS. **Sec**—ID. **IQ 60 and up.**
Gen Acad. Gr 1-12. Man_Arts & Shop. On-Job Trng. **Feat**—Sci.
Therapy: Lang Music Play Rec Speech. **Psychotherapy:** Art Dance Fam Group Indiv. **Counseling:** Educ.
Enr: 43. Bdg 16. Day 27. B 36. G 7. **Fac:** 6 (Full-time). Spec ed 5. Lay 1. **Est 1867.** Nonprofit.

Children who have been victims of abuse or neglect receive various residential and educational services through SCH. Capable of accommodating 80 children, the residential program provides therapy, guidance, support and care for survivors of traumatic childhoods. Most residents have lived in one or more foster homes prior to admittance. They also participate in day services and take part in individual and group therapy.

The Pat Anderson Education Center, SCH's educational program, combines academic instruction and therapy for emotionally troubled and mentally ill boys and girls, as well as those with major learning disabilities, in kindergarten through high school. (Students incur additional fees for speech and language therapy.) Emphasis at the school is on returning the child to a neighborhood school with the skills necessary for success.

SPRINGALL ACADEMY

Day — Coed Ages 5-21

San Diego, CA 92119. 6460 Boulder Lake Ave.
Tel: 619-460-5090. Fax: 619-460-5091.
www.springall.org   E-mail: hdierolf@springall.org
Heather Dierolf, PhD, Dir.
Conditions: Primary—ADHD Asp Au Dc Dg Dx ED LD Multi ON TBI. **Sec**—CP Ep ID S.
Gen Acad. Gr K-12. On-Job Trng. Interscholastic sports. **Expected outcome:** Return to local school.
Therapy: Lang Occup Speech Visual. **Psychotherapy:** Fam Group Indiv Parent. **Counseling:** Voc.
Enr: 80. B 65. G 15. **Fac:** 18 (Full-time). Spec ed 17. Lay 1.
Est 1972. Nonprofit.

The academy provides highly individualized developmental education for students with learning disabilities and behavioral problems. A full program of basic education in mathematics, reading and language arts is augmented by special services in adaptive physical education, sensorimotor training, behavior development, language and speech therapy, and independent living skills. Extracurricular activities aid in the development of self-esteem and the building of social skills.

STELLAR ACADEMY FOR DYSLEXICS

Day — Coed Ages 6-14

Newark, CA 94560. 38325 Cedar Blvd.
Tel: 510-797-2227. Fax: 510-797-2207.

www.stellaracademy.org   E-mail: stellaracademy@aol.com
Beth Mattsson-Boze, BA, MDiv, Dir.
   Conditions: Primary—Dg Dx. **Sec**—ADHD Db Dc Dpx Ep ID ODD SA. **Not accepted**—AN Anx Ap Apr Ar Asp Au B/VI Bu C CD CLP CP D D-B DS ED Hemo HI IP Lk MD Mood MS Nf OCD PDD Psy PTSD PW SB SC SO SP Sz TS.
   Gen Acad. Underachiever. Gr 1-8. **Feat**—ASL. **Expected outcome:** Return to local school (Avg length of stay: 2-4 yrs).
   Adm: Appl fee: $0. Appl due: Year-round. On-campus interview.
   Enr: 20. B 12. G 8. **Fac:** 4 (Full 2, Part 2). Spec ed 4.
   Tui '12-'13: Day $15,600/sch yr (+$650). **Aid:** School. State 1. **Summer prgm:** Day. Educ. Tui Day $1100. 4 wks.
   Class rms 3. Courts 1. Comp labs 1. Laptop prgm Gr 1-8.
   Est 1988. Nonprofit.

Stellar Academy enrolls students of average to above-average intelligence who have a primary diagnosis of dyslexia. The school employs the Slingerland approach, a sequential, simultaneous multisensory approach to language arts instruction. Programming addresses difficulties with oral language, spelling, written language and reading. Each pupil receives a laptop computer for school use.

STERNE SCHOOL

Day — Coed Ages 10-18

San Francisco, CA 94115. 2690 Jackson St.
Tel: 415-922-6081. Fax: 415-922-1598.
www.sterneschool.org   E-mail: emcmanis@sterneschool.org
Ed McManis, Head.
   Conditions: Primary—ADHD APD Dc Dg Dx LD NLD.
   Gen Acad. Gr 5-12. **Feat**—Span Econ Psych. SAT/ACT prep. **Expected outcome:** Graduation.
   Counseling: Voc.
   Adm: Appl fee: $0. Appl due: Rolling.
   Enr: 57 (Cap: 60). **Fac:** 13 (Full 10, Part 3).
   Tui '12-'13: Day $22,000-24,000/sch yr. **Aid:** School 20. State 2. **Summer prgm:** Day. Educ. Tui Day $420-790. 4 wks.
   Bldgs 1. Sci labs 1. Fields 1. Courts 1. Comp labs 1.
   Est 1976. Nonprofit.

Sterne's individualized program helps boys and girls with learning differences develop academically and socially by teaching them various skills and strategies. The curriculum emphasizes the mastery of basic skills. Mixed-grade classrooms allow boys and girls to learn at an appropriate level and pace. Career education and guidance counseling are available during the high school years.

VIA CENTER

Day — Coed Ages 5-21

Berkeley, CA 94710. 2126 6th St.
Tel: 510-848-1616. Fax: 510-848-1632.
www.viacenter.org E-mail: viacenter@viacenter.org
Anke VandenBosch, Exec Dir.
   Conditions: Primary—ADHD Ap Asp Au C CD CP ED Ep MS OCD ON PDD
   PW S TBI TS. **Sec**—B/VI D Db DS ID.
   Gen Acad. Voc. Ungraded. Support_Employ. **Feat**—Stats Performing_Arts
   Visual_Arts.
   Therapy: Hydro Lang Occup Phys Rec Speech. **Psychotherapy:** Art Dance.
   Enr: 18 (Cap: 25). B 10. G 8.
   Est 1988. Nonprofit.

Via Center provides a continuum of services for children and adults with developmental disabilities. The goal of programming is to help clients succeed in increasingly less restrictive environments, such as local school programs, agencies offering adult services, supported employment programs, supported living arrangements, and the individual's family and community.

Via School, which serves those ages 5-21, offers educational services and behavioral treatment for students with developmental disabilities who stand to benefit from a highly structured, behaviorally based program. Level of functioning varies, but pupils typically require more individualized attention and behavioral programming than is available through public school special-education programs.

VILLA ESPERANZA SERVICES

Day — Coed Ages 5-22

Pasadena, CA 91107. 2116 E Villa St.
Tel: 626-449-2919. Fax: 626-449-2850.
www.villaesperanzaservices.org
   E-mail: cgregg@villaesperanzaservices.org
Casey Gregg, Dir.
   Conditions: Primary—Au CP DS Ep ID Multi PDD. **Sec**—Ap Asp B/VI C D
   Db ED ON SB TBI.
   Gen Acad. Voc. Ungraded. **Expected outcome:** Graduation.
   Therapy: Lang Music Occup Rec Speech. **Psychotherapy:** Dance Parent.
   Adm: Appl due: Year-round.
   Enr: 79 (Cap: 96). B 53. G 26. **Fac:** 57 (Full 9, Part 48). Spec ed 9. Lay 48.
   Tui '12-'13: Day $125/day. **Aid:** State.
   Class rms 10. Comp labs 1.
   Est 1961. Nonprofit.

Villa Esperanza serves children and young adults with developmental disabilities. The school enrolls individuals with Down syndrome, cerebral palsy, seizure disorders, intellectual disabilities, autism and other learning handicapping conditions. Programming combines classroom work with recreation, speech therapy, language development and behavior modification. A team-teaching approach promotes expertise in academics, play/social skills and independent living.

The program also includes speech-language and occupational therapy services, as well as behavior intervention.

VISTA HILLS/BARON SCHOOL
FOR EXCEPTIONAL CHILDREN
Day — Coed Ages 3-22

Los Angeles, CA 90034. 3200 Motor Ave.
Tel: 310-836-1223. Fax: 310-204-4134.
www.vistadelmar.org/vistahills
Elias Lefferman, PhD, Pres.
  Conditions: Primary—ADHD Anx Ap Apr Asp Au CD Dc Dg Dx ED LD Mood ID OCD ODD PDD S SA TS. **Sec**—As CLP CP PTSD. **IQ 80-120. Not accepted**—B/VI CF D IP MD MS Nf SB SO.
  Gen Acad. Gr PS-12. **Feat**—Photog Theater Music Dance. **Expected outcome:** Return to local school (Avg length of stay: 1-3 yrs).
  Therapy: Occup Play Speech. **Psychotherapy:** Art Dance Fam Indiv. **Counseling:** Educ.
  Est 1916. Nonprofit. **Spons:** Vista Del Mar Child and Family Services.

These educational programs serve children with autism spectrum disorders and other developmental challenges from preschool through early adulthood. Enrolling children ages 3-9, the Baron School provides a therapeutic environment for boys and girls along the autism spectrum, as well as those with severe emotional and behavioral issues and developmental delays. Educational plans incorporate play therapy, sensory and motor skill integration, and speech and language therapy. The goal is to return the child to a mainstream setting as soon as possible.

Vista Hills Middle and High School combines academic opportunities with vocational skills training. Students receive instruction in the traditional classroom, while also engaging in independent skills training in a life skills laboratory. Regular community vocational opportunities and training are also part of the program.

Vista Elite, the young adult component of Vista Hills School, assists students in need of additional vocational, social and living skills prior to moving beyond high school. This transitional program features hands-on work experiences and independent living opportunities in on-campus apartments.

WESTVIEW SCHOOL
Day — Coed Ages 11-18

Los Angeles, CA 90025. 11801 Mississippi Ave.
Tel: 310-478-5544. Fax: 310-473-5235.
www.westviewschool.com   E-mail: info@westviewschool.com
Jackie Strumwasser, MA, Exec Dir. **Bonnie Aharoni,** Adm.
  Conditions: Primary—ADHD Anx Asp Dx ED LD. **Sec**—Dc Dg OCD SP. **IQ 80 and up.**

Col Prep. Gen Acad. Gr 6-12. **Feat**—Span Environ_Sci Computers Econ Govt Filmmaking Studio_Art Drama Music Health Study_Skills. Interscholastic sports. **Expected outcome:** Return to local school (Avg length of stay: 1-7 yrs). **Therapy:** Speech. **Psychotherapy:** Indiv. **Adm:** Appl due: Rolling. **Enr:** 100. B 70. G 30. **Fac:** 20 (Full-time). Spec ed 20. Libs 1. Sci labs 2. Art studios 1. Dance studios 1. Comp labs 1. **Est 1990.** Nonprofit.

A college prep school emphasizing precision teaching based upon social learning principles, Westview offers personalized instruction for children with learning disabilities, attentional disorders and mild emotional disturbances. In addition to college preparation, the program places significant emphasis on therapeutic support and the improvement of self-esteem. Students who remain at Westview through grade 12 earn a high school diploma upon completion of standard course requirements.

The school does not tolerate physical aggression or drug usage in its pupils. Length of enrollment typically ranges from one to seven years.

WINGS LEARNING CENTER
Day — Coed Ages 5-22

Redwood City, CA 94063. 411 Middlefield Rd.
Tel: 650-365-3250. **Fax:** 650-365-3267.
www.wingslearningcenter.org   **E-mail:** info@wingslearningcenter.org
Karen Kaplan, BS, MS, Exec Dir. **Laxmi Ghale,** BA, Educ Dir.
Conditions: Primary—Ap Apr Asp Au ID ON. **Sec**—ADHD.
Gen Acad. Gr K-12. **Feat**—Studio_Art Home_Ec.
Therapy: Lang Music Occup Speech.
Adm: Appl fee: $200. Appl due: Year-round.
Enr: 30. **Fac:** 4 (Full-time).
Tui '10-'11: Day $232/day. **Aid:** State.
Est 2000. Nonprofit.

Wings addresses the academic and social needs of children with autism and communication disorders, making it possible for them to interact, learn and live with typically developing children. The center seeks to create a learning environment where children can learn academic, social and interactive skills at an appropriately challenging pace. WLC also serves as a training facility for professionals interested in working with special-needs children.

COLORADO

DENVER ACADEMY
Day — Coed Ages 6-18

Denver, CO 80222. 4400 E Iliff Ave.
Tel: 303-777-5870. Fax: 303-777-5893.
www.denveracademy.org   E-mail: admissions@denveracademy.org
Kevin M. Smith, BS, MEd, Head. **Daniel A. Loan,** Adm.
  Conditions: Primary—ADHD LD. **IQ 90 and up.**
  Col Prep. Gen Acad. Underachiever. Gr 1-12. **Feat**—Span Calc Anat Astron
    Ecol Anthro Sociol Film Drama. ACT: Avg 20. Interscholastic sports.
  Expected outcome: Graduation.
  Psychotherapy: Parent. **Counseling:** Educ.
  Adm: Appl fee: $75. Appl due: Rolling. On-campus interview.
  Enr: 387. B 293. G 94. **Fac:** 69.
  Tui '12-'13: Day $23,025-24,900/sch yr (+$50). **Aid:** School 107 ($1,000,000).
    Educ. Rec. 5 wks.
  Acres 22. Bldgs 20. Libs 1. Sci labs 1. Lang labs 1. Theaters 1. Art studios 2.
    Music studios 1. Gyms 1. Fields 1. Comp labs 6.
  Est 1972. Nonprofit.

The school's curriculum is designed to meet the needs of children with learning differences or other problems that lead to underachievement. In the elementary and middle schools, instruction focuses on language skills and mathematics in a structured, nurturing environment. High school students can choose either the Core program or the Progressive track, which includes experiential, hands-on learning and the following community service requirements: 20 hours annually in grades 9-11 and 25 hours during senior year.

The academy's 22-acre campus is located near downtown; the Rocky Mountains provide opportunities for field trips and activities.

HAVERN SCHOOL
Day — Coed Ages 5-14

Littleton, CO 80123. 4000 S Wadsworth Blvd.
Tel: 303-986-4587. Fax: 303-986-0590.
www.havernschool.org   E-mail: nmann@havernschool.org
Cathleen M. Pasquariello, MEd, Head. **Nancy B. Mann,** Adm.
  Conditions: Primary—ADHD Dc Dg Dpx Dx LD NLD S. **Sec**—Anx Asp HI
    Mood OCD TS. **IQ 90 and up. Not accepted**—CD ED ID MR ODD Psy SO
    SP Sz.
  Gen Acad. Gr K-8. **Feat**—Computers Studio_Art Drama. **Expected outcome:**
    Return to local school (Avg length of stay: 2-4 yrs).
  Therapy: Lang Occup Speech.
  Adm: Appl fee: $75. Appl due: Mar.
  Enr: 85 (Cap: 85). **Fac:** 16.

Tui '12-'13: Day $18,500/sch yr. **Aid:** School. **Summer prgm:** Day. Educ. Rec. Ther. 6 wks. **Est 1966.** Nonprofit.

Havern serves children who have been diagnosed with specific learning disabilities and who have had difficulties succeeding in a traditional classroom setting. The integrated curriculum emphasizes skill development in the core academic areas of reading, spelling, writing and math. Individualized instruction and speech-language and occupational therapy are provided in a highly structured environment. The goal is to mainstream students into a regular school program, with the usual duration of treatment being two to four years.

TEMPLE GRANDIN SCHOOL
Day — Coed Ages 11-18

Boulder, CO 80301. 6446 Jay Rd.
Tel: 303-554-7363. Fax: 303-494-7558.
www.templegrandinschool.org   E-mail: info@templegrandinschool.org
Jen Wilger, BA, MA, Exec Dir. **Mark Inglis,** Adm.
Conditions: Primary—ADHD Asp Au Dg NLD PDD. **Sec—**Anx Apr Ar CLP CP Dc ED ID MD Mood MS OCD SB SP TBI TS. **IQ 85 and up. Not accepted—**CD Dpx IP Nf ODD Psy SO Subst Sz.
Col Prep. Gen Acad. Underachiever. Gr 6-12. **Feat—**ASL Lat. **Expected outcome:** Graduation.
Therapy: Lang Occup. **Psychotherapy:** Equine Fam Group Indiv Parent.
Counseling: Educ Nutrition Voc.
Adm: Appl fee: $100. Appl due: Year-round. On-campus interview.
Enr: 10 (Cap: 20). B 9. G 1. **Fac:** 6 (Part-time). Spec ed 4. Lay 2.
Tui '12-'13: Day $21,000/sch yr (+$200). **Aid:** School 4 ($38,000). **Summer prgm:** Day. Educ. Rec. Ther. Tui Day $325. 3 wks.
Est 2011. Nonprofit.

Named for the renowned Colorado State University professor, animal scientist and autism advocate, the school serves students with Asperger's syndrome and similar learning profiles. The curriculum condenses core classroom instruction into four days, with a fifth day dedicated to the creative arts, individualized enrichment, mentoring or service learning. The schoolwide social skills program focuses on building students' interpersonal, technology and workplace skills.

CONNECTICUT

AMERICAN SCHOOL FOR THE DEAF

Bdg — Coed Ages 8-21; Day — Coed 3-21

West Hartford, CT 06107. 139 N Main St.
Tel: 860-570-2300. TTY: 860-570-2222. Fax: 860-570-2301.
www.asd-1817.org   E-mail: asdinfo@asd-1817.org
Edward F. Peltier, Exec Dir. Fern Reisinger, Educ Dir. Cindy A. Paluch, Adm.
  Conditions: Primary—D. Sec—Asp Au CP DS ED IP ID LD TBI.
  Col Prep. Gen Acad. Voc. Gr PS-12. Culinary. Man_Arts & Shop. On-Job
    Trng. Feat—Fr Comp_Sci. Expected outcome: Graduation.
  Therapy: Hear Lang Occup Phys Speech. Psychotherapy: Indiv Parent.
    Counseling: Educ Voc.
  Adm: Appl due: Rolling.
  Enr: 236. Fac: 83 (Full 72, Part 11). Spec ed 66. Lay 17.
  Summer prgm: Day. Educ. Rec. 4 wks.
  Dorms 3. Libs 1. Gyms 2. Fields 1. Pools 1.
  Est 1817. Nonprofit.

Children who are deaf or deaf with other special needs take part in a total communication program that emphasizes language growth and development. ASD offers academic, vocational, residential, counseling and support programs. Three separate summer sessions will accept students from other schools. High school seniors perform 20 hours of required community service.

Outpatient services are available, as is home-based counseling for deaf and hard-of-hearing infants and their families. ASD also offers outreach and support services on a fee-for-service basis to deaf and hard-of-hearing individuals in other placements.

BEN BRONZ ACADEMY

Day — Coed Ages 7-18

West Hartford, CT 06107. 139 N Main St.
Tel: 860-236-5807. Fax: 860-233-9945.
www.benbronzacademy.org
  Conditions: Primary—Dc Dg Dx LD. Sec—ADHD Anx ED OCD ODD ON SB
    SP TS. IQ 90 and up.
  Col Prep. Gen Acad. Gr 2-12. Man_Arts & Shop. Feat—Study_Skills.
    Expected outcome: Return to local school (Avg length of stay: 2 yrs).
  Therapy: Lang Occup Phys Speech. Psychotherapy: Group Indiv.
    Counseling: Educ.
  Adm: Appl due: Year-round. On-campus interview.
  Enr: 60. B 40. G 20. Fac: 26.
  Est 1985. Inc. Spons: Learning Incentive.

BBA offers individualized academic programs for learning-disabled students of average to above-average intelligence. The program stresses cognitive abilities, language skills and independence training. Most subjects incorporate computers. Students work on problem solving and are taught to use strategies that facilitate their own learning. All pupils must take part in a structured study hall, except for those who prove they have acquired independent study skills or who maintain an "A" average. Parents participate in the program, and therapy and counseling are available.

An on-site clinic concentrates on academic remediation and skill improvement for both children and adults not enrolled in the day school program. The clinic also emphasizes independence and socialization skills. Classes are small and all work is individualized.

CEDARHURST SCHOOL

Day — Coed Ages 12-21

Hamden, CT 06517. 871 Prospect St.
Tel: 203-764-9314. Fax: 203-764-9321.
www.cedarhurst.yale.edu   E-mail: betsy.donovan@yale.edu
Mary E. Donovan, BS, MS, Dir.
  Conditions: Primary—ADHD CD ED LD OCD Psy SP Sz. **IQ 90 and up.**
  Col Prep. Gen Acad. Gr 7-12. Man_Arts & Shop. On-Job Trng. **Expected**
  outcome: Return to local school (Avg length of stay: 1 yr).
  Psychotherapy: Group.
  Enr: 47. **Fac:** 10.
  Est 1960. Spons: Yale University.

Cedarhurst, an affiliate of the Yale Department of Psychology, offers a special education program to students with moderate to severe emotional disturbances. The school serves partial hospital patients hospitalized at Yale New Haven Hospital, as well as commuting day students referred by local school districts. A complete junior/senior high school curriculum is offered in small classroom groups, with an emphasis on individualized instruction.

EAGLE HILL SCHOOL

Bdg — Coed Ages 10-16; Day — Coed 6-16

Greenwich, CT 06831. 45 Glenville Rd.
Tel: 203-622-9240. Fax: 203-622-0914.
www.eaglehillschool.org   E-mail: info411@eaglehill.org
Marjorie E. Castro, BA, MA, EdD, Head. **Thomas Cone,** Adm.
  Conditions: Primary—Dx LD. **Sec**—ADHD Dc Dg NLD. **IQ 95-135.**
  Gen Acad. Ungraded. **Feat**—Computers Study_Skills. Interscholastic sports.
  Expected outcome: Return to local school (Avg length of stay: 3-4 yrs).
  Therapy: Lang Occup Speech. **Psychotherapy:** Fam Group Indiv Parent.
  Counseling: Educ.
  Adm: Appl fee: $50. Appl due: Rolling.
  Enr: 250. Bdg 35. Day 215. B 157. G 93. **Fac:** 80 (Full 75, Part 5). Spec ed 80.
  Tui '12-'13: Bdg $78,075/sch yr (+$500). Day $59,125/sch yr. **Aid:** School 46
  ($1,650,000). **Summer prgm:** Day. Educ. Tui Day $3100. 5½ wks.
  Endow $15,000,000. Plant val $26,000,000. Acres 20. Bldgs 16. Dorms 1.

Dorm rms 18. Lib 15,000 vols. Sci labs 2. Tech ctrs 1. Auds 1. Theaters 1.
Art studios 1. Music studios 1. Gyms 1. Fields 4. Radio stations 1. Comp
labs 1.
Est 1975. Nonprofit.

The school offers boys and girls of average or above-average intelligence remediation for learning disabilities. Students have typically failed to reach potential in traditional educational environments. Eagle Hill also provides speech and language services, motor training, adaptive physical education classes and counseling services. In addition to various after-school activities, EHS offers an hourlong, proctored study hall on weekday afternoons.

EAGLE HILL-SOUTHPORT

Day — Coed Ages 6-14

Southport, CT 06890. 214 Main St.
Tel: 203-254-2044. Fax: 203-255-4052.
www.eaglehillsouthport.org   E-mail: info@eaglehillsouthport.org
Leonard Tavormina, BA, MA, Head. **Carolyn Lavender,** Adm.
  Conditions: Primary—ADHD APD Dc Dg Dx LD. **Sec**—Anx Mood OCD SP
  TS. **IQ 90 and up.**
  Gen Acad. Ungraded. **Feat**—Studio_Art Study_Skills. Interscholastic sports.
  Expected outcome: Return to local school (Avg length of stay: 2-3 yrs).
  Therapy: Lang.
  Adm: Appl fee: $100. Appl due: Rolling. On-campus interview.
  Enr: 112. B 82. G 30. **Fac:** 29 (Full 27, Part 2). Spec ed 29.
  Tui '11-'12: Day $40,700/sch yr. **Aid:** School 20 ($463,900). **Summer prgm:**
  Day. Educ. Tui Day $540-2500. 2-5 wks.
  Endow $7,727,000. Plant val $516,000. Acres 1. Bldgs 1 (100% ADA). Class
  rms 27. Comp/stud: 1:4.
  Est 1985. Nonprofit.

Eagle Hill provides a linguistically based language arts program for children of average or above-average intelligence with language/learning disabilities. Each child receives small-group tutorial instruction and attends small skills classes in a structured yet flexible environment. Students generally attend for two or three years, as the school aims to place children in a more traditional setting.   **See Also Page 30**

ELIZABETH IVES SCHOOL FOR SPECIAL CHILDREN

Day — Coed Ages 5-21

North Haven, CT 06473. 70 State St.
Tel: 203-234-8770. Fax: 203-234-7238.
www.elizabethivesschool.org
Linda Zunda, MS, MFT, Dir.
  Conditions: Primary—DS ED ID. **Sec**—ADHD Ap Asp Au Dc Dg Dx LD ODD
  ON Psy PTSD S SP Sz TBI TS. **IQ 60 and up.**

Col Prep. Gen Acad. Voc. Ungraded. On-Job Trng. **Expected outcome:** Return to local school.
Therapy: Lang Speech. **Psychotherapy:** Group Indiv. **Counseling:** Educ.
Enr: 21 (Cap: 25). **Fac:** 5 (Full-time). Spec ed 5.
Summer prgm: Day. Educ. Rec. 4 wks.
Est 1963. Nonprofit.

The Elizabeth Ives School offers a therapeutic academic program for children with emotional disturbances and neurological disabilities. Students are grouped according to ability, and the school maintains a favorable student-teacher ratio. Boys and girls choose from various therapeutic, prevocational and vocational services.

FORMAN SCHOOL

Bdg and Day — Coed Ages 14-18

Litchfield, CT 06759. 12 Norfolk Rd, PO Box 80.
Tel: 860-567-8712. Fax: 860-567-8317.
www.formanschool.org   E-mail: admission@formanschool.org
Adam K. Man, BA, MA, Head. **Sara Lynn Leavenworth,** Adm.
Conditions: Primary—ADHD Dc Dg Dx LD. **IQ 90 and up.**
Col Prep. Gen Acad. Gr 9-PG. **Feat**—ASL Fr Span Graphic_Arts Photog Studio_Art Visual_Arts. Avg SAT: CR/M 850. ESL. Interscholastic sports.
Expected outcome: Graduation.
Adm: Appl fee: $50. Appl due: Rolling. On-campus interview.
Enr: 173. Bdg 151. Day 22. **Fac:** 56.
Tui '12-'13: Bdg $61,700/sch yr. Day $50,400/sch yr. **Aid:** School 42 ($1,000,000).
Endow $3,500,000. Plant val $20,200,000. Acres 104. Bldgs 26. Dorms 12. Class rms 25. Lib 6000 vols. Sci labs 2. Auds 1. Art studios 1. Music studios 1. Art galleries 1. Gyms 1. Fields 4. Courts 6. Comp labs 1.
Est 1930. Nonprofit.

The school was founded by John N. Forman as a school for young boys who would benefit from close personal attention. An upper school was added in 1935, and a girls' school was incorporated in 1942 under the direction of Mrs. Forman.

Serving pupils with learning differences, the school offers a college preparatory curriculum with a wide variety of courses. Language and math training programs are specifically designed to help students with learning differences.

THE FOUNDATION SCHOOL

Day — Coed Ages 3-21

Milford, CT 06460. 91 Woodmont Rd.
Tel: 203-877-1426. Fax: 203-876-7531.
www.foundationschool.org   E-mail: stoddard@foundationschool.org
Nearby locations: 719 Derby Milford Rd, Orange 06477.
Conditions: Primary—Au ED LD.

Gen Acad. Ungraded. Man_Arts & Shop. On-Job Trng. **Feat**—Studio_Art
Music.
Therapy: Lang Occup Speech.
Adm: Appl due: Rolling.
Enr: 46.
Est 1966. Nonprofit.

Foundation School designs individualized programs with a team-teaching approach for students with a wide variety of developmental needs, learning deficits, autism spectrum disorders and behavioral challenges. Boys and girls may arrive at the school with deficiencies in perceptual and motor development, speech and language acquisition and processing, learning disabilities, social skills and emotional adjustment, or some combination of the above. A staff comprising special education teachers, speech and language pathologists, occupational therapists, specialty teachers and trained paraprofessionals formulate and implement an individualized program for each pupil. Children are grouped by social and achievement levels and study on a nongraded basis.

Students enroll from many locations in Connecticut and New York, including Westchester County and New York City. The lower and middle schools (ages 3-13) occupy a separate campus in Orange (203-795-6075).

THE GLENHOLME SCHOOL
DEVEREUX CONNECTICUT

Bdg and Day — Coed Ages 10-18

Washington, CT 06793. 81 Sabbaday Ln.
Tel: 860-868-7377. Fax: 860-868-7413.
www.theglenholmeschool.org
  E-mail: admissions@theglenholmeschool.org
Maryann Campbell, MEd, Exec Dir. **Kathi Fitzherbert,** Adm.
  Conditions: Primary—ADHD Asp ED. **Sec**—Anx Ap As Db Dc Dg Dx Ep LD
  Mood OCD ODD PTSD SP TS. **IQ 90 and up.**
  Gen Acad. Underachiever. Gr 5-PG. **Feat**—Span Studio_Art Music. Inter-
  scholastic sports. **Expected outcome:** Return to local school (Avg length
  of stay: 2-4 yrs).
  Therapy: Lang Milieu Music Occup Rec Speech. **Psychotherapy:** Fam Indiv
  Parent. **Counseling:** Educ.
  Adm: Appl fee: $150. Appl due: Rolling.
  Enr: 89. Bdg 83. Day 6. B 72. G 17. **Fac:** 20. Spec ed 7. Lay 13.
  Summer prgm: Res & Day. Educ. Rec. 3-7 wks.
  Acres 110. Bldgs 28. Dorms 9. Class rms 21. Libs 1. Sci labs 1. Theaters 1. Art
  studios 1. Music studios 1. Gyms 1. Fields 2. Courts 2. Pools 1. Riding rings
  1. Stables 1. Comp labs 1. Comp/stud: 1:1 Laptop prgm Gr 5-PG.
  Est 1968. Nonprofit. Spons: Devereux Foundation.

Glenholme uses an evidence-based treatment milieu in a structured therapeutic setting. The 12-month program serves boys and girls who have been diagnosed with such conditions as Asperger's, ADHD, PDD, OCD, Tourette's, depression and anxiety, as well as various learning differences.

The program builds competence socially and academically and integrates a learning approach into all activities, including the arts, an equestrian program, sports and various other interests. While providing a strong academic curriculum, Glenholme utilizes a positive behavior support model to promote relationships among peers, an understanding of boundaries and appropriate social behaviors. The supportive, small-class learning environment and individualized services are designed with higher education in mind.

GROVE SCHOOL

Bdg and Day — Coed Ages 12-19

Madison, CT 06443. 175 Copse Rd.
Tel: 203-245-2778. Fax: 203-245-6098.
www.groveschool.org   E-mail: mainoffice@groveschool.org
Richard L. Chorney, BA, MS, Pres. **Peter J. Chorney,** BA, MS, Exec Dir. **Lauren Seltzer,** Adm.
Conditions: Primary—ADHD Asp Dx ED Mood NLD OCD Psy Sz. **Sec**—LD. **IQ 90 and up. Not accepted**—ID MR.
Col Prep. Gen Acad. Gr 7-PG. Man_Arts & Shop. On-Job Trng. AP courses (Calc Bio US_Hist). **Feat**—Creative_Writing Span Botany Marine_Bio/Sci Biochem Comp_Networking Econ Psych Sociol Philos Ceramics Filmmaking Graphic_Arts Photog Sculpt Video_Production Stained_Glass. Avg SAT: CR/M 1000. ESL. Interscholastic sports. **Expected outcome:** Return to local school (Avg length of stay: 1½-2 yrs).
Therapy: Hear Lang Phys Speech. **Psychotherapy:** Fam Group Indiv Parent. **Counseling:** Educ.
Adm: Appl fee: $200. Appl due: Rolling.
Enr: 126. Bdg 105. Day 21. B 76. G 50. **Fac:** 30.
Tui '12-'13: Bdg $109,980/yr (+$3400). Day $80,900/yr (+$500).
Acres 90. Bldgs 25. Dorms 12. Class rms 20. Libs 1. Sci labs 1. Art studios 1. Gyms 1. Fields 1.
Est 1934. Inc.

Grove serves adolescents who have social, emotional and learning challenges through a therapeutic program that focuses on interpersonal relationships. The school's year-round program includes four two-week vacation periods; boys and girls complete intensive, individualized work during both the summer months and the traditional school year. Grove's clinical approach to psychodynamic psychotherapy features biweekly individual sessions, weekly group therapy, and family and milieu therapy. Boarders attend mandatory evening study periods and, if supplementary academic assistance is necessary, an after-school study hall.

Transitional dormitories are designed for older adolescents not yet ready to return home. The usual length of treatment is 18 to 24 months. Delinquent and violent acting-out youngsters may not enroll.

HIGH ROAD SCHOOLS

Day — Coed Ages 5-21

Wallingford, CT 06492. 29A Village Ln.
Tel: 203-265-5507. Fax: 203-265-5581.
www.highroadschool.com   E-mail: crevill@highroadschool.com
Michael Kaufman, Co-Admin. **Brooke Violante,** Co-Admin.
    Conditions: Primary—ADHD Anx Ap Apr As Asp Au C CP Dg Dx Ep IP LD
    MD Mood ID MS OCD ON PDD PTSD S SB SP TBI TS. **Sec**—B/VI CD D
    Db ED Psy SA Subst Sz.
    Col Prep. Gen Acad. Voc. Gr 1-12. On-Job Trng. **Feat**—Computers Studio_Art
    Music. Interscholastic sports.
    Therapy: Hear Lang Occup Phys Speech. **Counseling:** Voc.
    Enr: 101. **Fac:** 24 (Full-time). Spec ed 12. Lay 12.
    Est 1977. Spons: Specialized Education Services.

At multiple Connecticut locations, High Road serves students facing learning, language and social challenges. Each pupil follows an Individualized Education Program based upon his or her assessed needs. Small classes and a favorable faculty-student ratio facilitate progress. Elements of the program include a transitional component, integrated computer technology, a behavior management system and related services.

Occupational and physical therapy incurs an additional fee.

INSTITUTE OF LIVING
THE GRACE S. WEBB SCHOOL

Day — Coed Ages 5-21

Hartford, CT 06106. 200 Retreat Ave.
Tel: 860-545-7238. Fax: 860-545-7037.
www.instituteofliving.org   E-mail: klevingerdner@harthosp.org
    Nearby locations: 725 Jarvis St, Cheshire 06410.
Kikke Levin-Gerdner, EdD, Dir.
    Conditions: Primary—AN Anx Asp Au Bu ED Mood OCD ODD PDD Psy
    PTSD PW SP Sz TS. **Sec**—ADHD Ap Apr Ar As B/VI C CD CF CLP CP D
    Db Dc Dg DS Dx Ep Hemo LD MD MS Nf ON S SA SB SC SO TBI. **IQ 60
    and up.**
    Gen Acad. Voc. Gr K-12. Culinary. Hort. On-Job Trng. **Feat**—Comp_Sci
    Studio_Art Music Health. **Expected outcome:** Return to local school (Avg
    length of stay: 2-24 mos).
    Therapy: Lang Occup Speech. **Psychotherapy:** Group Indiv. **Counseling:**
    Educ Voc.
    Enr: 170. **Fac:** 40 (Full 37, Part 3). Spec ed 34. Lay 6.
    Summer prgm: Day. Ther. 4 wks.
    Est 1968. Nonprofit. Spons: Hartford Hospital.

The Webb School's primary emphasis is the diagnosis, treatment and education of children in the Greater Hartford area who have emotional disturbances. Children with learning disabilities and perceptual disorders may also enroll in the program. Boys and girls have access to a range of diagnostic and assessment services, and the Institute of Living provides such ancillary services as clinical case management, outreach, and community-based educational and behavioral consultations.

The main Webb School location accepts students in grades K-12, and the institute operates a satellite school for children in grades K-8, The Webb School at Cheshire (203-272-8395).

INTENSIVE EDUCATION ACADEMY
Day — Coed Ages 5-21

West Hartford, CT 06117. 840 N Main St.
Tel: 860-236-2049. Fax: 860-231-2843.
www.intensiveeducationacademy.org   E-mail: iea_education@comcast.net
Jill O'Donnell, Head.
  Conditions: Primary—ADHD Au B/VI ED HI LD ID Multi S TBI.
  Gen Acad. Gr K-12. Culinary. **Feat**—Sci Computers Soc_Stud Studio_Art
    Music.
  Therapy: Lang Occup Speech. **Psychotherapy:** Fam.
  Adm: Appl due: Rolling.
  Enr: 50. B 38. G 12.
  Summer prgm: Day. Educ. 5 wks.
  Est 1971. Nonprofit.

IEA serves children who have learning disabilities. The school, which maintains a low student-teacher ratio, attempts to help children gain confidence, recognize their strengths and weaknesses, and set and reach realistic goals. Activities such as music, art, cooking and drama supplement academics and promote leadership qualities and organizational skills development.

THE MARVELWOOD SCHOOL
Bdg and Day — Coed Ages 14-18

Kent, CT 06757. 476 Skiff Mountain Rd, PO Box 3001.
Tel: 860-927-0047, 800-440-9107. Fax: 860-927-0021.
www.marvelwood.org   E-mail: admissions@marvelwood.org
Arthur F. Goodearl, Jr., AB, MALS, Head. **Katherine Almquist,** Adm.
  Conditions: Primary—LD. IQ 90 and up.
  Col Prep. Underachiever. Gr 9-PG. AP courses (Calc Stats Chem Eur_Hist
    US_Hist). **Feat**—Creative_Writing Shakespeare Fr Lat Span Anat & P⊦   ⊐l
    Ecol Environ_Sci Ethology Limnology Ornithology Comp_Sci Asia⌐
    Psych Comp_Relig Art_Hist Ceramics Filmmaking Photog Stu⌐
    Drama Directing Music Public_Speak. ESL. Interscholastic
    Expected
    outcome: Graduation.
  Adm: Appl fee: $50. Appl due: Rolling. On-campus ˙
  Enr: 169. Bdg 152. Day 17. B 112. G 57. **Fac:** ⌐
  Tui '12-'13: Bdg $48,200/sch yr (+$1250). ⌐
    Aid: School 42 ($540,000). **Summe⌐**

$5600 (+$600). Tui Day $2000 (+$300). 4.
Endow $1,422,000. Plant val $10,000,000. Acres 83. Bldgs 17. Dorms 4.
Dorm rms 92. Class rms 25. Lib 8500 vols. Labs 3. Theaters 1. Art studios
2. Music studios 1. Wood shops 1. Gyms 1. Fields 5. Courts 6. Comp/stud:
1:16.9.
Est 1956. Nonprofit.

Marvelwood was founded by Robert A. Bodkin especially to help youngsters of average to above-average intelligence who have not lived up to academic potential in traditional school settings.

The college preparatory curriculum is sensitive to the individual who needs a structured program in order to fully realize his or her potential. One-quarter of the student body participates in a tutorial program designed to improve reading, writing, organizational and study skills. An extensive interscholastic sports program and many outdoor activities are offered. Graduates attend many different colleges.

In addition to a full range of competitive team sports, Marvelwood offers a year-round Wilderness Ways program that provides experiences in hiking, cross-country skiing, canoeing and mountain biking. All students participate in a weekly community service program.

OXFORD ACADEMY

Bdg — Boys Ages 14-20

Westbrook, CT 06498. 1393 Boston Post Rd.
Tel: 860-399-6247. Fax: 860-399-6805.
www.oxfordacademy.net   E-mail: admissions@oxfordacademy.net
Philip B. Cocchiola, BS, MS, Head. **Patricia Davis,** Adm.
   Conditions: Primary—ADHD Dc Dg Dx LD. **IQ 90 and up.**
   Col Prep. Gen Acad. Ungraded. AP courses (Eng US_Hist). **Feat**—Fr Ger
     Lat Span Calc Stats Botany Ecol Environ_Sci Marine_Bio/Sci Microbio
     Civil_War Holocaust Econ Pol_Sci Psych Sociol Art_Hist Drawing Painting
     Photog Study_Skills. Avg SAT: CR 476. M 544. W 495. **Expected outcome:**
     Return to local school (Avg length of stay: 6 mos-2 yrs).
   Counseling: Educ.
   Adm: Appl fee: $65. Appl due: Rolling. On-campus interview.
   Enr: 48. **Fac:** 18 (Full 17, Part 1).
   Tui '12-'13: Bdg $54,900/sch yr (+$2000). **Summer prgm:** Bdg. Educ. Rec. Tui
     Bdg $7298. 5 wks.
   Endow $200,000. Plant val $3,700,000. Acres 12. Bldgs 10. Dorms 2. Dorm
     rms 26. Class rms 20. Lib 3100 vols. Sci labs 2. Lang labs 1. Art studios 1.
     Gyms 1. Fields 2. Courts 3. Comp labs 1.
   Est 1906. Nonprofit.

Founded in Pleasantville, NJ, by Joseph M. Weidberg, this school moved to Westbrook in 1973, after a fire had destroyed the main building. The academy, which draws its enrollment from throughout the country and the world, has successfully developed and pursued a program of totally individualized instruction that prepares all of its students for college or further secondary preparation.

The school serves young men who have failed to thrive in traditional classrooms. Although students enroll for different reasons, Oxford is especially adept at assisting those with documented disabilities in the area of processing speed and executive function. Typically, these pupils have also been diagnosed with ADHD, anxiety, depression or a combination thereof. Despite the fact that many suitable students have strong verbal skills, they have struggled to keep pace in previous college preparatory settings.

The academy employs the Socratic method of teaching, and a full curriculum extends from basic courses through Advanced Placement. Each class consists of one student and one teacher. Independent study in the subject area follows 20 minutes of class time, and boys receive study skills instruction focusing on note taking, test preparation, stress-reduction strategies, organization and time management. Proctored study halls and access to teachers for extra help throughout the day are additional program features.

Extracurricular activities include trips to concerts, museums, movies, deep-sea fishing sites and nearby points of interest.

ST. THOMAS MORE SCHOOL

Bdg — Boys Ages 13-19

Oakdale, CT 06370. 45 Cottage Rd.
Tel: 860-859-1900. Fax: 860-823-3863.
www.stmct.org   E-mail: triordan@stmct.org
James Fox Hanrahan, Jr., BS, MEd, Head. **Todd Holt,** Adm.
   Conditions: Primary—LD. **IQ 90 and up.**
   Col Prep. Underachiever. Gr 8-PG. **Feat**—British_Lit Mythology Span Calc Environ_Sci Physiol Programming Comp_Relig Theol Fine_Arts Studio_Art. Avg SAT: CR/M 1010. ESL. Interscholastic sports. **Expected outcome:** Graduation.
   Adm: Appl fee: $75. Appl due: Rolling. On-campus interview.
   Enr: 200. **Fac:** 27 (Full-time).
   Tui '12-'13: Bdg $43,900/sch yr (+$1000). **Summer prgm:** Bdg. Educ. Tui Bdg $2998-5995. 2½-5 wks.
   Endow $9,100,000. Plant val $10,500,000. Acres 110. Bldgs 14. Dorms 3. Dorm rms 121. Class rms 18. Lib 6500 vols. Chapels 1. Sci labs 2. Lang labs 1. Auds 1. Art studios 1. Gyms 1. Fields 5. Courts 6. Pools 1. Tracks 1. Comp labs 2.
   Est 1962. Nonprofit. Roman Catholic.

St. Thomas More prepares boys for college entrance by emphasizing study and organizational skills, which are incorporated into the regular curriculum. The school typically enrolls underachieving students of average to above-average intelligence who have no chronic social, emotional or behavioral problems. Classes are small and highly structured.

The school maintains a postgraduate program offering separate English and math courses to prepare students for college-level work. Special emphasis is given to preparation for the SAT exam. International pupils, who may enroll in a grade 7 program that is reserved for them, take part in an intensive English as a Second Language program that provides preparation for the TOEFL.

SETON ACADEMY

Day — Coed Ages 10-20

Westport, CT 06880. 47 Long Lots Rd.
Tel: 203-341-4506. Fax: 203-227-9526.
www.setonacademyschool.org E-mail: afabbri@stvincents.org
Armand Fabbri, Head. **Bill Gluckman,** Educ Coord.
  Conditions: Primary—ADHD AN Anx Asp Bu ED HI Mood OCD PDD Psy
  PTSD SA SP Sz. **Sec**—Ap As Dc Dg Dpx Dx Ep ID LD Lk Multi NLD S TS.
  IQ 85 and up. Not accepted—Apr Ar Au B/VI C CD CF CLP CP D Db D-B
  DS Hemo IP MD MS Nf ODD ON PW SB SC SO Subst TBI.
  Gen Acad. Gr 6-12. **Feat**—Ital Lat Span Genetics Marine_Bio/Sci Govt Psych
  Film Studio_Art Music Music_Hist Health Study_Skills. **Expected outcome:**
  Return to local school (Avg length of stay: 7 mos).
  Therapy: Milieu Music. **Psychotherapy:** Art Group Indiv Parent.
  Adm: Appl due: Year-round. On-campus interview.
  Enr: 17 (Cap: 22). B 10. G 7. **Fac:** 5 (Full-time). Spec ed 3. Lay 2.
  Aid: State 17 (100% of tui). **Summer prgm:** Day. Educ. Ther. 6 wks.
  Bldgs 1. Class rms 4. Libs 1. Lang labs 1. Art studios 1. Music studios 1. Fields
  1. Courts 1.
  Est 1898. Nonprofit. Roman Catholic. **Spons:** Hall-Brooke Behavioral Health
  Services.

Seton provides an individualized educational program for students with emotional disorders or learning or adjustment problems. The academy attempts to mainstream the student and works closely with home school systems. Middle school and high school course work encompasses the traditional subject areas. The specific curriculum is based on requirements of the student's sending district, with modifications dictated by individual needs. An individualized program for each pupil includes both group and individual therapy.

VILLA MARIA SCHOOL

Day — Coed Ages 5-14

Stamford, CT 06903. 161 Sky Meadow Dr.
Tel: 203-322-5886. Fax: 203-322-0228.
www.villamariaedu.org E-mail: info@villamariaedu.org
Sr. Carol Ann Nawracaj, OSF, MA, Exec Dir. **Mary Ann Tynan,** Adm.
  Conditions: Primary—ADHD APD Dc Dg Dx LD NLD S. **Sec**—Anx Apr Asp
  CP Db Dpx Ep. **IQ 90 and up.**
  Gen Acad. Gr K-9. **Feat**—Computers Studio_Art Music Study_Skills.
  Expected outcome: Return to local school (Avg length of stay: 2-3 yrs).
  Therapy: Lang Occup Phys Speech.
  Adm: Appl fee: $100. Appl due: Year-round. On-campus interview.
  Enr: 70 (Cap: 88). B 46. G 24. **Fac:** 25 (Full 24, Part 1). Spec ed 25.
  Tui '12-'13: Day $41,000-42,750/sch yr. **Aid:** School 25 ($393,000). State 15.
  Acres 2. Bldgs 1. Class rms 22. Libs 1. Fields 1. Comp labs 1.
  Est 1973. Nonprofit. Roman Catholic.

Founded as an after-school and summer program, Villa Maria eventually instituted a full-time day school for children with specific learning disabilities in the areas of language arts, math and perception. The program utilizes a holistic approach within the context of a small, highly structured learning environment. The individualized, experiential program is flexible enough to accommodate pupils of varying learning styles, personalities, interests and levels of learning.

The nongraded educational program serves students of average to above-average intelligence who are emotionally sound and motivated to learn, but who have not achieved to potential in traditional school settings. In addition to language arts and math courses (in which a 5:1 teacher-student ratio is maintained), Villa Maria offers science, social studies, music, art, computer, language development, study skills, and auditory and visual perception in small groupings based primarily on grade level.

In addition to academics, the school places significant emphasis on the child's emotional and social growth. A formal social skills program, operated along with a guidance program and the student council, provides opportunities for strengthening relationships and developing communicational and leadership skills, responsibility and integrity.

WATERFORD COUNTRY SCHOOL

Bdg — Coed Ages 8-18; Day — Coed 8-21

Quaker Hill, CT 06375. 78 Hunts Brook Rd, PO Box 408.
Tel: 860-442-9454. Fax: 860-442-2228.
www.waterfordcountryschool.org   E-mail: info@waterfordcs.org
David B. Moorehead, MA, MSW, Exec Dir. **Sharon Butcher,** Educ Dir.
   Conditions: Primary—ED. **Sec**—As CD CP Dx Ep ID LD MD MS OCD ON
      Psy TBI. **IQ 80 and up. Not accepted**—B/VI D.
   Gen Acad. Voc. Ungraded. On-Job Trng. Shelt_Workshop. **Expected outcome:**
      Return to local school (Avg length of stay: 12-14 mos).
   Therapy: Lang Speech. **Psychotherapy:** Equine Fam Group Indiv Parent.
      Counseling: Educ.
   Enr: 70.
   Aid: State 70 (100% of tui).
   Acres 350.
   Est 1922. Nonprofit.

Located on a 350-acre campus, Waterford serves students with mild to severe emotional and learning problems through year-round treatment. Diagnostic-prescriptive techniques are used in the on-grounds school to match each child's program with his or her needs and abilities. Tutorial speech and reading assistance is provided, and there is an opportunity for work experiences both on grounds and in the community. A day school option is available for students not requiring intensive residential care. Psychiatric and psychological services are integrated into the entire program and are available on individual, group and crisis bases.

The recreational program includes sports, social activities and hobbies. Arts, crafts, music, farming, horseback riding, swimming and physical education are part of this program. The usual length of stay is 12 to 14 months. Actively psychotic and severely acting-out students are not accepted.

THE WOODHALL SCHOOL

Bdg and Day — Boys Ages 14-18

Bethlehem, CT 06751. 58 Harrison Ln, PO Box 550.
Tel: 203-266-7788. Fax: 203-266-5896.
www.woodhallschool.org   E-mail: woodhallschool@woodhallschool.org
Matthew C. Woodhall, BA, MA, Head.
   Conditions: Primary—ADHD Asp LD NLD. **IQ 90 and up.**
   Col Prep. Underachiever. Gr 9-12. AP courses (Eng Calc Bio Chem Eur_Hist
   US_Hist). **Feat**—Fr Greek Lat Span. Avg SAT: CR 600. M 540. W 550. ESL.
   Interscholastic sports. **Expected outcome:** Graduation.
   Adm: Appl fee: $100. Appl due: Rolling. On-campus interview.
   Enr: 42. Bdg 42. **Fac:** 16 (Full-time).
   Tui '12-'13: Bdg $59,500/sch yr. Day $45,810/sch yr.
   Endow $100,000. Plant val $7,500,000. Acres 38. Bldgs 8. Dorms 2. Dorm rms
   22. Class rms 15. Lib 3000 vols. Sci labs 2. Auds 1. Art studios 1. Gyms 1.
   Fields 1. Courts 2.
   Est 1983. Nonprofit.

Located on a 38-acre campus, the school enrolls boys who have not succeeded in traditional school environments. Woodhall accepts students of average to superior intellectual ability who have no serious emotional or behavioral problems and no chemical dependencies. Applicants may display one or more of the following characteristics: lack of motivation and low achievement; a mild learning disability; difficulty with reading, writing or math; poor concentration and attention; lack of self-confidence or poor self-esteem; long school absences due to illness; or school changes due to family mobility.

The school provides small classes within a core college preparatory or general secondary-level curriculum in English, math, social studies, science and foreign languages; remedial programs in language arts, reading, writing and math; and English as a Second Language instruction. The intensive academic program is integrated with proctored study periods, small study groups and an evening study hall.

Communications groups help students develop skills of self-expression, and a daily athletic program promotes physical fitness, sportsmanship and teamwork and includes interscholastic options. Each boy completes a compulsory service project every trimester. Woodhall conducts social and recreational activities and clubs on campus and in cooperation with nearby prep schools. Theater, concerts, and educational field trips to New Haven, Hartford and New York City complete the program.   **See Also Page 34**

DELAWARE

CENTREVILLE SCHOOL
Day — Coed Ages 3-14

Centreville, DE 19807. 6201 Kennett Pike.
Tel: 302-571-0230. Fax: 302-571-0270.
www.centrevilleschool.org   E-mail: centreville@centrevilleschool.org
Denise Orenstein, Head.
  Conditions: Primary—ADHD Dx LD. **IQ 100 and up.**
  Gen Acad. Ungraded. **Feat**—Computers Studio_Art Drama Music. Interscholastic sports. **Expected outcome:** Return to local school (Avg length of stay: 3½ yrs).
  Therapy: Lang Occup Speech.
  Adm: Appl fee: $75. Appl due: Rolling. On-campus interview.
  Enr: 127. B 85. G 42.
  Tui '12-'13: Day $26,775/sch yr. **Aid:** School.
  Est 1974. Nonprofit.

Centreville provides an elementary program for children of average to above-average intelligence who have learning disabilities. To facilitate individualized instruction, the school limits classes of younger students to six or seven; as pupils get older, the maximum class size increases to 10. Instructors teach children strategies to compensate for their learning disabilities, and the program emphasizes self-esteem development. Centreville's teaching approach provides each pupil with a team of specialists that work together to ameliorate areas of weakness and build on existing strengths.

Reading forms the foundation of the curriculum. At all grade levels, a specialized and systematic reading course is integral to the school day. Computers are an important learning tool for writing and review. In addition to the core subjects, the school offers a varied arts program that includes drawing, painting, sculpture, building, acting and singing.

THE PILOT SCHOOL
Day — Coed Ages 5-14

Wilmington, DE 19803. 100 Garden of Eden Rd.
Tel: 302-478-1740. Fax: 302-478-1746.
www.pilotschool.org   E-mail: info@pilotschool.org
Kathleen B. Craven, BS, MEd, Dir.
  Conditions: Primary—ADHD APD Dc Dg Dpx Dx LD. **IQ 90 and up.**
  Gen Acad. Gr K-8. **Feat**—Lib_Skills Computers. **Expected outcome:** Return to local school (Avg length of stay: 3-5 yrs).
  Therapy: Lang Music Occup Perceptual-Motor Phys Speech. **Psychotherapy:** Fam Parent. **Counseling:** Educ Nutrition.
  Adm: Appl fee: $75. Appl due: Rolling. On-campus interview.
  Enr: 153. B 103. G 50. **Fac:** 32 (Full 30, Part 2). Spec ed 30. Lay 2.
  Tui '12-'13: Day $24,090/sch yr. **Aid:** School 55 ($547,840). Educ. 4 wks.

Endow $823,000. Plant val $11,291,000. Bldgs 1. Class rms 24. Lib 10,000 vols. Sci labs 1. Auds 1. Art studios 1. Music studios 1. Gyms 1. Fields 2. Pools 1. Comp labs 1. Comp/stud: 1:1.7. **Est 1957.** Nonprofit.

Serving children of normal ability who are experiencing learning problems, Pilot School offers an individualized program with instruction in small groups and prescriptive teaching. The core of instruction is in language arts and mathematics; however, basic skills weaknesses in auditory, visual-perceptual and memory areas are also addressed. The school tailors each child's program to his or her level of ability and particular learning needs. Reading consultants work with the classroom teacher and the individual child.

The school's program also includes a full range of therapeutic and support services.

See Also Page 32

DISTRICT OF COLUMBIA

THE LAB SCHOOL OF WASHINGTON
Day — Coed Ages 6-19

Washington, DC 20007. 4759 Reservoir Rd NW.
Tel: 202-965-6600. Fax: 202-944-3088.
www.labschool.org   E-mail: alexandra.freeman@labschool.org
   Nearby locations: 1550 Foxhall Rd NW, Washington 20007.
Katherine A. Schantz, BA, MEd, Head. **Susan F. Feeley,** Adm.
   Conditions: Primary—ADHD APD Dc Dg Dpx Dx LD NLD. **IQ 90 and up.**
   Col Prep. Gr 1-12. Interscholastic sports. **Expected outcome:** Return to local
   school (Avg length of stay: 4+ yrs).
   Therapy: Lang Occup Speech. **Psychotherapy:** Group Indiv. **Counseling:**
   Educ Voc.
   Adm: Appl fee: $100. Appl due: Feb. On-campus interview.
   Enr: 340. B 219. G 121. **Fac:** 89 (Full 73, Part 16). Spec ed 89.
   Tui '12-'13: Day $35,000-38,000/sch yr. **Aid:** School 18 ($150,000). **Summer**
   prgm: Day. Educ. Rec. Ther. Tui Day $2850. 5 wks.
   Sci labs 2. Lang labs 1. Auds 1. Theaters 1. Art studios 3. Music studios 1. Dance
   studios 1. Wood shops 1. Gyms 1. Pools 1. Comp labs 1. Comp/stud: 1:1
   Est 1967. Nonprofit.

The Lab School primarily serves children of average to superior intelligence who have language-based learning disabilities and attentional disorders. The arts are central to the curriculum, and teaching methods are differentiated, experiential and multisensory. In the lower grades, the school's Academic Club Method utilizes visual, concrete activities to present topics in history, geography, civics, archaeology, literature and economics. High school students complete 100 hours of required community service prior to graduation.

The elementary division operates on Foxhall Road, with grades 5-12 conducted on the Reservoir Road campus.

FLORIDA

AMERICAN ACADEMY
PLANTATION

Day — Coed Ages 3-18

Plantation, FL 33325. 12200 W Broward Blvd.
Tel: 954-472-0022. Fax: 954-472-3088.
www.ahschool.com   E-mail: admissions@ahschool.com
William R. Laurie, BA, MEd, Pres. Jacqueline Davis, MAT, Head.
  Conditions: Primary—APD Dg Dpx Dx LD NLD. IQ 80 and up.
  Col Prep. Gen Acad. Gr 1-12. Feat—Span Comp_Sci. ESL. SAT/ACT prep.
    Interscholastic sports. Expected outcome: Graduation.
  Counseling: Educ.
  Adm: Appl due: Year-round. On-campus interview.
  Enr: 348. Fac: 34 (Full-time). Spec ed 34.
  Tui '12-'13: Day $25,418-29,399/sch yr. Aid: School. Summer prgm: Day.
    Educ. Tui Day $930. 3 wks.
  Acres 40. Bldgs 9. Class rms 2. Sci labs 2. Art studios 6. Music studios 4.
    Dance studios 2. Gyms 1. Comp labs 10.
  Est 1969.

Located on the campus of American Heritage Academy, the school serves students with average to gifted intelligence who are functioning below grade level, including children with mild to moderate learning disabilities. Small class sizes and individualized educational plans are integral to the curriculum, which also emphasizes fine arts and computers. Extracurricular activities include athletics, clubs and associations.

American Academy maintains a second campus in Delray Beach.

ATLANTIS ACADEMY
MIAMI

Day — Coed Ages 5-18

Miami, FL 33176. 9600 SW 107th Ave.
Tel: 305-271-9771. Fax: 305-271-7078.
www.miami.atlantisacademy.com   E-mail: esmith@esa-education.com
Carlos R. Aballi, BA, MS, EdS, Dir. Eric Smith, Adm.
  Conditions: Primary—ADHD Dx ED LD OCD. Sec—Asp Au Ep ID ON S SB.
  IQ 72 and up.
  Gen Acad. Gr K-12. Feat—Fr Span Computers Studio_Art. ESL. Interscholas-
    tic sports. Expected outcome: Graduation.
  Adm: Appl due: Rolling. On-campus interview.
  Enr: 180. B 96. G 84. Fac: 27. Spec ed 27.
  Summer prgm: Day. Educ. Rec. 8 wks.
  Acres 4. Bldgs 1. Class rms 22. Lib 7764 vols. Sci labs 1. Art studios 1. Fields 1.
    Courts 2. Comp labs 1.

Est 1976. Inc.

Students with reading and learning difficulties receive individualized instruction in small classes and a clinical setting at Atlantis. All students have access to computers, and pupils in grade 3 and above receive formal instruction in computer usage.

ATLANTIS ACADEMY
PALM BEACHES

Day — Coed Ages 5-22

West Palm Beach, FL 33406. 1950 Prairie Rd.
Tel: 561-642-3100. Fax: 561-969-1950.
www.palmbeaches.atlantisacademy.com
E-mail: mlogan@esa-education.com
Mary A. Joyner, BS, Dir. **Mary Teresa Logan,** Adm.
  Conditions: Primary—ADHD Asp Au Dc Dg Dx LD PTSD. **Sec**—AN Anx Apr Ar As Bu C CD CF Db ED Hemo ID MD Mood OCD ODD SA SC TBI TS. **IQ 75-125. Not accepted**—B/VI CLP CP D D-B DS Ep IP MS Nf ON Psy PW SB SO SP Subst Sz.
  Gen Acad. Gr K-12. **Feat**—Span Comp_Sci Studio_Art Journ. SAT/ACT prep. Interscholastic sports. **Expected outcome:** Graduation.
  Therapy: Lang Occup Phys Speech. **Psychotherapy:** Fam.
  Adm: Appl fee: $300. Appl due: Rolling. On-campus interview.
  Enr: 152 (Cap: 192). B 84. G 68. **Fac:** 15 (Full-time). Spec ed 15.
  Tui 2010: Day $8925-23,000/sch yr (+$500). **Aid:** School. State. **Summer prgm:** Day. Educ. Rec. 9 wks.
  Class rms 19. Libs 1. Sci labs 1. Art studios 1. Fields 1. Courts 1. Comp labs 1.
  Est 1937. Inc. **Spons:** Educational Services of America.

This structured school accommodates boys and girls with varying learning styles. Students progressing at the appropriate grade level take part in small classes that focus on individual needs; pupils who are working two to three years below grade level take part in self-contained classes. The academy reinforces positive behavior and teaches the organizational skills necessary for academic success. Students with learning disabilities engage in various school activities with boys and girls who are not.

Branches of the academy operate in Miami and Coral Springs (see separate listings).

CENTER ACADEMY

Day — Coed Ages 10-19

Pinellas Park, FL 33782. 6710 86th Ave N.
Tel: 727-541-5716. Fax: 727-544-8186.
www.mycenteracademy.com   E-mail: infopp@centeracademy.com
Stephen Kenney, BS, Dir.
  Conditions: Primary—ADHD Dc Dg Dx LD. **Sec**—Asp IP. **IQ 85-130.**
  Not accepted—AN Anx Apr Ar B/VI Bu C CD CLP CP D Db DS ED Ep Hemo ID MD Mood MR MS Nf OCD ODD ON Psy PTSD PW SA SB SC

SO SP Subst Sz TBI TS.
Col Prep. Gen Acad. Gr 5-12. AP courses (Environ_Sci). SAT/ACT prep.
Expected outcome: Return to local school (Avg length of stay: 1-2 yrs).
Counseling: Educ Voc.
Adm: Appl due: Rolling.
Enr: 100 (Cap: 105). B 70. G 30. **Fac:** 8 (Full 6, Part 2). Spec ed 2. Lay 6.
Summer prgm: Day. Educ. Tui Day $695. 5 wks.
Est 1968.

Enrolling children with attentional disorders, motivational problems and learning disabilities, the academy formulates educational programs for each student following consultation between neuropsychologists and school educators. In addition to improving motivation and self-esteem, the school teaches lifelong learning strategies for pupils to employ. Following assessment, instructors develop an academically appropriate curriculum for the child that addresses processing deficits. Staff members continually evaluate the student's progress and needs.

DEPAUL SCHOOL OF NORTHEAST FLORIDA
Day — Coed Ages 6-14

Jacksonville, FL 32224. 3044 S San Pablo Rd.
Tel: 904-223-3391. Fax: 904-223-8722.
www.depaulschool.com   E-mail: info@depaulschool.com
Connie Korte, Head. **Diane Hoffman,** Adm.
Conditions: Primary—ADHD APD Dc Dg Dx LD. **IQ 90 and up.**
Gen Acad. Gr 1-8. **Feat**—Studio_Art Drama. **Expected outcome:** Return to local school (Avg length of stay: 2-3 yrs).
Therapy: Speech. **Psychotherapy:** Parent. **Counseling:** Educ.
Adm: Appl fee: $250. Appl due: Year-round. On-campus interview.
Enr: 65 (Cap: 65). B 45. G 20. **Fac:** 8 (Full 6, Part 2). Spec ed 6. Lay 2.
Tui '12-'13: Day $8850/sch yr (+$400). Clinic $45 (Tutoring)/half hr.
  Aid: School 15 ($25,000). State.
Est 1980. Nonprofit.

The school uses a structured, multisensory method of teaching children with learning differences that includes repetition and drills. Emphasis is placed on returning the child to a conventional classroom setting, usually after two to three years. DePaul aims to establish a firm educational foundation and to build upon this base, thereby increasing the likelihood of future academic success. Tutoring and various therapies are available at additional cost.

EASTER SEALS SOUTH FLORIDA
EDUCATIONAL SERVICES
Day — Coed Ages Birth-22

Miami, FL 33125. 1475 NW 14th Ave.
Tel: 305-325-0470. Fax: 305-325-0578.
www.southflorida.easterseals.com

E-mail: sadhya-taylor@sfl.easterseals.com
Conditions: Primary—ADHD Asp Au D Dc Dg DS LD PDD PW SB SP TS.
Sec—As C CP Dx ED Ep ID S TBI. **IQ 70 and up.**
Gen Acad. Ungraded. Culinary. **Expected outcome:** Graduation.
Therapy: Hear Lang Occup Phys Speech. **Psychotherapy:** Fam Group Indiv.
Adm: Appl fee: $50. Appl due: Year-round. On-campus interview.
Enr: 103. **Fac:** 21 (Full-time). Spec ed 21.
Summer prgm: Day. Educ. 7 wks.
Libs 1. Pools 1.
Est 1967. Nonprofit.

ESSF conducts three distinct educational programs. The Child Development Center provides individualized, hands-on learning experiences for children from birth to school age who have various disabilities. Physical, occupational, speech and behavioral therapy is incorporated into the school day. Typical learners may also enroll in the program.

Serving children in grades K-5 with autism spectrum disorders, the Autism Elementary Demonstration School offers bilingual (English and Spanish) special education that incorporates various teaching methods, materials and techniques. Staff maintain a multisensory setting and formulate an Individualized Education Plan for each student. Programming places particular emphasis on the development of auditory, fine-motor, visual and perceptual development.

The Culinary Arts High School Program serves students ages 16-22 with autism, Down syndrome and other special needs. While completing course work necessary for a special diploma, boys and girls participate in culinary training both in the classroom and in the school's vocational kitchen. Course work addresses such culinary activities as sanitation, job preparation, store/stock room coordination and maintenance, and food preparation. Job coaches help graduates find and keep jobs in their fields.

KILLIAN OAKS ACADEMY

Day — Coed Ages 3-18

Miami, FL 33176. 10545 SW 97th Ave.
Tel: 305-274-2221. **Fax:** 305-279-5460.
www.killianoaksacademy.com
Conditions: Primary—Dx LD. **Sec**—ADHD S. **IQ 85 and up.**
Col Prep. Gen Acad. Ungraded. **Feat**—Studio_Art Drama Music Dance.
Expected outcome: Return to local school (Avg length of stay: 2-3 yrs).
Therapy: Speech.
Enr: 113.
Est 1970. Inc.

Killian Oaks provides an academic program, based on a modified open classroom concept, for children with disabilities in the areas of language development, reading and verbal behavior. Each student receives three hours of language arts instruction a day, with his or her progress evaluated continually. The academy attempts to mainstream children into regular schools as soon as possible, typically after two to three years.

LIGHTHOUSE POINT ACADEMY

Day — Coed Ages 8-18

Coconut Creek, FL 33073. 7600 Lyons Rd.
Tel: 954-247-0011. Fax: 954-247-0012.
www.nbps.org   E-mail: daltons@nbps.org
Jon Coyle, Dir. Jackie Fagan, Adm.
  Conditions: Primary—ADHD Dx LD. IQ 95 and up.
  Col Prep. Gr 3-12. AP courses (Eng Fr Span Calc Stats Comp_Sci Bio
    Chem Physics US_Govt & Pol Art_Hist Studio_Art Music_Theory).
    Feat—Creative_Writing Chin Anat & Physiol Ecol Marine_Bio/Sci Robot-
    ics Web_Design Drawing Film Painting Acting Theater_Arts Band Chorus
    Jazz_Ensemble Dance Debate Journ. Expected outcome: Graduation.
  Therapy: Speech.
  Adm: Appl fee: $150. Appl due: Rolling. On-campus interview.
  Enr: 100. Fac: 27 (Full-time).
  Tui '12-'13: Day $30,000-33,500/sch yr (+$200-950). Aid: School.
  Acres 80. Libs 3. Art studios 1. Music studios 1. Dance studios 1. Gyms 2.
    Fields 10. Pools 3. Laptop prgm Gr 6-12.
  Est 1978. Inc. Spons: North Broward Preparatory School.

The academy uses a multisensory approach in small, highly personalized classes. Each student uses computers extensively and may choose from a variety of enrichment courses. A mainstreaming program with the affiliated North Broward Preparatory School enables students to attend classes at both schools while making use of the shared facilities. NBPS' curriculum includes a selection of Advanced Placement and International Baccalaureate courses.

Boys and girls in grades 9-12 accumulate 100 hours of required community service.

MORNING STAR SCHOOL

Day — Coed Ages 5-15

Jacksonville, FL 32211. 725 Mickler Rd.
Tel: 904-721-2144. Fax: 904-721-1040.
www.morningstar-jax.org   E-mail: mss@morningstar-jax.org
Jean Barnes, Prin.
  Conditions: Primary—ADHD APD Asp Dx LD. Sec—Apr CP Dg ED ID S
    TBI. IQ 80 and up. Not accepted—B/VI D.
  Gen Acad. Ungraded. Feat—Relig Music Study_Skills. Expected outcome:
    Return to local school (Avg length of stay: 2-3 yrs).
  Therapy: Speech.
  Adm: Appl due: Rolling.
  Enr: 114. Fac: 15 (Full-time). Spec ed 15.
  Est 1958. Nonprofit. Roman Catholic.

Morning Star accepts children with learning disabilities, mild emotional disturbances and attentional disorders. The curriculum facilitates the development of academic and motor skills, promoting appropriate social, behavioral and personal relationships.

The preschool emphasizes self-care, readiness activities and group interaction. Academic areas, perceptual training and self-control are areas of emphasis in the primary grades. Intermediate-level and junior high students continue academic training, and the program focuses on skill acquisition and the development of self-directedness.

The school shares its campus with an adjoining parochial school, affording students part-time placement in regular classes. All pupils enroll on a trial basis that lasts for at least nine weeks.

MORNING STAR SCHOOL

Day — Coed Ages 6-15

Tampa, FL 33612. 210 E Linebaugh Ave.
Tel: 813-935-0232. Fax: 813-932-2321.
www.morningstartampa.org   E-mail: edaly@morningstartampa.org
Eileen Daly, MA, Prin. **Leslie Maggio,** Adm.
  Conditions: Primary—ADHD APD Apr Dc Dg Dpx Dx LD NLD S TBI.
    Sec—Anx Ap Ar As Asp Au CF CLP CP D Db Ep HI MD Mood MS Multi Nf
    OCD ON PDD SA SP TS. **IQ 90 and up. Not accepted**—AN B/VI Bu C CD
    DS ED Hemo ID IP Lk MR ODD Psy PTSD PW SB SC SO Subst Sz.
  Gen Acad. Ungraded. **Feat**—Lib_Skills Fine_Arts. **Expected outcome:**
    Return to local school.
  Therapy: Lang Occup Speech. **Counseling:** Educ.
  Adm: Appl fee: $150. Appl due: Year-round. On-campus interview.
  Enr: 70 (Cap: 75). B 40. G 30. **Fac:** 13 (Full 9, Part 4). Spec ed 9. Lay 4.
  Tui '12-'13: Day $10,506/sch yr (+$425-575). **Aid:** School 20 ($40,000).
    State 60.
  Bldgs 6. Class rms 9. Libs 1. Art studios 1. Music studios 1. Gyms 1. Fields 1.
    Courts 1.
  Est 1958. Nonprofit. Roman Catholic.

Morning Star enrolls children who are unable to function in a regular classroom due to learning disabilities or related difficulties. During the primary years (ages 6-9), pupils attend self-contained classes; departmentalization and ability grouping are employed in the intermediate (ages 9-12) and junior high (ages 12-15) divisions. The individualized curriculum strives to develop maximum efficiency in academics and motor skills connected with those areas, and to improve students' self esteem. Applicants must undergo a psychological evaluation.

NOVA SOUTHEASTERN UNIVERSITY
BAUDHUIN PRESCHOOL

Day — Coed Ages 2-5

Fort Lauderdale, FL 33314. 3301 College Ave.
Tel: 954-262-7100. Fax: 954-262-3936.
www.nova.edu/humandevelopment/earlylearning/baudhuin
  E-mail: baudhuin@nova.edu
Nancy Lieberman, Dir.

Conditions: Primary—Au. **Sec**—B/VI D Db. **IQ 80 and up.**
Gen Acad. Gr PS.
Therapy: Lang Occup Phys Speech. **Psychotherapy:** Fam Parent.
Enr: 150.
Aid: State 150 (100% of tui). **Summer prgm:** Day. Educ.
Nonprofit.

Baudhuin Preschool provides programming for children with autism. Preschoolers receive full funding from the county school district. The summer session serves only children enrolled in the school-year program.

PACE-BRANTLEY HALL SCHOOL

Day — Coed Ages 6-18

Longwood, FL 32779. 3221 Sand Lake Rd.
Tel: 407-869-8882. Fax: 407-869-8717.
www.pacebrantley.org   E-mail: info@pacebrantley.org
Kathleen Shatlock, BSE, MEd, Dir. **Barbara Winter,** Adm.
   Conditions: Primary—ADHD Dc Dg Dx LD. **Sec**—Nf. **IQ 80 and up.**
      Not accepted—AN B/VI Bu CD D DS ED ID MR ODD Psy PW SA SO SP Subst Sz.
   Gen Acad. Gr 1-12. **Feat**—ASL Span Environ_Sci Comp_Sci Studio_Art Speech. Avg SAT: CR 401. M 379. W 393. ACT: Avg 18. Interscholastic sports. **Expected outcome:** Graduation.
   Therapy: Lang Occup Speech. **Counseling:** Educ.
   Adm: Appl due: Rolling.
   Enr: 150. **Fac:** 26 (Full-time).
   Tui '12-'13: Day $13,920-14,409/sch yr (+$800-1000). **Aid:** School 10 ($13,000). **Summer prgm:** Day. Educ. Rec. 4 wks.
   Plant val $2,000,000. Acres 9. Bldgs 9. Class rms 32. Lib 12,000 vols. Sci labs 1. Arts ctrs 1. Fields 1. Courts 2. Playgrounds 2. Comp labs 1.
   Est 1972. Nonprofit.

PACE provides reading, language arts and math programs for the child with learning disabilities whose needs are not met in traditional school settings. Teaching methods combine three distinct learning approaches: auditory, visual and tactile. Frequently scheduled field trips enhance classroom learning.

THE VANGUARD SCHOOL

Bdg and Day — Coed Ages 10-18

Lake Wales, FL 33859. 22000 Hwy 27.
Tel: 863-676-6091. Fax: 863-676-8297.
www.vanguardschool.org   E-mail: vanadmin@vanguardschool.org
Cathy Wooley-Brown, BA, MA, EdS, PhD, Pres. **Derri Park,** MEd, EdS, Prin.
   Candi Medeiros, Adm.
   Conditions: Primary—ADHD APD Asp Dc Dg Dpx Dx LD NLD. **Sec**—AN

Anx B/VI Bu D HI Mood OCD ODD PDD PTSD S SA SP TBI. **IQ 80 and up. Not accepted**—AuCD D-B DS ED ON Psy SO Subst Sz.
Col Prep. Gen Acad. Underachiever. Gr 5-PG. Culinary. Man_Arts & Shop. Shelt_Workshop. AP courses (Calc Physics). **Feat**—Creative_Writing ASL Span Comp_Sci Econ Govt Filmmaking Studio_Art Accounting Journ Speech Woodworking Culinary_Arts. Interscholastic sports. **Expected outcome:** Graduation.
Therapy: Lang Speech. **Psychotherapy:** Art Group Indiv. **Counseling:** Educ.
Adm: Appl fee: $100. Appl due: Rolling. On-campus interview.
Enr: 100. Bdg 82. Day 18. B 75. G 25. **Fac:** 21. Spec ed 9. Lay 12.
Tui '12-'13: Bdg $44,000/sch yr (+$650). Day $22,500/sch yr (+$350). **Aid:** School 70 ($560,000). State 24. **Summer prgm:** Bdg. Educ. Rec. Tui Day $5400/4-wk ses. 8 wks.
Endow $3,000,000. Plant val $8,000,000. Acres 75. Bldgs 13. Dorms 3. Dorm rms 72. Class rms 20. Lib 6300 vols. Sci labs 1. Lang labs 3. Dark rms 1. Gyms 1. Athletic ctrs 1. Fields 3. Courts 2. Pools 1. Comp labs 2.
Est 1966. Nonprofit.

Vanguard provides an individualized program for students with dyslexia, attention deficit disorder and other learning disabilities through a combination of classroom instruction and individual tutorial sessions. Structured classes emphasize organizational skills, study habits and the acquisition of fundamental academic skills. The core subjects of reading, language arts and mathematics, complemented by science and social studies, form the basic curriculum. Spanish language study, American Sign Language, and electives in the creative, performing, culinary and industrial arts complete the program.

Two diploma programs are available in the upper school: one geared toward college-oriented academics, the other focusing on career-oriented practical studies.

THE VANGUARD SCHOOL OF COCONUT GROVE

Day — Coed Ages 6-14

Coconut Grove, FL 33133. 3939 Main Hwy.
Tel: 305-445-7992. Fax: 305-441-9255.
www.vanguardschool.com   E-mail: vangcg@aol.com
John R. Havrilla, BS, MS, Dir.
   Conditions: Primary—ADHD Dx LD.
   Gen Acad. Ungraded.
   Enr: 80. B 55. G 25. **Fac:** 11 (Full-time). Spec ed 11.
   Tui '11-'12: Day $16,200/sch yr.
   Est 1968. Nonprofit.

Vanguard offers a nontraditional education for students with atypical learning patterns or difficulties in the visual or auditory processing of information. Education is individualized and classes consist of a maximum of 10 students. The program stresses the development of homework skills, social and organizational skills, and the ability to think, write and communicate. The goal is to return pupils to traditional schools.

WOODLAND HALL ACADEMY
Day — Coed Ages 6-20

Tallahassee, FL 32309. 5246 Centerville Rd.
Tel: 850-893-2216. Fax: 850-893-2440.
www.woodlandhallacademy.org   E-mail: dri@talstart.com
Amber Mitchell, BS, Prin. **Robyn A. Rennick,** MS, Prgm Coord.
  Conditions: Primary—ADHD Ap APD Apr Asp Dc Dg Dpx Dx LD Multi Nf.
    Sec—CP HI. **IQ 90 and up. Not accepted**—D D-B DS ID MR.
  Col Prep. Gen Acad. Gr 1-12. **Feat**—World_Lit Ecol Computers FL_Hist
    Civics Econ Govt Study_Skills. **Expected outcome:** Return to local school
    (Avg length of stay: 3-4 yrs).
  Counseling: Educ Nutrition.
  Adm: Appl fee: $0. Appl due: Year-round. On-campus interview.
  Enr: 25 (Cap: 35). **Fac:** 7 (Full 6, Part 1).
  Tui '12-'13: Sliding-Scale Rate $14,000-19,000 (+$950). **Aid:** State 20.
    Summer prgm: Day. Educ. Tui Day $955. 4 wks.
  Endow $255,000. Acres 3. Bldgs 2 (100% ADA). Class rms 7. Libs 1. Fields 1.
    Courts 1. Comp labs 1.
  Est 1975. Nonprofit. **Spons:** Dyslexia Research Institute.

Woodland Hall, a division of the Dyslexia Research Institute, accepts children of average or above-average intelligence who have been diagnosed with dyslexia, attention deficit disorder or a related learning difference such as Asperger's syndrome. Math, reading, language, sensorial and perceptual skills are emphasized in the primary classes. A basic college preparatory curriculum is followed in the highly structured, nongraded advanced program.

Parental involvement is an integral part of Woodland's program. In addition to academics, the program emphasizes positive self-concept development, self-control, organizational skills, and acceptable social and behavioral adjustment. Pupils may undergo diagnostic testing and may attend one-on-one tutorial sessions.

GEORGIA

ATLANTA SPEECH SCHOOL
KATHERINE HAMM CENTER
Day — Coed Ages 2-8

Atlanta, GA 30327. 3160 Northside Pky NW.
Tel: 404-233-5332. TTY: 404-233-5332. Fax: 404-364-5326.
www.atlantaspeechschool.org
Shelley Carr, MEd, Coord.
Conditions: Primary—D HI. **Sec**—ADHD Apr LD Nf. **IQ 85 and up.**
Gen Acad. Ungraded. **Expected outcome:** Return to local school (Avg length of stay: 3 yrs).
Therapy: Hear Lang Occup Speech. **Counseling:** Educ.
Adm: Appl fee: $75. Appl due: Year-round.
Enr: 60 (Cap: 60). B 30. G 30. **Fac:** 16 (Full-time). Spec ed 16.
Tui '12-'13: Day $28,900/sch yr (+$60). Clinic $150/hr. **Aid:** School. **Summer prgm:** Day. Educ. Ther. Tui Day $1900. 5 wks.
Est 1938. Nonprofit.

This branch of Atlanta Speech School consists of three main components: a special school, a parent-infant program, and a resource program that provides one-on-one assistance for hearing-impaired children from regular school settings. Psycho-educational evaluations for hearing-impaired children are also available. A primary goal of the program is to develop residual hearing, both for better understanding of others and for further developing the child's own speech. The school program incorporates FM amplification systems.

Atlanta Speech School operates a children's cochlear implant center that, in conjunction with the Oral School, offers speech and auditory training to children being considered for implants and to those who have already received implants. Classroom teachers and members of the cochlear implant staff work together to maximize the benefits of the implant.

Other offerings of the facility include educational consultation and placement services as well as learning disabilities and speech/language/audiology clinics that offer diagnostic and remedial services.

ATLANTA SPEECH SCHOOL
WARDLAW SCHOOL
Day — Coed Ages 5-12

Atlanta, GA 30327. 3160 Northside Pky NW.
Tel: 404-233-5332. TTY: 404-233-5332. Fax: 404-266-2175.
www.atlantaspeechschool.org   E-mail: mdemko@atlspsch.org
Comer Yates, Exec Dir. **Gale Shafer,** Adm.
Conditions: Primary—APD Dc Dg Dx LD. **Sec**—ADHD S. **IQ 90 and up.**
Gen Acad. Gr K-6. **Feat**—Lib_Skills Computers Studio_Art Music Movement.
Expected outcome: Return to local school (Avg length of stay: 2-3 yrs).
Therapy: Lang Occup Speech. **Counseling:** Educ.

112   **Guide to Private Special Education**

Adm: Appl fee: $200. Appl due: Rolling. On-campus interview.
Enr: 184. B 109. G 75. **Fac:** 47 (Full 45, Part 2). Spec ed 47.
Tui '12-'13: Day $29,743/sch yr (+$150). **Aid:** School 25 ($336,538). **Summer prgm:** Day. Educ. Tui Day $450-2435. 1-7 wks.
Bldgs 1 (100% ADA). Class rms 20. Libs 1. Art studios 1. Gyms 1. Fields 2. Comp labs 2.
Est 1938. Nonprofit.

The Wardlaw School, a division of the Atlanta Speech School, serves children with mild to moderate language-based learning disabilities such as dyslexia. The program integrates individualized remediation with a comprehensive school program. Oral communication, language comprehension, vocabulary development and conversational skills are key components of the program. To allow for individualized programming, class size is kept small. Classes are nongraded and instructional groupings are based on age, social maturity, and general cognitive and skill levels.

The Wardlaw School uses a collaborative model that incorporates language-based instruction throughout the curriculum. Speech-language pathologists work with classroom teachers to design and implement the classroom curriculum, then work individually with children as needed. Reading specialists employ research-based, multisensory methods of instruction.

THE BEDFORD SCHOOL

Day — Coed Ages 6-16

Fairburn, GA 30123. 5665 Milam Rd.
Tel: 770-774-8001. Fax: 770-774-8005.
www.thebedfordschool.org   E-mail: bbox@thebedfordschool.org
Betsy E. Box, MEd, EdS, PhD, Exec Dir.
   Conditions: Primary—ADHD Dc Dg Dx LD. **Sec**—Anx As Asp CD Db ED Ep Mood OCD ODD PTSD SP TBI TS. **IQ 90 and up.**
   Gen Acad. Gr 1-9. **Feat**—Computers Studio_Art. **Expected outcome:** Return to local school (Avg length of stay: 2-4 yrs).
   Therapy: Occup Speech. **Counseling:** Educ.
   Adm: Appl fee: $100. Appl due: Year-round. On-campus interview.
   Enr: 135 (Cap: 150). B 95. G 40. **Fac:** 20 (Full 19, Part 1).
   Tui '12-'13: Day $16,350/sch yr (+$200). **Aid:** School. **Summer prgm:** Day. Educ. Rec. Tui Day $2750. 4 wks.
   Endow $2,000,000. Plant val $1,000,000. Acres 40. Bldgs 2 (100% ADA). Class rms 25. Lib 1000 vols. Art studios 1. Gyms 1. Fields 1. Pools 1. Comp labs 2.
   Est 1985. Nonprofit.

The goal of this school for pupils with learning disabilities is to remediate and return children to a mainstream classroom setting. Class size does not exceed 12 students, and Bedford groups children according to skill level. An activity period includes such classes as art, music, computer and social values.

Among extracurricular activities are athletics, yearbook, newspaper and martial arts. Individual speech and language therapy, hot lunches and after-school care are all available for an additional fee.

BRANDON HALL SCHOOL

Bdg — Boys Ages 12-19; Day — Coed 11-19

Atlanta, GA 30350. 1701 Brandon Hall Dr.
Tel: 770-394-8177. Fax: 770-804-8821.
www.brandonhall.org E-mail: admissions@brandonhall.org
John L. Singleton, BA, MA, EdD, Pres. Jeffrey S. Holloway, Adm.
Conditions: Primary—ADHD Dc Dg Dx LD. IQ 85 and up.
Col Prep. Gr 6-PG. AP classes (Eng Span Calc Chem Physics). Feat—
Comp_Sci Fine_Arts Studio_Art Drama Music SAT_Prep. ESL. SAT/ACT
prep. Interscholastic sports. Expected outcome: Return to local school
(Avg length of stay: 4 yrs).
Psychotherapy: Indiv. Counseling: Educ.
Adm: Appl fee: $75. Appl due: Rolling.
Enr: 140. Fac: 31 (Full-time).
Tui '12-'13: Bdg $49,995/sch yr. Day $26,095/sch yr. Aid: School 9
($155,800). Summer prgm: Bdg & Day. Educ. Tui Bdg $2500-7500. Tui Day
$1250-3750. 2-6 wks.
Endow $250,000. Plant val $9,500,000. Acres 27. Bldgs 10. Dorms 1. Dorm
rms 36. Class rms 20. Lib 5000 vols. Sci labs 3. Lang labs 1. Auds 1. The-
aters 1. Gyms 1. Fields 1. Courts 2. Comp labs 2. Comp/stud: 1:1 Laptop
prgm Gr 6-12.
Est 1959. Nonprofit.

Brandon Hall stresses college preparatory skills, independent study habits and personal self-discipline for the underachiever and for other bright students with different learning styles. Learning disabilities supported include dyslexia, ADHD, dyscalculia, dysgraphia and expressive language disorders. Reconstruction of basic skills and accelerated course work are elements of the program. All seniors receive SAT preparation. Class size varies from one-on-one instruction (offered in all courses) to small groups of four to eight. All instructors provide comprehensive E-mail updates each week.

CHATHAM ACADEMY

Day — Coed Ages 6-18

Savannah, GA 31406. 4 Oglethorpe Professional Blvd.
Tel: 912-354-4047. Fax: 912-354-4633.
www.chathamacademy.com E-mail: cainfo@chathamacademy.com
Carolyn M. Hannaford, MEd, Prin.
Conditions: Primary—ADHD Anx APD Dc Dg Dpx Dx LD NLD. Sec—Asp Au
C CD CF Db Ep Hemo Lk Mood OCD ODD PW S SC SP TS. IQ 75-130.
Not accepted—Apr Ar B/VI CLP CP D D-B IP MD MS Multi Nf ON SB.
Col Prep. Gen Acad. Underachiever. Gr 1-12. On-Job Trng. Feat—Writing
Span Visual_Arts. SAT/ACT prep. Interscholastic sports. Expected outcome:
Return to local school (Avg length of stay: 3-5).
Therapy: Lang Speech. Psychotherapy: Parent. Counseling: Educ.
Adm: Appl fee: $50. Appl due: Rolling. On-campus interview.
Enr: 80 (Cap: 105). B 60. G 20. Fac: 15 (Full 13, Part 2). Spec ed 15.

Tui '11-'12: Day $15,050/sch yr. **Aid:** School 48 ($155,000). State 34.
Summer prgm: Day. Educ. Tui Day $700. 5 wks.
Bldgs 1 (100% ADA). Libs 1. Art studios 1. Fields 2. Comp labs 1.
Est 1978. Nonprofit. **Spons:** Royce Learning Center.

The school provides special education for students with learning disabilities, ADHD or both. Chatham's individualized, small-group approach addresses various learning styles. Instructors utilize language-based and multisensory methods to teach academic skills, appropriate daily behavior and social skills. Field trips and interscholastic sports supplement classroom instruction. Depending upon the student's progress, some boys and girls transition back to traditional schools after three to five years, while others remain until graduation.

THE COTTAGE SCHOOL
Day — Coed Ages 11-18

Roswell, GA 30075. 700 Grimes Bridge Rd.
Tel: 770-641-8688. Fax: 770-641-9026.
www.cottageschool.org   E-mail: tcs@cottageschool.org
Jacque Digieso, PhD, Exec Dir. **Liz Scott,** Adm.
    Conditions: Primary—ADHD APD Dc Dg Dpx Dx LD NLD. **Sec**—AN Anx Apr Ar Asp Bu C CLP CP Db ED Ep Hemo HI ID Lk Mood Multi OCD ODD PDD PTSD S SA SC SP Subst TBI TS. **IQ 85-115. Not accepted**—Ap Au B/VI CD D D-B DS IP MD MS Nf ON Psy PW SB SO Sz.
    Col Prep. Gen Acad. Underachiever. Voc. Gr 6-12. Culinary. Hort. Man_Arts & Shop. On-Job Trng. **Feat**—Fr Span Photog Studio_Art Jewelry_Making Carpentry. SAT/ACT prep. Interscholastic sports. **Expected outcome:** Graduation.
    Counseling: Educ Voc.
    Adm: Appl fee: $200. Appl due: Year-round. On-campus interview.
    Enr: 156 (Cap: 200). B 108. G 48. **Fac:** 38 (Full 31, Part 7).
    Tui '12-'13: Day $22,950-23,950/sch yr. **Aid:** School 35 ($225,000). State 69.
        Summer prgm: Day. Educ. Tui Day $1000. 3 wks.
    Endow $570,000. Plant val $6,000,000. Acres 23. Bldgs 7 (70% ADA). Class rms 30. Lib 7500 vols. Sci labs 2. Lang labs 1. Art studios 2. Gyms 1. Comp labs 3.
    Est 1985. Nonprofit.

The school offers individualized educational programming for adolescents with a history of learning difficulties. The program features college preparatory academics, career and vocational studies, and attention to study skills and social skills development. Career development assistance is available.

GABLES ACADEMY
Bdg — Coed Ages 12-18; Day — Coed 9-18

Stone Mountain, GA 30083. 811 Gordon St.

Tel: 770-465-7500. Fax: 770-465-7700.
www.gablesacademy.com   E-mail: info@gablesacademy.com
James D. Meffen III, BA, MSEd, EdD, Head. **Brandy H. Highsmith,** Adm.
   Conditions: Primary—ADHD Asp Au Dc Dg Dx PDD. **Sec**—Anx CP ED SP
   Subst TBI TS. **IQ 90 and up.**
   Col Prep. Gen Acad. Voc. Gr 4-12. On-Job Trng. Support_Employ. Interscho-
   lastic sports. **Expected outcome:** Return to local school (Avg length of
   stay: 2 yrs).
   Therapy: Occup Perceptual-Motor Speech. **Psychotherapy:** Group Indiv.
   Counseling: Educ Voc.
   Enr: 34 (Cap: 45). Bdg 13. Day 21. B 29. G 5. **Fac:** 6 (Full 4, Part 2). Spec ed 6.
   Summer prgm: Bdg & Day. Educ. Rec. 8 wks.
   Est 1961. Nonprofit. Nondenom Christian.

Gables offers a full curriculum for children who have specific learning deficits. The emphasis is on strengthening basic skills through increased proficiency of learning. Each student receives individualized corrective or remedial instruction, in conjunction with larger group instruction.

In addition to conventional physical education, the academy conducts an outdoor challenge program that addresses self-confidence, coordination and problem solving skills. The curriculum also includes a fine arts program that comprises visual, literary and performing arts activities.

The academy schedules group and individual counseling sessions as needed.

THE HOWARD SCHOOL

Day — Coed Ages 5-18

Atlanta, GA 30318. 1192 Foster St NW.
Tel: 404-377-7436. Fax: 404-377-0884.
www.howardschool.org   E-mail: info@howardschool.org
Marifred Cilella, Head. **Anne Beisel,** Adm.
   Conditions: Primary—ADHD APD Dx LD. **Sec**—Apr CP Dc Dg Dpx.
   Not accepted—CD ODD.
   Col Prep. Gen Acad. Ungraded. **Feat**—ASL Span Film Studio_Art Music.
   Interscholastic sports.
   Therapy: Lang Speech.
   Adm: Appl fee: $150. Appl due: Year-round. On-campus interview.
   Enr: 240.
   Tui '12-'13: Day $25,500-26,750/sch yr. **Aid:** School. State. **Summer prgm:**
   Day. Educ. Rec. Ther. Tui Day $250-1300. 1-4 wks.
   Acres 15. Bldgs 2 (100% ADA). Libs 1. Sci labs 1. Auds 1. Theaters 1. Art stu-
   dios 2. Music studios 2. Gyms 1. Fields 1. Courts 2.
   Est 1950. Nonprofit.

Enrolling students with language-learning disabilities and learning differences, Howard conducts an individualized program that accounts for variations in learning style and processing ability. The program enables students to work at an appropriate learning pace as they build basic skills in reading and math. In addition, pupils develop higher-level thinking skills and learn self-monitoring strategies and self-evaluation skills.

The school's team of professionals includes classroom teachers, speech-language pathologists, literacy specialists, a math specialist and an assistive technology specialist. Art, music, and physical education are part of the curriculum.

Language-communication-speech services, specialized tutoring and professional development are among the school's community outreach services.

MILL SPRINGS ACADEMY

Day — Coed Ages 6-18

Alpharetta, GA 30004. 13660 New Providence Rd.
Tel: 770-360-1336. Fax: 770-360-1341.
www.millsprings.org   E-mail: sfitzgerald@millsprings.org
Robert W. Moore, BBA, Head. **Sheila FitzGerald**, Adm.

    Conditions: Primary—ADHD APD Dc Dg Dx LD Multi NLD. **Sec**—AN Anx Ap Asp B/VI Bu C Db Dpx Ep Hemo HI Lk OCD ON SC TS. **IQ 90 and up.**
    Not accepted—Apr Ar Au CD CLP CP DS ED ID IP MD Mood MR MS Nf ODD Psy PTSD SA SB SO SP Sz TBI.
    Col Prep. Gr 1-12. **Feat**—British_Lit Span Anat & Physiol Ecol Econ Pol_Sci Studio_Art Drama Band Chorus. Mid 50% SAT: CR 410-520. M 330-520. W 340-490. ACT: Mid 50% 15-22. Interscholastic sports. **Expected outcome:** Graduation.
    Therapy: Lang Speech. **Counseling:** Educ Voc.
    Adm: Appl fee: $100. Appl due: Rolling. On-campus interview.
    Enr: 299 (Cap: 350). B 221. G 78. **Fac:** 50 (Full 48, Part 2).
    Tui '12-'13: Day $20,570/sch yr (+$1800). **Aid:** School. State. **Summer prgm:** Day. Educ. Rec. 6 wks.
    Endow $132,000. Plant val $8,758,000. Acres 85. Bldgs 12 (100% ADA). Class rms 57. Lib 11,000 vols. Sci labs 4. Theaters 1. Art studios 2. Gyms 1. Fields 4. Courts 4. Comp labs 2. Laptop prgm Gr 4-12.
    Est 1981. Nonprofit.

Psychological and diagnostic evaluations form the basis of individualized prescriptive programs at the academy. Serving those who have failed to achieve to potential in traditional settings, Mill Springs generates learning strategies based upon psycho-educational evaluations, previous school records, diagnostic skills assessments and communications with professionals who have dealt with the pupil previously.

Within a structured setting, children receive instruction in age-appropriate groupings. Boys and girls must supply a laptop for school use beginning in grade 4. An extended-day program offers fencing, golf, tennis, yoga, and arts and crafts to children ages 6-14.

THE SCHENCK SCHOOL

Day — Coed Ages 5-12

Atlanta, GA 30327. 282 Mt Paran Rd NW.
Tel: 404-252-2591. Fax: 404-252-7615.
www.schenck.org   E-mail: office@schenck.org
Gena W. Calloway, MEd, Head. **Peggy Webb Hendrix**, Adm.

Conditions: Primary—Dx LD. **Sec**—ADHD. **IQ 100 and up.**
Gen Acad. Gr K-6. **Feat**—Lib_Skills Computers Studio_Art Music Study_Skills.
Expected outcome: Return to local school (Avg length of stay: 2-3 yrs).
Therapy: Lang Occup Speech.
Adm: Appl fee: $80. Appl due: Rolling.
Enr: 250. **Fac:** 56. Spec ed 56.
Tui '12-'13: Day $27,070-29,662/sch yr. **Aid:** School. **Summer prgm:** Day.
Educ. 5 wks.
Acres 6.
Est 1959. Nonprofit.

Schenck provides remedial training in a day school framework for children with dyslexia and other language disabilities. The educational program enables students to continue study in their basic school subjects while receiving concentrated instruction in reading, writing and spelling. The school conducts complete testing of students three times per year, and individual tutoring is available. The usual length of stay is two to three years.

HAWAII

ASSETS SCHOOL

Day — Coed Ages 5-18

Honolulu, HI 96818. 1 Ohana Nui Way.
Tel: 808-423-1356. Fax: 808-422-1920.
www.assets-school.net   E-mail: admissions@assets-school.net
Paul Singer, BA, MEd, Head. **Sandi Tadaki**, Adm.
   Conditions: Primary—ADHD Dx. **Sec**—Ap CP ED Ep S TBI. **IQ 90 and up.**
   Col Prep. Gen Acad. Gr K-12. **Feat**—Women's_Lit ASL Span Korean Calc
   Marine_Bio/Sci Computers Philos Graphic_Arts Photog Studio_Art Music
   Dance Study_Skills. Interscholastic sports. **Expected outcome:** Graduation.
   Therapy: Lang Speech. **Psychotherapy:** Fam Indiv.
   Adm: Appl fee: $75. Appl due: Rolling.
   Enr: 340. **Fac:** 59 (Full 57, Part 2).
   Tui '12-'13: Day $18,600-21,730/sch yr. **Summer prgm:** Day. Educ. 5 wks.
   Acres 3. Bldgs 24. Class rms 32. Lib 15,000 vols. Sci labs 3. Art studios 1.
   Music studios 1. Comp labs 2.
   Est 1969. Nonprofit.

This school for dyslexic children of average to superior intelligence offers a program consisting of intensive academic remediation, acceleration and enrichment in the mornings, followed by a departmentalized course of study in the afternoons. Assets also works at improving a child's self-concept through daily group counseling and ongoing individual counseling. Both initial diagnostic evaluations and continuous diagnostic and prescriptive services are available.

The school works in close conjunction with the Special Education Department of the University of Hawaii and utilizes both student teachers and field work placements as supplements to the faculty.

HORIZONS ACADEMY OF MAUI

Day — Coed Ages 5-20

Kihei, HI 96753. 2679 Wai Wai Pl, Ste 301, PO Box 171.
Tel: 808-575-2954. Fax: 808-575-9180.
www.horizonsacademy.org   E-mail: director@horizonsacademy.org
Beau Laughlin, Exec Dir.
   Conditions: Primary—ADHD Dc Dg Dx LD OCD SP. **Sec**—Au ED ID ODD S
   TS. **IQ 75-130.**
   Gen Acad. Ungraded. Culinary. On-Job Trng. Support_Employ. **Expected
   outcome:** Return to local school (Avg length of stay: 2-8 yrs).
   Therapy: Lang Music Occup Play Rec Speech Visual. **Psychotherapy:** Art
   Dance Fam Group Indiv. **Counseling:** Educ Nutrition Voc.
   Adm: Appl fee: $50. Appl due: Rolling. On-campus interview.
   Enr: 22 (Cap: 25). B 10. G 12. **Fac:** 10 (Full 2, Part 8). Spec ed 3. Lay 7.

Tui '12-'13: Day $23,000/sch yr (+$150). Clinic $25-40 (Tutoring); $60-90 (Therapy)/hr. **Aid:** School. State. Educ. Tui Day $225/wk. 8 wks. **Est 1993.** Nonprofit.

In a small-class setting, Horizons conducts an individualized program for students with learning disabilities. Staff develop an educational plan for each pupil, then regularly assess achievement to ensure that progress is being made. Ongoing adaptation of the program occurs as necessary. The academy addresses behavioral issues by providing instruction in social skills, problem solving, impulse control and anger management.

VARIETY SCHOOL OF HAWAII

Day — Coed Ages 5-13

Honolulu, HI 96816. 710 Palekaua St.
Tel: 808-732-2835. Fax: 808-732-4334.
www.varietyschool.org   E-mail: info@varietyschool.org
Duane Yee, MAT, Dir. **Jolene Nanod,** Adm.
   Conditions: Primary—ADHD Asp Au Dc Dg Dx LD PDD. **Sec**—CD ED OCD S.
   Gen Acad. Ungraded.
   Therapy: Lang Occup Perceptual-Motor Phys Speech. **Psychotherapy:** Dance.
   Adm: Appl fee: $50. Appl due: Year-round. On-campus interview.
   Enr: 35 (Cap: 50). **Fac:** 11 (Full-time). Spec ed 4. Lay 7.
   Tui '12-'13: Day $24,700-26,900/sch yr. **Aid:** School. **Summer prgm:** Day. Educ. Rec. Tui Day $1900. 6 wks.
   Est 1961. Nonprofit.

Variety School was established to meet the educational needs of children with mild autism or a learning disability attributable to neurological dysfunction. The program seeks to develop individual readiness, then successfully place each child in a traditional school setting.

Class work is highly individualized. Gross-motor training, visual-motor perceptual training, and speech and language therapies are planned to address the needs of the pupil. A required program for parents attempts to assist in understanding and solving everyday problems in the home.

Sessions before and after regular school hours are also available.

ILLINOIS

ACACIA ACADEMY
Day — Coed Ages 6-18

La Grange, IL 60525. 6425 S Willow Springs Rd.
Tel: 708-579-9040. Fax: 708-579-5872.
www.acaciaacademy.com   E-mail: eileen.petzold@acaciaacademy.com
Kathryn Fouks, MSEd, Prin. **Eileen Petzold,** Adm.
   Conditions: Primary—ADHD Dc Dg Dx LD. **Sec**—Anx Ap Asp Au ED ID S
   SP TS. **IQ 65 and up.**
   Col Prep. Gen Acad. Gr 1-12. **Feat**—Sci Computers Soc_Stud Fine_Arts
   Drama. SAT/ACT prep.
   Therapy: Lang Occup Perceptual-Motor Phys Play Rec Speech. **Counseling:**
   Educ.
   Enr: 100. B 65. G 35.
   Summer prgm: Day. Educ. Rec. Tui Day $425/wk. 6 wks.
   Acres 2.
   Est 1979. Inc.

The academy offers a full elementary and secondary academic program. Acacia enrolls
boys and girls with learning disabilities, autism, emotional or behavioral disorders, attentional disorders; slow learners; and accelerated or gifted students who wish to address
skills in a particular subject area. Diagnostic and tutorial services provided by the affiliated
Achievement Center include academic testing, psycho-educational diagnosis, psychological projective testing, and ACT and SAT exam preparation in a clinic setting.

BEACON THERAPEUTIC DAY SCHOOL
Day — Coed Ages 3-21

Chicago, IL 60643. 1912 W 103rd St.
Tel: 773-298-1243. Fax: 773-298-1078.
www.beacon-therapeutic.org   E-mail: beacon@beacon-therapeutic.org
   Nearby locations: 12440 S Ada St, Calumet Park 60827; 10650 S Longwood
   Dr, Chicago 60643.
Susan Reyna-Guerrero, LCSW, Pres. **Joan Gross,** EdD, Prin.
   Conditions: Primary—ADHD Anx Asp Au CD Dc Dg Dx ED LD Mood ID
   OCD ODD Psy PTSD S SA SP Sz. **Sec**—Ap C Db Ep Hemo Lk SC SO
   Subst TBI TS. **IQ 50-130.**
   Gen Acad. Voc. Gr PS-12. On-Job Trng. Support_Employ. **Expected out-
   come:** Return to local school (Avg length of stay: 2-5 yrs).
   Therapy: Lang Occup Speech. **Psychotherapy:** Fam Group Indiv.
   Counseling: Educ Voc.
   Adm: Appl due: Year-round. On-campus interview.
   Enr: 131 (Cap: 160). B 90. G 41. **Fac:** 24 (Full-time).
   Tui '10-'11: Day $180/day. **Aid:** State.

Est 1968. Nonprofit.

Beacon Therapeutic is a multi-service agency that provides behavioral and educational services for high-risk children and adolescents with multiple special needs. Local public schools place elementary and secondary students in Beacon Day School. These pupils' severe disabilities and attendant needs cannot be properly addressed in a public school setting. The goal of the educational program is to increase function to the point that the boy or girl can successfully return to a less restrictive school setting or to an employment or a vocational situation.

Also available through the agency is outpatient programming for children who are experiencing emotional or behavioral problems at home or in the community.

BREHM PREPARATORY SCHOOL

Bdg and Day — Coed Ages 11-21

Carbondale, IL 62901. 1245 E Grand Ave.
Tel: 618-457-0371. Fax: 618-529-1248.
www.brehm.org   E-mail: admissionsinfo@brehm.org
Richard G. Collins, PhD, Exec Dir. **Donna E. Collins,** Adm.
   Conditions: Primary—ADHD Anx Dc Dg Dx LD NLD. **Sec**—Ap Apr Asp CP
      ED Ep Mood OCD TBI TS. **IQ 90-130. Not accepted**—CD ID MR Psy SO
      Subst.
   Col Prep. Gen Acad. Gr 6-PG. **Feat**—British_Lit Creative_Writing Japan
      Span Anat Environ_Sci Comp_Sci Econ Psych Art_Hist Studio_Art
      Study_Skills. Interscholastic sports. **Expected outcome:** Return to local
      school (Avg length of stay: 2½-4 yrs).
   Therapy: Lang Speech.
   Adm: Appl due: Rolling.
   Enr: 86. Bdg 81. Day 5. **Fac:** 24. Spec ed 24.
   Tui '12-'13: Bdg $66,900/sch yr (+$3000). Day $41,400/sch yr (+$1500).
   Aid: State 29.
   Acres 80. Bldgs 10. Dorms 5. Dorm rms 36. Class rms 21. Sci labs 1. Gyms 1.
      Comp labs 3.
   Est 1982. Nonprofit.

Brehm offers a program of general academics for pupils with learning disabilities highlighted by microcomputers, laboratory science and course work required for college entrance. Remedial work, study habits and social skills are also stressed. A total curricular approach encourages students to utilize new skills in their daily living experiences.

The school administers psycho-educational diagnostic evaluations to determine individual program emphases. College and vocational counseling are also available for 12th graders and postgraduate students.

CHILD'S VOICE SCHOOL

Day — Coed Ages 3-9

Wood Dale, IL 60191. 180 Hansen Ct.

Tel: 630-595-8200. TTY: 630-595-8200. Fax: 630-595-8282.
www.childsvoice.org   E-mail: info@childsvoice.org
Michele Wilkins, EdD, Exec Dir.
   Conditions: Primary—D HI S. **IQ 90-135.**
   Gen Acad. Ungraded. **Feat**—Sci Soc_Stud. **Expected outcome:** Return to
      local school (Avg length of stay: 4-6 yrs).
   Therapy: Hear Lang Music Speech. **Psychotherapy:** Fam Group Indiv
      Parent. **Counseling:** Educ.
   Adm: Appl due: Year-round.
   Enr: 53. **Fac:** 13 (Full-time). Spec ed 12. Lay 1.
   Aid: State (100% of tui). **Summer prgm:** Day. Educ. Tui Day $199/day. 5 wks.
   Est 1996. Nonprofit.

This auditory/oral school teaches children who are deaf or hard of hearing to speak.
The school provides individualized instruction using speech therapy, auditory training, language development and knowledge of technological advances (such as cochlear implants).
The program goal is to mainstream the child into his or her local school with minimal
support.
   Funding from the student's sending school district typically covers tuition fees.

CLARE WOODS ACADEMY

Day — Coed Ages 3-22

Bartlett, IL 60103. 801 Carillon Dr.
Tel: 630-289-4221. Fax: 630-289-4390.
www.blcinc.org   E-mail: contact@blcinc.org
John Utterback, Prin.
   Conditions: Primary—ADHD Asp Au DS ED LD ID PDD PW TBI TS.
      Sec—Ap Apr As CD CP Dg Dpx Dx Ep MD MS Multi OCD ON S.
   Gen Acad. Voc. Ungraded. On-Job Trng. Shelt_Workshop. **Feat**—Studio_Art
      Music. **Expected outcome:** Return to local school.
   Therapy: Music Occup Play Speech. **Psychotherapy:** Art Group Indiv.
      Counseling: Educ Voc.
   Adm: Appl fee: $0. Appl due: Year-round. On-campus interview.
   Enr: 110 (Cap: 130). **Fac:** 20 (Full 13, Part 7). Spec ed 13. Lay 7.
   Summer prgm: Day. Educ. 5 wks.
   Est 1968. Nonprofit. Roman Catholic.

Founded and sponsored by the Sisters of St. Joseph, the academy offers remedial and
functional academics for boys and girls with mild to moderate intellectual disabilities.
Children may also have a learning disability or an emotional disturbance. Physical education is part of the curriculum. Applicants must be ambulatory and toilet trained.
   During both the school year and the summer program, Clare Woods offers one-on-one
instruction for an additional fee.

THE COVE SCHOOL

Day — Coed Ages 5-21

Northbrook, IL 60062. 350 Lee Rd.
Tel: 847-562-2100. Fax: 847-562-2112.
www.coveschool.org   E-mail: ssover@coveschool.org
Sally L. Sover, EdD, Exec Dir. **John Stieper,** Educ Dir.
Conditions: Primary—Dc Dg Dx LD. **Sec**—ADHD Anx Apr Db Ep NLD OCD
TBI TS. **IQ 85 and up.**
Col Prep. Gen Acad. Voc. Gr K-12. Culinary. On-Job Trng. Support_Employ.
Feat—Span Computers Photog Studio_Art Drama Chorus Music Journ.
Expected outcome: Return to local school (Avg length of stay: 2-4 yrs).
Therapy: Lang Music Occup Speech. **Psychotherapy:** Art Indiv. **Counseling:**
Educ Voc.
Adm: Appl fee: $75. Appl due: Year-round. On-campus interview.
Enr: 137 (Cap: 150). B 86. G 51. **Fac:** 31 (Full 30, Part 1). Spec ed 30. Lay 1.
Tui '12-'13: Day $38,000/sch yr. **Aid:** School. State 116. **Summer prgm:** Day.
Educ. Rec. 6 wks.
Acres 7. Bldgs 1 (100% ADA). Class rms 19. Libs 1. Sci labs 1. Lang labs 1.
Art studios 1. Music studios 1. Gyms 1. Fields 1. Comp labs 1. Laptop prgm
Gr 9-12.
Est 1947. Nonprofit.

The nation's first school designed exclusively for children with learning disabilities, Cove provides students having various learning problems with a specially designed educational environment. The program, which consists of elementary, junior high and high school divisions, utilizes an integrated academic program to develop children's critical-thinking, language and study skills. Teachers attempt to formulate an appropriate learning strategy for the pupil. Cove issues a laptop to each high school student for school use.

Social workers at the school provide individual and group counseling for those experiencing social and emotional problems. Cove's seeks to help each student develop the academic, language, social and practical skills necessary for the successful return to a traditional classroom.

ELIM CHRISTIAN SCHOOL

Day — Coed Ages 3-21

Palos Heights, IL 60463. 13020 S Central Ave.
Tel: 708-389-0555, 877-935-4627. Fax: 708-293-3673.
www.elimcs.org   E-mail: info@elimcs.org
Bill Lodewyk, MEd, PhD, Pres. **Mike Otte,** MS, Prin. **Carol Runge,** Adm.
Conditions: Primary—As Au CP DS ID Multi ON PDD S SB TBI.
Sec—ADHD AN Anx B/VI C D Db ED Ep Hemo HI LD Mood OCD ODD
Psy PTSD PW SA SC SP Sz TS. **IQ 25-70. Not accepted**—Bu CD SO
Subst.
Gen Acad. Voc. Ungraded. On-Job Trng. Shelt_Workshop. Support_Employ.
Feat—Studio_Art Music.
Therapy: Lang Occup Phys Rec Speech.

Adm: Appl fee: $0. Appl due: Year-round. On-campus interview.
Enr: 275. **Fac:** 35 (Full 33, Part 2). Spec ed 35.
Aid: State 275 (100% of tui).
Gyms 2. Pools 1.
Est 1948. Nonprofit. Nondenom Christian.

In a rural setting, Elim offers therapeutic education for boys and girls with developmental or physical disabilities or both. The school comprises elementary, middle school and high school programs, and students are grouped by age and ability level. In addition to educational services, prevocational training is available.

Elim's Autism Comprehensive Educational Program serves children along the autism spectrum who have heightened sensory, motor and communicational needs.

HOLY TRINITY SCHOOL FOR THE DEAF

Day — Coed Ages 3-15

Chicago, IL 60612. 1900 W Taylor St.
Tel: 312-243-8186. Fax: 312-243-8479.
www.copeace.pvt.k12.il.us/deaf_program.html
  E-mail: tlangelliercop@yahoo.com
Phyllis Winter, Pres. **Terri Langellier,** BA, MA, Prin.
  Conditions: Primary—D. **IQ 85 and up.**
  Gen Acad. Gr PS-8. **Feat**—Sci Soc_Stud Relig Fine_Arts.
  Therapy: Lang Speech.
  Tui '12-'13: Day $4300/sch yr (+$400).
  Est 1957. Nonprofit. Roman Catholic. **Spons:** Children of Peace School.

Elementary education for deaf and hard-of-hearing students is provided at Holy Trinity. The program emphasizes an individual approach that uses a total communication method of instruction. The school involves parents both in the structuring of the program and in communicative skills for use in the home. Speech and language services are also available. Children are mainstreamed into traditional schools.

THE HOPE SCHOOL LEARNING CENTER

Bdg and Day — Coed Ages 5-21

Springfield, IL 62712. 15 E Hazel Dell Ln.
Tel: 217-585-5437. TTY: 217-529-5766. Fax: 217-786-3356.
www.thehopeschool.org
Cliff Hathaway, Prin. **Amy Chase,** Adm.
  Conditions: Primary—Au LD ID ON PDD TBI. **Sec**—ADHD B/VI CP D Db
    DS Ep IP MD MS S SB. **IQ 0-70.**
  Voc. Ungraded. On-Job Trng.
  Therapy: Lang Occup Phys Rec Speech. **Psychotherapy:** Group Indiv.
  Enr: 177. Bdg 64. Day 113. **Fac:** 131.
  Acres 25.
  Est 1957. Nonprofit.

Located on a 25-acre, wooded campus in the central part of the state, Hope conducts an individualized residential program that serves children and young adults with multiple disabilities. Programs include a school; occupational, physical, recreational and speech therapy services; a vocational program that operates both on and off campus; assistive technology services; and nursing and medical services. Family involvement is integral to the program.

JOSEPH ACADEMY
Day — Coed Ages 5-21

Des Plaines, IL 60016. 1101 Gregory St.
Tel: 847-803-1930. Fax: 847-803-8669.
www.josephacademy.org   E-mail: information@josephacademy.org
   Nearby locations: 555 Wilson Ln, Des Plaines 60016; 1100 N 22nd Ave, Melrose Park 60160; 420 County Farm Rd, Wheaton 60187; 9003 S Kostner Ave, Hometown 60456.
Michael Schack, MBA, MA, Exec Dir.
   Conditions: Primary—CD ED LD. **Sec**—ADHD Dc Dg Dx ID Mood OCD. **IQ 60-120. Not accepted**—B/VI D.
   Gen Acad. Gr K-12. Man_Arts & Shop. **Feat**—Sci Soc_Stud. Interscholastic sports. **Expected outcome:** Return to local school (Avg length of stay: 2 yrs).
   Psychotherapy: Fam Group Indiv Parent.
   Enr: 85.
   Aid: State 85 (100% of tui).
   Est 1983. Nonprofit.

This therapeutic day school enrolls children with behavioral disorders and learning disabilities at five locations. The behavioral program follows the Boys' Town model. Academic credit is given for work-study program, and frequent academic field trips are available. The sending school district pays all tuition and transportation expenses.

In addition to the Gregory Street location, Joseph Academy also maintains another Des Plaines location, as well as schools in Melrose Park, Hometown and Du Page.

LT. JOSEPH P. KENNEDY SCHOOL
FOR EXCEPTIONAL CHILDREN
Bdg — Coed Ages 6 and up; Day — Coed 6-21

Tinley Park, IL 60487. 18350 Crossing Dr.
Tel: 708-342-5278. Fax: 708-342-2579.
www.stcolettas.com/kennedy-school   E-mail: info@stcolettasofil.com
Rosemary Kern, MEd, Educ Dir.
   Conditions: Primary—Anx APD Asp Au CD Db DS ED ID NLD PDD TBI TS. **Sec**—ADHD B/VI CP Dx LD OCD ODD ON PW S.
   Gen Acad. Voc. Ungraded. On-Job Trng. Shelt_Workshop. **Expected outcome:** Return to local school (Avg length of stay: 4-6 yrs).
   Therapy: Lang Occup Perceptual-Motor Phys Rec Speech. **Psychotherapy:** Indiv Parent. **Counseling:** Educ.

Enr: 51 (Cap: 91). Bdg 5. Day 46. B 30. G 21. **Fac:** 8 (Full-time). Spec ed 8.
Tui '10-'11: Day $145/day. **Summer prgm:** Day. Educ. 10 wks.
Est 1949. Nonprofit. Roman Catholic.

The school provides comprehensive special education and vocational training for mildly to moderately retarded children and adolescents. A program for nonacademic students that emphasizes the development of life skills is also offered. Student behavior is monitored by means of a life camera feed that can be observed by staff, parents and special education directors. Based upon these observations, staff develop and implement a behavior program.

SONIA SHANKMAN ORTHOGENIC SCHOOL
Bdg and Day — Coed Ages 6-20

Chicago, IL 60637. 1365 E 60th St.
Tel: 773-702-1203. Fax: 773-702-1304.
www.oschool.org   E-mail: kfriesen@uchicago.edu
Diana Kon, MEd, Co-Exec Dir. **Peter Myers,** PsyD, Co-Exec Dir. **Kristin Friesen,** Adm.
    Conditions: Primary—Anx Asp Au ED Mood OCD ODD Psy PTSD SP Sz TS. **Sec**—ADHD Ar As CD Db Dx LD. **IQ 80 and up.**
    Col Prep. Gen Acad. Voc. Ungraded. Man_Arts & Shop. On-Job Trng.
    Feat—Fr Span Calc Environ_Sci Econ Govt Painting Journ. SAT/ACT prep.
    Expected outcome: Return to local school (Avg length of stay: 3-5 yrs).
    Therapy: Milieu Occup Speech. **Psychotherapy:** Art Fam Group Indiv Parent.
    Counseling: Educ Voc.
    Adm: Appl fee: $0. Appl due: Year-round. On-campus interview.
    Enr: 60 (Cap: 60). Bdg 44. Day 16. B 38. G 22. **Fac:** 20 (Full 18, Part 2). Spec ed 12. Lay 8.
    Tui '10-'11: Bdg $140,000/yr. Day $207/day.
    Est 1930. Nonprofit. **Spons:** University of Chicago.

The Orthogenic School maintains an affiliation with the University of Chicago. Severely emotionally disturbed children of average intelligence and above receive individualized attention within small groups. Life activities are planned after results of repeated psychiatric and psychological evaluation and staff conferences. Milieu therapy is the basis of rehabilitation and includes both individual therapy and group work. Classroom groups are small, with each student working at a suitable pace. Individualized teaching enables students to reach educational goals similar to those instituted in public schools.

Sonia Shankman maintains close cooperation with appropriate departments of the University of Chicago. Children enrolled at the school may use the university's swimming pool. School is in session year-round, with home and parent visits arranged according to the child's emotional needs. Parents receive weekly reports and attend conferences to track their children's progress.

SUMMIT SCHOOL

Day — Coed Ages 2-21

Elgin, IL 60123. 333 W River Rd.
Tel: 847-468-0490. Fax: 847-468-9392.
www.summitinc.org   E-mail: jwhite@summitelgin.org
Johanna White, BA, MS, EdS, Prin. **Elaine Suitts,** Adm.
  Conditions: Primary—ADHD Asp Au Dc Dx Ep LD S. **Sec**—ED.
  Gen Acad. Voc. Gr PS-12. Man_Arts & Shop. On-Job Trng. **Feat**—Computers
    Studio_Art. **Expected outcome:** Return to local school.
  Therapy: Lang Occup Speech. **Psychotherapy:** Group Indiv. **Counseling:** Voc.
  Adm: Appl fee: $30.
  Enr: 94 (Cap: 120).
  Summer prgm: Day. Educ. Ther. 5 wks.
  Est 1968. Nonprofit.

Summit accepts children of average to superior intelligence who have learning difficulties. Individualized learning and coordinated motor, language and speech instruction form the foundation of the program. The school day ends early for those students who are being mainstreamed. Social skills and self-advocacy training is a secondary emphasis of the program.

The school's early learning center serves special-needs children ages 2-4.

TRANSITIONS SCHOOL

Day — Coed Ages 3-21

Quincy, IL 62305. 4409 Maine St.
Tel: 217-223-0413. Fax: 217-223-0461.
www.twi.org   E-mail: transitions@twi.org
J. Michael Rein, MA, Exec Dir.
  Conditions: Primary—ID. **Sec**—ADHD B/VI CP D ON TBI. **IQ** 0-35.
  Gen Acad. Ungraded. Shelt_Workshop.
  Therapy: Hear Lang Occup Phys Speech. **Psychotherapy:** Fam Group Indiv
    Parent. **Counseling:** Educ Voc.
  Adm: Appl fee: $0.
  Enr: 15. B 10. G 5. **Fac:** 4. Spec ed 4.
  Aid: State 15 (100% of tui).
  Est 1971. Nonprofit. **Spons:** Transitions of Western Illinois.

The school serves severely to children with profound intellectual disabilities who have not had their needs adequately met in public school systems. Individualized programs correspond with each child's requirements and capabilities, and parental involvement plays a major role at the school. Counseling, respite care and referral services are also available. The sending school district pays all tuition fees.

TRINITY SCHOOL
Day — Coed Ages 3-21

New Lenox, IL 60451. 13318 W Lincoln Hwy.
Tel: 815-463-0719.
www.trinity-services.org   E-mail: kvinquist@trinity-services.org
Kelly Vinquist, Dir.

    Conditions: Primary—Au ID. **Sec**—ADHD Asp B/VI CP D DS ED Ep LD PW
    S TS.
    Gen Acad. Ungraded.
    Therapy: Lang Occup Speech.
    Enr: 27. B 18. G 9.
    Aid: State 27 (100% of tui). **Summer prgm:** Day. Educ. 6 wks.
    Est 1950. Nonprofit. **Spons:** Trinity Services.

All children at the school have a developmental disability, such as cognitive impairment, autism or cerebral palsy. Program emphasis is to help the boy or girl function in society as independently as possible. As children have varying developmental levels, Trinity works with each child individually. Boys and girls learn to interact with one another and with other members of the community.

INDIANA

WORTHMORE ACADEMY
Day — Coed Ages 5-22

Indianapolis, IN 46220. 3535 Kessler Boulevard East Dr.
Tel: 877-700-6516. Fax: 317-251-6516.
www.worthmoreacademy.org E-mail: bjackson@worthmoreacademy.org
Brenda J. Jackson, BS, MS, Dir.
Conditions: Primary—ADHD Anx Ap APD Apr Asp Au Dc Dg Dpx Dx LD
ID Multi NLD ODD PDD S TBI. **Sec**—AN Ar As Bu CD CP Db DS ED Ep
Mood OCD ON SP TS. **IQ 80 and up.**
Gen Acad. Ungraded. **Expected outcome:** Return to local school (Avg length
of stay: 2-3 yrs).
Therapy: Occup Perceptual-Motor Phys Speech. **Counseling:** Educ.
Adm: Appl due: Rolling. On-campus interview.
Enr: 35 (Cap: 35). B 25. G 10. **Fac:** 10 (Full 8, Part 2).
Tui 2004: Day $900/mo. **Summer prgm:** Day. Educ. Tui Day $325/wk. 6 wks.
Acres 5. Bldgs 1. Class rms 10. Libs 1. Auds 1. Music studios 1. Comp labs 1.
Est 1988. Nonprofit.

Worthmore serves children with specific learning disabilities, among them dyslexia, attentional disorders, autism and auditory processing difficulties. The program is ungraded, with each pupil working at his or her ability level. Boys and girls may complete the academy's high school program in as little as three years or as many as six. After-school care is available for an additional monthly fee.

KANSAS

HEARTSPRING

Bdg — Coed Ages 5-21

Wichita, KS 67226. 8700 E 29th St N.
Tel: 316-634-8700, 800-835-1043. Fax: 316-634-0555.
www.heartspring.org   E-mail: carar@heartspring.org
Gary Singleton, Pres. **Cara Rapp,** Adm.
  Conditions: Primary—Ap Asp Au CP D DS ID Multi NLD ON PDD PW SB
    TBI. **Sec**—ADHD Anx B/VI Db Dx ED Ep OCD ODD PTSD TS.
  Gen Acad. Gr K-12. On-Job Trng. Shelt_Workshop. Support_Employ.
    Feat—Life_Skills. **Expected outcome:** Return to local school (Avg length
    of stay: 2-3 yrs).
  Therapy: Hear Lang Occup Phys Speech. **Psychotherapy:** Indiv.
  Adm: Appl due: Year-round.
  Enr: 47. B 42. G 5. **Fac:** 9. Spec ed 7. Lay 2.
  Tui '11-'12: Bdg $21,000/mo. Clinic $95 (Clinic)/ses. **Aid:** School. State.
    Summer prgm: Day. Ther. Tui Day $200. 2 wks.
  Acres 38. Bldgs 10. Class rms 8. Gyms 1.
  Est 1934. Nonprofit.

The school serves pupils with mental retardation who often have one or more accompanying disorders, among them autism, orthopedic and neurological conditions, visual and hearing problems, and attentional disorders. An interdisciplinary team of professionals designs and implements each student's program in the areas of behavior management, communication and health.

In addition to its school program, Heartspring operates a hearing center that provides comprehensive diagnostic hearing evaluations for pediatric patients.

MARILLAC

Bdg and Day — Coed Ages 6-17

Overland Park, KS 66213. 8000 W 127th St.
Tel: 913-951-4300.
www.marillac.org   E-mail: intakeservices@marillac.org
Joy Wheeler, Int Pres.
  Conditions: Primary—ADHD Anx Asp Au Bu Db Dx ED LD PDD PTSD SP
    Sz TS. **Sec**—As CD Ep Mood OCD Psy PW. **IQ 80 and up.**
    Not accepted—B/VI D.
  Gen Acad. Ungraded. **Expected outcome:** Return to local school (Avg length
    of stay: 9 mos-2 yrs).
  Therapy: Lang Music Occup Play Rec Speech. **Psychotherapy:** Art Fam
    Group Indiv Parent. **Counseling:** Educ.
  Enr: 132. Bdg 108. Day 24. B 93. G 39. **Fac:** 10 (Full-time). Spec ed 8. Lay 2.
  Est 1897. Nonprofit.

Marillac provides a therapeutic atmosphere of learning for emotionally disturbed children. The program includes individualized prescriptive educational programming, perceptual-motor training, psychotherapy, and a combination of individual and group therapy aimed at mainstreaming. Aftercare services are available for six months to both student and family.

KENTUCKY

THE DE PAUL SCHOOL
Day — Coed Ages 6-14

Louisville, KY 40205. 1925 Duker Ave.
Tel: 502-459-6131. Fax: 502-458-0827.
www.depaulschool.org   E-mail: dpinfo@depaulschool.org
Anthony R. Kemper, Head. **Peggy Woolley,** Adm.
  Conditions: Primary—ADHD APD Dc Dg Dx LD NLD. **IQ 100 and up.**
  Gen Acad. Gr 1-8. **Feat**—Humanities Lib_Skills Computers. Interscholastic
    sports. **Expected outcome:** Return to local school (Avg length of stay: 4 yrs).
  Therapy: Lang.
  Adm: On-campus interview.
  Enr: 262. **Fac:** 20.
  Tui '10-'11: Day $12,800/sch yr. **Aid:** School. **Summer prgm:** Day. Educ. 6 wks.
  Est 1970. Nonprofit.

The school provides diagnosis and remediation of dyslexia and other specific learning differences. De Paul's program focuses upon the acquisition of basic skills and the development of independent learning skills. Faculty members also address difficulties with social skills and self-esteem. Students, who must possess at least average intelligence, typically spend an average of four years at de Paul.

HEUSER HEARING & LANGUAGE ACADEMY
Day — Coed Ages 3-7

Louisville, KY 40203. 111 E Kentucky St.
Tel: 502-515-3320. TTY: 502-515-3323. Fax: 502-515-3325.
www.thehearinginstitute.org   E-mail: info@thehearinginstitute.org
Mona K. McCubbin, MS, Exec Dir.
  Conditions: Primary—D. **Sec**—ADHD Dx LD.
  Gen Acad. Gr PS-K. **Expected outcome:** Graduation.
  Therapy: Hear Lang Occup Phys Speech. **Counseling:** Educ.
  Enr: 150.
  Est 1948. Nonprofit. **Spons:** Heuser Hearing Institute.

Young children who have a hearing loss serious enough to require amplification and educational intervention may enroll at the school. Functioning as both a teaching and a diagnostic center, the academy provides daily activities that promote language, speech, listening and cognitive development. The school, which is part of the Heuser Hearing Institute, serves as a regional center for cochlear implant evaluation and post-implant rehabilitation.

HINDMAN SETTLEMENT SCHOOL

Day — Coed Ages 6-14

Hindman, KY 41822. 254 Hwy 160 S, PO Box 844.
Tel: 606-785-4044. Fax: 606-785-4044.
www.hindmansettlement.org   E-mail: lgibson@hindmansettlement.org
Brent D. Hutchinson, BA, MS, Exec Dir.
  Conditions: Primary—Dx LD. **Sec**—ADHD Dc Dg. **IQ 90 and up.**
  Gen Acad. Gr 1-8. **Expected outcome:** Return to local school (Avg length of
    stay: 2½ yrs).
  Adm: Appl fee: $75. Appl due: Rolling.
  Enr: 24 (Cap: 40). B 17. G 7. **Fac:** 5 (Full 4, Part 1). Spec ed 1. Lay 4.
  Summer prgm: Bdg & Day. Educ. Tui Bdg $4200. Tui Day $2100. 6 wks.
  Est 1902. Nonprofit.

Utilizing an explicit multisensory phonic approach to reading instruction, the school remediates dyslexia in children from the Appalachian region. The center comprises an elementary day school, after-school tutoring sessions, and a summer tutorial program. Parent volunteers and college students receive training that enables them to tutor children in Knott County and five surrounding counties.

The full-time school emphasizes reading and math in addition to writing, science and social studies. Students in the after-school program attend one evening each week for reading, auditory and social values instruction. The only fee associated with the school-year programs is one for after-school tutoring, if the child receives it.

The summer school provides an intense, structured remedial setting. It features one-on-one tutoring in reading and three-to-one tutoring in math for students ages 6-20. Many of the summer session's participants attend public school during the regular academic year.

STEWART HOME SCHOOL

Bdg — Coed Ages 6 and up

Frankfort, KY 40601. 4200 Lawrenceburg Rd.
Tel: 502-227-4821. Fax: 502-227-3013.
www.stewarthome.com   E-mail: info@stewarthome.com
Sandra Bell, BA, Dir.
  Conditions: Primary—DS ID PW TBI. **Sec**—ADHD Ap Asp Au B/VI Db ED
    Ep ODD PDD. **IQ 30 and up.**
  Gen Acad. Voc. Ungraded. On-Job Trng. Shelt_Workshop. **Feat**—Computers
    Fine_Arts Music.
  Therapy: Music Speech. **Psychotherapy:** Dance Equine.
  Enr: 400 (Cap: 400).
  Est 1893. Inc.

SHS provides care and training, including lifetime care, for children and adults with intellectual disabilities. All residents have an active, individually planned program that includes recreation, academics, vocational training, job placement, self-care and social skills. A community-based sheltered workshop is also available.

SUMMIT ACADEMY

Day — Coed Ages 5-14

Louisville, KY 40243. 11508 Main St.
Tel: 502-244-7090. Fax: 502-244-3371.
www:summit-academy.org   E-mail: info@summit-academy.org
Margaret Thornton, MEd, Head. **Barbara Waldrop,** Adm.
  Conditions: Primary—ADHD APD Apr As Asp Dc Dg Dpx Dx LD Multi NLD
    PDD. **Sec**—Anx Ar C CF CLP CP Db Ep Hemo HI Lk MD Mood MS Nf
    OCD ON PW SB SC SP TBI TS. **IQ 80 and up. Not accepted**—AN Ap Au
    B/VI Bu CD D D-B ED ID IP MR ODD Psy PTSD SA SO Subst Sz.
  Gen Acad. Underachiever. Gr PS-8. **Feat**—Computers Studio_Art Music.
    Expected outcome: Return to local school (Avg length of stay: 3-4 yrs).
  Therapy: Occup Perceptual-Motor Rec Speech. **Psychotherapy:** Dance Fam
    Group Indiv Parent. **Counseling:** Educ.
  Adm: Appl fee: $50. Appl due: Year-round. On-campus interview.
  Enr: 115 (Cap: 170). B 89. G 26. **Fac:** 24 (Full-time).
  Tui '10-'11: Day $9700-14,000/yr (+$250). Clinic $55 (Speech Therapy); $100
    (Occup Therapy)/ses. **Aid:** School 40 ($190,000). **Summer prgm:** Day.
    Educ. Rec. 12 wks.
  Acres 4. Bldgs 4. Class rms 17. Libs 1. Sci labs 1. Auds 1. Theaters 1. Art stu-
    dios 1. Music studios 1. Gyms 1. Fields 1. Courts 2. Comp labs 1.
  Est 1992. Nonprofit.

   The academy serves children with learning disabilities, as well as those who are at risk
of developing learning disabilities. Each child receives intensive instruction in a small
classroom setting. Staff use annual standardized testing results as a complement to ongoing performance assessments and criterion-referenced testing. Extracurricular activities
include soccer, basketball, drama, art, chess club and environmental club.

LOUISIANA

THE BRIGHTON SCHOOL
Day — Coed Ages 5-19

Baton Rouge, LA 70816. 12108 Parkmeadow Ave.
Tel: 225-291-2524. Fax: 225-291-8587.
www.thebrightonschool.org   E-mail: info@thebrightonschool.org
  Nearby locations: 9150 Bereford Dr, Baton Rouge 70809.
Kenneth B. Payne, MS, Exec Dir. Tim Penny, Adm.
  Conditions: Primary—APD Dg Dx LD. Sec—ADHD Dc. IQ 90 and up.
  Gen Acad. Gr K-12. Feat—Environ_Sci Comp_Sci Bible Studio_Art.
  Expected outcome: Return to local school (Avg length of stay: 4 yrs).
  Psychotherapy: Fam.
  Adm: Appl fee: $0. Appl due: Year-round. On-campus interview.
  Enr: 154. Fac: 22.
  Tui '12-'13: Day $9700-10,500/sch yr (+$910). Aid: School 20 ($40,000).
  Summer prgm: Day. Educ. 4 wks.
  Est 1972. Nonprofit. Spons: Dyslexia Association of Greater Baton Rouge.

The school specializes in the remediation of dyslexia. A structured teaching approach presents basic linguistic and mathematical symbols and skills, extending to a full curriculum as the child progresses. Involvement of parents is extensive, as they participate in tutoring, carpentry and fundraising.

The high school campus (grades 7-12), located on Parkmeadow Avenue, emphasizes practical life and job-related skills, along with preparation for postsecondary academics. Children in grades K-6 attend classes at a separate campus on Bereford Drive. The usual duration of treatment is four years, and Brighton does not accept children with primary emotional problems.

MAINE

SPURWINK

Bdg — Coed Ages 7 and up; Day — Coed 5 and up

Portland, ME 04103. 899 Riverside St.
Tel: 207-871-1200, 888-889-3903. TTY: 207-871-1233. Fax: 207-871-1232.
www.spurwink.org   E-mail: info@spurwink.org
   Nearby locations: Auburn; Brunswick; Casco; Chelsea; Cornville; Lewiston;
      Portland; Saco; South Portland; Westbrook.
Dawn Stiles, LCSW, Pres. **Cynthia Dodge,** PhD, Clin Dir. **Mary Melquist,** Adm.
   Conditions: Primary—ADHD Au CD ED ID OCD Psy Sz. **Sec**—Ap D Dx Ep
      LD ON S SB TBI. **IQ 40 and up.**
   Gen Acad. Voc. Ungraded. Man_Arts & Shop. On-Job Trng. Shelt_Workshop.
      Expected outcome: Return to local school (Avg length of stay: 2 yrs).
   Therapy: Hear Lang Milieu Occup Speech. **Psychotherapy:** Fam Group Indiv
      Parent.
   Enr: 216.
   Est 1960. Nonprofit.

   At locations throughout Maine, Spurwink offers year-round residential and day services
for children, adolescents and adults who have a developmental disability or autism, or who
are functionally limited by emotional or behavioral difficulties. Programs are community
based, with residential locations emphasizing a natural home setting. Day treatment takes
place in small classes, where eclectic teaching methods focus on a dynamic understanding
of the personality and social development of the students. The usual duration of enrollment
is two years.

MARYLAND

THE BENEDICTINE SCHOOL

Bdg and Day — Coed Ages 5-21

Ridgely, MD 21660. 14299 Benedictine Ln.
Tel: 410-634-2112. Fax: 410-634-2640.
www.benschool.org   E-mail: admissions@benschool.org
Julie Hickey, MSpEd, Prin. Cindy Thornton, Adm.
   Conditions: Primary—Asp Au DS ID Multi PDD. Sec—ADHD Anx Ap Apr Ar
   As B/VI CP D Db ED Ep HI LD OCD ODD ON PTSD PW S TBI TS.
   Not accepted—AN Bu D-B SO Subst.
   Voc. Ungraded. Hort. On-Job Trng. Shelt_Workshop. Support_Employ.
   Feat—Lib_Skills Computers Studio_Art Embroidery. Expected outcome:
   Graduation.
   Therapy: Aqua Hear Lang Music Occup Phys Rec Speech. Psychotherapy:
   Art Fam Group Indiv. Counseling: Educ Voc.
   Adm: Appl fee: $100. Appl due: Year-round. On-campus interview.
   Enr: 80 (Cap: 92). Bdg 71. Day 9. B 59. G 21. Fac: 17 (Full-time). Spec ed 15.
   Lay 2.
   Tui '10-'11: Bdg $99,000-172,000/yr. Day $59,000-95,000/yr.
   Acres 600.
   Est 1959. Nonprofit. Roman Catholic.

Located on a 600-acre campus in Caroline County, Benedictine serves children and young adults with mild to severe intellectual disabilities, autism or multiple handicaps. Benedictine's approach is to create a supportive therapeutic environment that assists the individual with reaching his or her potential. The year-round program seeks to help individuals gain as much independence as possible, learn to make wise use of leisure time, and learn to live and work in a community setting.

Comprehensive and integrated programming is supplemented by psychological, psychiatric, social work, counseling, vocational/transitional, and speech and language services; assistive technology; computer training; adaptive physical education and aquatics; home management; 24-hour nursing; and occupational and physical therapy. Teaching, residential and related service staff work together in an integrated fashion to address pupils' needs.

CHELSEA SCHOOL

Day — Coed Ages 10-18

Silver Spring, MD 20910. 711 Pershing Dr.
Tel: 301-585-1430. Fax: 301-585-0245.
www.chelseaschool.edu   E-mail: information@chelseaschool.edu
Katherine Fedalen, BA, MEd, Head. Deborah Lourie, Adm.
   Conditions: Primary—Dx LD. Sec—ADHD Dc Dg S. IQ 90 and up.
   Not accepted—Au CD D DS ED ID Mood MR ODD PDD Psy SO SP Sz
   TBI.

Col Prep. Gr 5-12. AP courses (Eng Comp_Sci). **Feat**—Span Anat & Physiol Govt Ceramics Graphic_Arts Performing_Arts Studio_Art Video_Production Music_Theory. Interscholastic sports. **Expected outcome:** Graduation. **Therapy:** Lang Occup Speech. **Psychotherapy:** Indiv. **Counseling:** Educ. **Adm:** Appl fee: $50. Appl due: Rolling.
Enr: 74. **Fac:** 19 (Full-time).
Tui '12-'13: Day $36,060/sch yr. Clinic $111-117 (Therapy)/hr. **Aid:** School 13 ($240,203). State 63.
Plant val $2,486,000. Acres 5. Bldgs 3 (0% ADA). Class rms 31. Lib 10,000 vols. Sci labs 2. Art studios 2. Music studios 1. Gyms 1. Fields 1. Courts 1. Comp labs 4.
Est 1976. Nonprofit.

The school provides a full middle through high school curriculum for students with learning disabilities who possess average to above-average intelligence. The program supports students in a highly structured environment that teaches academic and social skills and further develops self-confidence. Small classes and tutorials assist in meeting these goals. Diagnostic assessments and counseling services are available.

For older high schoolers, Chelsea offers a careers program that provides information and counseling on career choices. The program includes some on-the-job training in the form of internships and work-study opportunities.

Boys and girls accumulate 60 hours of required community service prior to graduation.

CHIMES SCHOOL

Day — Coed Ages 6-21

Baltimore, MD 21215. 4810 Seton Dr.
Tel: 410-358-8270. Fax: 410-358-8271.
www.chimesmd.org   E-mail: mschaefer@chimes.org
Mary Schaefer, Prin.
　　Conditions: Primary—Au DS ID Multi. **Sec**—ADHD Ap CD CP ED Ep Mood OCD ODD ON Psy Sz TBI. **IQ 25-70.**
　　Gen Acad. Voc. Ungraded. On-Job Trng. Shelt_Workshop. **Feat**—Studio_Art Music. **Expected outcome:** Graduation.
　　Therapy: Lang Occup Phys Speech. **Psychotherapy:** Group Indiv.
　　Enr: 69. B 47. G 22. **Fac:** 28 (Full-time).
　　Est 1947. Nonprofit.

Chimes offers a comprehensive educational program for children and young adults who have intellectual disabilities, multiple disabilities or autism. The curriculum provides each student with the opportunity to develop to his or her potential in the areas of basic academic skills and prevocational training. Programming comprises recreational activities and training in speech and language development, practical living skills and sequential motor development.

The school also provides social work and counseling services for both pupils and their families in individual and group settings.

THE FORBUSH SCHOOL AT GLYNDON

Bdg — Coed Ages 11-18; Day — Coed 3-21

Reisterstown, MD 21136. 407 Central Ave.
Tel: 410-517-5400. Fax: 410-517-5600.
www.sheppardpratt.org   E-mail: info@sheppardpratt.org
Kathleen Ourand, Prin.
   Conditions: Primary—AN Anx Asp Au Bu CD ED Mood OCD ODD Psy PTSD PW SA SP Sz TS. **Sec**—ADHD Dx LD.
   Col Prep. Gen Acad. Voc. Gr PS-12. Culinary. Hort. Man_Arts & Shop. On-Job Trng. **Feat**—Studio_Art. **Expected outcome:** Return to local school (Avg length of stay: 2 yrs).
Therapy: Lang Occup Speech. **Psychotherapy:** Fam Group Indiv Parent.
Counseling: Educ Voc.
Enr: 160 (Cap: 160). **Fac:** 50 (Full-time). Spec ed 50.
Est 1968. Nonprofit. **Spons:** Sheppard Pratt Health System.

A therapeutic educational program with psychotherapy for severely emotionally disturbed and (for an additional fee) autistic children is provided at Forbush, part of the Sheppard Pratt Health System. The school provides individual psychotherapy and family counseling, in addition to a broad curriculum that includes courses in the areas of studio art, industrial arts, technology and computers. Peer mediation is integral to the program. The usual length of enrollment at the school is two years.

THE FROST SCHOOL

Day — Coed Ages 5-21

Rockville, MD 20853. 4915 Aspen Hill Rd.
Tel: 301-933-3452. Fax: 301-933-3350.
www.frostschool.org   E-mail: chobbes@frostschool.org
Claire Cohen, Dir. **Laura Pickard,** Prin. **Carol Hobbes,** Adm.
   Conditions: Primary—Asp Au CD ED Mood OCD ODD Psy PTSD SP Sz TS. **Sec**—ADHD AN Dx LD.
   Col Prep. Gen Acad. Voc. Gr K-12. On-Job Trng. Interscholastic sports.
   Expected outcome: Return to local school (Avg length of stay: 2 yrs).
Therapy: Lang Occup Speech. **Psychotherapy:** Fam Group.
Adm: On-campus interview.
Enr: 58.
Aid: State 58 (100% of tui).
Est 1976. Nonprofit. **Spons:** Sheppard Pratt Health System.

This year-round school offers education and counseling for young people with severe emotional disturbances. Traditional academic courses such as English, math, social studies and science are integrated with daily counseling sessions. Parents and siblings participate in family and group sessions once a week.

GATEWAY SCHOOL

Day — Coed Ages 3-12

Baltimore, MD 21215. 5900 Metro Dr.
Tel: 410-318-6780. Fax: 410-318-6754.
www.hasa.org   E-mail: gateway@hasa.org
Jill Berie, MS, Educ Dir. **Veronica Williams,** Adm.
   Conditions: Primary—Ap Apr Asp Au D ON PDD S. **Sec**—ADHD Anx As C
   CP Db Dc Dg Dx ED Ep IP ID LD MD Mood MS Nf OCD PTSD PW SB SP
   TBI TS. **IQ 70-120.**
   Gen Acad. Gr PS-6. **Feat**—Lib_Skills Computers Studio_Art Music. **Expected
   outcome:** Return to local school (Avg length of stay: 1-5 yrs).
   Therapy: Hear Lang Occup Phys Play Rec Speech. **Psychotherapy:** Art Dance
   Fam Indiv Parent.
   Adm: Appl fee: $0. Appl due: Year-round. On-campus interview.
   Enr: 46 (Cap: 70). **Fac:** 21 (Full-time).
   Tui '12-'13: Day $56,000/sch yr. **Aid:** School 5 ($75,000). State 42. **Summer
   prgm:** Day. Educ. 5 wks.
   Bldgs 1 (100% ADA). Class rms 13. Libs 1. Auds 1. Art studios 1. Music stu-
   dios 1. Gyms 1. Comp labs 1.
   Est 1957. Nonprofit. **Spons:** The Hearing and Speech Agency.

Gateway offers special education for children with moderate to severe speech, language
or communicative disabilities. The school maintains small classes while offering an 11-
month program than emphasizes the remediation of language deficits that interfere with
academic development and the acquisition of appropriate social behavior. Language experiences and direct instruction facilitate language, cognition and academic readiness for preschoolers, while the curriculum for older children incorporates language learning within
the subject areas of reading, written language, math, science and social studies.

The school emphasizes social and life skills development at all grade levels. Field trips
and special events enrich the curriculum.

HANNAH MORE SCHOOL

Day — Coed Ages 11-21

Reisterstown, MD 21136. 12039 Reisterstown Rd.
Tel: 410-526-5000. Fax: 410-526-7631.
www.hannahmore.org   E-mail: hmsinfo@hannahmore.org
Mark Waldman, BS, MEd, Pres. **Mike Kerins,** Educ Dir.
   Conditions: Primary—ADHD AN Anx Asp Au Bu CD Dg Dx ED LD Mood
   OCD PDD Psy PW SP Sz TS. **Sec**—Ap B/VI D Db.
   Gen Acad. Voc. Gr 6-12. Culinary. Hort. On-Job Trng. Support_Employ.
   Feat—Computers Studio_Art Music Life_Skills. **Expected outcome:**
   Return to local school (Avg length of stay: 3 yrs).
   Therapy: Lang Music Occup Rec Speech. **Psychotherapy:** Art Fam Group
   Indiv. **Counseling:** Educ Voc.
   Adm: Appl fee: $0. Appl due: Year-round. On-campus interview.
   Enr: 91.

Aid: State 91 (100% of tui). **Summer prgm:** Day. Educ. Rec. 5 wks. Acres 21. **Est 1977.** Nonprofit.

The school conducts a psycho-educational program consisting of academics, vocational education, counseling programs and a behavioral management system. The program provides each student with individual goals and objectives that are regularly monitored and revised to meet the child's emotional and educational needs.

Hannah More conducts a comprehensive program for middle and high school students diagnosed with pervasive developmental disorder. During the middle school years, each self-contained classroom features a teacher and a teacher assistant. Pragmatic language, leisure and life skills supplement standard course work. The high school program comprises two models: the first is similar to the middle school program, as it continues the use of self-contained classrooms, while the second approach serves students identified with Asperger's syndrome or with pervasive developmental disorder who have functioned academically close to grade level. Students in the latter section participate in a departmentalized curriculum. Activities outside the classroom such as recreational opportunities and various types of therapy round out the program.

The school also provides special education at the middle and high school levels for students with such emotional disabilities as depression, schizophrenia, anxiety, and mood, behavior and personality disorders. Many pupils with emotional disabilities have also been diagnosed with chronic mental illnesses. While students may enroll for anywhere from six months to six years, the average length of stay is three years.

In addition to its traditional high school program, Hannah More also offers a vocational high school program with classes in horticulture, culinary arts, communications, building trades and automotive repair.

THE HARBOUR SCHOOL

Day — Coed Ages 6-21

Annapolis, MD 21401. 1277 Green Holly Dr.
Tel: 410-974-4248. Fax: 410-757-3722.
www.harbourschool.org   E-mail: info@harbourschool.org
 Nearby locations: 11251 Dolfield Blvd, Owings Mills 21117.
Linda J. Jacobs, EdD, Exec Dir. **Yvonne B. Callaway,** Adm.
 Conditions: Primary—ADHD Anx Ap Asp Au Dx LD PTSD PW S SP TBI TS.
  Sec—ED Mood OCD. **IQ 70 and up.**
 Col Prep. Gen Acad. Voc. Gr 1-12. Man_Arts & Shop. On-Job Trng.
  Feat—Comp_Sci Video_Production Drama Dance. Interscholastic sports.
  Expected outcome: Return to local school (Avg length of stay: 3 yrs).
 Therapy: Lang Occup Phys Rec Speech. **Psychotherapy:** Art Dance Fam
  Group Indiv Parent. **Counseling:** Educ Voc.
 Adm: Appl fee: $50. Appl due: Year-round. On-campus interview.
 Enr: 263. B 180. G 83. **Fac:** 39. Spec ed 29. Lay 10.
 Tui '12-'13: Day $36,556/sch yr (+$200). Clinic $80 (Occup Therapy)/wk.
  Summer prgm: Day. Educ. Rec. Ther. 4 wks.
 Endow $3,000,000. Plant val $12,000,000. Acres 7. Bldgs 3 (100% ADA).
  Class rms 45. Libs 1. Sci labs 1. Auds 2. Theaters 2. Art studios 1. Music
  studios 1. Dance studios 1. Gyms 2. Fields 2. Courts 2. Comp labs 1.

Est 1982. Nonprofit.

Children who have been diagnosed with learning problems receive personalized instruction in reading, math and language arts at this school. Other academic subjects are taught in a group setting. The program emphasizes social skill development at all grade levels. High school programming seeks to ease the student's transition into college or a career, with graduates earning a high school diploma. Pupils accumulate 75 hours of required community service prior to graduation, 30 of which must be served on site.

Counseling, speech and psychological services, and occupational therapy are available, and boys and girls spend an average of three years at the school. Harbour maintains a second campus in Owings Mills.

THE IVYMOUNT SCHOOL

Day — Coed Ages 4-21

Rockville, MD 20854. 11614 Seven Locks Rd.
Tel: 301-469-0223. Fax: 301-469-0778.
www.ivymount.org E-mail: sdesibour@ivymount.org
Janet Wintrol, MEd, Dir. **Stephanie deSibour,** Adm.
  Conditions: Primary—Asp Au LD ID PDD. **Sec**—Ap CP ON.
  Voc. Ungraded. On-Job Trng. **Expected outcome:** Return to local school (Avg length of stay: 2-6 yrs).
  Therapy: Hear Lang Music Occup Phys Speech. **Psychotherapy:** Fam Group. **Counseling:** Educ Voc.
  Adm: Appl due: Rolling.
  Enr: 200. B 130. G 70.
  Summer prgm: Day. Educ. Ther. 4 wks.
  Est 1961. Nonprofit.

Ivymount provides therapeutic education for children with such disabilities as developmental delays, speech and language deficits, learning disabilities, health impairments and autism/pervasive developmental disorder. Through early diagnosis and individualization of programs geared to the child's learning style, the school attempts to improve the client's social and emotional health, as well as his or her intellectual potential. The areas emphasized are sensorimotor functioning, visual/auditory perception and processing, language development, academic skills, functional living skills, social behavior and emotional development.

In most cases, the sending school district covers tuition expenses, but some families pay private tuition.

THE JEMICY SCHOOL

Day — Coed Ages 6-18

Owings Mills, MD 21117. 11 Celadon Rd.
Tel: 410-653-2700. Fax: 410-653-1972.
www.jemicyschool.org E-mail: psutz@jemicyschool.org
  Nearby locations: 11202 Garrison Forest Rd, Owings Mills 21117.

Ben Shifrin, BS, MEd, Head. **Patricia Utz,** Adm.
Conditions: Primary—Dg Dx LD. **Sec**—ADHD Dc. **IQ 100 and up.**
Col Prep. Gr 1-12. **Feat**—British_Lit Stats Genetics Robotics Photog Visual_Arts
Drama Music Dance. Interscholastic sports. **Expected outcome:** Graduation.
Therapy: Speech.
Adm: Appl fee: $50. Appl due: Jan.
Enr: 295. **Fac:** 82.
Tui '12-'13: Day $30,535-31,825/sch yr. **Aid:** School 68. **Summer prgm:** Day.
Educ. Rec. 5 wks.
Endow $13,900,000.
Est 1973. Nonprofit.

Jemicy works with above-average to gifted students with dyslexia and other language-based learning differences. Employing a variety of proven research-based, multisensory teaching techniques, faculty work with students in small groups and individually to develop reading, writing, spelling and organizational skills. A strong arts and athletic program complements the core curriculum. Pupils accumulate 40 hours of required community service prior to graduation.

The upper school (grades 9-12) occupies a separate, 57-acre campus on Garrison Forest Road, four miles from the lower and middle school location.

LAUREL HALL SCHOOL

Day — Coed Ages 5-20

Hagerstown, MD 21742. 13218 Brook Lane Dr, PO Box 1945.
Tel: 301-733-0330, 800-342-2992. Fax: 301-733-4106.
www.brooklane.org   E-mail: curt.miller@brooklane.org
  Nearby locations: 4540B Mack Ave, Frederick 21703.
R. Lynn Rushing, CEO. **Catherine Byers,** Educ Dir.
  Conditions: Primary—ADHD AN Anx Asp Au Bu ED Mood OCD PDD Psy
  PTSD SA SP Sz TS. **Sec**—As CD Dc Dg Dpx Dx Ep HI ID LD Multi ODD
  Subst TBI.
  Gen Acad. Underachiever. Voc. Gr 1-12. On-Job Trng. Support_Employ.
  Feat—Span. **Expected outcome:** Return to local school.
  Therapy: Occup Speech. **Psychotherapy:** Art Fam Group Indiv Parent.
  Counseling: Educ Voc.
  Enr: 70 (Cap: 90). **Fac:** 13 (Full-time). Spec ed 13.
  Tui '10-'11: Day $175-278/day. **Aid:** State.
  Est 1945. Nonprofit. Mennonite. **Spons:** Brook Lane Health Services.

Laurel Hall, which is under the auspices of Brook Lane Health Services, includes among its offerings inpatient and partial hospitalization services. The school provides special education for individuals diagnosed as emotionally disturbed who require a highly structured and individualized setting, in addition to psychiatric support services. All boys and girls receive group therapy and individual therapy. Additionally, students may receive substance abuse counseling, art therapy or family therapy. Psychological services and medical management are provided as needed.

A second Laurel Hall campus in Frederick maintains an enrollment capacity of 45.

THE MARYLAND SCHOOL FOR THE BLIND

Bdg — Coed Ages 7-21; Day — Coed 3-21

Baltimore, MD 21236. 3501 Taylor Ave.
Tel: 410-444-5000. TTY: 410-319-5703. Fax: 410-319-5700.
www.mdschblind.org   E-mail: info@mdschblind.org
Michael J. Bina, EdD, Pres. **Ruth Ann Hynson,** Adm.
  Conditions: Primary—B/VI. **Sec**—ADHD Ap Apr As Asp Au CP D Ep ID LD MD MS Nf ON PDD S TBI.
  Gen Acad. Voc. Gr PS-PG. Man_Arts & Shop. On-Job Trng. **Feat**—Theater Music Dance Health. Interscholastic sports.
  Therapy: Hear Lang Music Occup Phys Rec Speech. **Psychotherapy:** Fam Group Indiv Parent. **Counseling:** Educ Voc.
  Enr: 184. Bdg 120. Day 64. **Fac:** 56 (Full 53, Part 3).
  Tui '12-'13: Clinic No Fee. **Summer prgm:** Bdg & Day. Educ. Ther. 4 wks.
  Est 1853. Nonprofit.

Educational opportunities for children who are blind or visually impaired and have additional impairments are available through MSB, which offers a curriculum paralleling that of public schools. Students who are incapable of fulfilling academic requirements for graduation enter an independence or developmental skills program.

Maryland residents attend free of charge, while out-of-state pupils pay tuition charges.

THE ODYSSEY SCHOOL

Day — Coed Ages 5-14

Stevenson, MD 21153. 3257 Bridle Ridge Ln.
Tel: 410-580-5551. Fax: 410-580-5352.
www.theodysseyschool.org   E-mail: mnesbitt@theodysseyschool.org
Martha H. Sweeney, MS, Head. **Martha D. Nesbitt,** Adm.
  Conditions: Primary—Dx LD S. **Sec**—ADHD Apr Ar CLP CP Db Dc Dg Dpx Ep Hemo SC. **IQ 90 and up. Not accepted**—AN Anx Ap Asp Au Bu C CD CF D D-B DS ED ID IP Lk MD Mood MR MS Multi Nf NLD OCD ODD ON PDD Psy PTSD PW SA SB SO SP Subst Sz TBI TS.
  Gen Acad. Gr K-8. **Feat**—Computers Studio_Art Music Dance.
  Adm: Appl fee: $100. Appl due: Jan. On-campus interview.
  Enr: 165 (Cap: 165).
  Tui '12-'13: Day $29,250/sch yr. **Aid:** School. **Summer prgm:** Day. Rec. Tui Day $2400-3400. 5 wks.
  Acres 42. Bldgs 1. Libs 1. Sci labs 1. Auds 1. Theaters 1. Art studios 2. Music studios 1. Gyms 1. Fields 2. Comp labs 1.
  Est 1994.

This elementary school's hands-on, multisensory program serves children of average to superior intelligence who have language-based learning differences. An intensive daily tutoring program addresses phonological awareness, fluency, vocabulary, comprehension, reference skills, decoding, encoding, written expression, and study and organizational skills. Odyssey's curriculum features various visual arts offerings, as well as recorder training and exposure to the violin. The school's early intervention program provides assessment services for five- and six-year-olds who appear to be dyslexic.

THE PATHWAYS SCHOOLS

Day — Coed Ages 11-21

Silver Spring, MD 20902. 1106 University Blvd W.
Tel: 301-649-0778. Fax: 301-649-2598.
www.pathwayschools.org   E-mail: info@pathwayschools.org
Helen C. Williams, MA, EdD, Exec Dir.
  Conditions: Primary—ED. **Sec**—Asp Au ID LD PDD TBI. **IQ 65 and up.**
  Gen Acad. Gr 6-12. On-Job Trng. **Expected outcome:** Return to local school
  (Avg length of stay: 18 mos).
  Therapy: Lang Occup Rec Speech. **Psychotherapy:** Fam Group Indiv.
  Adm: On-campus interview.
  Fac: 52 (Full 51, Part 1). Spec ed 23. Lay 29.
  Est 1982. Nonprofit.

Pathways operates six schools in Anne Arundel, Montgomery and Prince George's counties utilize a holistic approach to the remediation of emotional deficits. Each school enrolls no more than 40 students. The network comprises middle schools serving students ages 11-14 and secondary programs that may focus on general academics, work-entry skills development, helping pupils return to the public school system or community-based living skills. The curriculum at each site combines academics, therapy, life and transitional skills, field trips and recreational activities. Counseling and parental support groups are also available.

THE RIDGE SCHOOL OF MONTGOMERY COUNTY

Bdg and Day — Coed Ages 11-18

Rockville, MD 20850. 14901 Broschart Rd.
Tel: 301-251-4500. Fax: 301-251-4588.
www.adventistbehavioralhealth.com
Melissa Thompson, Educ Dir. **Tori Mills,** Adm.
  Conditions: Primary—ADHD CD Dx ED LD Mood OCD PTSD SP. **IQ 50 and**
  up.
  Gen Acad. Gr 6-12. **Expected outcome:** Return to local school (Avg length of
  stay: 15 mos).
  Therapy: Lang Occup Speech. **Psychotherapy:** Art Fam Group Indiv Parent.
  Enr: 116. Bdg 80. Day 36. B 80. G 36.
  Summer prgm: Bdg & Day. Educ. 4 wks.
  Nonprofit. Seventh-day Adventist. **Spons:** Adventist HealthCare.

The Ridge School provides therapeutic educational services for residential and day students with emotional disabilities, multiple disabilities, specific learning disabilities and other health impairments. Ridge maintains an individualized learning environment in which boys and girls also learn effective strategies for use in other settings. Cognitively and behaviorally based therapeutic services accompany academics. Various recreational activities complete the program.

ST. ELIZABETH SCHOOL

Day — Coed Ages 6-21

Baltimore, MD 21218. 801 Argonne Dr.
Tel: 410-889-5054. Fax: 410-889-2356.
www.stelizabeth-school.org   E-mail: info@stelizabeth-school.org
Christine Manlove, EdD, Exec Dir. **Judy Malin,** Adm.
   Conditions: Primary—Anx APD Asp Au CP DS ED Ep Mood ID Multi OCD ODD ON PDD Psy PTSD PW S SB SP Sz TBI. **Sec**—ADHD Ap Apr Ar As B/VI C CF CLP Db Dc Dg Dpx Dx Hemo HI LD Lk MD MS Nf NLD SC Subst TS. **IQ 25-89. Not accepted**—AN Bu CD D D-B IP SA SO.
   Gen Acad. Voc. Gr 1-12. Culinary. Hort. Man_Arts & Shop. On-Job Trng. Support_Employ. **Feat**—Span Computers Studio_Art Woodworking.
   Expected outcome: Graduation.
   Therapy: Lang Occup Phys Speech. **Psychotherapy:** Art Fam Group Indiv Parent. **Counseling:** Voc.
   Adm: Appl fee: $0. Appl due: Year-round. On-campus interview.
   Enr: 119 (Cap: 125). B 86. G 33. **Fac:** 64 (Full-time). Spec ed 23. Lay 41.
   Tui '11-'12: Day $313/day. Clinic $114 (Therapy)/hr.
   Acres 3. Bldgs 2 (100% ADA). Class rms 22. Auds 1. Art studios 1. Gyms 1. Greenhouses 1. Comp labs 2.
   Est 1961. Nonprofit. Roman Catholic.

Operating 11 months per year, St. Elizabeth provides education, counseling, vocational training and placement for middle and high school students with special needs. Pupils who complete program requirements earn a certificate of completion from their local school systems or a high school diploma. High schoolers complete 75 hours of required community service prior to graduation.

THE SUMMIT SCHOOL

Day — Coed Ages 6-14

Edgewater, MD 21037. 664 E Central Ave.
Tel: 410-798-0005. Fax: 410-798-0008.
www.thesummitschool.org   E-mail: info@thesummitschool.org
Jane R. Snider, EdD, Exec Dir. **Joan A. Mele-McCarthy,** Head.
   Kathleen Heefner, Adm.
   Conditions: Primary—Dc Dg Dx LD. **IQ 90 and up.**
   Gen Acad. Gr 1-8. **Feat**—Sci Soc_Stud. **Expected outcome:** Return to local school (Avg length of stay: 2 yrs).
   Therapy: Occup Speech.
   Adm: Appl fee: $50. Appl due: Rolling. On-campus interview.
   Enr: 100. B 69. G 31. **Fac:** 31 (Full 24, Part 7). Spec ed 31.
   Tui '12-'13: Day $27,647/sch yr (+$100). **Aid:** School 28. **Summer prgm:** Day.

Educ. Rec. Tui Day $1650. 4 wks.
Acres 15.
Est 1989. Nonprofit.

Summit provides an elementary program that addresses learning difficulties and provides academic challenge. The curriculum employs a multisensory teaching approach that introduces and reinforces auditory, visual, tactile and kinesthetic skills.

UCP DELREY SCHOOL

Day — Coed Ages 2-21

Baltimore, MD 21227. 3610 Commerce Dr, Ste 804-807.
Tel: 410-314-5000. Fax: 410-314-5015.
www.delreyschool.org   E-mail: delreyschool@ucp-cm.org
Mimi M. Wang, MEd, Prin. **Dorothy Lemon-Thompson,** Adm.
Conditions: Primary—CP Multi ON PDD SB. **Sec**—Au S.
Gen Acad. Ungraded. **Expected outcome:** Return to local school.
Therapy: Hear Lang Occup Phys Speech. **Psychotherapy:** Fam Parent.
Adm: Appl due: Year-round.
Enr: 40 (Cap: 45). B 23. G 17. **Fac:** 6 (Full-time). Spec ed 5. Lay 1.
Tui '12-'13: Day $238/day. **Aid:** State. **Summer prgm:** Day. Educ. Ther. 5 wks.
Est 1964. Nonprofit.

Delrey serves children, adolescents and young adults based upon their Individualized Education Program needs. A preschool program aims to prepare children educationally, physically and emotionally for entrance into the public school system. In addition, Delrey provides educational programs and functional therapies for children and young adults up to age 21. Services include sensory integration therapy, therapeutic feeding, assistive technology, a wheelchair clinic, community daycare and social work services.

MASSACHUSETTS

ARCHWAY

Bdg — Coed Ages 10-22

Leicester, MA 01524. 77 Mulberry St.
Tel: 508-892-4707. Fax: 508-892-0259.
www.archwayinc.org   E-mail: sesber@archwayinc.org
Sonya Esber, MSPC, Exec Dir. **Lucy Tresisi,** Prgm Dir.
    Conditions: Primary—Au ID PDD. **Sec**—ADHD CD Ep Mood OCD ODD
      PTSD TS. **Not accepted**—AN Anx Ap As Asp B/VI Bu C CF CLP CP D Db
      Dc Dg Dx Hemo IP MD MS Nf Psy PW SA SB SC SO SP Subst Sz TBI.
    Gen Acad. Voc. Ungraded. **Feat**—Computers Studio_Art Health. **Expected
    outcome:** Graduation.
    Therapy: Occup Speech.
    Adm: Appl fee: $0. Appl due: Year-round. On-campus interview.
    Enr: 13 (Cap: 13). B 9. G 4. **Fac:** 3 (Full 2, Part 1). Spec ed 3.
    Tui '12-'13: Bdg $374/day.
    Bldgs 1 (0% ADA). Gyms 1. Pools 1.
    Est 1978. Nonprofit.

   Founded by several families of autistic children, ARCHway is a small residential school that helps students with autism to lead productive lives. The program integrates the child's natural characteristics with functional skills to maximize growth and learning. Each pupil's program includes the following: functional academics that are tailored to the child's abilities, prevocational and vocational skills instruction in preparation for future employment, work on communicational skills, daily living skills instruction, and frequent opportunities for recreation and socialization.

THE ARLINGTON SCHOOL

Day — Coed Ages 12-20

Belmont, MA 02478. 115 Mill St.
Tel: 617-855-2125. Fax: 617-855-2757.
www.thearlingtonschool.org   E-mail: sloughlin@partners.org
Suzanne Loughlin, Dir. **Maureen Principe,** BSBA, MSEd, Educ Dir.
    Conditions: Primary—ADHD Anx ED LD Mood OCD Psy PTSD Sz.
      Sec—AN Asp Bu C Db Dx SA SO SP Subst. **IQ 100 and up.**
      Not accepted—Ap Au B/VI D DS ID MR.
    Col Prep. Gen Acad. Gr 7-12. **Feat**—Creative_Writing Comp_Graphics
      Ceramics Photog Studio_Art Drama. **Expected outcome:** Return to local
      school (Avg length of stay: 1-4 yrs).
    Therapy: Milieu. **Psychotherapy:** Group. **Counseling:** Educ.
    Adm: Appl due: Year-round.
    Enr: 46 (Cap: 48). B 24. G 22. **Fac:** 9 (Full-time). Spec ed 4. Lay 5.
    Summer prgm: Day. Educ. 4 wks.

Est 1961. Nonprofit. **Spons:** McLean Hospital.

Arlington School is a comprehensive secondary school for boys and girls with moderate to severe emotional disturbances and learning disabilities. The school emphasizes individualized attention while tailoring its program to the student's ability level. The program's goal is to facilitate the pupil's return to his or her public or private school system. The student's home school district typically pays tuition fees.

Students may elect a course of study stressing either college or career preparation. The traditional academic curriculum includes creative arts courses, and career exploration classes are available. Graduates move on to employment, two- and four-year colleges, and vocational training schools.

BEACON HIGH SCHOOL
Day — Coed Ages 14-22

Watertown, MA 02472. 917 Belmont St.
Tel: 617-993-5100. Fax: 617-993-5101.
www.beaconhighschool.org E-mail: ptravers@beaconhighschool.org
Pamela J. Travers, MEd, Dir.
    Conditions: Primary—ADHD Anx Asp Bu Dc Dg Dpx Dx ED Mood NLD OCD PTSD SP. **Sec—**LD Psy SA Subst Sz. **IQ 95 and up. Not accepted—**APD Au CD ID MR Multi ODD ON PDD PW SO.
    Col Prep. Gr 9-12. **Feat—**Creative_Writing Poetry Comp_Relig Drawing Painting Sculpt Stained_Glass. Avg SAT: CR 538. M 548. W 518. ACT: Avg 29. SAT/ACT prep. **Expected outcome:** Graduation.
    Therapy: Milieu. **Psychotherapy:** Fam Group Indiv. **Counseling:** Educ Nutrition.
    Adm: Appl due: Year-round. On-campus interview.
    Enr: 65 (Cap: 66). B 30. G 35. **Fac:** 11 (Full-time). Spec ed 6. Lay 5.
    Tui '11-'12: Day $45,000/yr. **Aid:** State 62.
    Bldgs 1. Libs 1. Sci labs 2. Art studios 1. Music studios 1. Comp labs 1.
    Est 1971. Nonprofit.

Beacon is an alternative, therapeutic school for students who have displayed academic promise in previous years but who have undergone events in their lives that have rendered traditional academic programs inadequate. Boys and girls participate in compulsory individual and group therapy, and crisis management support is available at all times. Pupils typically take part in creative pursuits, among them printmaking, drama, school publications, and music compositions and performances.

Students accumulate 20 hours of compulsory service—10 of which must take place at the school—prior to graduation.

BEVERLY SCHOOL FOR THE DEAF
Day — Coed Ages 3-22

Beverly, MA 01915. 6 Echo Ave.
Tel: 978-927-7070. TTY: 978-927-7200. Fax: 978-927-6536.

www.beverlyschoolforthedeaf.org
E-mail: jocelynclark@beverlyschoolforthedeaf.org
Mark E. Carlson, MEd, MBA, Exec Dir.
Conditions: Primary—Apr Asp Au D DS LD ON PDD. **Sec**—Ar CLP CP ED
Ep IP ID MD MS Nf OCD ODD PTSD S SB TBI. **IQ 70 and up.**
Gen Acad. Voc. Ungraded. On-Job Trng. Shelt_Workshop.
Therapy: Hear Lang Occup Phys Speech. **Counseling:** Educ.
Adm: Appl due: Rolling.
Enr: 32. B 20. G 12. **Fac:** 39 (Full 29, Part 10).
Summer prgm: Day. Educ. 6 wks.
Est 1876. Nonprofit.

The school's educational program for deaf and hard-of-hearing children emphasizes
social/emotional growth and development. Counseling is available, and a summer session
for preschoolers and kindergartners will accept enrollment from the regular program only.

BOSTON COLLEGE CAMPUS SCHOOL
Day — Coed Ages 3-21

Chestnut Hill, MA 02467. 140 Commonwealth Ave, Campion Hall, Rm 197.
Tel: 617-552-3460. Fax: 617-552-6465.
www.bc.edu/campusschool   E-mail: odonnesn@bc.edu
Don Ricciato, PhD, Dir.
Conditions: Primary—Au CP D-B ID Multi ON TBI. **Sec**—B/VI.
Gen Acad. Ungraded. **Expected outcome:** Return to local school (Avg length
of stay: 5-8 yrs).
Therapy: Lang Music Occup Phys Speech Visual.
Adm: Appl fee: $0. Appl due: Year-round. On-campus interview.
Enr: 45 (Cap: 49). B 26. G 19. **Fac:** 7 (Full-time). Spec ed 7.
Tui '11-'12: Day $361/day.
Bldgs 2 (100% ADA). Libs 1. Pools 1.
Est 1970. Nonprofit.

The Campus School offers individualized educational, therapeutic and healthcare services for children, adolescents and young adults with multiple disabilities and complex
needs. Special needs generally involve the cognitive, communicative and physical areas.
Academic remediation and various therapies prepare students for community life. When
appropriate, boys and girls are mainstreamed into public schools.

BOSTON HIGASHI SCHOOL
Bdg and Day — Coed Ages 3-22

Randolph, MA 02368. 800 N Main St.
Tel: 781-961-0800. Fax: 781-961-0888.
www.bostonhigashi.org   E-mail: admissions@bostonhigashi.org
Michael Kelly, Exec Dir. **Deborah Donovan,** MEd, Prin. **Amy Carter,** Adm.
Conditions: Primary—Asp Au PDD. **Sec**—ADHD Anx Ap Apr As CLP CP D

Db Dc Dg Dx Ep ID LD Mood OCD ODD ON PW SP TBI TS. **IQ 40-120.**
Not accepted—Ar Bu CD DS ED IP MD MS Nf PTSD SA SB SO Subst Sz.
Gen Acad. Voc. Gr PS-12. Culinary. Hort. Man_Arts & Shop. On-Job Trng.
Support_Employ. **Feat**—Computers Studio_Art Music. **Expected outcome:**
Graduation.
Therapy: Lang Occup Phys Speech.
Adm: Appl due: Rolling.
Enr: 129 (Cap: 144). **Fac:** 62 (Full-time). Spec ed 31. Lay 31.
Est 1987. Nonprofit.

This international school—which bases its teaching method upon the tenets of Daily Life Therapy, as developed by Kiyo Kitahara—serves children and young adults with a diagnosis along the autism spectrum. Daily Life Therapy acknowledges that children with autism tend to be socially isolated, anxious and sensitive. To address these issues, the methodology employs group dynamics in an effort to further develop communicational and daily living skills, thereby promoting social independence. Emotional stability and self-care skills are the school's primary focus, while extensive physical exercise (as a self-control mechanism) represents a secondary focus.

The age-appropriate curriculum features instruction in language arts, math and the social sciences, and staff make necessary modifications to the program to account for differences in ability. Creative activities in the areas of art and music play an important role in the curriculum.

BRANDON SCHOOL
AND RESIDENTIAL TREATMENT CENTER
Bdg and Day — Boys Ages 7-18

Natick, MA 01760. 27 Winter St.
Tel: 508-655-6400. Fax: 508-650-9431.
www.brandonschool.org   E-mail: rporter@brandonschool.org
Timothy M. Callahan, EdD, Exec Dir. **Karen McCarthy,** MEd, Prin.
Rebecca Porter, Adm.
Conditions: Primary—Anx ED LD Mood NLD ODD PDD PTSD SA SO SP.
Sec—ADHD Asp CD CP Db Dx Ep HI ID OCD Psy S SC Subst Sz TS. **IQ
70-135. Not accepted**—Au.
Gen Acad. Underachiever. Gr 2-12. Culinary. On-Job Trng. **Feat**—Studio_Art
Dance. Interscholastic sports. **Expected outcome:** Return to local school
(Avg length of stay: 2 wks to 1 yr).
Therapy: Milieu Music Occup Play Rec Speech. **Psychotherapy:** Art Fam
Group Indiv Parent. **Counseling:** Educ.
Adm: Appl fee: $0. Appl due: Year-round.
Enr: 85 (Cap: 85). Bdg 75. Day 10. **Fac:** 40. Spec ed 15. Lay 25.
Tui '10-'11: Bdg $411/day. Day $129/day. **Aid:** State. **Summer prgm:** Bdg &
Day. Educ. Rec. Ther. 6 wks.
Acres 35. Bldgs 8. Dorms 7. Class rms 12. Libs 1. Auds 1. Gyms 1. Fields 2.
Est 1966. Nonprofit.

Located on a 35-acre campus, Brandon offers residential and day services for young and adolescent boys with emotional and behavioral problems. The center specializes in the assessment and the treatment of fire setters and boys displaying inappropriate sexual behavior. The learning environment approximates that of a public school, but Brandon's small enrollment allows for additional supports and structure. The program seeks to improve students' academic and social skills, to develop more appropriate behavioral controls, and to improve self-esteem levels. Psychotherapists and graduate clinical interns administer psychotherapy and family services.

Brandon's residential program offers several levels of treatment, ranging from more restrictive to less restrictive. All residents utilize group meetings, family-style meals, study halls and privilege levels. Acute services, including diagnostic services and emergency placements, are also available.

CARDINAL CUSHING SCHOOL
Bdg and Day — Coed Ages 6-22

Hanover, MA 02339. 405 Washington St.
Tel: 781-829-1205. Fax: 781-826-1559.
www.cushingcenters.com   E-mail: mmarkowitz@cushingcenters.org
Jo Ann Simons, MSW, Pres. Roberta M. Pulaski, Educ Dir.
   Michelle Markowitz, Adm.
   Conditions: Primary—ADHD Au DS ID Multi PDD. Sec—Anx As Asp B/VI
      CP Dx ED Ep LD Mood NLD OCD ON PTSD TBI TS. IQ 40-85.
      Not accepted—SO.
   Gen Acad. Voc. Ungraded. Culinary. Hort. On-Job Trng. Shelt_Workshop.
      Hospitality Retail. Feat—Computers Studio_Art Music Life_Skills.
      Expected outcome: Return to local school (Avg length of stay: 6-8 yrs).
   Therapy: Milieu Music Occup Phys Speech. Psychotherapy: Art Group Indiv.
   Adm: Appl fee: $0. Appl due: Year-round.
   Enr: 102 (Cap: 130). Bdg 72. Day 30. B 70. G 32. Fac: 16 (Full-time). Spec
      ed 16.
   Tui '10-'11: Bdg $444/day. Day $272/day. Aid: State. Summer prgm: Bdg &
      Day. Educ. Rec. Ther. 6 wks.
   Acres 200. Bldgs 20. Libs 1. Auds 1. Art studios 1. Music studios 1. Gyms 1.
      Fields 1. Courts 1. Pools 1. Comp labs 1.
   Est 1947. Nonprofit. Roman Catholic. Spons: Cardinal Cushing Centers.

The school offers education and vocational programs within a therapeutic milieu for children and adults with mild to severe intellectual disabilities. The 12-month program includes functional academics, music, arts, crafts, and fine- and gross-motor therapy, as well as crisis intervention, respite care, counseling and extensive vocational opportunities. The goal is to teach the skills and provide the experience necessary for students to integrate into the community to the best of their abilities.

CARROLL SCHOOL
Day — Coed Ages 6-15

Lincoln, MA 01773. 25 Baker Bridge Rd.
Tel: 781-259-8342. Fax: 781-259-8852.

www.carrollschool.org   E-mail: admissions@carrollschool.org
Nearby locations: 1841 Trapelo Rd, Waltham 02451.
Stephen M. Wilkins, BA, MEd, PhD, Head. **Lesley Fowler Nesbitt,** Adm.
Conditions: Primary—Dx LD. **IQ 95 and up.**
Gen Acad. Gr 1-9. **Feat**—Computers Studio_Art Drama Music Woodworking.
Interscholastic sports. **Expected outcome:** Return to local school.
Adm: Appl fee: $75. Appl due: Rolling. On-campus interview.
Enr: 370. B 236. G 134. **Fac:** 132.
Tui '12-'13: Day $39,838/sch yr. **Aid:** School 60. State 106. **Summer prgm:** Day.
Educ. Rec. Tui Day $4275-5100. 5 wks.
Endow $4,900,000. Plant val $13,500,000. Acres 23. Bldgs 5. Auds 2. Art
studios 2. Gyms 2. Fields 3. Comp labs 5. Laptop prgm Gr 6-9.
Est 1967. Nonprofit.

Carroll specializes in the education and the remediation of children of average to superior intelligence who have been diagnosed with dyslexia or a language-based learning disability. The program helps the language-disabled child grow to the point where he or she can successfully return to a regular public or private school setting. Children are grouped according to language competency and grade. In all subjects, teachers use a multisensory approach to learning and place emphasis on improving reading, writing and organizational skills.

A full academic program includes language, math, science, social studies, performing arts, drama, art, woodworking and an Outward Bound-type program. Sports and physical education are offered at all levels, with interscholastic competition available in cross-country, soccer, basketball, lacrosse and track. After-school electives are numerous and entail additional fees. Computers are employed in all classes.

The day camp complements the academic summer school. The academic summer program includes one-on-one tutoring and small-group instruction in language and math; in addition to a choice of electives, it offers a full range of activities aimed at building self-confidence.

In the fall of 2010, Carroll opened a new lower school campus (grades 1-5) in Waltham. The same year, the middle school program in Lincoln grew with the addition of grade 9.

See Also Page 29

THE CHILDREN'S STUDY HOME
Bdg — Boys Ages 6-19; Day — Coed 6-19

Springfield, MA 01109. 44 Sherman St.
Tel: 413-739-5626. Fax: 413-732-5457.
www.studyhome.org   E-mail: ecrescentini@studyhome.org
Eliza Crescentini, Exec Dir. **James Fay,** Educ Dir.
   Conditions: Primary—ADHD CD ED. **Sec**—Anx Mood OCD PTSD. **IQ 75-129. Not accepted**—ID MR Psy.
   Gen Acad. Voc. Gr 1-12. Hort. Man_Arts & Shop. On-Job Trng. **Expected outcome:** Return to local school (Avg length of stay: 1-2 yrs).
   Therapy: Milieu. **Psychotherapy:** Fam Group Indiv Parent. **Counseling:** Educ Voc.
   Enr: 85. Bdg 20. Day 65. B 73. G 12.
   Aid: State 85 (100% of tui).

Est 1865. Nonprofit.

This multiservice agency specializes in four areas: residential treatment, special education, community-based services and family support services. The residential program serves children and adolescents with emotional and behavioral challenges. Psychological counselors, social workers, nurses, psychiatrists and psychologists provide daily support and individual treatment plans. The special education programs offer traditional academic programming, life skills and a vocational training curriculum. The home schedules therapy and family counseling on a regular basis.

Community-based programs assist families who are considered to be at risk or who are homeless. The aim of the program is to assist the family in reaching economic independence. In cooperation with the Department of Social Services, the home provides an array of programs designed to educate and support families in crisis. These services offer supervision and instruction to help families function healthily and independently.

Sending school districts pay program fees.

CLARKE SCHOOLS FOR HEARING AND SPEECH
NORTHAMPTON CAMPUS
Day — Coed Ages 4-14

Northampton, MA 01060. 47 Round Hill Rd.
Tel: 413-584-3450. TTY: 413-584-3450. Fax: 413-584-8273.
www.clarkeschools.org   E-mail: info@clarkeschools.org
Bill Corwin, Pres. **Martha A. deHahn,** Adm.
   Conditions: Primary—D.
   Gen Acad. Gr PS-8. **Feat**—Studio_Art Drama Music. **Expected outcome:**
      Return to local school.
   Therapy: Hear Lang Speech.
   Adm: Appl fee: $0. Appl due: Year-round. On-campus interview.
   Enr: 36 (Cap: 60). B 20. G 16. **Fac:** 8 (Full-time).
   Aid: State 36 (100% of tui). **Summer prgm:** Day. Educ. Rec. 2 wks.
   Libs 1. Art studios 1. Gyms 1. Fields 1.
   Est 1867. Nonprofit.

The educational program for profoundly deaf children at the Clarke Schools utilizes an auditory and oral method of instruction. The program seeks to prepare students for entrance into a mainstream setting. Early intervention, preschool and outreach programs are available. During the summer, Clarke offers theme-oriented, camplike programs to students with hearing impairments (and their siblings).

CLEARWAY SCHOOL
Day — Coed Ages 11-18

West Newton, MA 02465. 61 Chestnut St.
Tel: 617-964-6186. Fax: 617-964-5680.
www.clearwayschool.org   E-mail: clearway@clearwayschool.org
Mary Ryan, BA, Admin. **Peter Rosen,** BA, MEd, Educ Dir.

Conditions: Primary—ADHD Dc Dg Dx LD. **Sec**—Asp ED S. **IQ 85 and up.**
Col Prep. Gen Acad. Gr 6-12. On-Job Trng. **Feat**—Ceramics Photog Studio_Art
Music Woodworking.
Therapy: Lang Speech.
Adm: Appl due: Rolling.
Enr: 30 (Cap: 30). B 19. G 11. **Fac:** 6 (Full-time). Spec ed 4. Lay 2.
Est 1975. Nonprofit.

Clearway's highly individualized program features regularly scheduled one-on-one tutorials as well as speech and language services. The curriculum incorporates vocational offerings (including a community-based work-study program) and numerous electives. Vocational and educational counseling are integrated into the student's routine, and therapy is also available. Some students attend the school for one or two years and then return to a public school setting, while others remain at Clearway through graduation.

CORNERSTONES SCHOOL

Bdg and Day — Coed Ages 6-14

Ipswich, MA 01938. 35 Mitchell Rd.
Tel: 978-356-9321. Fax: 978-356-9724.
www.hes-inc.org/cornerstones-ipswich.html
Conditions: Primary—ADHD Anx Asp CD Dc Dg Dx ED LD Mood OCD Psy
PTSD SP Sz TS. **Sec**—AN Bu D Db. **IQ 68 and up.**
Gen Acad. Gr K-8. **Expected outcome:** Return to local school.
Therapy: Milieu Music Occup Perceptual-Motor Play Rec Speech.
Psychotherapy: Art Dance Fam Group Indiv Parent. **Counseling:** Educ.
Adm: Appl due: Year-round.
Enr: 15 (Cap: 24).
Tui '10-'11: Day $212/day. **Aid:** State.
Nonprofit. **Spons:** Health & Education Services.

Serving children with behavioral, learning and psychiatric special needs who have not had success in traditional school settings, Cornerstones enrolls boys and girls who stand to benefit from an intensive and highly structured environment. Students often are abuse victims who have developed behavioral problems as a result of their mistreatment. The educational program spans the entire year.

THE CORWIN-RUSSELL SCHOOL
AT BROCCOLI HALL

Day — Coed Ages 11-19

Sudbury, MA 01776. 142 North Rd.
Tel: 978-369-1444. Fax: 978-369-1026.
www.corwin-russell.org   E-mail: brochall@corwin-russell.org
Jane-Elisabeth Jakuc, AB, MEd, Head. **Chesley Wendth,** Adm.
Conditions: Primary—ADHD Asp Dx LD. **Sec**—Anx Db ED Mood OCD. **IQ
100 and up.**

Col Prep. Gen Acad. Gr 7-12. **Feat**—Fr Ger Japan Span Comp_Sci Studio_Art Drama Music Study_Skills. SAT/ACT prep.
Therapy: Lang. **Counseling:** Educ.
Adm: Appl due: Rolling.
Enr: 55. **Fac:** 22 (Full 17, Part 5).
Tui '12-'13: Day $33,950/sch yr (+$400). Educ. Rec. Tui Day $4000/2-wk ses. 4 wks.
Bldgs 2 (100% ADA). Class rms 13. Libs 1. Sci labs 1. Theaters 1. Art studios 2. Music studios 1. Fields 1. Ponds 1. Comp labs 1. Comp/stud: 1:2.
Est 1970. Nonprofit.

This small school serves college-bound students of superior intelligence who display a variety of learning styles. Multi-modal instruction is available in all traditional academic areas, and CRS also offers foreign language study, career education and social service opportunities. Students engage in visual and performing arts activities, technology, outdoor education and study partnerships with area cultural institutions and colleges. A tutorial program assists boys and girls with organizational needs and provides opportunities for course replacement, SAT preparation and skill advancement.

COTTING SCHOOL

Day — Coed Ages 3-22

Lexington, MA 02421. 453 Concord Ave.
Tel: 781-862-7323. Fax: 781-861-1179.
www.cotting.org   E-mail: info@cotting.org
David W. Manzo, BA, MEd, Pres. **Elizabeth Fay Russell,** Adm.
  Conditions: Primary—Apr Asp CP DS LD MD Nf ON PW SB. **Sec**—ADHD Ap As B/VI C D Db Dx Ep IP ID MS S TBI. **IQ 60 and up.**
  Col Prep. Gen Acad. Voc. Gr PS-12. Man_Arts & Shop. On-Job Trng.
  Expected outcome: Return to local school (Avg length of stay: 4-8 yrs).
Therapy: Hear Lang Occup Perceptual-Motor Phys Speech. **Psychotherapy:** Indiv. **Counseling:** Educ Voc.
Adm: Appl due: Year-round.
Enr: 120. **Fac:** 33 (Full 29, Part 4). Spec ed 33.
Est 1893. Nonprofit.

Cotting's objective is to provide the necessary educational, vocational and therapeutic programs for children and adolescents with communication deficits, medical disabilities, moderate to severe learning disabilities, multiple physical disabilities and posttraumatic head and spinal cord injuries.

The program includes individualized academic, prevocational, vocational and enrichment experiences. Comprehensive therapy and medical support services (including occupational, communication and physical therapies) are available on site, as are vision and dental clinic services. Children have access to appropriate assistive technologies.

CRYSTAL SPRINGS SCHOOL

Bdg — Coed Ages 3-22

Assonet, MA 02702. 38 Narrows Rd, PO Box 372.
Tel: 508-644-3101. Fax: 508-644-2008.
www.crystalspringsinc.org   E-mail: info@crystalspringsinc.org
Spencer Moore, PhD, CEO. Cheryl Tsimprea-Andrade, Adm.
  Conditions: Primary—ID. **Sec**—As Au B/VI C CF CP D Db DS Ep HI IP MD
  Multi ON SB TBI TS.
  Gen Acad. Voc. Ungraded. Shelt_Workshop. **Expected outcome:** Graduation.
  Therapy: Lang Music Occup Phys Rec Speech.
  Adm: Appl fee: $0. Appl due: Year-round.
  Enr: 41 (Cap: 63). **Fac:** 29 (Full-time). Spec ed 7. Lay 22.
  Tui '11-'12: Bdg $247,167/yr.
  Acres 45. Bldgs 20. Dorms 2. Class rms 7. Libs 1. Gyms 1. Fields 1. Courts 1.
    Pools 1.
  Est 1953. Nonprofit.

The school offers an educationally based program for students with severe to profound developmental disabilities who have accompanying medical, physical and behavioral disabilities. Pre-academic, prevocational and life skills programs are offered. Services include psychological assessments and family services. Speech and language evaluations and various forms of therapy are available. A 24-hour, self-contained behavioral unit serves students with severe behavioral disorders.

DEARBORN ACADEMY

Day — Coed Ages 5-22

Arlington, MA 02474. 34 Winter St.
Tel: 781-641-5992. Fax: 781-641-5997.
www.dearbornacademy.org   E-mail: hrossman@sfcinc.org
Howard Rossman, PhD, Dir.
  Conditions: Primary—ADHD Anx ED LD Mood NLD PTSD.
  Gen Acad. Ungraded. Man_Arts & Shop. On-Job Trng. Shelt_Workshop.
    Feat—Computers Indus_Arts. **Expected outcome:** Graduation.
  Psychotherapy: Fam Group Indiv.
  Adm: On-campus interview.
  Enr: 120 (Cap: 125). B 90. G 30.
  Aid: State 120 (100% of tui). Educ. Rec. 6 wks.
  Est 1949. Nonprofit. **Spons:** Schools for Children.

The academy offers a psycho-educational program that serves children with emotional, behavioral and learning problems. Dearborn's blend of educational and clinical services is designed to help students identify and achieve individual goals, and to assume responsibility for their behavior. Programming emphasizes academic achievement, hands-on learning experiences, academic remediation, and social and emotional growth. The upper school curriculum includes a shop program and a transitional program that prepares students to assume productive roles in the community when they graduate.

All students receive individual and group therapy, and family treatment is available both on site and in the community.

DOCTOR FRANKLIN PERKINS SCHOOL

Bdg — Coed Ages 5-21; Day — Coed 5-18

Lancaster, MA 01523. 971 Main St.
Tel: 978-365-7376. Fax: 978-368-8861.
www.perkinschool.org   E-mail: admissions@perkinschool.org
Charles P. Conroy, EdD, Exec Dir. **David A. Cook,** MEd, Educ Dir.
  Frank Boegemann, Adm.
  Conditions: Primary—ADHD Anx Asp ED LD Mood NLD OCD ODD PTSD
  Sz. **Sec**—AN Bu Dx ID Psy SA Subst. **IQ 80 and up.**
  Gen Acad. Voc. Gr K-12. **Feat**—Computers Studio_Art Drama Music.
  Expected outcome: Return to local school (Avg length of stay: 12-18 mos).
  Therapy: Lang Occup Speech. **Psychotherapy:** Equine Fam Group Indiv
  Parent.
  Enr: 164 (Cap: 189). **Fac:** 40. Spec ed 18. Lay 22.
  Est 1896. Nonprofit.

Perkins provides year-round, 24-hour care to clients who are coping with varying degrees of trauma, behavioral disturbances, psychiatric disturbance, family dysfunction and previous failed placements. Individuals may have deficits in self-care, community awareness and interpersonal skills. Services are available in a continuum of settings. Treatment programs seek to improve the client's behavioral controls and insight, interpersonal relationships, and life and leisure skills.

Year-round educational programming is available to both residents and day students. The curriculum features course work in the traditional disciplines, a young children's readiness class, computer training, job skills instruction, art, music, physical education, swimming, a therapeutic riding program and fitness instruction.

EAGLE HILL SCHOOL

Bdg and Day — Coed Ages 13-19

Hardwick, MA 01037. 242 Old Petersham Rd, PO Box 116.
Tel: 413-477-6000. Fax: 413-477-6837.
www.ehs1.org   E-mail: admission@ehs1.org
Peter John McDonald, BS, MEd, EdD, Head. **Dana M. Harbert,** Adm.
  Conditions: Primary—ADHD LD NLD. **IQ 90 and up.**
  Col Prep. Gen Acad. Gr 8-12. **Feat**—British_Lit Creative_Writing Sci_Fiction
  Fr Lat Russ Span Calc Anat & Physiol Botany Environ_Sci Forensic_Sci
  Oceanog Zoology Meteorology Microbio Web_Design Civil_War Holo-
  caust Middle_Eastern_Hist Vietnam_War WWI WWII Psych Child_Dev
  Gender_Stud World_Relig Film Filmmaking Painting Studio_Art Directing
  Music_Theory Journ Woodworking Health. ACT: Avg 22. Interscholastic
  sports. **Expected outcome:** Graduation.
  Therapy: Lang Speech. **Psychotherapy:** Indiv.

Adm: Appl fee: $100. Appl due: Rolling. On-campus interview.
Enr: 184. Bdg 166. Day 18. B 108. G 76. **Fac:** 45.
Tui '12-'13: Bdg $62,532/sch yr (+$4500). Day $44,257/sch yr (+$1000).
Aid: School 4 ($230,000). **Summer prgm:** Bdg. Educ. Rec. Tui Bdg $8332
(+$800). 5 wks.
Endow $6,000,000. Plant val $31,000,000. Acres 210. Bldgs 16 (94% ADA).
Dorms 4. Dorm rms 145. Class rms 48. Lib 5000 vols. Sci labs 6. Dark rms
1. Art studios 3. Wood shops 1. Gyms 1. Athletic ctrs 1. Fields 1. Tennis
courts 3. Pools 1. Ropes crses 1. Comp labs 5. Comp/stud: 1:1 .
Est 1967. Nonprofit.

One of the few independent schools designed for the adolescent who has been diagnosed with a specific learning disability, attention deficit disorder or both, Eagle Hill accepts only students of average or above-average intelligence who are free of primary emotional and behavioral difficulties. The college preparatory program allows faculty to take advantage of the pupil's strengths while also providing remediation of learning deficits. An important aspect of the curriculum is the Pragmatics Program, which assists students with their verbal and nonverbal communicational skills. Eagle Hill also conducts a student leadership program.

Specialized training in perceptual speech and language development is available. In addition, the residential program facilitates the development of organizational, time management and social skills.

Students in grades 9-12 satisfy a 10-hour annual community service requirement.

FARR ACADEMY

Day — Coed Ages 12-18

Cambridge, MA 02139. 71 Pearl St.
Tel: 617-492-4922. Fax: 617-547-8301.
www.farracademy.org   E-mail: farr@farracademy.org
Thomas F. Culhane, MEd, Exec Dir. **Bonnie K. Culhane,** Dir.
  Conditions: Primary—ADHD Anx Dc Dg Dx ED LD Mood PTSD SP.
    Sec—OCD TS. **IQ 90 and up.**
  Col Prep. Gen Acad. Gr 7-12. Man_Arts & Shop. **Feat**—Creative_Writing
    Mythology Span Anat Astron Computers Studio_Art Journ Woodworking.
    SAT/ACT prep. **Expected outcome:** Graduation.
  Psychotherapy: Fam Group Indiv Parent. **Counseling:** Educ Voc.
  Adm: On-campus interview.
  Enr: 36.
  Est 1972. Nonprofit.

The academy provides a therapeutic day school program for students with one or more learning, emotional or behavioral difficulties. Intensive individualized programs aim to develop the student's academic skills while alternatives within the program encourage success in nonacademic areas. The program also includes comprehensive physical education and elective components, as well as frequent overnight weekend camping trips. Homeroom teacher/counselors conduct individual and small-group counseling sessions.

FRANCISCAN HOSPITAL FOR CHILDREN
KENNEDY HOPE ACADEMY
Bdg — Coed Ages 5-21

Brighton, MA 02135. 30 Warren St.
Tel: 617-254-3800. Fax: 617-779-1119.
www.fhfc.org
Rui Carreiro, MEd, Prgm Dir. **Jonathan Parkhurst,** Adm.
  Conditions: Primary—As Au C CP Ep IP MD ON SB TBI. **Sec**—ADHD Ap
    Dx ID LD S.
  Voc. Gr K-12.
  Therapy: Hear Lang Music Occup Phys Speech. **Psychotherapy:** Fam Group
    Indiv Parent. **Counseling:** Educ.
  Enr: 17 (Cap: 17).
  Playgrounds 2. Comp labs 1.
  Est 1963. Nonprofit.

In conjunction with McLean Hospital, Kennedy operates a 17-bed residential school for children with multiple disabilities or medical challenges in one or more of the following areas: physical/motor, perceptual, language/communication, cognitive/learning and attention/interaction. Hospital services are coordinated with a team approach in designing individualized programs.

The spectrum of integrated offerings includes an augmentative communication team, assistive/computer technology, music therapy (and various other therapies), life skills/vocational training, family resource services, adaptive physical education, audiology, speech-language pathology, psychological services and reading services.

FREDERIC L. CHAMBERLAIN SCHOOL
Bdg and Day — Coed Ages 11-20

Middleboro, MA 02346. 1 Pleasant St, PO Box 778.
Tel: 508-947-7825. Fax: 508-947-0944.
www.chamberlainschool.org   E-mail: admissions@chamberlainschool.org
William J. Doherty, Exec Dir. **John Mendonca,** Adm.
  Conditions: Primary—ADHD Anx Asp Au ED LD Mood NLD OCD PTSD.
    Sec—As CD Dx Ep ODD Psy SP TS. **IQ 95 and up.**
  Col Prep. Gen Acad. Voc. Gr 6-12. On-Job Trng. **Feat**—Studio_Art. **Expected
    outcome:** Return to local school (Avg length of stay: 2 yrs).
  Therapy: Hear Lang Occup Play Speech. **Psychotherapy:** Fam Group Indiv.
  Adm: Appl due: Rolling. On-campus interview.
  Enr: 105. Bdg 85. Day 20. B 74. G 31. **Fac:** 34 (Full-time).
  Summer prgm: Bdg & Day. Educ. Rec. Ther. 6 wks.
  Acres 15.
  Est 1976. Nonprofit.

This therapeutic, highly structured boarding and day school, located on a 15-acre, rural campus, provides 24-hour care for students with learning, emotional and psychological special needs. Therapeutic services are coordinated with the school's individualized academic programming. Boys and girls, who typically have experienced significant difficulties in school, at home or in the community, receive individual, group and family counseling, as well as psychiatric therapy.

THE GIFFORD SCHOOL
Day — Coed Ages 8-22

Weston, MA 02493. 177 Boston Post Rd.
Tel: 781-899-9500. Fax: 781-899-4515.
www.gifford.org   E-mail: admin@gifford.org
Michael J. Bassichis, LICSW, Exec Dir. **Kevin McKenna,** Prin. **Ann Fry,** Adm.
Conditions: Primary—ADHD AN Anx Asp Bu CD Dc Dg Dx ED LD Mood OCD Psy PTSD PW SP Sz TS. **Sec**—TBI. **IQ 75 and up.**
Col Prep. Gen Acad. Ungraded. Culinary. Man_Arts & Shop. **Feat**—Computers Studio_Art Drama Music Woodworking. Interscholastic sports. **Expected outcome:** Return to local school (Avg length of stay: 2-3 yrs).
Therapy: Lang Milieu Speech.
Adm: On-campus interview.
Enr: 100. B 75. G 25. **Fac:** 43.
Summer prgm: Day. Educ. Rec. Ther. 3 wks.
Acres 26.
Est 1965. Nonprofit.

Gifford offers special education for students with mild to severe social and emotional problems and learning disabilities. Students are assigned to small classroom groups according to their skills, age and peer-group relations. Courses in art, shop and sports are integrated into the curriculum, as is individual tutoring. High school diplomas are awarded to students completing a prescribed course of study.

The clinical staff collaborates with teachers in understanding intellectual, social and emotional factors affecting the student's learning and overall functioning. In most cases, the student's sending school district covers all program and transportation costs.

THE GUILD FOR HUMAN SERVICES LEARNING CENTER
Bdg and Day — Coed Ages 6-22

Waltham, MA 02452. 411 Waverley Oaks Rd, Ste 104.
Tel: 781-893-6000. Fax: 781-893-1171.
www.theguildschool.org   E-mail: admissions@theguildschool.org
Thomas Belski, MS, CEO. **Sharon DiGrigoli,** Educ Dir.
Conditions: Primary—Anx Asp Au B/VI CP HI LD Mood ID OCD ODD PDD PTSD.
Voc. Ungraded. On-Job Trng. Shelt_Workshop.
Therapy: Lang Occup Speech. **Psychotherapy:** Indiv.
Enr: 54. Bdg 48. Day 6. B 33. G 21.
Est 1952. Nonprofit.

The Learning Center offers programs for individuals with social and behavioral problems, communicative disorders and medical conditions that interfere with the ability to learn. Using a behavioral approach, a clinical team develops an individual program for each student. Students acquire academic skills through classroom activities, realistic practice and computer-assisted learning. Personal hygiene and household skills, as well as community living skills, are employed.

Extracurricular opportunities include on-site activities and special outings. Family involvement is encouraged through participation in activities and clubs.

HILLSIDE SCHOOL
Bdg and Day — Boys Ages 10-15

Marlborough, MA 01752. 404 Robin Hill Rd.
Tel: 508-485-2824. Fax: 508-485-4420.
www.hillsideschool.net   E-mail: admissions@hillsideschool.net
David Z. Beecher, BA, Head. **Kristen J. Naspo,** Adm.
  Conditions: Primary—ADHD LD. **IQ 90 and up.**
  Gen Acad. Underachiever. Gr 5-9. **Feat**—Fr Lat Span Studio_Art Music
    Study_Skills. ESL. Interscholastic sports. **Expected outcome:** Graduation.
  Psychotherapy: Indiv.
  Adm: Appl fee: $50. Appl due: Rolling. On-campus interview.
  Enr: 140. Bdg 95. Day 45. **Fac:** 35 (Full-time).
  Tui '11-'12: Bdg $49,500/sch yr (+$1000). Day $29,500/sch yr (+$500).
    Aid: School 29 ($1,000,000).
  Endow $3,300,000. Plant val $20,000,000. Acres 200. Bldgs 15. Dorms 6.
    Dorm rms 30. Class rms 14. Lib 7000 vols. Sci labs 2. Auds 1. Art studios 1.
    Music studios 1. Gyms 1. Fields 2. Courts 2. Pools 1. Farms 1. Comp labs 1.
  Est 1901. Nonprofit.

Hillside provides a structured and supportive environment for traditional learners and boys of average to above-average intelligence who have learning differences, attentional disorders or both. In grades 7-9, the academic program includes English, history, science, math, studio art, wood shop, and foreign language; children in grades 5 and 6 receive instruction in math, language arts, social studies, reading, art, music and science. The curriculum is supplemented with organizational, socialization and subject-specific tutorials for those students in need of additional support. Regular evaluations of each pupil's social and academic behavior is another important element of school life.

All students must participate in a sport or an athletic activity each trimester. Selected boys who are interested in assisting with the farm program may live on the farm and are responsible for getting up early each morning to feed and provide water for the animals.

THE IVY STREET SCHOOL
Bdg and Day — Coed Ages 13-22

Brookline, MA 02446. 200 Ivy St.
Tel: 617-620-7779. Fax: 617-739-5110.
www.ivystreetschool.org   E-mail: admissions@ivystreetschool.org
Ron Allen, PhD, Dir. **Mayumi Migitaka,** Educ Dir. **Tunzel Hayes,** Adm.
  Conditions: Primary—Asp ED Ep ID ON TBI. **Sec**—ADHD Mood TS.

Gen Acad. Ungraded. Culinary. Man_Arts & Shop. On-Job Trng. Shelt_Workshop. **Therapy:** Hear Lang Milieu Music Occup Perceptual-Motor Phys Rec Speech. **Psychotherapy:** Art Dance Group Indiv Parent. **Enr:** 28. Bdg 28. B 18. G 10. **Est 1993.** Nonprofit.

This year-round therapeutic day and residential school addresses the educational and behavioral needs of children and adolescents who have either suffered traumatic brain injuries or experienced other neurologically based difficulties. Ivy Street offers specialized education programs, along with rehabilitative therapies, vocational services, psychotherapy and neurobehavioral management. All boys and girls take part in the culinary arts program.

Sending school districts typically pay tuition costs, although private-pay students occasionally enroll.

KENNEDY-DONOVAN CENTER SCHOOL

Day — Coed Ages 3-22

New Bedford, MA 02740. 19 Hawthorn St.
Tel: 508-992-4756. Fax: 508-999-5367.
www.kdcschool.org   E-mail: info@kdcschool.org
Karen Dobbins, Prgm Dir.
   Conditions: Primary—Ap Apr As Asp Au B/VI C CP D DS Ep IP MD Mood ID MS OCD PDD PTSD PW S SB TBI. **Sec**—ADHD Anx CD Db Dc Dg Dx ED LD SP TS.
   Gen Acad. Ungraded.
   Therapy: Occup Phys Speech.
   Enr: 53. **Fac:** 33 (Full-time). Spec ed 7. Lay 26.
   Aid: State 53 (100% of tui).
   Est 1969. Nonprofit.

Kennedy-Donovan serves students who are medically fragile or face cognitive, physical or behavioral challenges. The school provides year-round education, therapy and support services, while also maintaining an after-school program.

LANDMARK SCHOOL

Bdg — Coed Ages 13-20; Day — Coed 7-20

Prides Crossing, MA 01965. 429 Hale St, PO Box 227.
Tel: 978-236-3000. Fax: 978-927-7268.
www.landmarkschool.org   E-mail: admission@landmarkschool.org
   Nearby locations: 167 Bridge St, PO Box 1489, Manchester-by-the-Sea 01944.
Robert J. Broudo, BA, MEd, Head. **Carolyn Orsini Nelson,** Adm.
   Conditions: Primary—Dx LD. **Sec**—ADHD. **IQ 95 and up.**
   Col Prep. Gr 2-12. **Feat**—Anat & Physiol Environ_Sci Marine_Bio/Sci Anthro Psych Sociol Studio_Art Acting Drama Chorus Dance Woodworking

Study_Skills. Avg SAT: CR 447. M 425. W 445. Interscholastic sports.
Expected outcome: Graduation.
Therapy: Lang Speech. **Psychotherapy:** Indiv. **Counseling:** Educ.
Adm: Appl due: Rolling.
Enr: 461. Bdg 159. Day 302. B 301. G 160. **Fac:** 222 (Full-time).
Tui '12-'13: Bdg $64,200/sch yr (+$1600). Day $48,200/sch yr (+$200).
Summer prgm: Bdg & Day. Educ. Tui Bdg $7775. Tui Day $4625-6450.
4-6 wks.
Endow $10,000,000. Plant val $40,000,000. Acres 45. Bldgs 27. Dorms 6.
Dorm rms 89. Class rms 81. Libs 2. Sci labs 3. Art studios 2. Music studios
1. Dance studios 1. Gyms 2. Fields 4. Comp labs 5.
Est 1971. Nonprofit.

Landmark is designed to help those intellectually capable and emotionally healthy students who are not able to achieve in school because of language-based learning disabilities. The school is not capable of addressing the needs of boys and girls with more pervasive learning disabilities such as nonverbal learning disabilities, Asperger's syndrome, pervasive developmental disorder, bipolar disorder and developmental delay.

An intensive program of diagnostic prescriptive teaching based on one-on-one tutorials is provided. The school offers remedial, expressive language and college preparatory programs on two campuses along Boston's North Shore: the high school campus in Prides Crossing and the elementary and middle schools in Manchester-by-the-Sea.

LEAGUE SCHOOL OF GREATER BOSTON

Bdg and Day — Coed Ages 3-22

Walpole, MA 02032. 300 Boston Providence Tpke.
Tel: 508-850-3900. Fax: 508-660-2442.
www.leagueschool.org   E-mail: info@leagueschool.com
Frank Gagliardi, EdD, Exec Dir. **Patrick Fuller,** Adm.
Conditions: Primary—Asp Au PDD. **Sec**—ADHD ED ID Mood NLD OCD.
Voc. Ungraded. Culinary. On-Job Trng. Shelt_Workshop. Support_Employ.
Feat—Studio_Art Music. **Expected outcome:** Graduation.
Therapy: Lang Occup Phys Speech. **Counseling:** Educ Voc.
Adm: Appl fee: $0. Appl due: Year-round. On-campus interview.
Enr: 84 (Cap: 110). Bdg 16. Day 68. B 74. G 10. **Fac:** 48 (Full-time). Spec ed
15. Lay 33.
Tui '12-'13: Bdg $158,209/yr. Day $74,267/yr. **Aid:** State.
Plant val $10,000,000. Acres 12. Bldgs 1 (100% ADA). Class rms 18. Libs 1.
Auds 1. Art studios 1. Music studios 1. Gyms 1. Comp labs 1.
Est 1966. Nonprofit.

This comprehensive, year-round school provides a full range of educational and rehabilitative services for children and young adults with autism and related developmental disabilities who require specialized services not currently available in local public school systems. The program seeks to return the student to his or her community and public school system equipped with the skills necessary for achievement of maximum possible independence.

As the school's two homes occupy residential neighborhoods, each student participates in the care and upkeep of the home. Residents may also take advantage of various recreational and cultural activities during weekend, evening and vacation periods.

THE LEARNING CENTER FOR DEAF CHILDREN

Bdg — Coed Ages 12-22; Day — Coed 3-22

Framingham, MA 01701. 848 Central St.
Tel: 508-879-5110. TTY: 508-879-5110. Fax: 508-875-9203.
www.tlcdeaf.org E-mail: inquiries@tlcdeaf.org
Judith Vreeland, Pres. **Judy Jacobs,** Educ Dir.
   Conditions: Primary—D ED Mood OCD ODD PTSD. **Sec**—ADHD Au Bu CD ID Psy SP Sz TS. **Not accepted**—SO.
   Col Prep. Gen Acad. Gr PS-12. Man_Arts & Shop. On-Job Trng. AP courses (Eng). **Feat**—Computers Filmmaking Studio_Art. SAT/ACT prep. Interscholastic sports. **Expected outcome:** Return to local school (Avg length of stay: 1-3 yrs).
   Therapy: Hear Lang Occup Phys Speech. **Psychotherapy:** Fam Group Indiv.
   Adm: Appl fee: $0. Appl due: Year-round.
   Enr: 206. **Fac:** 65.
   Aid: State 206 (100% of tui).
   Acres 14. Bldgs 16. Libs 1. Sci labs 2. Art studios 1. Fields 1. Courts 1. Pools 2.
   Est 1970. Nonprofit.

The school provides comprehensive treatment and educational services for deaf children and youth with severe social and emotional difficulties resulting from childhood trauma, mental illness and organic dysfunctions. Students receive individualized care and therapy in an environment in which approximately half of the staff are deaf, and all are proficient in American Sign Language. The program combines a full range of academic and enrichment courses with social and work training skills. Accommodating adolescent pupils ages 12 and up, the five-day residential program facilitates the development of communicational, social and independent living skills.

TLC comprises two schools: a comprehensive preschool through high school program in Framingham that serves a majority of the students, and Walden School, a therapeutic treatment program for deaf students who also have severe emotional, behavioral or developmental disturbances (at the same Framingham address; 508-626-8581).

Sending school districts or state agencies fund all TLC placements.

LEARNING PREP SCHOOL

Day — Coed Ages 7-22

West Newton, MA 02465. 1507 Washington St.
Tel: 617-965-0764. Fax: 617-527-1514.
www.learningprep.org E-mail: dworcester@learningprep.org
Cynthia Papoulias DeAngelis, BA, MEd, Exec Dir.
   Conditions: Primary—APD LD PDD. **Sec**—ADHD Anx Apr As Asp Au CP Db Dc Dg Dpx Dx ED IP Mood Nf NLD OCD ON S SP TBI TS. **IQ 75-125.**

Gen Acad. Voc. Gr 2-12. Man_Arts & Shop. On-Job Trng. Support_Employ.
Feat—Calc Environ_Sci Engineering Comp_Sci Studio_Art Health.
Therapy: Lang Occup Speech. **Psychotherapy:** Group Indiv.
Counseling: Educ.
Adm: Appl due: Rolling.
Enr: 310. **Fac:** 75 (Full-time). Spec ed 70. Lay 5.
Tui '12-'13: Day $39,312/sch yr.
Est 1970. Nonprofit.

Students with language and learning differences who have accompanying secondary handicaps receive academic and work/job training at the school. Children follow an individualized program. The high school curriculum incorporates work-study opportunities and vocational training while stressing personal responsibility and social skills development.

LIGHTHOUSE SCHOOL
Day — Coed Ages 3-22

North Chelmsford, MA 01863. 25 Wellman Ave.
Tel: 978-251-4050. Fax: 978-251-8950.
www.lighthouseschool.org   E-mail: office@lighthouseschool.org
Michael Pappafagos, EdD, Pres.
　　Conditions: Primary—ADHD AN Anx APD Asp Au Bu CD DS ED Mood ID Multi OCD ODD ON PDD Psy PTSD PW SA SP Subst Sz TBI TS. **Sec**— Apr Ar C CLP CP D Db Dg Dpx Dx Ep Hemo HI IP LD Lk MD MS Nf NLD S SB SC SO. **Not accepted**—B/VI D-B.
　　Gen Acad. Voc. Gr PS-PG. On-Job Trng. Shelt_Workshop. **Expected outcome:** Return to local school (Avg length of stay: 2-5 yrs).
　　Therapy: Lang Milieu Occup Speech. **Psychotherapy:** Fam Group Indiv Parent. **Counseling:** Educ Voc.
　　Adm: Appl fee: $0. Appl due: Year-round. On-campus interview.
　　Enr: 243. B 203. G 40. **Fac:** 85 (Full 48, Part 37).
　　Tui '11-'12: Day $329/day.
　　Acres 33. Bldgs 1. Class rms 55. Libs 1. Sci labs 1. Lang labs 1. Gyms 1. Fields 3. Courts 1. Comp labs 2.
　　Est 1967. Nonprofit. ·

Lighthouse provides educational services for students with various special needs by means of an approach called APEX. Development of positive self-perception, quality interpersonal relationships and a sense of motivation is central to the program. The life development technology seeks to improve functional adaptation ability across all dimensions of life experience. The usual duration of treatment is two to five years.

MAY CENTER FOR CHILD DEVELOPMENT
Bdg and Day — Coed Ages 3-22

Randolph, MA 02368. 41 Pacella Park Dr.

Tel: 781-440-0400, 800-778-7601. **TTY:** 781-440-0461. **Fax:** 781-437-1301.
www.mayinstitute.org   E-mail: jhoover@mayinstitute.org
 Nearby locations: 596 Summer St, Brockton 02302; 511 Main St, West
  Springfield 01089; 10-R Commerce Way, Woburn 01801.
Jamie Hoover, BA, Exec Dir.
 Conditions: Primary—Asp Au PDD. **Sec**—DS ID LD.
 Gen Acad. Voc. Ungraded.
 Therapy: Lang Occup Phys Speech.
 Enr: 58. Day 58.
 Est 1955. Nonprofit. **Spons:** May Institute.

This year-round program comprises early intervention, educational and consultative services for children and young adults with autism and their families. The early intervention program serves both preschoolers and school-age children. Educational services are integral to the center's program, and school- and home-based consultations are also available.
   Other special education sites operate in Brockton, West Springfield and Woburn.

NEARI SCHOOL

Day — Coed Ages 7-22

Holyoke, MA 01040. 70 N Summer St.
Tel: 413-540-0712. **Fax:** 413-540-1915.
www.neari.com   E-mail: sbengis@gmail.com
Steven Bengis, EdD, LCSW, Exec Dir.
 Conditions: Primary—ADHD AN Anx As Asp Au Bu CD Dc Dg Dx ED LD
  Mood OCD Psy PTSD SA SB SP Subst Sz TBI TS. **Sec**—ID. **IQ 65-130.**
 Gen Acad. Voc. Gr K-12. Man_Arts & Shop. On-Job Trng. Support_Employ.
  Feat—Studio_Art Music. **Expected outcome:** Return to local school (Avg
  length of stay: 18-24 mos).
 Therapy: Lang Occup Speech. **Psychotherapy:** Group Indiv. **Counseling:**
  Educ Voc.
 Adm: Appl fee: $0. Appl due: Year-round. On-campus interview.
 Enr: 47 (Cap: 55). B 32. G 15. **Fac:** 15 (Full-time). Spec ed 8. Lay 7.
 Aid: State 47 (100% of tui).
 Acres 2. Bldgs 2 (50% ADA). Libs 1. Art studios 1. Comp labs 2.
 Est 1985. Nonprofit. **Spons:** New England Adolescent Research Institute.

The New England Adolescent Research Institute provides year-round educational, clinical, recreational and prevocational services for children, adolescents and young adults facing severe challenges, as well as those with developmental delays. The institute also provides training opportunities and resources for professionals who work with at-risk individuals.
   NEARI's special education day school enrolls young people with severe emotional disturbances and learning disabilities. A training and consulting center for at-risk children that specializes in the care of sexually abusive students is a component of the school program, as is an after-school prevention program for highly at-risk boys and girls.
   The sending school district typically pays all tuition fees.

PERKINS SCHOOL FOR THE BLIND

Bdg — Coed Ages 5-22; Day — Coed 3-22

Watertown, MA 02472. 175 N Beacon St.
Tel: 617-924-3434. Fax: 617-926-2027.
www.perkins.org   E-mail: info@perkins.org
Steven M. Rothstein, MBA, Pres. **Christopher Underwood**, Adm.
Conditions: Primary—B/VI D D-B. **Sec**—ADHD HI ID Multi ON PDD.
Col Prep. Gen Acad. Voc. Ungraded. Hort. Man_Arts & Shop. On-Job Trng.
  Shelt_Workshop. Interscholastic sports. **Expected outcome:** Return to
  local school.
Therapy: Hear Lang Music Occup Phys Play Speech Visual Orientation &
  Mobility. **Psychotherapy:** Art Group Indiv. **Counseling:** Educ Nutrition Voc.
Adm: Appl fee: $0. Appl due: Rolling.
Enr: 200.
Aid: State 200 (100% of tui). **Summer prgm:** Bdg. Educ. Voc. 5 wks.
Libs 1. Sci labs 1. Lang labs 1. Auds 1. Theaters 1. Art studios 1. Music studios
  1. Gyms 1. Fields 1. Pools 1. Comp labs 1.
Est 1829. Nonprofit.

Chartered through the efforts of Dr. John D. Fisher and a committee of interested citizens, Perkins accepts children who are blind—with or without additional disabilities— or deaf-blind. An interdisciplinary treatment team comprises teachers, clinicians, and residential and support staff. The school's academic experience is similar to that found in a traditional school, but boys and girls have access to specialized services that aid in their development.

Staff formulate an Individualized Education Plan for each pupil, with the goal of maximizing independence and self-reliance. Skill-building activities incorporate prevocational training and physical and language therapy, while also addressing independent living skills. Enrollment options range from ungraded classes to an accredited high school program. Students rarely spend their entire school careers at Perkins, with most enrolling for a few years before or after attending public school. Group pursuits such as chorus, dramatic productions, and horticultural projects in the school's greenhouse and gardens complement academics.

The student's sending school district typically pays all tuition fees.

REED ACADEMY

Bdg and Day — Boys Ages 7-14

Framingham, MA 01701. 1 Winch St.
Tel: 508-877-1222. Fax: 508-877-7477.
www.reedacademy.net   E-mail: reed.academy@verizon.net
Edward A. Cohen, EdD, Exec Dir. **Maura Flanagan**, Prgm Coord.
Conditions: Primary—ADHD Anx APD Asp Au ED LD Mood NLD OCD ODD
  ON PDD PTSD SP TBI. **Sec**—As Dx Ep ID S TS.
Gen Acad. Ungraded. **Feat**—Computers Studio_Art Health. **Expected outcome:**
  Return to local school (Avg length of stay: 3 yrs).
Therapy: Lang Occup Speech. **Psychotherapy:** Fam Group Indiv Parent.

Adm: Appl due: Year-round. On-campus interview.
Enr: 21 (Cap: 24). Bdg 15. Day 6. **Fac:** 9 (Full 7, Part 2). Spec ed 7. Lay 2.
Tui '11-'12: Bdg $70,792/yr. Day $53,991/yr. **Aid:** State. **Summer prgm:** Bdg
& Day. Educ. Rec. Ther. 6 wks.
Est 1975. Nonprofit.

The five-day residential school and day program focuses on promoting developmental and academic growth, as well as behavioral changes. Enrichment courses, workshop skills, household chores and supervised social activities are part of a highly structured program. The day program includes 24-hour emergency support. All students participate in psychotherapy sessions. The usual length of stay is three years. A six-week summer camp emphasizes socialization skills.

RIVERVIEW SCHOOL
Bdg and Day — Coed Ages 11-23

East Sandwich, MA 02537. 551 Rte 6A.
Tel: 508-888-0489. Fax: 508-833-7001.
www.riverviewschool.org   E-mail: admissions@riverviewschool.org
Maureen B. Brenner, BA, MEd, Head. Jeanne M. Pacheco, Adm.
  Conditions: Primary—LD. **Sec**—ADHD CP Dc Dg Dpx Ep ID NLD S TBI.
    IQ 70-100.
  Col Prep. Ungraded. Man_Arts & Shop. **Feat**—Computers Photog Studio_Art
    Drama Indus_Arts. Interscholastic sports. **Expected outcome:** Graduation.
  Therapy: Lang Speech.
  Adm: Appl fee: $75. Appl due: Rolling.
  Enr: 207. Bdg 187. Day 20. B 117. G 90. **Fac:** 48 (Full 45, Part 3).
  Tui '11-'12: Bdg $69,750/sch yr. Day $41,674/sch yr. **Aid:** School 24
    ($330,000). State. **Summer prgm:** Res & Day. Educ. Rec. Tui Bdg $6984.
    Tui Day $4260. 5 wks.
  Endow $4,500,000. Plant val $30,000,000. Acres 16. Bldgs 20 (50% ADA).
    Dorms 10. Dorm rms 62. Class rms 29. Libs 1. Sci labs 1. Dark rms 1. Auds
    1. Art studios 1. Music studios 1. Gyms 1. Athletic ctrs 1. Fields 1. Courts 1.
    Greenhouses 1. Comp labs 3. Comp/stud: 1:1
  Est 1957. Nonprofit.

Riverview serves adolescents without significant behavioral or emotional problems who have complex language, learning and cognitive disabilities. Students typically have experienced lifelong difficulties in academics and in making friends. The thematic, integrated program features academic, remedial and computer course work, while also addressing independent living skills and social skills development.

The program includes small, individualized academic classes, as well as reading, speech and language therapies. Speech/language pathologists and reading specialists provide assistance as needed. Structured evening and weekend programs offer support and are an important element of Riverview's predictable learning environment.

All juniors take part in a weekly community service program.

ST. COLETTA DAY SCHOOL

Day — Coed Ages 3-22

Braintree, MA 02184. 85 Washington St.
Tel: 781-848-6250. Fax: 781-848-0640.
www.cushingcenters.com   E-mail: rshepherd@cushingcenters.org
Ron Shepherd, Educ Dir.
   Conditions: Primary—DS ID PDD. **Sec**—Ap Au CP ED Ep MD OCD ODD
   ON S.
   Voc. Ungraded. On-Job Trng. Shelt_Workshop. **Feat**—Studio_Art Music.
   Therapy: Hear Lang Music Occup Perceptual-Motor Phys Speech Visual.
   Psychotherapy: Art Dance Indiv.
   Enr: 23. **Fac:** 50 (Full 43, Part 7).
   Acres 4.
   Est 1948. Nonprofit. **Spons:** Cardinal Cushing Centers.

Located 15 minutes from Boston on a four-acre site, St. Coletta offers a year-round academic program for moderately to severely retarded children and young adults. Students acquire functional daily living skills for home and community living and take part in practical academic, prevocational, vocational and recreational programs. The academic program addresses speech and communication skills, as well as perceptual-motor development.

SCHWARTZ CENTER FOR CHILDREN DAY SCHOOL

Day — Coed Ages 3-21

Dartmouth, MA 02747. 1 Posa Pl.
Tel: 508-996-3391. TTY: 508-996-3397. Fax: 508-996-3397.
www.schwartzcenter.org   E-mail: mmaiato@schwartzcenter.org
Margaret M. Maiato, BS, MS, Dir.
   Conditions: Primary—Ap Au CP DS IP ID Multi ON PDD S TBI. **Sec**—B/VI D
   HI MD MS SB.
   Gen Acad. Ungraded.
   Therapy: Hydro Lang Occup Phys Speech.
   Adm: Appl fee: $0. Appl due: Year-round. On-campus interview.
   Enr: 51 (Cap: 57). B 28. G 23. **Fac:** 8 (Full-time). Spec ed 7. Lay 1.
   Tui '11-'12: Day $46,457/sch yr. **Aid:** State.
   Bldgs 1 (100% ADA). Class rms 9. Libs 1.
   Est 1956. Nonprofit.

Schwartz Center provides evaluations and treatment for children with many types of disabilities, including physical handicaps, developmental impairments, medical conditions and communicative disorders. In addition to the day school, the center offers these services: audiology, occupational therapy, physical therapy, speech and language pathology, and early intervention.

SOUTHEAST ALTERNATIVE SCHOOL

Day — Coed Ages 14-18

Middleboro, MA 02346. 49 Plymouth St.
Tel: 508-947-0131. Fax: 508-947-1569.
www.communitycareservices.org
 E-mail: sas.middleboro@communitycareservices.org
 Nearby locations: 117 Stowe Rd, Sandwich 02563.
Timothy Hurley, MEd, Dir.
 Conditions: Primary—ADHD CD Dx ED LD NLD.
 Gen Acad. Voc. Gr 9-12. Man_Arts & Shop. **Expected outcome:** Return to
 local school (Avg length of stay: 1-2 yrs).
 Therapy: Speech. **Psychotherapy:** Fam Group Indiv.
 Adm: Appl due: Year-round. On-campus interview.
 Enr: 40. **Fac:** 8. Spec ed 3. Lay 5.
 Aid: State 40 (100% of tui).
 Est 1952. Nonprofit.

SAS provides flexible, individualized educational programming for students with learning and social/emotional disabilities. Pupils work toward their high school degrees and explore vocational interests as they prepare for independent living. Boys and girls typically spend one or two years at the school before returning to a public school setting.

SAS also maintains a Cape Cod campus in Sandwich (508-420-6401).

STETSON SCHOOL

Bdg — Boys Ages 9-21

Barre, MA 01005. 455 South St, PO Box 309.
Tel: 978-355-4541. Fax: 978-355-6335.
www.stetsonschool.org   E-mail: koconnor@stetsonschool.org
Kathleen Lovenbury, MA, Exec Dir. **Robert Fitzgerald,** Adm.
 Conditions: Primary—ED SO. **Sec**—ADHD Anx As Asp Au C CD CP Db Dg
 Dx Ep ID Mood OCD Psy PTSD SC SP Sz TBI TS. **IQ 55 and up.**
 Gen Acad. Voc. Ungraded. Man_Arts & Shop. **Feat**—Comp_Sci Studio_Art
 Woodworking. SAT/ACT prep. Interscholastic sports. **Expected outcome:**
 Return to local school (Avg length of stay: 18 mos).
 Therapy: Milieu Occup Play Rec Speech. **Psychotherapy:** Art Fam Group
 Indiv Parent. **Counseling:** Educ Nutrition Voc.
 Adm: Appl fee: $0. Appl due: Year-round.
 Enr: 111 (Cap: 120). **Fac:** 47.
 Tui '10-'11: Bdg $460/day. **Aid:** State.
 Acres 200. Bldgs 8 (50% ADA). Dorms 4. Dorm rms 117. Class rms 16. Libs 1.
 Sci labs 1. Gyms 1. Fields 2. Pools 1. Comp labs 1.
 Est 1899. Nonprofit.

Stetson serves boys and adolescent males who have a history of sexually abusive behaviors, including sexual acting out and sexual misconduct. Treatment, which takes place in a secure rehabilitative environment, addresses the emotional, behavioral, social, familial and cognitive domains. Structured external behavioral controls are in place to assist the boy with developing self-control, and the multidisciplinary, integrated treatment model incorporates milieu treatment, psychotherapy, academics, health services and recreation. The ultimate program goal is the client's successful reintegration into his community.

Offered through Stetson's Robinson Education Center, educational services mirror those found in public schools. An extended, 216-day school year allows for flexibility in course scheduling, staff training and summer programming. The curriculum incorporates prevocational course work in such areas as woodworking, computer technology, and building and grounds maintenance. Annual Individual Education Plan meetings constitute an important part of the educational process.

SWANSEA WOOD SCHOOL

Bdg — Coed Ages 12-22

Swansea, MA 02777. 789 Stevens Rd.
Tel: 508-672-6560. Fax: 508-672-6595.
www.jri.org/swansea   E-mail: mbalzanoaugust@jri.org
Maribeth Balzano-August, Prgm Dir.
   Conditions: Primary—ADHD Anx CD ED LD Mood ID ODD PTSD SA.
     Sec—As CP Dx Ep ON TBI. **IQ 60-85.**
   Voc. Ungraded. Man_Arts & Shop. On-Job Trng. **Feat**—Computers Theater
     Woodworking Health. **Expected outcome:** Return to local school (Avg
     length of stay: 12-18 mos).
   Therapy: Hear Occup Phys Rec Speech. **Psychotherapy:** Group Indiv.
   Enr: 26. B 15. G 11. **Fac:** 6 (Full-time). Spec ed 3. Lay 3.
   Tui '10-'11: Bdg $410/day. **Aid:** State.
   Acres 6.
   Est 1987. Nonprofit. **Spons:** Justice Resource Institute.

Located on six acres of wooded land, Swansea Wood serves adolescents who have struggled with significant and chronic past trauma, organic mental illness or both and who have mild to moderate cognitive impairments. As students often display emotional problems, at-risk behavior, behavioral issues, academic problems and, at times, psychosis, SWS modifies its academic program and provides therapeutic services to address individual educational, behavioral and developmental needs.

Services include educational, vocational and social skills training, including close interaction with the community. The school organizes specialized groups for certain behavioral difficulties.

VALLEY VIEW SCHOOL

Bdg — Boys Ages 11-16

North Brookfield, MA 01535. 91 Oakham Rd, PO Box 338.
Tel: 508-867-6505. Fax: 508-867-3300.
www.valleyviewschool.org   E-mail: valview@aol.com
Philip G. Spiva, AB, MA, PhD, Dir.
   Conditions: Primary—ADHD Anx ED Mood ODD SP. **Sec**—AN Asp Db Dc
     Dg Dx HI LD Multi NLD OCD PDD SA TS. **IQ 90 and up.**

Not accepted—Ap Apr Ar As Au B/VI C CD CF CLP CP D D-B DS Ep Hemo ID IP Lk MD MR MS Nf ON Psy PTSD PW S SB SC SO Subst Sz TBI.
Col Prep. Gen Acad. Gr 5-12. **Feat**—Span Computers Studio_Art Drama.
Expected outcome: Return to local school (Avg length of stay: 2-3 yrs).
Therapy: Milieu Speech. **Psychotherapy:** Group Indiv. **Counseling:** Educ.
Adm: Appl due: Year-round. On-campus interview.
Enr: 50 (Cap: 56). **Fac:** 11.
Tui '11-'12: Bdg $65,900/yr. **Aid:** State 4.
Endow $500,000. Plant val $4,000,000. Acres 215. Bldgs 8. Dorms 5. Dorm rms 29. Class rms 11. Sci labs 1. Theaters 1. Art studios 1. Gyms 1. Fields 1. Courts 2. Comp labs 1.
Est 1970. Nonprofit.

Located on 215 acres of timberland and fields, Valley View offers a year-round therapeutic environment for adolescent boys with adjustment difficulties. A large percentage of the school's population arrives with a history of oppositional behavior and attentional problems.

A school program emphasizes the remediation of academic and motivational difficulties, encouraging boys to return to a more traditional educational setting. Boys participate in community activities and maintain contact with their families. Activities on campus include organized athletics, creative arts and crafts, computer lab, photography and indoor sports. As an extension of the philosophy of providing boys with a wide variety of success-oriented experiences, travel opportunities are offered both locally and abroad.

Counseling and a full range of psychotherapeutic services are provided. The usual duration of stay is two to three years.

WALKER

Bdg and Day — Coed Ages 3-14

Needham, MA 02492. 1968 Central Ave.
Tel: 781-449-4500. Fax: 781-449-5717.
www.walkerschool.org   E-mail: ldanovitch@walkerschool.org
Susan Getman, LICSW, Exec Dir. **Lisa Danovitch,** Adm.
   Conditions: Primary—ADHD Anx APD Asp Au CD ED Mood NLD OCD ODD PDD Psy PTSD SA SP. **Sec**—AN Ap Apr As Bu Db Dc Dg Dx Ep LD S TS.
   IQ 70 and up.
   Gen Acad. Gr K-8. **Expected outcome:** Graduation.
   Therapy: Lang Milieu Occup Play Rec Speech. **Psychotherapy:** Art Fam Group Indiv.
   Adm: Appl due: Year-round. On-campus interview.
   Enr: 85 (Cap: 85). **Fac:** 11 (Full 10, Part 1). Spec ed 9. Lay 2.
   Aid: State 85 (100% of tui). **Summer prgm:** Bdg & Day. Educ. Rec. Ther. 7 wks.
   Est 1961. Nonprofit.

Located adjacent to the Charles River, Walker is a day and residential treatment center that serves children with severe emotional, behavioral and learning disorders.

Residential units provide three levels of services: intensive residential, with a goal of stepping down to less restrictive programs; residential services, with a goal of increased community involvement; and acute residential services for children ages 3-10, with a goal of stabilization and assessment at times of crisis. The year-round school includes afternoon activities and summer programs. The treatment approach emphasizes milieu, family, individual and group therapy; specialized pediatric and psychiatric care; and a strong academic curriculum with emphasis on the remediation of language-based learning disabilities.

Through its division of Walker Partnerships, Walker offers transition and support services to students, families and educators involved in public school inclusion.

WHITNEY ACADEMY

Bdg — Boys Ages 10-22

East Freetown, MA 02717. PO Box 619.
Tel: 508-763-3737. Fax: 508-763-5300.
www.whitneyacademy.org
George E. Harmon, MEd, Exec Dir. **Ben Allen,** Adm.
   Conditions: Primary—Anx Asp CD ED Mood ID OCD ODD Psy PTSD SA SO Sz. **Sec**—ADHD As DS Dx LD SP TS. **IQ 50-80. Not accepted**—AN B/VI Bu D Hemo SC.
   Gen Acad. Voc. Gr 5-12. Culinary. Man_Arts & Shop. **Feat**—Sci Computers Soc_Stud. **Expected outcome:** Return to local school (Avg length of stay: 2 yrs).
   Therapy: Hear Lang Milieu Phys Play Rec Speech. **Psychotherapy:** Dance Fam Group Indiv Parent.
   Enr: 42 (Cap: 42). **Fac:** 12 (Full-time). Spec ed 6. Lay 6.
   Est 1986. Nonprofit.

The academy provides year-round care for dually diagnosed children while maintaining a 2:1 staff-student ratio. Patients with mild to moderate intellectual disabilities and psychiatric diagnoses receive academic training and interdisciplinary treatment. Whitney also conducts a program that serves both sex offenders and victims of sexual offenses. Counseling and individual and group therapies are available, and the average length of stay is two years.

WILLIE ROSS SCHOOL FOR THE DEAF

Day — Coed Ages 3-22

Longmeadow, MA 01106. 32 Norway St.
Tel: 413-567-0374. TTY: 413-567-0374. Fax: 413-567-8808.
www.willierossschool.org   E-mail: labbate@willierossschool.org
Louis E. Abbate, EdD, Pres. **Veronica Miller,** Adm.
   Conditions: Primary—D HI. **Sec**—ADHD Apr Asp Au ED ID S. **Not accepted**—SO.
   Col Prep. Gen Acad. Voc. Gr PS-12. On-Job Trng. SAT/ACT prep. Interscholastic sports. **Expected outcome:** Graduation.
   Therapy: Hear Lang Occup Phys Speech. **Psychotherapy:** Indiv Parent.
   Counseling: Educ Voc.
   Adm: Appl fee: $0. Appl due: Year-round. On-campus interview.

Enr: 63. B 34. G 29. **Fac:** 13 (Full-time). Spec ed 13.
Tui '12-'13: Day $226/day. **Summer prgm:** Day. Educ. 5 wks.
Acres 2. Bldgs 2. Fields 1.
Est 1967. Nonprofit.

The school provides a full continuum of services for deaf and hard-of-hearing children who reside in western Massachusetts. WRSD employs a total communication approach and places emphasis on the development of spoken language. Staff attempt to maximize residual hearing.

WRSD's integrated model, incorporating both center-based and local public school settings, allows deaf and hard-of-hearing students to share many experiences of regular education with their hearing peers.

WILLOW HILL SCHOOL

Day — Coed Ages 11-19

Sudbury, MA 01776. 98 Haynes Rd.
Tel: 978-443-2581. Fax: 978-443-7560.
www.willowhillschool.org   E-mail: mfoley@willowhillschool.org
Stanley V. Buckley, EdS, Head. **Melissa Foley-Procko,** Adm.
Conditions: Primary—ADHD Asp Dc Dg Dx LD NLD. **IQ 90 and up.**
Col Prep. Gr 6-12. **Feat**—Computers Filmmaking Photog Studio_Art Drama Music. Interscholastic sports. **Expected outcome:** Graduation.
Counseling: Educ.
Adm: Appl fee: $0. Appl due: Rolling.
Enr: 60. B 43. G 17. **Fac:** 17 (Full 16, Part 1).
Tui '11-'12: Day $48,574/sch yr.
Plant val $4,928,000. Acres 26. Bldgs 4. Class rms 17. Lib 5300 vols. Sci labs 2. Art studios 1. Arts ctrs 1. Gyms 1. Comp labs 2. Comp/stud: 1:1 Laptop prgm Gr 6-12.
Est 1970. Nonprofit.

The school offers comprehensive educational services for students of average to high intelligence who have been diagnosed with learning disabilities, nonverbal learning disabilities or Asperger's syndrome. The college preparatory curriculum includes course work in art, drama and technology. Willow Hill also provides highly individualized one-on-one and small-group tutorials, sports, a wilderness exploration program and extracurricular activities.

THE WINCHENDON SCHOOL

Bdg and Day — Coed Ages 14-20

Winchendon, MA 01475. 172 Ash St.
Tel: 978-297-1223, 800-622-1119. Fax: 978-297-0911.
www.winchendon.org   E-mail: admissions@winchendon.org
John A. Kerney, BS, MS, MEd, Head. **David Flynn,** Adm.
Conditions: Primary—LD. **Sec**—ADHD Dc Dg Dx. **IQ 95 and up.**

Col Prep. Underachiever. Gr 9-PG. AP courses (Calc). **Feat**—British_Lit Fr
Span Stats Forensic_Sci Comp_Sci Psych Ceramics Drawing Painting
Drama Public_Speak. Avg SAT: CR 550. M 600. W 500. ESL. Interscholastic
sports. **Expected outcome:** Graduation.
Adm: Appl fee: $50. Appl due: Jan. On-campus interview.
Enr: 240. Bdg 218. Day 22. B 188. G 52. **Fac:** 36 (Full 25, Part 11). Spec ed 3.
Lay 33.
Tui '12-'13: Bdg $48,600/sch yr. Day $27,600/sch yr. **Aid:** School
($2,000,000). **Summer prgm:** Bdg & Day. Educ. Tui Bdg $6500 (+$330).
6 wks.
Endow $21,000,000. Plant val $29,000,000. Acres 350. Bldgs 35. Dorms 5.
Dorm rms 162. Class rms 27. Lib 15,000 vols. Sci labs 4. Art studios 2.
Music studios 1. Dance studios 1. Gyms 1. Athletic ctrs 1. Fields 4. Courts
2. Pools 1. Rinks 1. Golf crses 1. Comp labs 1.
Est 1926. Nonprofit.

Through personal attention to the academic capabilities of each student, Winchendon
seeks to aid those who have not previously developed sound study habits. Various types of
students enroll, from bright underachievers to those with basic learning deficits.

The curriculum is college preparatory, with emphasis on small, student-centered classes.
The school offers daily tutorials in English and math, and one-on-one remedial programs
are available. Instructors administer grades each day in in every course, and counselors
provide services daily.

MICHIGAN

ETON ACADEMY
Day — Coed Ages 6-19

Birmingham, MI 48009. 1755 E Melton Rd.
Tel: 248-642-1150. Fax: 248-642-3670.
www.etonacademy.org   E-mail: contact@etonacademy.org
Pete Pullen, Head.
   Conditions: Primary—ADHD Dx LD. **IQ 85 and up.**
   Col Prep. Gen Acad. Voc. Gr 1-12. **Feat**—Span Econ Studio_Art Health.
   Expected outcome: Return to local school (Avg length of stay: 3 yrs).
   Therapy: Hear Lang Occup Phys Speech.
   Adm: Appl fee: $100. Appl due: Rolling. On-campus interview.
   Enr: 185.
   Tui '12-'13: Day $21,700-23,300/sch yr. **Aid:** School.
   Est 1986. Nonprofit.

Eton offers academic instruction to children with dyslexia and related learning problems through individualized lessons and classes of no more than eight students. The program emphasizes the development of mathematics, reading, language, communicative and study skills. Physical education, computer instruction, art and curriculum enrichment programs are available. The usual duration of enrollment is three years.

MONTCALM SCHOOL FOR BOYS AND GIRLS
Bdg — Boys Ages 12-21, Girls 12-18

Albion, MI 49224. 13725 Starr Commonwealth Rd.
Tel: 517-630-2512, 866-244-4321. Fax: 517-630-2352.
www.montcalmschool.org   E-mail: info@montcalmschool.org
Kelley Jones, BS, MA, Dir.
   Conditions: Primary—ADHD Anx Asp CD ED Mood ODD PDD. **IQ 70 and up. Not accepted**—Ep SO.
   Gen Acad. Gr 7-12. **Expected outcome:** Return to local school (Avg length of stay: 12 mos).
   Psychotherapy: Fam Group.
   Tui '12-'13: Bdg $7000/mo. **Aid:** School.
   Acres 350. Gyms 1. Pools 1. Tracks 1.
   Nonprofit. **Spons:** Starr Commonwealth.

Montcalm's specially structured residential program for adolescents with emotional and behavioral problems offers therapeutic and growth experiences as it promotes intellectual development. Individualized treatment and education plans address the needs of each student. Fine arts, athletics and adventure education round out the core program.
   The program also provides treatment for substance abuse.

MINNESOTA

FRASER SCHOOL

Day — Coed Ages 6wks-6

Minneapolis, MN 55423. 2400 W 64th St.
Tel: 612-861-1688. Fax: 612-861-6050.
www.fraser.org   E-mail: fraser@fraser.org
Diane S. Cross, STM, Pres. **Deedee Stevens-Neal,** MEd, Dir.
   Conditions: Primary—ADHD Anx As Asp Au B/VI C CLP CP D DS ED Ep IP
   LD MD Mood ID OCD ON PDD PW S SB TBI TS.
   Gen Acad. Gr PS-K.
   Therapy: Music Occup Phys Speech.
   Enr: 300.
   Est 1935. Nonprofit.

Within a fully inclusive environment, Fraser places children in an age-appropriate classroom regardless of their disability or lack thereof. Focus areas include cognition, gross- and fine-motor development, communication, social and emotional development, and social skills development, all provided in a developmentally and individually appropriate curriculum. All pupils participate in music therapy.

GROVES ACADEMY

Day — Coed Ages 6-18

St Louis Park, MN 55416. 3200 Hwy 100 S.
Tel: 952-920-6377. Fax: 952-920-2068.
www.grovesacademy.org   E-mail: luffeya@grovesacademy.org
John Alexander, BA, MA, Head. **Teresa Smith, Upper & Middle Sch Adm;**
   Debbie Moran, Lower Sch Adm.
   Conditions: Primary—ADHD APD Dc Dg Dpx Dx LD NLD S. **Sec**—Anx Ap
   Asp CP Db Ep HI PDD. **IQ 85 and up.**
   Col Prep. Gen Acad. Gr 1-12. Man_Arts & Shop. **Feat**—Studio_Art Theater
   Music Health Home_Ec. **Expected outcome:** Return to local school (Avg
   length of stay: 3 yrs).
   Therapy: Lang Occup Speech. **Counseling:** Educ.
   Adm: Appl fee: $75. Appl due: Rolling.
   Enr: 220. **Fac:** 45 (Full 43, Part 2). Spec ed 38. Lay 7.
   Tui '12-'13: Day $22,500-23,400/sch yr. **Aid:** School 87 ($850,000). **Summer**
   prgm: Day. Educ. Rec. 4 wks.
   Endow $1,000,000. Plant val $7,200,000. Acres 5. Bldgs 100% ADA. Class
   rms 37. Libs 1. Sci labs 2. Art studios 1. Ceramics studios 1.Wood shops 2.
   Gyms 2. Fields 1. Weight rms 1. Comp labs 1. Comp/stud: 1:1 Laptop prgm
   Gr 7-12.
   Est 1972. Nonprofit.

The academy accepts students with learning disabilities and attentional disorders of normal or higher intelligence with the goal of returning them to the educational mainstream. Pupils may also remain through grade 12 and earn a high school diploma at Groves. Individualized instruction and remediation are tailored to each student's learning characteristics.

Prior to admission, staff members conduct a diagnostic assessment of the educational, psychological, social and physical factors of the student's learning disorders. Course offerings include reading, writing, math, science, social studies, art, physical education and computer, and various extracurricular activities supplement class work. The school also offers a basic skills tutorial for children, teens and adults after school. A summer session open to all pupils provides intensive remediation for academic deficits and also includes recreational and social skills programming.

MISSISSIPPI

THE EDUCATION CENTER SCHOOL
Day — Coed Ages 6-21

Jackson, MS 39216. 4080 Old Canton Rd.
Tel: 601-982-2812. Fax: 601-982-2827.
www.educationcenterschool.com   E-mail: edcenter@bellsouth.net
Lynn T. Macon, MEd, Dir. Deborah J. Stamper, Prin.
Conditions: Primary—ADHD Asp CD Dc Dx ED LD SP. IQ 90 and up.
Col Prep. Gen Acad. Gr 1-12. Feat—Lat Span Psych Sociol. ACT: Avg 22.
SAT/ACT prep. Expected outcome: Graduation.
Psychotherapy: Fam Parent. Counseling: Educ.
Adm: Appl due: Year-round.
Enr: 150. Fac: 15 (Full 12, Part 3).
Tui '12-'13: Day $8400/sch yr. Summer prgm: Day. Educ. 4 wks.
Bldgs 2 (100% ADA). Class rms 14. Lib 6000 vols. Sci labs 1. Comp labs 1.
Est 1964.

The school provides special academic instruction in a small-class setting, as well as diagnostic and prescriptive education, for students with learning differences. The program emphasizes the development of reading skills, learning strategies and study skills. Preliminary vocational counseling and screening are also available, as are summer courses, tutoring and evening classes. Students perform 100 hours of required community service prior to graduation.

MISSOURI

CENTRAL INSTITUTE FOR THE DEAF

Day — Coed Ages 3-12

St Louis, MO 63110. 825 S Taylor Ave.
Tel: 314-977-0132, 877-444-4574. TTY: 314-977-0037. Fax: 314-977-0023.
www.cid.edu   E-mail: aosman@cid.edu
Robin M. Feder, MS, Exec Dir. Barbara Lanfer, MAEd, Co-Prin. Andrea Osman, Adm.
Conditions: Primary—D HI. IQ 80 and up.
Gen Acad. Ungraded. Feat—Computers Studio_Art Music. Expected outcome: Return to local school.
Therapy: Hear Lang Music Occup Speech. Psychotherapy: Dance Fam Parent. Counseling: Educ.
Adm: Appl fee: $50. Appl due: Year-round.
Enr: 125. B 75. G 50. Fac: 21 (Full 19, Part 2). Spec ed 20. Lay 1.
Tui '12-'13: Day $163/day. Sliding-Scale Rate $10-28,600/yr. Aid: State.
Summer prgm: Day. Educ. Rec. Tui Day $163/day. 5 wks.
Bldgs 1 (100% ADA). Libs 1. Gyms 1. Playgrounds 1.
Est 1914. Nonprofit.

CID offers a variety of instructional styles and learning sequences suited to children with varying degrees of hearing impairment, language-learning ability and academic achievement. The use of a hearing aid or cochlear implant is an important part of the hearing-impaired child's educational and social program.

The CID School provides a broad range of extracurricular activities, academics and nonacademic classes, among them computer, art and physical education. The CID Family Center combines instruction and counseling for parents with an initial nursery school experience for their children. Early intervention and diagnostic services are available.

CHURCHILL CENTER & SCHOOL

Day — Coed Ages 8-16

St Louis, MO 63131. 1021 Municipal Center Dr.
Tel: 314-997-4343. Fax: 314-997-2760.
www.churchillstl.org   E-mail: info@churchillstl.org
Sandra K. Gilligan, BS, MS, Dir. Anne Evers, Adm.
Conditions: Primary—Dx LD. IQ 90 and up.
Gen Acad. Gr 2-10. Feat—Computers Fine_Arts. Expected outcome: Return to local school (Avg length of stay: 3 yrs).
Adm: Appl fee: $75. Appl due: Rolling. On-campus interview.
Enr: 120. B 81. G 39.
Summer prgm: Day. Educ. 6 wks.
Est 1977. Nonprofit.

Churchill serves high-potential children with specific learning disabilities. The school's primary goals are to help children achieve to full academic potential and to prepare them for a successful return to a traditional classroom setting as soon as possible. Each student attends a 50-minute daily tutorial, and pupils receive small-group instruction in all other classes.

LOGOS SCHOOL
Day — Coed Ages 11-21

St Louis, MO 63132. 9137 Old Bonhomme Rd.
Tel: 314-997-7002. Fax: 314-997-6848.
www.logosschool.org   E-mail: skolker@logosschool.org
Kathy Boyd-Fenger, BA, MA, PhD, Head. **Stephanie Kolker,** Adm.
  Conditions: Primary—ADHD AN Anx Asp Bu CD Dc Dg Dx ED LD Mood OCD PDD Psy PTSD SP Sz TBI TS. **Sec**—Ap Au B/VI Db ID ODD ON S SA. **IQ 70 and up.**
  Col Prep. Underachiever. Gr 6-12. AP courses (Eng). **Feat**—Span Computers Ceramics Fine_Arts Mosaic_Art Mural_Painting. ACT: Avg 27.4. Interscholastic sports. **Expected outcome:** Return to local school (Avg length of stay: 18 mos).
  Therapy: Lang Occup Rec Speech. **Psychotherapy:** Art Group Indiv Parent. **Counseling:** Educ.
  Adm: Appl due: Year-round.
  Enr: 150. B 90. G 60. **Fac:** 23 (Full-time).
  Tui '08-'09: Day $22,000/yr (+$2000). **Aid:** School.
  Plant val $600,000. Acres 5. Bldgs 2. Class rms 13. Libs 1. Sci labs 1. Auds 1. Art studios 2. Gyms 2. Fields 1. Comp labs 1.
  Est 1970. Nonprofit.

Logos provides a program of therapeutic counseling, accredited academics and parental involvement for students who have had difficulty succeeding in traditional school settings. Features include a favorable student-teacher ratio, individualized education, and therapeutic treatment plans specializing in ADHD, learning disabilities, behavioral disorders and emotional problems. Boys and girls perform 120 hours of community service prior to graduation. Students may enroll at any time during the 12-month school year.

THE MIRIAM SCHOOL
Day — Coed Ages 4-14

St Louis, MO 63119. 501 Bacon Ave.
Tel: 314-968-5225. Fax: 314-968-7338.
www.miriamschool.org   E-mail: admissions@miriamschool.org
Joan Holland, MEd, Dir. **Megan Gibson,** Adm.
  Conditions: Primary—ADHD APD Apr Asp Dc Dg Dx LD Multi NLD.
    Sec—Ap Au D TS. **IQ 90 and up. Not accepted**—AN Bu CD DS ED ID MR Psy PTSD PW SA SO SP Sz.
  Gen Acad. Gr PS-8. **Feat**—Study_Skills. **Expected outcome:** Return to local

school (Avg length of stay: 3-5 yrs).
Therapy: Lang Occup Speech.
Adm: Appl fee: $65. Appl due: Year-round.
Enr: 96. **Fac:** 13 (Full-time). Spec ed 10. Lay 3.
Tui '12-'13: Day $24,000/sch yr. **Aid:** School 55 ($660,000). **Summer prgm:** Day.
Educ. Rec. Tui Day $600/2-wk ses. 4 wks.
Laptop prgm Gr PS-8.
Est 1951. Nonprofit. **Spons:** Miriam Foundation.

Miriam School conducts a program for children with average to above-average intellectual potential who evidence mild to moderate learning problems. An individualized learning approach emphasizes the development of academic, social and self-advocacy skills. The program is highly structured and addresses basic academic skills and appropriate social and classroom behavior.

The school also provides parental classes and a broad community program, serving as a consultant to preschools, daycare centers and public school systems to help children with developmental problems. The usual duration of enrollment is three to five years.

RAINBOW CENTER DAY SCHOOL

Day — Coed Ages 3-21

Blue Springs, MO 64015. 900 NW Woods Chapel Rd.
Tel: 816-229-3869. Fax: 816-229-4260.
www.rainbow-center.org E-mail: peggy.britton@rainbow-center.org
Marilu W. Herrick, MS, CCC-SLP, Exec Dir.
 Conditions: Primary—ADHD Ap Apr Asp Au CP DS Dx LD ID PDD S.
 Sec—As CD ED Ep Mood OCD ODD ON PW SA TS. **IQ 40-115.**
Gen Acad. Ungraded.
Therapy: Hear Lang Music Occup Phys Speech.
Enr: 116. **Fac:** 9 (Full-time). Spec ed 8. Lay 1.
Summer prgm: Day. Educ. Rec. Ther. 8 wks.
Est 1977. Nonprofit.

The school provides therapeutic intervention within an academic setting for children and young adults with autism, cerebral palsy, Down syndrome, learning disabilities, and other behavioral and developmental disabilities. Individualized programming and a favorable student-teacher ratio are program characteristics. In addition to its school-day programming, Rainbow Center provides before- and after-school care and a summer session.

RIVENDALE CENTER FOR AUTISM
AND INSTITUTE OF LEARNING

Day — Coed Ages 3-18

Springfield, MO 65807. 1613 W Elfindale Dr.
Tel: 417-864-7921. Fax: 417-864-6024.
www.rivendaleinstitute.com E-mail: lbarboa@sesi-schools.com
 Nearby locations: 1720 W Elfindale Dr, Springfield 65807.

Brooke Violante, Dir. **Linda Barboa,** PhD, Educ Dir.
Conditions: Primary—ADHD Ap APD Apr Asp Au Dc Dg Dx Ep LD Multi
   NLD PDD S TBI. **Sec**—ED OCD TS.
Gen Acad. Gr PS-12. **Expected outcome:** Return to local school (Avg length
   of stay: 2-3 yrs).
Therapy: Lang Music Occup Speech. **Psychotherapy:** Art. **Counseling:** Educ.
Adm: Appl due: Year-round. On-campus interview.
Enr: 38 (Cap: 40). **Fac:** 8 (Full-time). Spec ed 3. Lay 5.
Bldgs 2 (100% ADA). Class rms 10.
Est 1985. Inc.

Rivendale provides a year-round alternative to public education for students with learn-ing differences or autism. Individual instruction is designed to meet each child's needs for development in academic, cognitive, perceptual, language and personal/social areas. Student-teacher ratios do not exceed 8:1 in the general classrooms, or 2:1 in the classes for children with autism. Rivendale utilizes applied behavioral analysis for children with autism.

An after-school program offers diagnosis and remediation for language development and learning disabilities, as well as for all academic areas. An instrumental enrichment program for junior high and high school students supplements traditional course work.

The Center for Autism occupies down the street from the Institute of Learning at 1720 W. Elfindale Dr.

ST. JOSEPH INSTITUTE FOR THE DEAF

Bdg — Coed Ages 5-15; Day — Coed 3-15

Chesterfield, MO 63017. 1809 Clarkson Rd.
Tel: 636-532-3211, 866-751-3211. TTY: 636-532-3211. Fax: 636-532-4560.
www.sjid.org   E-mail: mkrug@sjid.org
Dawn Gettemeier, BA, MAEd, Int Prin.
   Conditions: Primary—D. **Sec**—ADHD Apr Asp CLP Dx. **IQ 90 and up.**
   Gen Acad. Gr PS-8. **Feat**—Computers Studio_Art. **Expected outcome:**
      Return to local school (Avg length of stay: 3-5 yrs).
   Therapy: Hear Lang Speech. **Psychotherapy:** Indiv.
   Enr: 79 (Cap: 90). Bdg 10. Day 69. B 46. G 33. **Fac:** 27 (Full 23, Part 4). Spec
      ed 23. Lay 4.
   Summer prgm: Day. Educ. Ther. 4 wks.
   Est 1837. Nonprofit. Roman Catholic.

A private Catholic school for severely and profoundly hearing-impaired children, the institute offers an educational program that includes speech, language and regular aca-demic courses, taught through speech reading and auditory-oral development. Children are mainstreamed into regular educational facilities as they progress, typically after three to five years.

Early intervention programs for children (birth to age 3) and counseling for both parents and students are also available. In addition, clinical services are in place for children and adults.

MONTANA

ELK MOUNTAIN ACADEMY
Bdg — Boys Ages 14-18

Heron, MT 59844. 54 Serenity Ln, PO Box 330.
Tel: 406-847-4400. Fax: 406-847-0034.
www.elkmountainacademy.org   E-mail: info@elkmountainacademy.org
Loretta Olding, Exec Dir. **Kim Wright,** Educ Dir.
    Conditions: Primary—ADHD CD ED Mood OCD ODD Subst. **Sec**—Dx SP.
    Not accepted—SO.
    Gen Acad. Gr 8-12. **Expected outcome:** Return to local school (Avg length of
    stay: 1 yr).
    Psychotherapy: Fam Group Indiv. **Counseling:** Educ.
    Enr: 26 (Cap: 26).
    Est 1994. Nonprofit.

Based on the Twelve-Step Program, this therapeutic boarding school treats boys for an average of one year. The program emphasizes academic success, spiritual awareness, the ability to deal with social and emotional obstacles, and strategies to overcome addictive behavior.

NEBRASKA

MADONNA SCHOOL
Day — Coed Ages 5-21

Omaha, NE 68104. 6402 N 71st Plz.
Tel: 402-556-1883. Fax: 402-556-7332.
www.madonnaschool.org   E-mail: murban@madonnaschool.org
Jay Dunlap, Pres. Michelle Urban, Prin.
Conditions: Primary—ADHD Asp Au Dx ED Ep LD ID ON SB. **Sec**—Ap CD D Mood OCD TS. **IQ 30-75.**
Voc. Ungraded. On-Job Trng. Shelt_Workshop. **Feat**—Sci Computers Soc_ Stud Relig Music Home_Ec.
Therapy: Lang Music Speech. **Counseling:** Voc.
Adm: Appl fee: $0. Appl due: Rolling. On-campus interview.
Enr: 58 (Cap: 80). **Fac:** 10 (Full 5, Part 5). Spec ed 10.
Tui '12-'13: Day $4000/sch yr (+$123). **Aid:** School.
Est 1961. Nonprofit. Roman Catholic.

Children with mild or moderate levels of mental retardation or specific severe learning disabilities may enroll at the school. Madonna also can accept students with minimal emotional disturbances and developmental disorders. Programming emphasizes academic and social adaptation. The school operates a work site used for vocational evaluation: Students age 15 and older participate in a community vocational placement.

NEVADA

NEW HORIZONS ACADEMY
Day — Coed Ages 5-18

Las Vegas, NV 89146. 6701 W Charleston Blvd.
Tel: 702-876-1181. Fax: 702-365-7807.
www.nhalv.org   E-mail: info@nhalv.org
Jody Mayville, MAEd, Exec Dir.
Conditions: Primary—ADHD Anx APD Ar Asp Au CP Db Dc Dg Dpx Dx HI
   LD Mood ID Multi NLD OCD PDD PTSD S SB TBI TS. **Sec**—As. **IQ 72-**
   130. Not accepted—AN B/VI Bu C CD D ED ODD ON Psy PW SA SO SP
   Subst Sz.
Gen Acad. Gr K-12. **Feat**—Comp_Sci Govt Studio_Art Music. **Expected out-**
   come: Return to local school.
Counseling: Educ Voc.
Adm: Appl fee: $100. Appl due: Year-round. On-campus interview.
Enr: 65 (Cap: 100). **Fac:** 9 (Full-time). Spec ed 7. Lay 2.
Tui '12-'13: Day $13,500-14,500/sch yr (+$1000).
Bldgs 100% ADA. Lib 3000 vols. Art studios 1. Fields 1. Basketball courts 1.
   Tennis courts 1. Comp labs 2.
Est 1974. Nonprofit.

New Horizons offers specific educational programs for students with such learning differences as processing difficulties and attentional problems. Multi-aged classes enable the
school to place children according to academic, social and emotional needs, not simply
chronological age.

NEW HAMPSHIRE

DAVENPORT SCHOOL

Bdg — Girls Ages 13-18

Jefferson, NH 03583. 30 Davenport Rd, PO Box 209.
Tel: 603-586-4328. Fax: 603-586-7867.
www.nafi.com   E-mail: jenniferaltieri@nafi.com
Jennifer Altieri, Prgm Dir.
Conditions: Primary—Anx ED Mood PTSD SA. **IQ 70 and up.**
Gen Acad. Underachiever. Voc. Gr 8-12. Feat—Fr. **Expected outcome:**
Return to local school (Avg length of stay: 2-8 mos).
Therapy: Milieu Rec. **Psychotherapy:** Fam Group Indiv. **Counseling:** Educ
Nutrition Voc.
Adm: Appl fee: $0. Appl due: Year-round. On-campus interview.
Enr: 10 (Cap: 15). **Fac:** 4. Spec ed 3. Lay 1.
Tui '10-'11: Bdg $356/day.
Acres 13. Bldgs 3. Dorms 1. Dorm rms 6. Class rms 3. Libs 1. Ropes crses 1.
Comp labs 1.
Nonprofit. **Spons:** NFI North.

This residential special education school serves girls with various emotional and behavioral special needs. Individualized programming addresses adaptive coping skills, appropriate peer and family relations, and community living and social skills. Counseling and therapeutic services are available.

GRANITE HILL SCHOOL

Day — Coed Ages 11-21

Newport, NH 03773. 135 Elm St, PO Box 25.
Tel: 603-863-0697. Fax: 603-863-1574.
www.granitehillschool.org   E-mail: principal@granitehillschool.org
Mark C. Bissell, BS, MA, PhD, CEO. Danielle Paranto, BS, MEd, Prin.
Conditions: Primary—ADHD CD ED OCD ODD SA. **Sec**—Anx Asp Dx LD
Mood NLD PTSD SO SP TS. **IQ 90-125. Not accepted**—Psy Subst Sz.
Gen Acad. Voc. Gr 6-12. Man_Arts & Shop. On-Job Trng. Support_Employ.
Therapy: Lang Phys Speech. **Psychotherapy:** Group Indiv. **Counseling:**
Educ Voc.
Enr: 30. **Fac:** 6 (Full 4, Part 2). Spec ed 3. Lay 3.
Tui '12-'13: Day $43,562/sch yr (+$1000/sch yr). Clinic $56 (Therapy)/half hr.
Summer prgm: Day. Educ. Tui Day $5317. 7 wks.
Est 1996. Nonprofit. **Spons:** Orion Group.

GHS provides a specialized therapeutic environment for students whose academic progress has been slowed by social difficulties. Typically, pupils have not previously been in a placement outside the home or traditional school environment. Social skills training is integrated into the curriculum to develop students' moral reasoning, anger management and problem solving skills. The school places emphasis on interactive and experiential learning in all subjects.

Granite Hill's residential program encourages social interaction through such recreational activities as downhill skiing, kayaking, swimming, ice skating and team sports. Individual occupational, physical and speech therapy is available for an additional fee.

HAMPSHIRE COUNTRY SCHOOL
Bdg — Boys Ages 8-18

Rindge, NH 03461. 28 Patey Cir.
Tel: 603-899-3325. Fax: 603-899-6521.
www.hampshirecountryschool.org
  E-mail: admissions@hampshirecountryschool.net
Bernd Foecking, BA, MEd, Head. **William Dickerman,** Adm.
  Conditions: Primary—Asp LD NLD. **Sec**—ADHD ED OCD SP TS. **IQ 115 and up.**
  Col Prep. Gen Acad. Underachiever. Gr 3-12. **Feat**—Fr Anat & Physiol Environ_Sci 20th-Century_Hist. **Expected outcome:** Return to local school (Avg length of stay: 3-4 yrs).
  Adm: Appl fee: $0. Appl due: Rolling. On-campus interview.
  Enr: 23. **Fac:** 10 (Full 9, Part 1). Lay 10.
  Tui '12-'13: Bdg $49,000/sch yr (+$1000).
  Plant val $2,000,000. Acres 1700. Bldgs 7. Dorms 4. Dorm rms 20. Class rms 7. Lib 3000 vols. Sci labs 1. Theaters 1. Music studios 1. Fields 1. Tennis courts 1. Comp labs 1. Comp/stud: 1:5.
  Est 1948. Nonprofit.

This small boarding school serves boys of high ability who have not succeeded in other settings, often due to problems related to this advanced ability. Students typically enroll at middle school age and remain at the school for three or four years before transferring to a larger, more competitive school, although some complete their high school studies at HCS. The school can accommodate such special needs as hyperactivity, difficulty in dealing with peers or adults, unusually timid or fearful behavior, school phobia, nonverbal learning disability and Asperger's syndrome. A low student-teacher ratio meets the needs of students who require extra structure and attention.

Located on 1700 acres of farm and woodland, the school offers an activities program that includes recreational sports, board games, farm animal care, hiking, canoeing, sledding and skiing.

THE HUNTER SCHOOL
Bdg and Day — Coed Ages 5-15

Rumney, NH 03266. 768 Doetown Rd, PO Box 600.
Tel: 603-786-9427. Fax: 603-786-2221.
www.hunterschool.org   E-mail: info@hunterschool.org
Laurie Ferris, Adm.
  Conditions: Primary—ADHD Asp ED ID ODD PDD S TS. **Sec**—Anx As Au

CD Db Dc Dg Dx Mood OCD PTSD SA SP. **IQ 90 and up. Not accepted—** B/VI Hemo SC.
Gen Acad. Gr K-8. **Feat**—Studio_Art Music Health. **Expected outcome:** Return to local school (Avg length of stay: 1-3 yrs).
Therapy: Lang Occup Phys Speech. **Psychotherapy:** Group Indiv.
Adm: Appl due: Rolling. On-campus interview.
Enr: 28 (Cap: 28). Bdg 10. Day 18. B 22. G 6. **Fac:** 6 (Full 5, Part 1). Spec ed 1. Lay 5.
Summer prgm: Bdg & Day. Educ. Rec. Ther. 6 wks.
Acres 137. Dorms 1.
Est 1998. Nonprofit.

Situated on a rural, 137-acre tract, Hunter serves children with attention deficit disorder and, frequently, coexisting disabilities. Staff formulate an individual education program for the student following an initial comprehensive academic and social assessment. Previous educational experiences, previous testing and input from the pupil's family are all taken into consideration.

Hunter's residential component features such wilderness experiences as hiking, camping and snowshoeing, as well as such athletic options as skiing, swimming, skating and team sports. Nearby Dartmouth College and Plymouth State College provide cultural options, while students may also participate in community-based pursuits and recreational activities.

SECOND START ALTERNATIVE HIGH SCHOOL
Day — Coed Ages 14-18

Concord, NH 03301. 450 N State St.
Tel: 603-225-3318. Fax: 603-226-0842.
www.second-start.org   E-mail: ahs@second-start.org
Ted Lambrukos, Dir.
  Conditions: Primary—ADHD Dx ED LD ODD. **Sec**—ID. **IQ 75 and up.**
  Gen Acad. Gr 9-12. On-Job Trng. Support_Employ. **Expected outcome:** Return to local school (Avg length of stay: 1-2 yrs).
  Adm: On-campus interview.
  Enr: 48. B 25. G 23. **Fac:** 6 (Full 5, Part 1). Spec ed 2. Lay 4.
  Aid: State 48 (100% of tui).
  Est 1979. Nonprofit.

The AHS program at Second Start serves children with emotional handicaps and mild learning disabilities that have interfered with their functioning in a traditional educational setting. Treatment strives to combine an individual academic and counseling program with group work and small classes. The primary objective is to develop basic academic skills, thereby improving self-image and social development. AHS does not grant diplomas to its graduating seniors; instead, Second Start works with the sending school district to arrange course credit and the high school of origin issues a diploma.

A transitional employment and training program, which aims to develop positive job-related attitudes and behaviors, is available. Educational counseling and an alcohol and drug abuse program are also offered. The usual length of enrollment for adolescents at AHS is one to two years.

NEW JERSEY

ALPHA SCHOOL

Day — Coed Ages 3-21

Jackson, NJ 08527. 2210 W County Line Rd, Ste 1.
Tel: 732-370-1150. Fax: 732-901-0736.
www.alphaschool.com   E-mail: deturom@alphaschool.com
Monica Walsh DeTuro, BA, MA, Prin.
  Conditions: Primary—ADHD Anx Asp Au CD DS Dx ED Ep LD Mood ID
    Multi OCD PDD Psy PW S SP Sz TBI TS. Sec—AN Ap Apr As B/VI Bu C
    CP D Db Dc Dg IP MD MS Nf ON SB.
  Gen Acad. Ungraded. On-Job Trng. Feat—Computers Studio_Art Music
    Health. Expected outcome: Graduation.
  Therapy: Hear Lang Music Occup Perceptual-Motor Phys Speech.
  Adm: Appl due: Rolling.
  Enr: 75 (Cap: 100). B 60. G 15. Fac: 12 (Full 11, Part 1). Spec ed 10. Lay 2.
  Aid: State 75 (100% of tui).
  Est 1980. Inc.

The school program is designed to remediate problems in academic achievement, motor skills, and speech and language for children with various special needs. Individualized Education Programs include adaptive physical education and a sensorimotor integration program. Social counseling is provided. Accepted students enroll at no cost, as tuition is paid by the student's sending school district.

Similar programs operate at Harbor School in Eatontown (240 Broad St., 07724) and at Gateway School in Carteret (60 High St., 07008).

THE ARC KOHLER SCHOOL

Day — Coed Ages 3-11

Mountainside, NJ 07092. 1137 Globe Ave.
Tel: 973-518-0021. Fax: 973-518-0636.
www.arckohlerschool.org   E-mail: soregan@arckohlerschool.org
Frank X. Caragher, BA, MEd, Actg Prin. Shannon O'Regan, Educ Dir.
  Conditions: Primary—ADHD Dc Dg Dx LD ID PDD PW. Sec—B/VI CD D Db
    ED OCD ON TS. Not accepted—C.
  Gen Acad. Gr PS-5.
  Therapy: Lang Occup Phys Speech.
  Enr: 60 (Cap: 75). B 35. G 25. Fac: 6 (Full-time).
  Aid: State 60 (100% of tui). Summer prgm: Day. Educ. 7 wks.
  Est 1963. Nonprofit. Spons: Arc of Union County.

A program of the Arc of Union County, the school follows a diagnostic-prescriptive teaching approach that employs several developmental profiles. A multidisciplinary team of teachers, therapists and other educational professionals formulates and implements an individualized instructional program for each student. Daily and weekly collaborative schedules then arise from the instructional program.

Active learning through sensorimotor and psychomotor experiences and play characterizes the curriculum. Speech, physical and occupational therapies form an integral part of the curriculum. An extended school year option is available, and children may enroll in the summer program only.

The sending school district typically pays tuition fees.

THE ARCHWAY SCHOOLS

Day — Coed Ages 3-21

Atco, NJ 08004. 280 Jackson Rd, PO Box 668.
Tel: 856-767-5757. Fax: 856-768-5562.
www.archwayprograms.org   E-mail: info@archwayprograms.org
   Nearby locations: 185 Raymond Ave, Evesham 08053.
Douglas Otto, Dir. **Robert Ruberton,** Adm.
   Conditions: Primary—As Au CD ED Multi ON. **Sec**—ADHD B/VI D Dx ID LD OCD ODD Psy S Sz.
   Gen Acad. Voc. Ungraded. Culinary. Hort. On-Job Trng. Shelt_Workshop. Support_Employ. **Feat**—Computers Studio_Art Music. Interscholastic sports.
   Expected outcome: Return to local school.
   Therapy: Aqua Hear Lang Occup Phys Speech. **Psychotherapy:** Art Group Indiv. **Counseling:** Educ Voc.
   Adm: Appl fee: $0. Appl due: Rolling. On-campus interview.
   Enr: 191 (Cap: 235). **Fac:** 45. Spec ed 35. Lay 10.
   Tui '11-'12: Day $34,380/sch yr. **Aid:** State. **Summer prgm:** Day. Educ. Tui Day $191/day. 7 wks.
   Acres 45. Bldgs 4 (100% ADA). Libs 2. Art studios 2. Gyms 2. Fields 2. Pools 2. Comp labs 3.
   Est 1965. Nonprofit.

Archway offers treatment for boys and girls with autism or learning, language, behavioral or multiple disabilities through highly structured, individual programs of education and therapy. Educational and personal counseling is available to all clients. A special-education program serves preschoolers.

The upper school (ages 8-21) occupies a separate campus in Evesham.

BANYAN SCHOOL

Day — Coed Ages 6-18

Fairfield, NJ 07004. 12 Hollywood Ave.
Tel: 973-439-1919. Fax: 973-439-1396.
www.banyanschool.com   E-mail: msaunders@banyanschool.com
   Nearby locations: 471 Main St, Little Falls 07424.
Mary Jo Saunders, MA, Dir.
   Conditions: Primary—ADHD APD Dx LD. **Sec**—AN As Asp B/VI Bu C D Db Dc Dg Hemo OCD PW SC SP TS. **IQ 75-130. Not accepted**—Anx CD ED

Mood ODD Psy PTSD SA SO Sz.
Gen Acad. Gr 1-12. **Feat**—Sci Soc_Stud Studio_Art Drama Music Life_Skills.
Therapy: Occup Speech. **Psychotherapy:** Group.
Adm: Appl due: Year-round.
Enr: 98. B 76. G 22.
Tui '10-'11: Day $32,868/sch yr. **Aid:** School. **Summer prgm:** Day. Educ. 4 wks.
Est 1993. Nonprofit.

Banyan offers a highly structured elementary and middle school program for students of average to above-average intelligence with learning disabilities. The elementary program is designed to fully develop basic academic and social skills. The middle school program focuses upon the application of these skills while emphasizing organizational and study techniques. Banyan also provides therapy and assists pupils with social skills development.

Banyan's high school division, located in Little Falls, opened in fall 2006.

BROOKFIELD SCHOOLS
Day — Coed Ages 5-21

Cherry Hill, NJ 08034. 1009 Berlin Rd.
Tel: 856-795-8228. Fax: 856-795-3009.
www.brookfieldschools.org   E-mail: dkvh@comcast.net
   Nearby locations: PO Box 200, Blackwood 08012; 800 Kings Hwy, Haddon Heights 08035.
Dorothy K. Van Horn, MA, EdD, Exec Dir. **Ed Travis,** Adm.
   Conditions: Primary—ADHD Anx Asp Bu ED LD Mood OCD ODD SP Subst TS. **Sec**—AN Db ID Psy SA Sz. **IQ 75-135.**
   Col Prep. Gen Acad. Underachiever. Voc. Gr K-12. Culinary. Hort. On-Job Trng. **Expected outcome:** Return to local school (Avg length of stay: 1-4 yrs).
   Therapy: Occup Phys Speech. **Psychotherapy:** Art Equine Group Indiv Parent. **Counseling:** Educ Voc.
Adm: Appl fee: $0. Appl due: Year-round. On-campus interview.
Enr: 110 (Cap: 140). B 70. G 40. **Fac:** 32. Spec ed 24. Lay 8.
Aid: State 110 (100% of tui). **Summer prgm:** Day. Educ. 4 wks.
Bldgs 2 (40% ADA). Libs 1. Auds 1. Gyms 1. Fields 1. Comp labs 2.
Est 1975. Nonprofit.

Brookfield Schools accommodate boys and girls who are experiencing personality disorders or adjustment or behavioral problems. Programs are Brookfield Elementary (ages 5-14), which operates in Haddon Heights (856-546-1388); Brookfield Academy (ages 14-20), which is conducted on the Cherry Hill campus; and Transition to College, a program based at Camden County College in Blackwood (856-401-2642) that enables students to fulfill their high school graduation requirements while concurrently taking college courses.

Pupils enroll from Atlantic, Burlington, Camden, Gloucester and surrounding counties. The sending school district pays all tuition costs.

CALAIS SCHOOL

Day — Coed Ages 5-21

Whippany, NJ 07981. 45 Highland Ave.
Tel: 973-884-2030. Fax: 973-884-0460.
www.thecalaisschool.org
 E-mail: josephine.mucciolo@thecalaisschool.org
David F. Leitner, LCSW, Exec Dir. **Diane Manno,** EdD, Prin.
 Conditions: Primary—ADHD Anx Asp Au Dx ED LD Mood OCD PDD PTSD
 SP TS. **Sec**—AN As Bu CP Db ON.
 Col Prep. Gen Acad. Gr K-12. On-Job Trng. **Feat**—Span Fine_Arts Perform-
 ing_Arts.
 Psychotherapy: Group Indiv. **Counseling:** Educ.
 Adm: Appl due: Rolling. On-campus interview.
 Enr: 160. B 126. G 34. **Fac:** 42 (Full-time). Spec ed 42.
 Summer prgm: Day. Educ. Rec. Ther. 4 wks.
 Est 1970. Nonprofit.

This school for special-needs children offers a highly structured behavioral modification program and individualized instruction to address the academic, emotional, social and
psychological needs of the student. A team of cognitive-behavioral therapists provide both
emotional support and cognitive strategies for dealing with stressful situations.

Special programs offered at the school include speech and language therapy (in both
diagnostic and remedial formats), therapeutic interventions, prescriptive learning services,
prevocational training and transitional education programs.

CAMBRIDGE SCHOOL

Day — Coed Ages 5-14

Pennington, NJ 08534. 100 Straube Center Blvd.
Tel: 609-730-9553. Fax: 609-730-9584.
www.thecambridgeschool.org
 E-mail: admissions@thecambridgeschool.org
Deborah C. Peters, BA, MA, Head. **Melody Lorenz,** Adm.
 Conditions: Primary—ADHD APD Dc Dg Dx LD S. **Sec**—Anx Ap Apr Asp
 Dpx NLD. **IQ 90 and up. Not accepted**—Au CD ED ID Mood MR ODD Psy
 SO Subst Sz.
 Gen Acad. Gr K-8. **Feat**—Computers Studio_Art Drama Music.
 Therapy: Lang Occup Speech. **Psychotherapy:** Art. **Counseling:** Educ.
 Adm: Appl fee: $475. Appl due: Rolling.
 Enr: 125. **Fac:** 27. Spec ed 27.
 Tui '12-'13: Day $39,175/sch yr. **Aid:** School. State. Educ. 4 wks.
 Est 2001. Inc.

The school provides a specially formulated educational environment for children who
have been diagnosed with primary language-based learning differences. Instruction is based
on the Orton-Gillingham method, and it incorporates the Wilson Reading and Lindamood-
Bell learning processes. The individualized, comprehensive, multisensory and structured
curriculum is representative of that found at a traditional elementary and middle school.

CHANCELLOR ACADEMY

Day — Coed Ages 11-18

Pompton Plains, NJ 07444. 157 West Pky, PO Box 338.
Tel: 973-835-4989. Fax: 973-835-0768.
www.chancellorhs.com E-mail: dfrench@chancellorhs.com
Kevin McNaught, Co-Dir. **Christopher Pagano,** Co-Dir.
Conditions: Primary—ED.
Gen Acad. Voc. Gr 6-12. Culinary. Hort. Man_Arts & Shop. **Feat**—Span Environ_Sci Marine_Bio/Sci Computers Film Photog Studio_Art Video_Production Drama Music Health. Interscholastic sports. **Expected outcome:** Return to local school.
Psychotherapy: Fam Group.
Enr: 96. **Fac:** 9.
Est 1983. Inc.

The academy enrolls middle and high school students with emotional or social issues who have not been successful in traditional public schools. Opportunities for active participation in student government, community service and interscholastic athletics are available. A varied curriculum and daily individual and group counseling are integral parts of the program. Staff seek to promote emotional maturity, social development and academic progress. Tuition rates are determined by the state.

COLLIER HIGH SCHOOL

Day — Coed Ages 11-18

Wickatunk, NJ 07765. 160 Conover Rd.
Tel: 732-946-4771. Fax: 732-946-3519.
www.collierhighschool.com
    E-mail: contactcollier@collieryouthservices.org
Sr. Deb Drago, MSW, Dir. **Bob Szafranski,** Adm.
    Conditions: Primary—ADHD Anx Asp ED Mood OCD ODD PTSD SA Subst.
    Sec—B/VI. **IQ 70 and up. Not accepted**—CD Psy.
    Col Prep. Gen Acad. Voc. Gr 6-12. Culinary. Hort. Man_Arts & Shop. On-Job Trng. **Feat**—British_Lit Mythology Span Calc Environ_Sci Psych Philos Photog Sculpt Drama Music Dance. **Expected outcome:** Return to local school (Avg length of stay: 18 mos).
    Psychotherapy: Fam Group Indiv.
    Adm: Appl fee: $0. Appl due: Year-round. On-campus interview.
    Enr: 110. B 55. G 55. **Fac:** 30 (Full-time).
    Aid: State 110 (100% of tui). **Summer prgm:** Day. Educ. Rec. Ther. 6 wks.
    Acres 260. Bldgs 4 (100% ADA). Class rms 30. Libs 1. Sci labs 1. Art studios 1. Music studios 1. Dance studios 1. Gyms 1. Fields 1. Courts 1. Pools 1. Comp labs 1.
    Est 1927. Nonprofit. **Spons:** Collier Services.

Emotionally disturbed adolescents follow individualized educational programs and receive individual, group and family counseling at the school. The program highlights both

college and career preparation. Various extracurricular activities supplement academic work. The average duration of enrollment is 18 months.
The sending school district pays all tuition fees.

COMMUNITY HIGH SCHOOL

Day — Coed Ages 14-21

Teaneck, NJ 07666. 1135 Teaneck Rd.
Tel: 201-862-1796. Fax: 201-862-1791.
www.communityhighschool.org
  E-mail: tbraunstein@communityhighschool.org
Toby Braunstein, MA, Dir.
  Conditions: Primary—ADHD Dx LD. **IQ 90 and up.**
  Col Prep. Underachiever. Gr 9-12. **Feat**—Span Psych Photog Studio_Art Video_Production Drama Music Bus Journ. Interscholastic sports.
  Expected outcome: Graduation.
  Therapy: Lang Speech. **Psychotherapy:** Indiv.
  Adm: Appl fee: $65. Appl due: Rolling. On-campus interview.
  Enr: 185. **Fac:** 80 (Full-time).
  Tui '09-'10: Day $40,901/sch yr.
  Sci labs 2. Art studios 1. Music studios 1. Gyms 1.
  Est 1967. Nonprofit.

Community School provides a traditional college preparatory program geared to students with learning and attentional difficulties. One-on-one and small-class instruction addresses SAT preparation, remediation, study skills, and tutoring in reading, language and speech. The curriculum includes courses in computers, photography, graphics, industrial arts, typing and driver education. Interscholastic and intramural sports are also available.

An enriched elementary program, conducted on West Forest Avenue (separately listed), closely resembles that of the high school.

THE COMMUNITY SCHOOL

Day — Coed Ages 5-14

Teaneck, NJ 07666. 11 W Forest Ave.
Tel: 201-837-8070. Fax: 201-837-6799.
www.communityschool.k12.nj.us   E-mail: office@communityschool.us
Isabel Shoukas, Dir. **Christine Gill,** Adm.
  Conditions: Primary—ADHD Dc Dg Dx LD. **Sec**—Anx Ap Apr As Asp Ep Mood OCD SP. **IQ 90 and up.**
  Gen Acad. Gr K-8. **Feat**—Computers. **Expected outcome:** Return to local school (Avg length of stay: 5 yrs).
  Therapy: Lang Perceptual-Motor Speech. **Psychotherapy:** Group. **Counseling:** Educ.
  Adm: Appl fee: $65. Appl due: Rolling. On-campus interview.
  Enr: 136. B 88. G 48.
  Aid: State.

Est 1968. Nonprofit.

Community School offers an elementary and junior high school program for students of average to above-average intelligence with specific learning disabilities, attentional disorders, hyperactivity and accompanying mild behavior problems. The curriculum is individualized to meet students' needs and learning styles. Small classes and close supervision are important characteristics of the program. Extracurricular activities and field trips round out the program.

Local sending school districts typically pay tuition costs.

THE CRAIG SCHOOL

Day — Coed Ages 8-19

Mountain Lakes, NJ 07046. 10 Tower Hill Rd.
Tel: 973-334-1295. Fax: 973-334-1299.
www.craigschool.org   E-mail: info@craigschool.org
   Nearby locations: 200 Comly Rd, Lincoln Park 07035.
Eric M. Caparulo, EdD, Head. **Marci Taub,** Adm.
   Conditions: Primary—ADHD Dx LD. **Sec**—Dc Dg. **IQ 90 and up.**
   Col Prep. Gen Acad. Gr 3-12. **Feat**—Creative_Writing Lat Span Psych
   Art_Hist Studio_Art Bus Public_Speak Health. SAT/ACT prep. **Expected**
   outcome: Return to local school (Avg length of stay: 4 yrs).
   Therapy: Lang Occup Speech. **Counseling:** Voc.
   Adm: Appl fee: $50. Appl due: Rolling. On-campus interview.
   Enr: 151. **Fac:** 34 (Full 28, Part 6). Spec ed 33. Lay 1.
   Summer prgm: Day. Educ. Rec. Tui Day $600-1425. 2-3 wks.
   Est 1980. Nonprofit.

Craig provides an education for children with learning disabilities in a structured setting. Taught in small classes, the core curriculum is supplemented by educational field trips and assemblies. Staff set individual goals and objectives for each child and then monitor progress closely, with parent-teacher conferences held regularly. The program strengthens social skills and self-esteem throughout the program and reinforces them through a mentor system. Consistent, positive behavior management is employed. High school pupils satisfy a 20-hour annual community service requirement.

The lower school (grades 3-8) operates in Mountain Lakes, while the high school (grades 9-12) occupies separate quarters in Lincoln Park (973-305-8086).

DOROTHY B. HERSH HIGH SCHOOL

Day — Coed Ages 14-21

Tinton Falls, NJ 07712. 1158 Wayside Rd.
Tel: 732-493-3563. Fax: 732-493-3427.
www.arcofmonmouth.org/hersh   E-mail: info@arcofmonmouth.org
   Conditions: Primary—DS ID. **Sec**—ADHD As Au CD Dx ED LD OCD ON
   PDD S. **IQ 30-85.**
   Voc. Ungraded. On-Job Trng. Shelt_Workshop. **Feat**—Studio_Art Speech.

Therapy: Occup Phys Speech. **Psychotherapy:** Indiv. **Counseling:** Voc.
Adm: On-campus interview.
Enr: 19. B 11. G 8.
Aid: State 19 (100% of tui). **Summer prgm:** Day. Educ. 6 wks.
Est 1949. Nonprofit. **Spons:** Arc of Monmouth.

Hersh High School provides academic and vocational training for students with intellectual and developmental disabilities. The school seeks to develop in pupils the skills and attitudes necessary to successfully function within the adult community. Hersh High's curriculum addresses academic skills, independent learning skills, social skills, vocational training, job exposure and employment training, supplemental services and family life education. An extended school year option is available.

Tuition and transportation charges are paid by the sending school district.

EAST MOUNTAIN SCHOOL
Bdg and Day — Coed Ages 12-19

Belle Mead, NJ 08502. 252 Rte 601.
Tel: 908-281-1415. Fax: 908-281-1663.
www.carrierclinic.org
Phillip A. Haramia, Exec Dir.
   Conditions: Primary—Asp CD ED OCD PDD Psy Sz. **Sec**—LD. **IQ 80 and up.**
   Col Prep. Gen Acad. Gr 7-12. **Feat**—Span Computers Robotics. **Expected outcome:** Return to local school (Avg length of stay: 2 yrs).
   Therapy: Speech. **Psychotherapy:** Fam Group Indiv.
   Enr: 80. Day 80.
   Aid: State 80 (100% of tui).
   Est 1981. Nonprofit. **Spons:** Carrier Clinic.

The school offers psycho-educational special education at the secondary school level for boys and girls with severe emotional disturbances. The school's goal is to return the student to an appropriate vocational or high school setting within two years.

A psycho-educational/humanistic approach to learning is utilized, and learning strategies are applied to instruction. Small educational classes emphasize individualized instruction. A status system reinforces positive behaviors. Group counseling with a psychologist, a social worker and a drug counselor is required, and parental support groups are available.

Tuition fees are typically paid by the sending school district.

THE FELICIAN SCHOOL FOR EXCEPTIONAL CHILDREN
Day — Coed Ages 3-21

Lodi, NJ 07644. 260 S Main St.
Tel: 973-777-5355. Fax: 973-777-0725.
www.fsec.org   E-mail: felicianschool@fsec.org
Sr. Rose Marie Smiglewski, CSSF, Dir.
   Conditions: Primary—Au CD DS ED ID. **Sec**—PW. **IQ 0-65.**

Gen Acad. Voc. Ungraded. On-Job Trng. **Expected outcome:** Graduation.
Therapy: Hear Lang Music Occup Phys Speech. **Psychotherapy:** Group
Indiv.
Enr: 121 (Cap: 150). B 75. G 46. **Fac:** 17 (Full-time). Spec ed 12. Lay 5.
Est 1971. Nonprofit.

The Felician School provides an educational program designed to offer individualized instruction to cognitively impaired children, as well as those with emotional disturbances and autism. Emphasis is placed on the development of cognitive, language-perceptual, self-help and social skills to prepare students for entrance into a more structured classroom setting.

A prevocational program offers training in specific job skills. Group physical education and individualized physical therapy aid students with neuro-developmental difficulties.

FIRST CHILDREN SCHOOL
Day — Coed Ages 3-12

Fanwood, NJ 07023. 330 South Ave.
Tel: 908-654-2470. Fax: 908-654-2483.
www.firstchildrenschools.com E-mail: info@firstchildrenschools.com
Kathleen Gorski, BS, MAT, MEd, Prin.
 Conditions: Primary—Anx Ap APD Apr Asp Au C CD CF CP D Db Dc Dg
  DS Dpx Dx ED Ep HI Hemo IP LD MD Mood ID Lk MS Multi Nf NLD OCD
  ODD ON PDD Psy PTSD S SB SC SP Sz TBI TS. **Sec**—AN Ar B/VI Bu
  CLP D-B PW SA SO Subst.
 Gen Acad. Underachiever. Gr PS-6. Hort. **Expected outcome:** Graduation.
 Therapy: Hear Lang Music Occup Perceptual-Motor Phys Play Rec Speech
  Visual. **Psychotherapy:** Art Dance. **Counseling:** Educ Nutrition Voc.
 Adm: Appl due: Year-round. On-campus interview.
 Enr: 60 (Cap: 85).
 Tui '12-'13: Day $344/day. **Summer prgm:** Day. Educ. Rec. Ther. Tui Day
  $344. 7 wks.
 Est 2009. Inc.

The school provides comprehensive preschool and primary educational programming for children with developmental delays related to autism, communicational, orthopedic, learning, behavioral or medical issues. A team of professionals and paraprofessionals works with students to address their educational, therapeutic, medical, physical, sensory, social/emotional and communicational needs, and also seeks to meet Individualized Education Program goals.

The curriculum, which follows state standards, features multisensory activities and course content that revolves around weekly themes. Field trips and special events reinforce classroom learning.

THE FORUM SCHOOL
Day — Coed Ages 3-16

Waldwick, NJ 07463. 107 Wyckoff Ave.
Tel: 201-444-5882. Fax: 201-444-4003.
www.theforumschool.com   E-mail: info@theforumschool.com
Alice Keener, MA, Dir. **Brian Detlefsen,** Prin. **Meryl Segal,** Adm.
   Conditions: Primary—ADHD Ap Apr Asp Au Dc Dg Dx ED OCD Psy Sz.
      Sec—Ep ID Mood ODD PW SP TS. **IQ 60-130.**
   Gen Acad. Underachiever. Ungraded. **Feat**—Computers. **Expected outcome:**
      Return to local school.
   Therapy: Lang Music Speech. **Psychotherapy:** Art. **Counseling:** Educ.
   Adm: Appl due: Year-round. On-campus interview.
   Enr: 120 (Cap: 150). **Fac:** 20 (Full 16, Part 4). Spec ed 16. Lay 4.
   Tui '11-'12: Day $44,627/sch yr. **Aid:** State. **Summer prgm:** Day. Educ. Tui
      Day $4672. 3½ wks.
   Est 1954. Nonprofit.

Forum offers therapeutic education for children diagnosed with one or more of the following conditions: autism, Asperger's syndrome, an emotional disturbance, ADD, ADHD or communicational disorders. The school offers a structured program to meet the student's individual needs. This includes the fostering of emotional, verbal, cognitive, physical and vocational growth. A primary goal is to increase the child's self-esteem while strengthening inner controls.

Through a psycho-educational approach, Forum aims to return students to a public school setting or to the least restrictive environment possible. A summer session is available only to students enrolled in the school-year program.

GARFIELD PARK ACADEMY
Day — Coed Ages 5-21

Willingboro, NJ 08046. 24 Glenolden Ln, PO Box 189.
Tel: 609-877-4111. Fax: 609-877-5551.
www.garfieldparkacademy.org   E-mail: smorse@garfieldparkacademy.org
Steven Morse, EdD, Exec Dir.
   Conditions: Primary—ADHD AN Anx Ap APD Apr As Asp Au Bu C CD CP
      Db Dc Dg Dpx Dx ED Ep LD MD Mood Multi Nf NLD OCD PDD Psy PTSD
      PW S SA SP Subst Sz TBI TS. **Sec**—ID. **IQ 65 and up.**
   Col Prep. Gen Acad. Voc. Gr K-12. Culinary. Hort. Man_Arts & Shop. On-Job
      Trng. Support_Employ. **Expected outcome:** Return to local school (Avg
      length of stay: 1-2 yrs).
   Therapy: Lang Music Occup Perceptual-Motor Phys Play Rec Speech. **Psy-
      chotherapy:** Art Dance Equine Fam Group Indiv Parent. **Counseling:**
      Educ Nutrition Voc.
   Enr: 280. B 200. G 80. **Fac:** 80 (Full 77, Part 3).
   Summer prgm: Day. Educ. Rec. Ther. 6 wks.
   Acres 16. Bldgs 2. Class rms 26. Libs 1. Sci labs 1. Lang labs 1. Art studios 1.
      Dance studios 1. Gyms 1. Fields 1. Courts 1. Riding rings 1. Comp labs 1.

Est 1992. Nonprofit.

This family-oriented school serves children with learning and emotional problems. GPA's behavioral management system, together with its intensive counseling services, allows for effective remediation of psychiatric and behavioral problems. Individual and group therapies are both part of the daily program, and art, music, speech and language therapies are also available.

Boys and girls enroll from Burlington, Mercer, Gloucester, Camden and surrounding counties. In most cases, the sending school district covers costs, although GPA also accepts students on private tuition.

GLENVIEW ACADEMY

Day — Coed Ages 5-12

Fairfield, NJ 07004. 24 Dwight Pl.
Tel: 973-808-9555. Fax: 973-227-8626.
www.glenview.org
John Kazmark, Exec Dir. **Rachel Herrington,** Prin.
   Conditions: Primary—ADHD AN Anx As Bu CD Dx ED LD Mood OCD ODD PTSD S SA SP Subst TBI. **IQ 60-120. Not accepted**—Asp Au B/VI D ID MR PDD.
   Gen Acad. Ungraded. **Feat**—Studio_Art. Interscholastic sports.
   Therapy: Lang Play Speech. **Psychotherapy:** Art Group Indiv. **Counseling:** Educ Voc.
   Enr: 168 (Cap: 168). B 138. G 30. **Fac:** 14. Spec ed 14.
   Aid: State 168 (100% of tui). **Summer prgm:** Day. Educ. Rec. Ther. 4 wks.
   Est 1985. Inc.

Glenview enrolls boys and girls who have educational disabilities that cannot be adequately addressed in the public schools. The academy's curriculum, which meets New Jersey standards, addresses both academic and social/emotional needs of the students. Individual, small-group and multimodal instruction employs diagnostic and direct teaching techniques. In addition to gaining a grounding in the fundamental skills, pupils learn to use technology as a tool and develop problem solving and critical-thinking abilities.

THE GRAMON SCHOOL

Day — Coed Ages 12-21

Fairfield, NJ 07004. 24 Dwight Pl.
Tel: 973-808-9555. Fax: 973-227-8626.
www.gramon.org
John Kazmark, Exec Dir. **Rachel Herrington,** Prin. **Kim Saunders,** Adm.
   Conditions: Primary—ADHD CD ED Mood Multi OCD ODD SP Sz. **Sec**—Anx LD ON PTSD S SA. **IQ 60 and up. Not accepted**—B/VI.
   Col Prep. Gen Acad. Ungraded. **Feat**—Visual_Arts.
   Therapy: Speech. **Psychotherapy:** Group Indiv. **Counseling:** Educ.
   Adm: On-campus interview.

Enr: 80 (Cap: 84). B 65. G 15. **Fac:** 21 (Full-time). Spec ed 7. Lay 14.
Aid: State 80 (100% of tui). **Summer prgm:** Day. Educ. Rec. Ther. 6 wks.
Est 1939.

The school follows a program built around a homelike, nonpressuring atmosphere. Individualized and small-group instruction, participation in small-group activity and flexible curricula, including independent study, are stressed in helping students work to potential. Achievement motivation and reality therapy are also utilized.

In addition to a full academic program, activities such as adaptive physical education, computer, prevocational laboratories, counseling, advisory groups and art are offered. Swimming, roller skating, interscholastic sports, yearbook and similar cocurricular and extracurricular activities are also available. Gramon holds special classes for those with neurological impairments and emotional disturbances.

An affiliated elementary school, Glenview Academy, enrolls boys and girls ages 5-15 (see separate listing).

GREEN BROOK ACADEMY

Day — Coed Ages 10-21

Bound Brook, NJ 08805. 151 Vosseller Ave, PO Box 947.
Tel: 732-469-8677. Fax: 732-469-0035.
www.greenbrookacademy.org   E-mail: cmotzel@greenbrookacademy.com
Constance A. Dougherty, BA, Dir. **Colleen D. Motzel,** MA, Prin. **Louise M.**
  Mancino, Adm.
  Conditions: Primary—ED. **Sec**—ADHD Anx Dx LD Mood OCD ODD TBI TS.
  IQ 70 and up.
  Gen Acad. Ungraded. **Expected outcome:** Return to local school (Avg length
  of stay: 2-3 yrs).
  Therapy: Speech. **Psychotherapy:** Art Group Indiv. **Counseling:** Educ.
  Adm: On-campus interview.
  Enr: 72. B 54. G 18. **Fac:** 17 (Full-time). Spec ed 8. Lay 9.
  Bldgs 4. Class rms 2. Gyms 1. Basketball courts 1. Weight rms 1.
  Est 1979. Inc.

Green Brook helps emotionally disturbed students return to their schools or complete their formal education and directly enter the job market. The individualized curriculum is developed in cooperation with the district's child study team and approved by the student's parents or legal guardian. The academy also offers a physical education program, vocational guidance and various therapies.

HARBOR SCHOOL

Day — Coed Ages 5-21

Eatontown, NJ 07724. 240 Broad St.
Tel: 732-544-9394. Fax: 732-544-0245.
www.harborschool.com   E-mail: agunteski@harborschool.com
Anne Gunteski, BMusEd, MS, EdD, Prin.

Conditions: Primary—ADHD Ap APD Asp Au Dg DS Dpx Dx LD ID Multi Nf NLD PDD S TBI. **Sec**—Anx Apr Ar As B/VI C CD CF CLP CP D Db D-B ED Ep Hemo HI IP Lk Mood OCD ODD ON PW SA SB SC SP Sz TS. **IQ 50-110.**

Voc. Ungraded. Culinary. On-Job Trng. Shelt_Workshop. Support_Employ. **Feat**—Computers Studio_Art Music Health. **Expected outcome:** Return to local school.

Therapy: Hear Lang Music Occup Phys Speech. **Psychotherapy:** Art Dance Group Indiv. **Counseling:** Educ.

Adm: Appl due: Rolling.

Enr: 90. B 50. G 40. **Fac:** 15 (Full-time). Spec ed 13. Lay 2.

Aid: State 90 (100% of tui).

Bldgs 1. Class rms 15. Gyms 1.

Est 1968. Inc.

The school provides academic instruction for children with neurological impairments, communicational disorders, autism or multiple disabilities. In addition to basic academics, the curriculum includes science, social studies, health and prevocational activities. An adaptive physical education program offers swimming instruction. The developmental program provides auditory, visual, perceptual, and gross- and fine-motor training.

Similar programs are conducted in Jackson at Alpha School (2210 W. County Line Rd., Ste. 1, 08527) and at Gateway School, in Carteret (60 High St., 07008).

HOLMSTEAD SCHOOL

Day — Coed Ages 13-18

Ridgewood, NJ 07450. 14 Hope St.
Tel: 201-447-1696. Fax: 201-447-4608.
www.holmstead.org   E-mail: mail@holmstead.org
Patricia G. Whitehead, MEd, Dir.

Conditions: Primary—ED ODD SP. **Sec**—LD. **IQ 115 and up.**

Col Prep. Gen Acad. Gr 8-12. **Feat**—Writing Fr Span Calc Computers Econ Psych Drawing Film Studio_Art Music_Theory Bus Health. **Expected outcome:** Return to local school (Avg length of stay: 3 yrs).

Psychotherapy: Fam Group Indiv. **Counseling:** Educ.

Enr: 77. B 56. G 21. **Fac:** 13 (Full-time). Spec ed 10. Lay 3.

Aid: State 77 (100% of tui).

Est 1970. Nonprofit.

Holmstead offers an alternative educational program for adolescents with intellectual ability who are not succeeding in a traditional academic setting because of emotional disturbances. It is primarily a college preparatory program. For individuals with learning disabilities, the school provides remediation and tutorial help in the development of skills and compensatory techniques. Every student takes six subjects within a multidisciplinary curriculum.

Adjunct services such as testing and vocational and college counseling, as well as individual psychotherapy, are readily available. The usual duration of treatment is three years.

LAKEVIEW SCHOOL

Day — Coed Ages 3-21

Edison, NJ 08837. 10 Oak Dr.
Tel: 732-549-6187. Fax: 732-549-0629.
www.cpamc.org/lakeview.htm   E-mail: lynn.sikorski@cpamc.org
Lynn Sikorski, BA, MA, Dir.
  Conditions: Primary—Ap Apr CP Ep IP MD MS ON SB TBI. **Sec**—As B/VI C
    D ID.
  Gen Acad. Ungraded. Shelt_Workshop.
  Therapy: Lang Occup Phys Speech. **Psychotherapy:** Indiv Parent. **Counseling:** Nutrition.
  Enr: 178. B 86. G 92. **Fac:** 28 (Full 26, Part 2). Spec ed 24. Lay 4.
  Summer prgm: Day. Educ. Ther. 6 wks.
  Est 1949. Nonprofit.

Lakeview serves severely and multiply disabled children. The school offers an individualized special education program specific to the learning needs of each student. Individualized therapy and monthly medical clinics in orthopedics and pediatrics support educational placement. Psychological assessment for students with multiple disabilities, comprehensive assessment and training in adaptive technologies for mobility, and Activities of Daily Living are also part of the program.

Local sending school districts typically pay tuition costs.

LEHMANN SCHOOL

Day — Coed Ages 3-21

Lakewood, NJ 08701. 1100 Airport Rd.
Tel: 732-905-7200. Fax: 732-905-1403.
www.ladacin.org
  Conditions: Primary—Apr CP Ep IP MD MS SB TBI. **Sec**—Ap B/VI D ID.
  Gen Acad. Voc. Ungraded. **Feat**—Computers Studio_Art Music.
  Therapy: Music Occup Phys Rec Speech. **Psychotherapy:** Art.
  Enr: 42. B 21. G 21.
  Aid: State 42 (100% of tui).
  Est 1953. Nonprofit. **Spons:** LADACIN Network.

A branch of the LADACIN Network, this year-round educational program serves students with developmental and multiple physical disabilities. Training and vocational preparation are elements of the program.

THE LEWIS SCHOOL AND CLINIC

Day — Coed Ages 5 and up

Princeton, NJ 08540. 53 Bayard Ln.
Tel: 609-924-8120. Fax: 609-924-5512.
www.lewisschool.org

Marsha Gaynor Lewis, MA, Dir. **Maureen H. Curran,** Adm.
  Conditions: Primary—ADHD APD Dx LD. **IQ 100 and up.**
  Col Prep. Gr K-PG. **Feat**—Studio_Art Music. Interscholastic sports. **Expected
    outcome:** Graduation.
  Therapy: Lang Speech.
  Adm: Appl due: Rolling. On-campus interview.
  Enr: 150.
  Educ. Tui Day $2600-3700 (+$650-1500). 4 wks.
  Est 1973. Nonprofit.

The Lewis School and Clinic evaluates and educates individuals with dyslexia. Diagnostic and educational testing services, evaluation of speech pathology, and early childhood screening are available at the facility. The school educates its students in a small, structured classroom setting within a regular school. Study skills instruction complements other academic courses. Faculty members provide personal support in helping students deal with frustration accompanying dyslexia.

High school seniors and postgraduate students complete a demanding course of study. The usual duration of the program is two to three years, with most students going on to public or private schools and colleges.

LORD STIRLING SCHOOL
Day — Coed Ages 7-20

Basking Ridge, NJ 07920. 99 Lord Stirling Rd, PO Box 369.
Tel: 908-766-1786. Fax: 908-766-9443.
www.lordstirling.org   E-mail: info@lordstirling.org
Joseph E. Gorga, MA, Exec Dir. **Barbara Strickarz,** Adm.
  Conditions: Primary—CD ED ODD. **Sec**—ADHD Ap Asp Dc Dg Dx LD Mood
    Multi OCD Psy PTSD SA SO SP Subst Sz TBI TS. **IQ 80 and up. Not
    accepted**—As Au CF CP DS IP MD MS Nf ON SB.
  Gen Acad. Ungraded. On-Job Trng. **Expected outcome:** Return to local
    school (Avg length of stay: 1-3 yrs).
  Therapy: Occup Speech. **Psychotherapy:** Group Indiv. **Counseling:** Educ
    Voc.
  Adm: Appl fee: $0. Appl due: Year-round. On-campus interview.
  Enr: 46 (Cap: 56). B 40. G 6. **Fac:** 22 (Full-time).
  Aid: State 46 (100% of tui). **Summer prgm:** Day. Educ. Ther. Tui Day $397/
    day. 6 wks.
  Acres 11. Bldgs 3. Class rms 6. Art studios 1. Music studios 1. Gyms 1. Fields
    1. Pools 1. Comp labs 1.
  Est 1964. Nonprofit.

Lord Stirling provides a special learning environment for mildly to severely disturbed children, with the goal of mainstreaming. Both individual and group psychotherapy and speech therapy are provided in the program. Parental participation is encouraged. A comprehensive transition program is provided for older students. The usual duration of enrollment is one to three years.

The student's sending school district typically covers all tuition costs.

MATHENY MEDICAL AND EDUCATIONAL CENTER

Bdg and Day — Coed Ages 3-21

Peapack, NJ 07977. 65 Highland Ave, PO Box 339.
Tel: 908-234-0011. Fax: 908-719-2137.
www.matheny.org   E-mail: info@matheny.org
Steven M. Proctor, Pres. **Deborah Andreoni,** Adm.
   Conditions: Primary—CP MD ON SB. **Sec**—Ap B/VI D Db D-B Ep HI ID S.
   IQ 40 and up.
   Voc. Gr PS-12. On-Job Trng. Shelt_Workshop. **Expected outcome:** Gradua-
   tion.
   Therapy: Music Occup Phys Rec Speech. **Psychotherapy:** Indiv.
   Adm: Appl due: Year-round.
   Enr: 101 (Cap: 140). **Fac:** 25.
   Acres 78.
   Est 1946. Nonprofit.

Founded by Walter and Marguerite Matheny, this year-round school occupies 78 acres in rural New Jersey, providing treatment and special education for children and young adults with medically complex developmental disabilities. Matheny specializes in the treatment of cerebral palsy and other neurological impairments. The educational component combines academics with functional life skills.

Clients receive a combination of services through an interdisciplinary team, including several therapies and comprehensive healthcare. Outpatient services are also available.

THE MIDLAND SCHOOL

Day — Coed Ages 5-21

North Branch, NJ 08876. 94 Readington Rd, PO Box 5026.
Tel: 908-722-8222. Fax: 908-722-1547.
www.midlandschool.org   E-mail: info@midlandschool.org
Philip M. Gartlan, MA, Exec Dir. **Barbara Barkan,** Prin.
   Conditions: Primary—ADHD Asp Dc Dx LD ID Multi PDD S. **Sec**—Apr As B/
   VI C CP D Db DS ED Ep HI Mood OCD ON Psy PW SB TBI TS. **IQ 50-100.**
   Gen Acad. Ungraded. Hort. Man_Arts & Shop. On-Job Trng. Shelt_Workshop.
   Support_Employ. **Feat**—Studio_Art Music Speech Indus_Arts. **Expected**
   outcome: Graduation.
   Therapy: Lang Occup Speech. **Psychotherapy:** Group Indiv Parent.
   Adm: Appl due: Year-round. On-campus interview.
   Enr: 200 (Cap: 229). B 130. G 70. **Fac:** 37 (Full-time). Spec ed 37.
   Aid: State 200 (100% of tui). **Summer prgm:** Day. Educ. 6 wks.
   Acres 57. Bldgs 3 (100% ADA). Class rms 30. Libs 1. Art studios 1. Music stu-
   dios 1. Dance studios 1. Gyms 1. Fields 1. Courts 1. Pools 1. Comp labs 1.
   Est 1960. Nonprofit.

This rehabilitation facility serves the special educational needs of children with learning disabilities, communicative disorders or maladaptive behavior. Midland provides early delineation of problems and careful planning to help these children develop their abilities and work to educational potential.

Midland teaches the child to compensate for his or her special needs, to overcome learning difficulties and to discover new capabilities. The school offers counseling for students and their parents, while also providing a comprehensive career education program, job training and placement services.

The sending school district pays all tuition fees.

MOUNT CARMEL GUILD ACADEMY
Day — Coed Ages 5-21

West Orange, NJ 07052. 100 Valley Way.
Tel: 973-325-4400. Fax: 973-669-8450.
www.mcgschools.com
Allan J. Daul, MSW, Exec Dir.
  Conditions: Primary—ADHD Asp Au CD ED PDD. **IQ 70-100.**
  Gen Acad. Ungraded. Culinary. **Feat**—Computers Fine_Arts Music. **Expected outcome:** Return to local school.
  Therapy: Music Occup Speech. **Psychotherapy:** Group Indiv Parent. **Counseling:** Educ.
  Enr: 59. B 50. G 9.
  Est 1967. Nonprofit.

MCGA seeks to help students reach an age-appropriate development, then return them to their home schools with adequate behavioral, social, academic and emotional coping skills. The program features structure, incremental learning, corrective feedback and small classes of no more than eight students.

NEWGRANGE SCHOOL OF PRINCETON
Day — Coed Ages 7-21

Hamilton, NJ 08629. 526 S Olden Ave.
Tel: 609-584-1800. Fax: 609-584-6166.
www.thenewgrange.org   E-mail: info@thenewgrange.org
Gordon F. Sherman, PhD, Exec Dir. **Bob Hegedus,** MA, Prin.
  Conditions: Primary—Dx LD NLD. **Sec**—S. **IQ 90 and up.**
  Col Prep. Gen Acad. Ungraded. Man_Arts & Shop. **Feat**—Comp_Sci Studio_Art Music Health Study_Skills. **Expected outcome:** Return to local school (Avg length of stay: 3 yrs).
  Therapy: Lang Occup Speech. **Psychotherapy:** Indiv.
  Adm: Appl fee: $0. Appl due: Rolling.
  Enr: 120. **Fac:** 55 (Full 50, Part 5).
  Tui '11-'12: Day $46,134/sch yr. **Aid:** State. Educ. 6 wks.
  Bldgs 2. Class rms 11. Libs 1. Sci labs 1. Lang labs 5. Music studios 1. Gyms 1. Comp labs 1. Comp/stud: 1:1
  Est 1977. Nonprofit.

Newgrange offers an individualized, intensive and full-time academic program for students with language-based learning difficulties. Basic skills and problem solving are stressed, and a full remedial and tutorial program is available. The average length of stay is three years; some students remain until graduation, while others move on to district or other schools.

ROCK BROOK SCHOOL

Day — Coed Ages 5-14

Skillman, NJ 08558. 109 Orchard Rd.
Tel: 908-431-9500. Fax: 908-431-9503.
www.rock-brook.org   E-mail: info@rock-brook.org
Mary Caterson, MS, Dir. **Katie Hardgrove,** MEd, Prin.
   Conditions: Primary—ADHD Ap Au D DS Dx LD ON S. **Sec**—Anx As CP Ep ID MD OCD SB.
   Gen Acad. Ungraded. **Feat**—Studio_Art Music. **Expected outcome:** Return to local school (Avg length of stay: 4-5 yrs).
   Therapy: Lang Music Occup Phys Play Speech. **Psychotherapy:** Art Dance Parent.
   Adm: Appl due: Year-round. On-campus interview.
   Enr: 60 (Cap: 60). **Fac:** 10.
   Tui '10-'11: Day $246/day. **Aid:** State. **Summer prgm:** Day. 6 wks.
   Acres 10. Bldgs 1.
   Est 1974. Nonprofit.

Rock Brook takes a team-teaching approach to the treatment of children with multiple disabilities and communication impairments. The school's program offers speech and language remediation, as well as help with academic skills. Outpatient services are available, and the usual duration of treatment is four to five years.

The sending school district typically pays tuition fees, although some boys and girls attend on a private-pay basis.

THE RUGBY SCHOOL AT WOODFIELD

Day — Coed Ages 5-21

Wall, NJ 07719. Belmar Blvd & Woodfield Ave, PO Box 1403.
Tel: 732-681-6900. Fax: 732-681-4867.
www.rugbyschool.org   E-mail: ddesanto@therugbyschool.org
Dolores DeSanto, BA, Exec Dir. **Anthony Aquilino,** MEd, Dir.
   Conditions: Primary—ADHD Anx As Asp Dc Dg Dx ED LD Mood OCD ODD PDD PTSD SP TS. **Sec**—ON. **IQ 79 and up.**
   Col Prep. Gen Acad. Voc. Gr K-12. Culinary. On-Job Trng. **Feat**—Creative_Writing Environ_Sci Performing_Arts Photog Visual_Arts Music. **Expected outcome:** Graduation.
   Therapy: Music Occup Rec Speech. **Psychotherapy:** Art Fam Group Indiv Parent. **Counseling:** Educ Nutrition Voc.
   Enr: 115 (Cap: 118). B 85. G 30. **Fac:** 22 (Full-time). Spec ed 14. Lay 8.
   Est 1977. Nonprofit.

Through an intensive academic program, individualized counseling and a structured environment, the Rugby School provides comprehensive academic and vocational programs for young people of normal intelligence with special needs. Specific programs focus upon college preparation, cooperative trade and industry, office occupation, career exploration and health services. Other services include behavior management and full clinical services.

The school maintains small, structured classes to help students develop necessary life and interpersonal skills while they prepare for college or the work force. Faculty tailor instruction to each student's skills, needs and capabilities. The curriculum features specialized programs in photography, music, art, drama, environmental science, culinary arts, creative writing, journalism, cosmetology, comprehensive behavior management and art therapy, as well as workshops, lectures, hands-on activities and one-on-one tutoring sessions.

ST. JOSEPH'S SCHOOL FOR THE BLIND
CONCORDIA LEARNING CENTER

Bdg — Coed Ages 5-21; Day — Coed Birth-21

Jersey City, NJ 07307. 761 Summit Ave.
Tel: 201-876-5432. Fax: 201-876-5430.
www.sjsnj.org   E-mail: info@sjsnj.org
Judy Ortman, Exec Dir.
   Conditions: Primary—B/VI Multi. **Sec**—ADHD As C CP Ep ID LD ON S TBI.
   Gen Acad. Voc. Ungraded. On-Job Trng.
   Therapy: Aqua Music Occup Phys Speech Visual. **Psychotherapy:** Fam
      Indiv. **Counseling:** Educ Nutrition Voc.
   Adm: Appl due: Year-round.
   Enr: 63. Bdg 11. Day 52. B 35. G 28. **Fac:** 29 (Full-time). Spec ed 9. Lay 20.
   Aid: State 63 (100% of tui). **Summer prgm:** Bdg & Day. Educ. Ther. 4 wks.
   Est 1891. Nonprofit.

Blind children in the New Jersey area with multiple special needs area take part in the educational program and receive the training necessary for them to achieve to potential. The basic curriculum addresses language development, activities of daily living, sensorimotor skills, prevocational skills, and personal and social skills.

SEARCH DAY PROGRAM

Day — Coed Ages 3-21

Ocean, NJ 07712. 73 Wickapecko Dr.
Tel: 732-531-0454. Fax: 732-531-5934.
www.searchdayprogram.com   E-mail: info@searchdayprogram.com
Katherine Solana, MA, Exec Dir.
   Conditions: Primary—Au PDD.
   Gen Acad. Ungraded. Man_Arts & Shop. On-Job Trng. Shelt_Workshop.
      Expected outcome: Graduation.
   Therapy: Lang Occup Speech. **Psychotherapy:** Fam Group Indiv.
   Adm: Appl due: Rolling.

Enr: 60.
Tui '12-'13: Bdg $0/day. Day $0/day.
Est 1971. Nonprofit.

SEARCH is a multiservice agency (school, adult activities and group home) that provides comprehensive year-round services for individuals with autism, beginning with pre-school-age programs and running through adulthood. A favorable staff-client ratio is a characteristic of all services.

Speech and language therapy, adaptive physical education, occupational therapy, behavioral support, daily living skills and transitional planning, job coaching, community work programs, swimming, computer programs, community opportunities, home training, outreach and consultations, and consulting psychologist and psychiatrist are all available through the agency. Fees are paid by the sending school districts or the Division of Developmental Disabilities.

THE SISTER GEORGINE SCHOOL

Day — Coed Ages 5-21

Ewing, NJ 08638. 180B Ewingville Rd.
Tel: 609-771-4300. Fax: 609-771-8521.
www.srgeorgineschool.org   E-mail: sgs@srgeorgineschool.org
Sr. Barbara Furst, BS, MA, Prin.
  Conditions: Primary—ADHD CP DS Dx ID ON. **Sec**—Ap As Au TBI. **IQ 25-55.**
  Voc. Ungraded. On-Job Trng. Shelt_Workshop.
  Therapy: Speech.
  Enr: 18. B 7. G 11.
  Est 1969. Nonprofit. Roman Catholic.

Boys and girls with developmental disabilities follow a specially designed curriculum that emphasizes the following: readiness skills, functional academics, life skills, transitional planning, and prevocational and work skills. Class size ranges from four to nine students, and each classroom features both a special education teacher and a full-time teacher assistant. Enrichment opportunities include art, computers, library skills, music, gardening, Special Olympics and field trips.

SUMMIT SPEECH SCHOOL

Day — Coed Ages 3-5

New Providence, NJ 07974. 705 Central Ave.
Tel: 908-508-0011. TTY: 908-508-0011. Fax: 908-508-0012.
www.summitspeech.org   E-mail: info@summitspeech.org
Pamela A. Paskowitz, PhD, Exec Dir.
  Conditions: Primary—D HI.
  Gen Acad. Gr PS. **Expected outcome:** Return to local school (Avg length of stay: 3 yrs).
  Therapy: Hear Lang Occup Phys Speech. **Psychotherapy:** Indiv.

Adm: Appl due: Year-round. On-campus interview.
Enr: 20. **Fac:** 21 (Full 13, Part 8). Spec ed 21.
Aid: State 20 (100% of tui). **Summer prgm:** Day. Educ. Tui Day $120/day. 6 wks.
Est 1967. Nonprofit.

Summit Speech provides speech, language and auditory training for children with hearing impairments through a preschool program that employs the auditory-oral method. Boys and girls at the school do not use sign language. Children too young for the preschool program may participate in a parent-infant early intervention program. Parents also learn how to instill listening and speaking skills at home. Preschool activities include art and music classes, gym and field trips.

Additional offerings include mainstream support and audiological services, as well as speech, physical and occupational therapies.

THE TITUSVILLE ACADEMY
Day — Coed Ages 5-18

Titusville, NJ 08560. 86 River Dr.
Tel: 609-737-7733. Fax: 609-737-3343.
www.titusvilleacademy.com   E-mail: titusinfo@titusac.org
Deborah R. Zerbib, Dir. **Charles Cunningham,** EdD, Int Prin.
  Conditions: Primary—ADHD Asp Dx ED LD PDD Subst TS. **Sec**—D-B. **Not accepted**—Apr B/VI CP D IP MD MS Nf SB Sz.
  Col Prep. Gen Acad. Gr K-12. **Feat**—Computers Studio_Art Music. Interscholastic sports.
  Therapy: Speech. **Psychotherapy:** Group Indiv Parent. **Counseling:** Educ Voc.
  Adm: Appl fee: $0. Appl due: Year-round. On-campus interview.
  Enr: 96 (Cap: 96). B 89. G 7. **Fac:** 32 (Full 31, Part 1).
  Aid: State 96 (100% of tui).
  Est 1971. Nonprofit.

Titusville provides a highly structured, individualized, noncompetitive academic environment for students with learning and behavioral difficulties. The academy also offers clinical services in an effort to integrate the students social and emotional development with the educational process. Sending school districts cover all tuition costs.

THE WINSTON SCHOOL
Day — Coed Ages 8-14

Short Hills, NJ 07078. 30 East Ln.
Tel: 973-379-4114. Fax: 973-379-3984.
www.winstonschool.org   E-mail: plewis@winstonschool.org
Peter S. Lewis, BA, MA, MEd, PhD, Head. **Paula Lordy,** Adm.
  Conditions: Primary—Dx LD. **Sec**—ADHD. **IQ 90 and up.**
  Gen Acad. Gr 3-8. **Feat**—Computers Studio_Art Music. **Expected outcome:**

Graduation.
Therapy: Lang Occup Speech. **Psychotherapy:** Indiv.
Adm: Appl fee: $100. Appl due: Year-round. On-campus interview.
Enr: 70 (Cap: 80). B 36. G 34. **Fac:** 21 (Full-time). Spec ed 15. Lay 6.
Tui '11-'12: Day $35,000/sch yr (+$900). **Aid:** School 5 ($35,000). State 6.
Educ. Rec. Tui Day $400/wk. 4 wks.
Endow $3,000,000. Gyms 1. Fields 1. Laptop prgm Gr 6-8.
Est 1981. Nonprofit.

Drawing children of average to above-average intelligence from area public and private schools, Winston serves students with language-based learning disabilities. Individualized programs accommodate varying learning styles, and instructors place an emphasis on reading and related language arts skills. Instructional groups are small (two to four students) and the staff works closely with families. Community-wide programs include monthly meetings with school professionals and a counseling program that provides guidance for parents seeking appropriate high school placements for their children.

WOODCLIFF ACADEMY

Day — Coed Ages 8-18

Wall, NJ 07753. 1345 Campus Pky.
Tel: 732-751-0240. Fax: 732-751-0243.
www.woodcliff.com   E-mail: mail@woodcliff.com
Scott Corbett, BA, Dir.
  Conditions: Primary—ADHD Anx APD Asp Au C Db Dc Dg Dpx Dx ED Ep LD Mood NLD OCD ON PW S SA SP Sz TBI TS. **Sec**—ID. **IQ 100 and up. Not accepted**—Subst.
  Col Prep. Gen Acad. Underachiever. Gr 3-12. **Feat**—Span Computers Studio_Art Music. Avg SAT: CR 400. M 400. **Expected outcome:** Return to local school (Avg length of stay: 2 yrs).
  Therapy: Lang Speech. **Psychotherapy:** Group Indiv Parent. **Counseling:** Educ Voc.
  Enr: 80 (Cap: 90). B 50. G 30. **Fac:** 31 (Full 25, Part 6). Spec ed 31.
  Aid: State 80 (100% of tui).
  Plant val $2,000,000. Acres 1. Bldgs 1 (100% ADA). Class rms 14. Gyms 1.
  Est 1949. Nonprofit.

This state-approved school serves New Jersey pupils with various academic and mild emotional conditions. The academy utilizes applied cognitive behavior modification to encourage more appropriate school behavior. The sending school district typically pays all tuition costs.

NEW YORK

ANDERSON CENTER FOR AUTISM

Bdg and Day — Coed Ages 5-21

Staatsburg, NY 12580. 4885 Rte 9, PO Box 367.
Tel: 845-889-4034. Fax: 845-889-3104.
www.andersoncenterforautism.org   E-mail: info@acenterforautism.org
Neil J. Pollack, BA, MS, Exec Dir.
   Conditions: Primary—Au. **Sec**—ADHD Ap As Asp B/VI C CD CP D Dx ED
      Ep ID LD OCD ON Psy SB Sz TBI.
   Gen Acad. Ungraded. Man_Arts & Shop. On-Job Trng. Shelt_Workshop.
      Expected outcome: Return to local school (Avg length of stay: 5-7 yrs).
   Therapy: Lang Occup Phys Speech. **Psychotherapy:** Indiv. **Counseling:**
      Educ Voc.
   Adm: Appl due: Rolling.
   Enr: 136. Bdg 124. Day 12. B 117. G 19.
   Aid: State 136 (100% of tui).
   Est 1924. Nonprofit.

Anderson provides year-round educational, residential and treatment services for individuals having a primary diagnosis of autism. The program seeks to prepare students to return to a mainstream school setting, while providing career education opportunities for pupils age 14 and up.

BLOCK INSTITUTE SCHOOL

Day — Coed Ages 3-8

Brooklyn, NY 11214. 376 Bay 44th St.
Tel: 718-906-5400. Fax: 718-714-0197.
www.blockinstitute.org   E-mail: jsilverstein@blockinstitute.org
Scott L. Barkin, PhD, Exec Dir. **Jay Silverstein,** PhD, Dir.
   Conditions: Primary—ADHD Ap Apr Asp Au CP Db Dc Dg DS Dx ED IP LD
      ID ON PDD PW S SB TBI. **Sec**—AN As C CD CF CLP Ep MD Mood MS Nf
      OCD ODD SP TS. **IQ 0-45.**
   Gen Acad. Ungraded. Shelt_Workshop.
   Therapy: Aqua Lang Occup Perceptual-Motor Phys Play Speech. **Psycho-**
      therapy: Fam Group Indiv Parent.
   Enr: 177. B 112. G 65. **Fac:** 80. Spec ed 20. Lay 60.
   Aid: State 177 (100% of tui). **Summer prgm:** Day. Educ. Rec. Tui Day $0. 6
      wks.
   Est 1963. Nonprofit.

The school provides educational and therapeutic services for children and young adults diagnosed with a variety of developmental disabilities and neuromuscular disorders. Psychological and speech-language services, as well as occupational and physical therapy, are available. The curriculum emphasizes pre-academic, social/emotional, gross- and fine-motor, and literacy skills.

BUFFALO HEARING AND SPEECH CENTER
Day — Coed Ages 3-5

Buffalo, NY 14203. 50 E North St.
Tel: 716-885-8318. Fax: 716-885-4229.
www.askbhsc.org   E-mail: info@askbhsc.org
Joseph J. Cozzo, Pres.
   Conditions: Primary—ADHD Ap Asp Au D LD S. **Sec**—CLP ED ON.
   Gen Acad. Gr PS. **Expected outcome:** Graduation.
   Therapy: Hear Lang Occup Phys Speech. **Psychotherapy:** Fam Group Indiv.
   Est 1953. Nonprofit.

BHSC provides diagnosis and treatment of hearing and speech impairments and related special education services. The center's oral deaf education preschool serves children from who are deaf or hard of hearing. Early intervention services for children with speech-language impairments or developmental disabilities are also available.

THE CHILD SCHOOL/LEGACY HIGH SCHOOL
Day — Coed Ages 5-21

Roosevelt Island, NY 10044. 587 Main St.
Tel: 212-223-5055. Fax: 212-223-5031.
www.thechildschool.org   E-mail: dshine@thechildschool.org
Salvatore Ferrera, Exec Dir. **Doug Shine,** Adm.
   Conditions: Primary—ADHD Anx Ap Asp CD Dc Dg Dx ED Mood OCD PDD
      PTSD S SP. **Sec**—Apr As C CP Ep MD MS ON SB TBI TS. **IQ 80 and up.**
   Col Prep. Gen Acad. Gr K-12. **Feat**—Mythology Sci Computers Econ Govt
      Soc_Stud Studio_Art Music Journ Health Home_Ec.
   Therapy: Lang Occup Speech. **Psychotherapy:** Indiv. **Counseling:** Educ.
   Adm: Appl fee: $50.
   Enr: 280. B 165. G 115.
   Est 1973. Nonprofit.

The school comprises four divisions: elementary school (grades K-6), middle school (grades 7 and 8), academy (grades 9-12) and Legacy High School (also grades 9-12). Each division addresses the progressive academic, emotional and psychological development of its students. Curricula include physical education, computer science, fine arts and music. Psychological services, speech and language therapy, and occupational therapy are available on an individual or group basis or both in all divisions.

THE CHILDREN'S SCHOOL FOR EARLY DEVELOPMENT
Day — Coed Ages 3-5

Hawthorne, NY 10532. 40 Saw Mill River Rd.
Tel: 914-347-3227. Fax: 914-347-4216.
www.westchesterarc.org/services/early_childhood.html
  E-mail: fporcaro@westchesterarc.org
Frances B. Porcaro, MA, Educ Dir.
Conditions: Primary—Au DS ID PDD. **Sec**—S.
Gen Acad. Gr PS.
Therapy: Hear Occup Phys Speech. **Psychotherapy:** Fam.
Enr: 185.
Aid: State 185 (100% of tui).
Est 1963. Spons: Westchester ARC.

CSED provides various services for children residing in Westchester County who have developmental delays. Center-based and inclusion classes, among them classes designed specifically for children diagnosed with PDD or autism, are tailored to the individual's particular needs. In addition, the school offers early-intervention services and full-inclusion parent-child groups for children from birth to age 3 and their families.

THE CHURCHILL SCHOOL AND CENTER
Day — Coed Ages 5-21

New York, NY 10016. 301 E 29th St.
Tel: 212-722-0610. Fax: 212-722-1387.
www.churchillschool.com   E-mail: wfederico@churchillschool.com
Robert C. Siebert, EdD, Head. **Wendy Federico,** Adm.
Conditions: Primary—LD S. **IQ 90 and up.**
Gen Acad. Gr K-12. **Feat**—Pol_Sci Psych Sociol Philos Filmmaking Photog
  Studio_Art Theater_Arts Music Dance Health. Interscholastic sports.
Therapy: Lang Occup Speech. **Psychotherapy:** Group Indiv.
Adm: Appl fee: $75. Appl due: Rolling. On-campus interview.
Enr: 396. B 264. G 132.
Educ. Tui Day $1500. 4 wks.
Sci labs 3. Auds 1. Art studios 3. Gyms 1. Playgrounds 1. Comp labs 2.
Est 1972. Nonprofit.

The school program utilizes individually prescribed educational approaches, including multisensory teaching of reading, writing and spelling, within an informal but structured classroom setting. Specialists in the fields of learning disabilities, speech and language therapy, sensorimotor integration, curriculum development and adaptive physical education provide appropriate remediation and a varied curriculum.

The middle school program (grades 6-8) includes some departmentalization and emphasizes organizational and study skills. The college preparatory high school division, which offers a program that resembles that found in mainstream high schools, provides individualized support for developing compensatory learning strategies and honing organizational and study skills.

THE CLEAR VIEW SCHOOL DAY TREATMENT PROGRAM
Day — Coed Ages 3-21

Briarcliff Manor, NY 10510. 480 Albany Post Rd.
Tel: 914-941-9513. Fax: 914-941-2339.
www.clearviewschool.org   E-mail: info@clearviewschool.org
Debbie Lauro-Conn, BA, MSW, LCSW-R, Exec Dir.
   Conditions: Primary—AN Anx Bu CD ED Mood OCD Psy PTSD SP Sz TS.
   Sec—Ap Asp Au ID LD ON. **IQ 60 and up.**
   Col Prep. Gen Acad. Voc. Gr PS-12. Man_Arts & Shop. On-Job Trng.
   Expected outcome: Return to local school (Avg length of stay: 5 yrs).
   Therapy: Lang Speech. **Psychotherapy:** Fam Group Indiv Parent. **Counseling:** Educ Voc.
   Enr: 117. B 87. G 30. **Fac:** 51 (Full 50, Part 1). Spec ed 19. Lay 32.
   Est 1968. Nonprofit.

Clear View enrolls children with severe emotionally disturbances. The principle mode of treatment is psycho-educational therapy, with emphases on psychotherapy, conjoint mother-child therapy and family counseling. Children suffering from a variety of developmental disorders are accepted if they also have an emotional disturbance. Students residing in Westchester County who cannot attend public school receive admission priority. The usual duration of treatment is five years.

CLEARY SCHOOL FOR THE DEAF
Day — Coed Ages 3-21

Nesconset, NY 11767. 301 Smithtown Blvd.
Tel: 631-588-0530. TTY: 631-588-0530. Fax: 631-588-0016.
www.clearyschool.org   E-mail: kmorseon@clearyschool.org
Kenneth Morseon, MS, Supt. **Ellen McCarthy,** MA, Prin.
   Conditions: Primary—D D-B HI. **Sec**—ADHD AN Anx Apr Ar As Asp Au
   B/VI Bu CD CF CLP CP Db Dc Dg Dpx DS Dx ED Ep Hemo IP ID LD Lk
   MD Mood MS Nf NLD OCD ODD ON PDD Psy PTSD PW S SA SB SC SP
   Subst Sz TBI TS.
   Col Prep. Gen Acad. Voc. Ungraded. Culinary. Hort. Man_Arts & Shop. On-Job Trng. **Feat**—Lib_Skills ASL Comp_Sci Studio_Art Dance. SAT/ACT prep. Interscholastic sports. **Expected outcome:** Return to local school.
   Therapy: Hear Lang Occup Perceptual-Motor Phys Speech. **Psychotherapy:** Dance Parent. **Counseling:** Educ Voc.
   Adm: Appl fee: $0. Appl due: Year-round. On-campus interview.
   Enr: 95 (Cap: 105). **Fac:** 18 (Full 16, Part 2). Spec ed 9. Lay 9.
   Aid: State 95 (100% of tui). **Summer prgm:** Day. Educ. Tui Day $0. 6 wks.
   Acres 5. Bldgs 3 (100% ADA). Class rms 15. Lib 25,000 vols. Art studios 1.
   Gyms 1. Comp labs 1.
   Est 1930. Nonprofit.

Profoundly deaf children from Suffolk and Nassau counties receive a total communication approach to learning at Cleary. The curriculum includes traditional academic subjects, in addition to speech reading, auditory training, finger spelling and signs. Programming also includes instruction in art, photography, visual perception, cognitive training, vocational job training and visual communication. Each student undergoes an evaluation each year to determine if he or she is ready for mainstreaming into a traditional school.

An infant program provides educational services for parents and their children (birth to age 3). The secondary program operates at East Islip High School in Islip Terrace.

The State of New York pays all tuition, fees and transportation costs.

COARC
THE STARTING PLACE
Day — Coed Ages 3-5

Hudson, NY 12534. 65 Prospect Ave.
Tel: 518-828-3890. Fax: 518-828-4195.
www.coarc.org E-mail: info@coarc.org
Kenneth R. Stall, Exec Dir.
  Conditions: Primary—ID. **Sec**—CP Ep LD MD MS ON S SB TBI.
  Gen Acad. Gr PS.
  Therapy: Hear Lang Occup Phys Speech. **Psychotherapy:** Fam Indiv.
  Enr: 30. **Fac:** 15 (Full-time). Spec ed 3. Lay 12.
  Aid: State 30 (100% of tui).
  Est 1983. Nonprofit. **Spons:** Columbia County Association for Retarded
    Citizens.

The Columbia County Association for Retarded Citizens offers a preschool program to children with developmental disabilities and to those who exhibit severe delays in speech, movement, learning or behavior. Early intervention, diagnosis and treatment are provided. Improvement is directed toward growth in communicational skills; fine- or gross-motor development; self-care; and socialization. Programming is provided to educate both parent and child. Parental counseling is available.

COBB MEMORIAL SCHOOL
Bdg and Day — Coed Ages 5-21

Altamont, NY 12009. 100 Mt Presentation Way, PO Box 503.
Tel: 518-861-6446. Fax: 518-861-5228.
www.cobbmemorialschool.org E-mail: cobbmemorialschool@verizon.net
  Conditions: Primary—ID.
  Gen Acad. Ungraded.
  Therapy: Occup Phys Play Speech. **Psychotherapy:** Indiv. **Counseling:** Voc.
  Enr: 36 (Cap: 36).
  Acres 40.
  Est 1962. Nonprofit.

Located on a wooded, 40-acre campus in the Helderberg Mountains, this school serves children with intellectual disabilities who fall in the trainable to severe range. Educational training strives to develop work habits, reliability and integrity. A multidisciplinary mental health team works with both children and their parents. The school employs various methods of communication to address the needs of its many nonverbal children.

THE FAMILY FOUNDATION SCHOOL

Bdg — Coed Ages 13-19

Hancock, NY 13783. 431 Chapel Hill Rd.
Tel: 845-887-5213. Fax: 845-887-4939.
www.thefamilyschool.com   E-mail: info@thefamilyschool.com
Rita Argiros, PhD, Prgm Dir. **Jeff Brain,** Adm.
   Conditions: Primary—ADHD Anx ED Mood OCD ODD PTSD SA. **IQ 95 and up.**
   Col Prep. Gr 9-12. **Feat**—Russ Span Calc Stats Econ Relig Photog Studio_Art Drama Band Chorus Journ Woodworking. Avg SAT: CR 501. M 500. W 518. ACT: Avg 22. SAT/ACT prep. Interscholastic sports. **Expected outcome:** Return to local school (Avg length of stay: 1½-2 yrs).
   Psychotherapy: Fam Group Indiv Parent. **Counseling:** Educ.
   Adm: Appl fee: $0. Appl due: Year-round. On-campus interview.
   Enr: 105 (Cap: 120). B 75. G 30. **Fac:** 35 (Full-time). Spec ed 1. Lay 34.
   Tui '12-'13: Bdg $6300/mo (+$4000/yr). **Aid:** School. Educ. Ther. 6 wks.
   Acres 150. Bldgs 6. Dorms 2. Libs 1. Sci labs 1. Art studios 2. Music studios 1. Dance studios 1. Gyms 1. Fields 3. Courts 2.
   Est 1982. Inc. **Spons:** Education Plus.

This therapeutic boarding school serves intelligent teens who are struggling with behavioral or emotional difficulties. Programming integrates academics, daily psychotherapy and character education that draws upon 12-Step Program principles. FFS offers tutoring and other learning support, honors courses, various journalism and arts classes, peer support and community service opportunities. The therapeutic environment seeks to facilitate personal development and improve student-family relationships.

GERSH ACADEMY

Day — Coed Ages 5-21

Huntington, NY 11743. 21 Sweet Hollow Rd.
Tel: 631-385-3342. Fax: 631-427-6332.
www.gershacademy.org   E-mail: info@gershacademy.org
   Nearby locations: 254-04 Union Tpke, Glen Oaks 11004; 385 Hoffman Ln, Hauppauge 11788; 465 Payne Ave, North Tonowanda 14120.
Kevin Gersh, Pres. **Daniel Selmer,** LCSW-R, Prgm Dir. **Yvonne Waskewicz,** Adm.
   Conditions: Primary—ADHD Anx Asp Au Dc Dg Dx LD Mood OCD PDD TS. **Sec**—CD ED NLD ODD PTSD SP.
   Col Prep. Gen Acad. Voc. Gr K-12. Culinary. Hort. On-Job Trng. Support_ Employ. **Feat**—Studio_Art Drama Music. **Expected outcome:** Graduation.
   Therapy: Music Occup Phys Speech. **Psychotherapy:** Equine Group Indiv Parent. **Counseling:** Educ Voc.
   Adm: Appl due: Year-round.

Enr: 120 (Cap: 150). **Fac:** 25 (Full 20, Part 5). Spec ed 15. Lay 10.
Tui '12-'13: Day $37,500-76,000/sch yr. **Aid:** State. **Summer prgm:** Day.
Educ. Rec. Tui Day $10,000-16,000. 6 wks.
Est 1999. Inc.

Designed for high-functioning students with neurobiological disorders, the academy provides a full elementary and secondary program within a flexible environment that helps boys and girls develop their strengths and work on their weaknesses. A cognitive-behavioral approach teaches pupils to better manage and regulate their behavior.

In grades K-8, the school formulates an Individualized Educational Plan for each student in coordination with the home school district. The multidisciplinary elementary curriculum features course work in music, art and foreign language, and field trips provide enrichment. During the high school years, boys and girls work toward the high school diploma, and the academy also administers New York State Regent and SAT examinations. Vocational training and transition planning are aspects of the high school program.

Gersh also provides educational services in Hauppauge, Glen Oaks and North Tonowanda.

THE GOW SCHOOL
Bdg — Boys Ages 12-18; Day — Coed 12-18

South Wales, NY 14139. 2491 Emery Rd, PO Box 85.
Tel: 716-652-3450. Fax: 716-652-3457.
www.gow.org   E-mail: admissions@gow.org
M. Bradley Rogers, Jr., BA, MA, Head. Robert Garcia, Adm.
   Conditions: Primary—ADHD APD Dc Dg Dx LD. **IQ 90 and up.**
   Col Prep. Gr 7-12. **Feat**—Comp_Sci Robotics Econ Fine_Arts Drama Music
      Bus Journ. Avg SAT: CR 450. M 460. W 400. Interscholastic sports.
   Adm: Appl fee: $100. Appl due: Rolling. On-campus interview.
   Enr: 130. **Fac:** 38 (Full 33, Part 5).
   Tui '12-'13: Bdg $54,500/sch yr (+$2500). Day $35,000/sch yr (+$2500).
      Aid: School ($800,000). **Summer prgm:** Bdg & Day. Educ. Tui Bdg $6800.
      Tui Day $3200-4300. 5 wks.
   Endow $7,100,000. Plant val $15,142,000. Acres 100. Bldgs 21. Dorms 6.
      Dorm rms 75. Class rms 32. Lib 10,000 vols. Comp ctrs 5. Auds 1. Theaters
      1. Art studios 2. Music studios 1. Gyms 1. Fields 5. Tennis courts 7. Squash
      courts 3. Weight rms 1. Comp labs 1. Laptop prgm Gr 7-PG.
   Est 1926. Nonprofit.

The school was established by Peter Gow as a college preparatory institution for those with dyslexia or similar language learning differences. Although primarily a boys' boarding school, Gow maintains a small day division for pupils of both genders. All programs are individually planned, and nearly all graduates enter college.

The school serves students of average to above-average intelligence who have specific language difficulties. Classes are small, averaging three to seven pupils each. The core of the program at Gow is "reconstructive language" and multisensory mathematics, both of which are designed to improve and extend the student's academic ability within a college preparatory setting.

Boys and girls attend classes six days each week. An Outward Bound-type outdoors program is one of Gow's activities.   **See Also Page 31**

GREEN CHIMNEYS
Bdg — Coed Ages 6-17; Day — Coed 5-17

Brewster, NY 10509. 400 Doansburg Rd, Box 719.
Tel: 845-279-2995. Fax: 845-279-3077.
www.greenchimneys.org   E-mail: info@greenchimneys.org
Joseph Whalen, MS, MBA, Exec Dir. **Debbie Moore,** Prin. **Eleanor Rothen-berger,** Adm.
  Conditions: Primary—ADHD Anx Asp ED Mood PDD PTSD SP. **Sec**—As CD Dx Ep ID LD OCD Psy S Sz. **IQ 70 and up.**
  Gen Acad. Gr K-12. Hort. Man_Arts & Shop. On-Job Trng. Support_Employ.
  Expected outcome: Return to local school (Avg length of stay: 20 mos).
  Therapy: Lang Milieu Music Occup Perceptual-Motor Rec Speech.
  Psychotherapy: Art Group Indiv. **Counseling:** Educ.
  Enr: 180. Bdg 88. Day 92. **Fac:** 75 (Full 67, Part 8). Spec ed 31. Lay 44. Acres 200.
  Est 1947. Nonprofit.

Green Chimneys provides a year-round therapeutic milieu for children with emotional, behavioral and educational handicaps. There is a full range of social service, clinical and educational programs, including psychotherapy and diagnostic evaluations. The program incorporates the use of a farm as a therapeutic modality, with animal- and plant-facilitated therapy.

Enrollment is restricted to children residing in New York State. Although the sending school district typically pays tuition costs, private-pay students may also enroll.

THE HAGEDORN LITTLE VILLAGE SCHOOL
Day — Coed Ages 3-12

Seaford, NY 11783. 750 Hicksville Rd.
Tel: 516-520-6000. Fax: 516-796-6341.
www.littlevillage.org   E-mail: information@littlevillage.org
Jon Feingold, PhD, Exec Dir. **Patricia Pizza,** MS, Prin.
  Conditions: Primary—ADHD Ap APD Apr Asp Au CF CP DS Dpx Dx LD ID Multi NLD PDD S. **Sec**—Anx As B/VI C D ED Ep HI IP MD MS Nf ON PW SB TBI TS.
  Gen Acad. Ungraded. **Feat**—Adaptive_Phys_Ed. **Expected outcome:** Return to local school (Avg length of stay: 3 yrs).
  Therapy: Lang Occup Perceptual-Motor Phys Play Rec Speech Visual.
  Psychotherapy: Dance Group Indiv Parent.
  Adm: Appl fee: $0. Appl due: Year-round. On-campus interview.
  Enr: 230. **Fac:** 92 (Full 30, Part 62). Spec ed 80. Lay 12.
  Aid: State 230 (100% of tui). **Summer prgm:** Day. Educ. Ther. Tui Day $0. 6 wks.
  Est 1969. Nonprofit.

Affiliated with the special-education graduate programs at Hofstra and Adelphi universities, HLVS groups children in classes of six, nine or 12. The program includes prescriptive teaching, self-help and life skills, gross- and fine-motor training, remediation and therapy. Parental counseling is available, as are outpatient services. The usual duration of enrollment is three years.

Little Village also offers an early intervention program for parents with children under age 3 that includes home visitation and various therapies.

THE HALLEN SCHOOL

Day — Coed Ages 5-21

New Rochelle, NY 10801. 97 Centre Ave.
Tel: 914-636-6600. Fax: 914-633-4294.
www.thehallenschool.net   E-mail: info@thehallenschool.net
Carol LoCascio, MEd, PhD, Exec Dir. **Stephanie Dalbey,** Adm.
   Conditions: Primary—ADHD Ap Apr Ar As Asp Au B/VI C Dc Dg Dx ED LD
      Mood Multi Nf OCD ODD PW SP TBI TS. **Sec**—AN Anx Db ID.
   Gen Acad. Voc. Gr K-12. Hort. Man_Arts & Shop. On-Job Trng. **Feat**—Art_Hist
      Studio_Art Music Health. **Expected outcome:** Graduation.
   Therapy: Lang Occup Speech. **Psychotherapy:** Art Dance Fam Group Indiv.
      Counseling: Educ Voc.
   Adm: Appl due: Year-round. On-campus interview.
   Enr: 315 (Cap: 328).
   Aid: State 315 (100% of tui). **Summer prgm:** Day. Educ. Ther. 6 wks.
   Bldgs 1. Gyms 1.
   Est 1972. Inc.

Hallen provides early diagnosis, remediation and education for children with learning disabilities. The curriculum emphasizes emotional growth and the development of academic skills. Individual and group therapy are integrated with academics and are incorporated into the student's weekly schedule. In addition to the prescribed curriculum, the school offers creative art, manual arts, music and business courses, in addition to supportive work and career education. Hallen strongly encourages active parental participation.

HAWTHORNE COUNTRY DAY SCHOOL

Day — Coed Ages 3-21

Hawthorne, NY 10532. 5 Bradhurst Ave.
Tel: 914-592-8526. Fax: 914-592-3227.
www.hawthornecountryday.org
   Nearby locations: 156 William St, New York 10038.
Tina Marie Covington, PhD, Exec Dir. **Ann Marie Babcock,** Adm.
   Conditions: Primary—ADHD Asp Au ID Multi PDD PW S. **Sec**—ON. **Not**
      accepted—AN Apr Ar CLP CP D D-B ED IP MD MS Nf Psy SA SB SO Sz.
   Col Prep. Gen Acad. Voc. Ungraded. On-Job Trng. Shelt_Workshop. Support_Employ.
   Therapy: Lang Occup Phys Speech.

Adm: Appl fee: $0. Appl due: Rolling. On-campus interview.
Enr: 171 (Cap: 172). **Fac:** 70 (Full-time). Spec ed 20. Lay 50.
Tui '12-'13: Day $36,972-41,338/sch yr. **Summer prgm:** Day. Educ. Tui Day
    $5996-6702. 6 wks.
Bldgs 4. Class rms 30. Libs 2. Gyms 1. Pools 1. Comp labs 2.
Est 1976. Nonprofit. **Spons:** Hawthorne Foundation.

This state-approved school serves special-needs children with autism/pervasive developmental disorder, intellectual disabilities, speech and language impairments, and multiple disabilities. Various academic, vocational and language-building programs are taught within the framework of applied behavior analysis.

Teaching methods emphasize positive reinforcement, continuous measurement of learning and strategic/tactical data analysis based upon graphic data displays. HCDS' programming addresses verbal behavior, reading and literacy, social skills, self-management and problem-solving skills. Staff analyze socially inappropriate behavior, such as aggression, self-injury and noncompliance, then work to systematically reinforce alternative behaviors. The school typically treats behavior problems as instructional opportunities rather than manifestations of an underlying pathology.

A separate location in Manhattan (212-281-6531) serves children ages 5-12 who have autism.

HEBREW ACADEMY FOR SPECIAL CHILDREN

Bdg — Coed Ages 5 and up; Day — Coed 3-21

Brooklyn, NY 11219. 5902 14th Ave.
Tel: 718-686-5930. Fax: 718-686-5935.
www.hasc.net   E-mail: chaya.miller@hasc.net
Samuel Kahn, Dir. **Judah Mischel,** Prgm Dir. **Chaya Miller,** Adm.
    Conditions: Primary—DS ID Multi. **Sec**—ADHD Ar As Asp Au B/VI CLP CP
        D Db D-B Ep HI IP LD MD ON S SB TBI. **Not accepted**—AN Anx APD Apr
        Bu C CD CF Dg Dpx Dx ED Hemo Lk Mood MS NLD OCD ODD Psy PTSD
        PW SA SC SO SP Subst Sz TS.
    Gen Acad. Ungraded. Culinary. Hort. On-Job Trng. Shelt_Workshop.
        Feat—Creative_Arts.
    Therapy: Aqua Hear Hydro Lang Music Occup Phys Rec Speech.
        Psychotherapy: Art Dance Indiv. **Counseling:** Educ Voc.
    Adm: Appl due: Mar.
    Enr: 275. Bdg 250. Day 25. B 155. G 120. **Fac:** 25. Spec ed 20. Lay 5.
    Tui '12-'13: Bdg $6000-7500/sch yr. Day $0/sch yr. **Summer prgm:** Res &
        Day. Educ. Rec. Ther. 7 wks.
    Est 1964. Nonprofit. Jewish.

HASC provides educational and clinical services for individuals from infancy through adulthood who exhibit developmental delays. The no-fee early intervention program, for children from birth to age 3, offers year-round evaluations and services at the child's home, a daycare setting or one of HASC's centers. Children ages 3-5 may participate in half- or full-day preschool programs; if the child's school district grants its approval, the preschool incurs no fee.

The school-age educational program (ages 5-21) emphasizes functional skills such as Activities of Daily Living, academic achievement and socialization. In addition, the curriculum includes a prevocational component that incorporates travel training, community integration, socialization techniques, exploration of postgraduate programs, volunteer job experiences, workshop skills and hand-on work experiences. Therapy and psychological services are part of this program.

Over the summer, Camp HASC offers sleep-away and day camp experiences for individuals of all ages who have mental or physical handicaps. The camp synthesizes academic and recreational programming.

THE HEBREW ACADEMY FOR SPECIAL CHILDREN SCHOOL AGE PROGRAM

Day — Coed Ages 5-21

Brooklyn, NY 11219. 6220 14th Ave.
Tel: 718-331-1624. Fax: 718-234-1763.
www.hasc.net   E-mail: cs.mandel@hasc.net
Debra Mandel, MS, Prgm Dir. **Zipora Rokeach**, Adm.
  Conditions: Primary—CP DS ID Multi PDD TBI. **Sec**—ADHD Ap Au B/VI C CLP Db D-B Ep Hemo HI IP Lk MD MS Nf SB SC TS. **IQ 0-49.**
  Not accepted—AN Anx Asp Bu CD D Dc Dg Dpx Dx ED Mood NLD OCD ODD Psy PTSD PW SA SO SP Subst Sz.
  Gen Acad. Ungraded. On-Job Trng. Shelt_Workshop. Support_Employ.
  Feat—Studio_Art Music. **Expected outcome:** Graduation.
  Therapy: Hear Music Occup Phys Speech Visual. **Psychotherapy:** Group Indiv. **Counseling:** Educ.
  Adm: Appl due: Year-round. On-campus interview.
  Enr: 72. **Fac:** 11 (Full-time). Spec ed 11.
  Aid: State 72 (100% of tui). **Summer prgm:** Res. Educ. Rec. Tui Bdg $6500-7500. 7 wks.
  Bldgs 1.
  Est 1963. Nonprofit.

Serving mono- and bilingual children with intellectual disabilities, Hebrew Academy's School Age Program focuses on development in such functional areas as academic skills, socialization and activities of daily living. Prevocational training constitutes an integral part of instruction; programming incorporates various transitional services and seeks to address students' futures in adult society.

Programs include travel training, community integration, socialization techniques, job-searching tactics, exploration of post-school programs, volunteer job experience, workshop skills and hands-on experience. Assistive technology and adaptive computers enhance learning. Psychological services and various therapies are available.

HENRY VISCARDI SCHOOL

Day — Coed Ages 3-21

Albertson, NY 11507. 201 I U Willets Rd.

Tel: 516-465-1696.
www.henryviscardischool.org   E-mail: jglover@henryviscardischool.org
Patrice McCarthy Kuntzler, Exec Dir.
Conditions: Primary—CP MD ON SB. **Sec**—S.
Col Prep. Gen Acad. Voc. Gr PS-12. Man_Arts & Shop. On-Job Trng.
Expected outcome: Graduation.
Therapy: Hear Occup Phys Speech. **Psychotherapy:** Fam Group Indiv.
Enr: 184.
Aid: State 184 (100% of tui).
Acres 15. Libs 1. Pools 1. Comp labs 1.
Est 1962. Nonprofit.

This state-supported school serves severely physically handicapped children who are excluded from public schools and placed on homebound instruction. A primarily academic program, HVS' curriculum includes college preparatory, general academic and remedial courses, as well as technical and vocational training.

HOLY CHILDHOOD SCHOOL PROGRAM

Day — Coed Ages 5-21

Rochester, NY 14623. 100 Groton Pky.
Tel: 585-359-3710. Fax: 585-359-3722.
www.holychildhood.org   E-mail: mbyrne@holychildhood.org
Donna Dedee, Pres. **Melanie Byrne,** Prin.
Conditions: Primary—Asp Au DS ID PDD. **IQ 30-75.**
Voc. Ungraded. Man_Arts & Shop. Shelt_Workshop. **Feat**—Home_Ec Adaptive_Phys_Ed Life_Skills.
Therapy: Lang Music Occup Rec Speech. **Psychotherapy:** Dance Group Indiv.
Enr: 106 (Cap: 116). B 63. G 43. **Fac:** 23 (Full-time). Spec ed 19. Lay 4.
Est 1946. Nonprofit.

Founded by the Sisters of St. Joseph of Rochester, this school serves individuals with mental retardation in Monroe County. Intensive education features all basic subjects, and class size averages 10 students. Prevocational and vocational training supplements standard academics. Courses in cooking, sewing, woodworking, weaving and ceramics are part of the curriculum. Emphasis is also placed on physical fitness, exercise and recreation.

In addition to sports-oriented activities, students may also participate in programs designed to enhance perceptual ability and coordination. The school does not accept pupils with severe emotional or physical special needs.

THE HOUSE OF THE GOOD SHEPHERD

Bdg — Boys Ages 6-17, Girls 12-17; Day — Coed 6-18

Utica, NY 13502. 1550 Champlin Ave.
Tel: 315-235-7600. Fax: 315-235-7609.
www.hgs-utica.com   E-mail: info@hgs-utica.com

William F. Holicky, Jr., MSW, Exec Dir. **Mark T. Ruffing,** Intake.
  Conditions: Primary—ADHD Anx CD ED Mood PTSD SP TS. **Sec**—As D Db
  LD OCD S. **IQ 65-120.**
  Gen Acad. Gr K-12. Man_Arts & Shop. **Expected outcome:** Return to local
  school (Avg length of stay: 6-12 mos).
  Therapy: Lang Milieu Occup Play Rec Speech. **Psychotherapy:** Fam Group
  Indiv.
  Enr: 180. Bdg 170. Day 10. B 116. G 64. **Fac:** 12 (Full-time). Spec ed 10. Lay 2.
  Acres 27. Libs 1. Gyms 1. Comp labs 1.
  Est 1872. Nonprofit.

The House provides children and families with the treatment, education and support services designed to help them succeed individually, within the family and as part of the community. Tilton School, the 12-month special education day school that forms an integral part of the overall program, consists of two divisions: Tilton East, for children ages 6-13 (grades 1-8), and Tilton West, for teenagers ages 14-18. Educational support services for all students include occupational therapy, speech and language therapy, and a learning center.

Aside from the educational program, HGS operates two group homes, two boarding homes, a residential treatment center and a residential treatment facility. Preventive, aftercare, diagnostic, emergency housing, nonsecure detention and foster care services are also available. Referrals come from public agencies. Both residential and day service programs operate year-round, with the usual duration of treatment being six to 12 months.

THE KARAFIN SCHOOL

Day — Coed Ages 13-21

Mount Kisco, NY 10549. 40-1 Radio Cir, PO Box 277.
Tel: 914-666-9211. Fax: 914-666-9868.
www.karafinschool.com   E-mail: karafin@optonline.net
Bart A. Donow, PhD, Dir.
  Conditions: Primary—ADHD Anx Asp Au CD Dc Dg Dx ED LD Mood Multi
  OCD ODD PDD PTSD SA SP TBI TS. **Sec**—Psy Sz. **IQ 80 and up.**
  Not accepted—ID MR Subst.
  Col Prep. Gen Acad. Underachiever. Gr 9-12. **Feat**—Ital Span Computers
  Studio_Art Music. Avg SAT: CR 600. M 600. W 575. SAT/ACT prep. **Expected
  outcome:** Return to local school (Avg length of stay: 2½ yrs).
  Therapy: Speech. **Psychotherapy:** Group Indiv. **Counseling:** Educ.
  Adm: Appl fee: $0. Appl due: Year-round. On-campus interview.
  Enr: 84 (Cap: 84). **Fac:** 26. Spec ed 22. Lay 4.
  Tui '11-'12: Day $27,945/sch yr.
  Bldgs 100% ADA.
  Est 1958. Inc.

A school for underachievers and children with learning and emotional disabilities who have been unable to achieve to potential in the regular school environment, Karafin provides a specialized, individualized structure that addresses the particular needs of each child. The goal is to remediate learning disabilities and to develop skills, confidence and motivation so that students are able to make the transition back to a mainstream setting.

Karafin devises each student's program after testing by the pupil's school district and reports and evaluations from psychologists, psychiatrists and neurologists.

KILDONAN SCHOOL
Bdg — Coed Ages 11-19; Day — Coed 7-19

Amenia, NY 12501. 425 Morse Hill Rd.
Tel: 845-373-8111. Fax: 845-373-9793.
www.kildonan.org   E-mail: info@kildonan.org
Kevin Pendergast, BA, JD, Head. **Beth Rainey**, Adm.
  Conditions: Primary—Dx LD.
  Col Prep. Gr 2-12. Man_Arts & Shop. **Feat—**Computers Robotics Studio_Art. Interscholastic sports. **Expected outcome:** Return to local school (Avg length of stay: 2 yrs).
  Therapy: Lang Speech. **Psychotherapy:** Indiv.
  Adm: Appl fee: $50. Appl due: Rolling. On-campus interview.
  Enr: 95. **Fac:** 63 (Full 62, Part 1).
  Tui '12-'13: Bdg $63,800/sch yr (+$1500). Day $46,900/sch yr (+$500).
  Aid: School 41 ($485,000). **Summer prgm:** Bdg & Day. Educ. Rec. Tui Bdg $10,000 (+$500). Tui Day $5000-7500 (+$250). 6 wks.
  Endow $636,000. Plant val $1,500,000. Acres 325. Bldgs 18. Dorms 3. Dorm rms 93. Class rms 21. Lib 14,975 vols. Sci labs 1. Art studios 2. Athletic ctrs 1. Fields 4. Courts 3. Riding rings 1. Stables 1. Comp labs 1. Laptop prgm Gr 2-12.
  Est 1969. Nonprofit.

Located on a 325-acre campus, the school serves boys and girls of average to above-average intelligence with dyslexia and language-based learning differences. Each student receives daily, one-to-one Orton-Gillingham tutoring. Other notable aspects of the program include college preparatory classes, opportunities in the arts and interscholastic athletics.

Dunnabeck at Kildonan, the country's oldest camp for children with dyslexia, operates on campus. Established to address the needs of intelligent boys and girls who are under-achieving or failing in their academic work due to dyslexia, this summer program's educational programming also centers around one-to-one Orton-Gillingham tutoring. Recreational activities at Dunnabeck include horseback riding, arts and crafts, and water-skiing.

LAVELLE SCHOOL FOR THE BLIND
Day — Coed Ages 3-21

Bronx, NY 10469. 3830 Paulding Ave.
Tel: 718-882-1212. Fax: 718-882-0005.
www.lavelleschool.org   E-mail: administration@lavelleschool.org
Frank Simpson, Supt.
  Conditions: Primary—B/VI D-B.
  Gen Acad. Ungraded. Man_Arts & Shop. **Expected outcome:** Graduation.
  Therapy: Hear Occup Phys Speech. **Psychotherapy:** Indiv.
  Enr: 90.

Summer prgm: Day. Educ. 6 wks.
Est 1904. Nonprofit.

Education of the legally blind at Lavelle consists of an academic program, training in braille techniques, music, manual arts, gymnastics, typing, dramatics and cane travel. Counseling is available. The length of stay varies.

THE LOWELL SCHOOL

Day — Coed Ages 6-21

Flushing, NY 11355. 142-45 58th Rd.
Tel: 718-445-4222. Fax: 718-353-6942.
www.thelowellschool.com   E-mail: rwasserman@thelowellschool.com
  Nearby locations: 203-05 32nd Ave, Bayside 11361.
Dede Proujansky, Exec Dir. **Rona Wasserman & Ruth Joseph,** Adms.
  Conditions: Primary—Dx LD Multi S. **Sec**—ED OCD. **IQ 70 and up.**
  Gen Acad. Gr 1-12. On-Job Trng. **Feat**—Creative_Writing ASL Marine_Bio/
    Sci Robotics Law Photog Studio_Art Drama Music. Interscholastic sports.
  Expected outcome: Return to local school.
  Therapy: Hear Lang Occup Phys Speech. **Psychotherapy:** Art Group Indiv.
  Counseling: Educ Voc.
  Adm: Appl fee: $50. Appl due: Rolling. On-campus interview.
  Enr: 240. **Fac:** 35.
  Summer prgm: Day. Educ. 6 wks.
  Est 1968. Nonprofit.

The school emphasizes intensive one-on-one sessions with specialists for building basic reading and math skills, language development and perceptual-motor skills. Each student participates in full academic, art and music programs. Counseling is offered, and Lowell encourages strong parental participation.

The improvement of the student's day-to-day performance and a placement in a less restrictive environment are program goals. Pupils who remain at Lowell through grade 12 typically enter the workforce, attend college or proceed to a vocational training program.

The elementary and middle schools occupy a separate campus in the Bayside section of Queens.

MAPLEBROOK SCHOOL

Bdg and Day — Coed Ages 11-21

Amenia, NY 12501. 5142 Rte 22.
Tel: 845-373-9511. Fax: 845-373-7029.
www.maplebrookschool.org   E-mail: jscully@maplebrookschool.org
Donna M. Konkolics, MA, Head. **Jennifer L. Scully,** Adm.
  Conditions: Primary—ADHD Ap LD S. **Sec**—Apr Dc Dg Dx Ep ON TBI.
    IQ 70-95. Not accepted—CD ED.
  Gen Acad. Underachiever. Ungraded. On-Job Trng. **Feat**—Span Computers
    Econ Govt Psych Performing_Arts Studio_Art Journ Home_Ec. Interscho-

lastic sports. **Expected outcome:** Return to local school (Avg length of stay: 4 yrs).
Therapy: Lang Perceptual-Motor Speech. **Counseling:** Educ.
Adm: Appl fee: $0. Appl due: Rolling. On-campus interview.
Enr: 116. Bdg 109. Day 7. B 56. G 60. **Fac:** 30 (Full 27, Part 3).
Tui '12-'13: Bdg $57,000-59,000/sch yr (+$400). Day $38,150/sch yr (+$200).
Aid: School 29 ($150,000). **Summer prgm:** Bdg. Educ. Rec. Tui Bdg $8000. 6 wks.
Acres 98. Bldgs 29. Dorms 8. Dorm rms 58. Class rms 17. Lib 7100 vols. Sci labs 1. Lang labs 1. Theaters 1. Art studios 1. Music studios 1. Gyms 1. Fields 3. Courts 2. Pools 1. Rinks 1. Comp labs 1.
Est 1945. Nonprofit.

Maplebrook offers academic and social programs to adolescents who are unable to thrive in traditional school settings or whose learning differences require more individual attention. The program emphasizes multisensory instruction and the development of social skills and self-esteem. CAPS (The Center for the Advancement of Post Secondary Studies), a postsecondary program providing either vocational or college programming, is available to students ages 18-21 for an additional fee. All students in CAPS use laptop computers, purchased independently or through the school.

MARY MCDOWELL FRIENDS SCHOOL
Day — Coed Ages 5-17

Brooklyn, NY 11201. 20 Bergen St.
Tel: 718-625-3939. Fax: 718-625-1456.
www.marymcdowell.org   E-mail: heatherb@mmfsnyc.org
   Nearby locations: 133-135 Summit St, Brooklyn 11231; 23 Sidney Pl, Brooklyn 11201.
Debbie Zlotowitz, BA, MS, Head. **Heather Burchyns,** Adm.
   Conditions: Primary—ADHD Dc Dg Dx LD. **Sec**—ON S TS. **IQ 90 and up.**
   Gen Acad. Gr K-11. **Feat**—Lib_Skills Span Comp_Sci Visual_Arts Music Movement. **Expected outcome:** Graduation.
   Therapy: Lang Occup Perceptual-Motor Speech. **Psychotherapy:** Dance Indiv Parent. **Counseling:** Educ.
   Adm: Appl fee: $90. Appl due: Rolling.
   Enr: 196 (Cap: 250).
   Tui '12-'13: Day $49,177/sch yr. **Aid:** School.
   Est 1984. Nonprofit. Religious Society of Friends.

This Quaker school offers education and therapy to children of average to above-average intelligence with learning disabilities. Classes are small and are grouped by skill level and age. Enrichment classes include computers, drama/music, library, movement, science, Spanish and physical education. Middle school students are grouped in grades 6-8. Social skills groups are available for an additional fee.

The three school divisions occupy separate campuses, with the elementary school located on Bergen Street, the middle school on Summit Street (718-625-3939) and the upper school on Sidney Place (718-855-0141).

MARYHAVEN CENTER OF HOPE CHILDREN'S SERVICES

Bdg and Day — Coed Ages 5-21

Port Jefferson, NY 11777. 450 Myrtle Ave.
Tel: 631-474-3400. Fax: 631-474-4181.
www.maryhaven.chsli.org E-mail: robin.dwyer@chsli.org
Robin Dwyer, LMSW, Exec Dir. **Miriam Fortunoff**, Adm.
Conditions: Primary—Asp Au DS ID PDD. **Sec**—ADHD Anx Ap Apr As CD
CP Db Dc Dg Dx ED Ep LD Mood OCD ON PTSD PW TS. **IQ 0-70.**
Voc. Ungraded. On-Job Trng. Shelt_Workshop. Support_Employ. **Expected
outcome:** Graduation.
Therapy: Lang Occup Perceptual-Motor Phys Play Rec Speech. **Psychother-
apy:** Group Indiv. **Counseling:** Educ Voc.
Adm: Appl due: Year-round. On-campus interview.
Enr: 121. Bdg 110. Day 11. B 79. G 42. **Fac:** 59 (Full-time). Spec ed 16. Lay 43.
Aid: State 121 (100% of tui).
Acres 14. Bldgs 4. Dorms 4. Dorm rms 45. Class rms 14. Libs 1. Auds 1. Art
studios 1. Music studios 1. Gyms 1. Fields 1. Courts 1. Pools 1.
Est 1934. Nonprofit. Roman Catholic. **Spons:** Catholic Health Services of
Long Island.

Maryhaven offers educational, residential, recreational and clinical services to children
with intellectual disabilities, autism or multiple disabilities. The integrated team of teachers, residential counselors, nurses and clinical professionals maintain a consistent approach
while addressing the child's needs. Residential services operate year-round.

MILL NECK MANOR SCHOOL FOR THE DEAF

Day — Coed Ages 3-21

Mill Neck, NY 11765. 40 Frost Mill Rd.
Tel: 516-922-4100, 800-264-0662. TTY: 516-922-4750. Fax: 516-922-4172.
www.millneck.org E-mail: info@millneck.org
Mark R. Prowatzke, PhD, Exec Dir. **Kathleen Kerzner**, Prin.
Conditions: Primary—D. **Sec**—Au CP LD ON PDD S. **IQ 50 and up.**
Col Prep. Gen Acad. Voc. Gr PS-12. Man_Arts & Shop. On-Job Trng.
Feat—Lib_Skills Comp_Sci Web_Design Law Drawing Painting Studio_Art
Journ Health.
Therapy: Hear Lang Occup Phys Speech. **Psychotherapy:** Fam Group Indiv.
Counseling: Educ Voc.
Enr: 200. **Fac:** 43 (Full-time). Spec ed 35. Lay 8.
Tui '12-'13: Day $0/day. **Summer prgm:** Day. Educ. 6 wks.
Est 1951. Nonprofit. Lutheran.

Mill Neck Manor accepts severely to profoundly deaf children who have been evaluated
by the assessment team. Services are available for both deaf infants and their families. The
school maintains an early childhood center for preschoolers with communicational and
language delays.

An alternative program for deaf children with multiple disabilities offers preparation for independent living. The school is state supported and enrollment is not limited to Lutherans.

NEW INTERDISCIPLINARY SCHOOL

Day — Coed Ages 3-5

Yaphank, NY 11980. 430 Sills Rd.
Tel: 631-924-5583. Fax: 631-924-5687.
www.niskids.org   E-mail: info@niskids.org
Helen C. Wilder, MA, Exec Dir. **Betsy Kaplan,** Educ Dir.
  Conditions: Primary—ADHD Anx APD Apr Asp Au CD CLP CP DS Dpx Dx ED LD MD ID Multi NLD ODD ON PDD PW SB Sz TBI TS. **Sec**—Ap As C CF D Db Ep Hemo IP Lk MS Nf S SA SC Subst.
  Gen Acad. Gr PS-K. **Expected outcome:** Return to local school.
  Therapy: Hear Lang Music Occup Perceptual-Motor Phys Play Speech.
    Psychotherapy: Art Dance Fam Group Indiv Parent.
  Enr: 350. B 200. G 150. **Fac:** 23 (Full-time). Spec ed 18. Lay 5.
  Aid: State 350 (100% of tui). **Summer prgm:** Day. Rec. 6 wks.
  Acres 6. Bldgs 1. Class rms 20. Gyms 1.
  Est 1976. Nonprofit.

NIS provides education for young children with and without disabilities. Therapy is available at the school, at home and in the community. The length of treatment varies according to the child's needs, and there is no fee for children with disabilities who reside in Suffolk County.

NEW YORK SCHOOL FOR THE DEAF

Day — Coed Ages 3-21

White Plains, NY 10603. 555 Knollwood Rd.
Tel: 914-949-7310. TTY: 914-949-7310. Fax: 914-949-8260.
www.nysd.net   E-mail: brobinson@nysd.net
Janet Dickinson, Exec Dir. **Barbara McRae Robinson,** Adm.
  Conditions: Primary—D. **Sec**—ADHD CP Dx LD MD MS ON.
  Col Prep. Gen Acad. Voc. Gr PS-PG. Man_Arts & Shop. On-Job Trng.
    Feat—Studio_Art. Interscholastic sports.
  Therapy: Hear Lang Occup Phys Speech. **Psychotherapy:** Indiv.
    Counseling: Educ.
  Enr: 155.
  Aid: State 155 (100% of tui).
  Est 1817. Nonprofit.

NYSD offers a complete academic program for children who are profoundly deaf, as well as vocational, psychiatric and psychological casework and special training. Career and transition services are available at all grade levels, particularly for pupils age 14 and up.

THE NORMAN HOWARD SCHOOL

Day — Coed Ages 10-21

Rochester, NY 14623. 275 Pinnacle Rd.
Tel: 585-334-8010. Fax: 585-334-8073.
www.normanhoward.org   E-mail: info@normanhoward.org
Rosemary M. Hodges, MS, MEd, Co-Head. Linda Lawrence, Co-Head.
 Julie Murray, Adm.
 Conditions: Primary—ADHD AN Anx APD Asp Au Dc Dg Dpx Dx LD NLD
  PDD SP TS. Sec—Ap Ar As Bu C CF CLP CP D Db Ep Hemo HI Lk MD
  Mood MS Nf OCD ON S SC TBI. IQ 80 and up. Not accepted—B/VI CD
  DS ED ID MR ODD Psy PW SA SB SO Subst Sz.
 Col Prep. Gen Acad. Voc. Gr 5-12. Feat—Computers Fine_Arts Photog
  Music Indus_Arts. Expected outcome: Return to local school.
 Therapy: Lang Speech. Psychotherapy: Indiv. Counseling: Educ Voc.
 Adm: Appl fee: $50. Appl due: Year-round. On-campus interview.
 Enr: 129 (Cap: 160). B 94. G 35. Fac: 42 (Full-time). Spec ed 28. Lay 14.
 Tui '12-'13: Day $26,000/sch yr. Aid: School. State.
 Bldgs 1. Class rms 40. Libs 1. Sci labs 1. Theaters 1. Art studios 2. Gyms 1.
 Est 1980. Nonprofit.

The school offers remedial work to children of average and above intelligence who have learning disabilities. Programming combines learning strategies with remediation in an individualized learning environment. NHS' curriculum stresses college preparation in the areas of reading, writing, spelling, math and organizational skills. High school seniors fulfill a community service requirement as part of the government/economics curriculum.

OAK HILL SCHOOL

Day — Coed Ages 5-14

Scotia, NY 12302. 39 Charlton Rd.
Tel: 518-399-5048. Fax: 518-399-6140.
www.oakhill.org   E-mail: oakhill@oakhill.org
 Conditions: Primary—ED. Sec—CD OCD. IQ 90 and up.
 Gen Acad. Gr K-8. Man_Arts & Shop. Feat—Computers Studio_Art.
  Expected outcome: Return to local school (Avg length of stay: 2-3 yrs).
 Therapy: Speech. Psychotherapy: Fam.
 Adm: On-campus interview.
 Enr: 24. B 21. G 3.
 Aid: State 24 (100% of tui).
 Acres 8.
 Est 1970. Nonprofit.

The Oak Hill program is designed for children who have severe learning problems, behavioral disorders or both. Remedial education in all subjects, combined with field trips, camping and group discussions, aims to improve the child's self-understanding and academic and socializing skills. The usual duration of enrollment is two to three years, and the sending district pays tuition charges.

ORANGE COUNTY AHRC
JEAN BLACK SCHOOL

Day — Coed Ages 5-21

Middletown, NY 10940. 28 Ingrassia Rd.
Tel: 845-341-0700. Fax: 845-341-0788.
www.orangeahrc.org   E-mail: mmusante@orangeahrc.org
Michael Musante, Dir.
   Conditions: Primary—Apr Asp Au CP DS Ep ID ON PDD TBI. **Sec**—ADHD
   Anx Ap As B/VI C CD D Db Dg Dx ED IP LD MD Mood MS Nf OCD PTSD
   PW S SB TS.
   Gen Acad. Ungraded. **Feat**—Sci Computers Soc_Stud Music Life_Skills.
   Therapy: Aqua Occup Phys Speech. **Psychotherapy:** Art Fam. **Counseling:**
   Educ Voc.
   Enr: 51. **Fac:** 5 (Full-time). Spec ed 4. Lay 1.
   Tui '10-'11: Bdg $23,042/sch yr.
   Nonprofit. **Spons:** Orange County Association for the Help of Retarded
   Citizens.

Jean Black School provides comprehensive services, advocacy and assistance for students with developmental disabilities. Services include adaptive music; adaptive physical education; family counseling and support services; occupational, physical, and speech and language therapy; psychological services; and student counseling. One-on-one tutoring is available for an additional fee.

PARKSIDE SCHOOL

Day — Coed Ages 5-11

New York, NY 10023. 48 W 74th St.
Tel: 212-721-8888. Fax: 212-721-1547.
www.parksideschool.org   E-mail: parksideschool@parksideschool.org
Albina Miller, MA, Co-Head. **Leslie Thorne,** MA, Co-Head.
   Conditions: Primary—ADHD Ap APD Apr Asp Dc Dg Dpx Dx LD NLD.
   Sec—Anx.
   Gen Acad. Ungraded. **Expected outcome:** Graduation.
   Therapy: Lang Occup Perceptual-Motor Play Speech. **Counseling:** Educ.
   Adm: Appl fee: $75. Appl due: Dec. On-campus interview.
   Enr: 80 (Cap: 80). B 45. G 35. **Fac:** 27 (Full 24, Part 3).
   Tui '12-'13: Day $42,000/sch yr. **Summer prgm:** Day. Educ. Rec. Tui Day
   $8500. 6 wks.
   Bldgs 1. Class rms 10. Libs 1. Auds 1. Art studios 1. Music studios 1. Gyms 1.
   Est 1986. Nonprofit.

This elementary school enrolls children with language-based learning difficulties. Parkside's curriculum consists of three essential components: direct involvement and active participation in the classroom; supported communication methods, which incorporate such visual cues as sign language, symbols, pictures and photographs; and integrated, thematically organized hands-on learning experiences. Interventions address issues related to the child's social and emotional development, cognition, motor/sensory functioning and communication.

PLEASANTVILLE COTTAGE SCHOOL

Bdg — Coed Ages 7-15

Pleasantville, NY 10570. 1075 Broadway, PO Box 237.
Tel: 914-769-0164. Fax: 914-741-4565.
www.jccany.org   E-mail: ressvcs@jccany.org
  Conditions: Primary—ED.
  Col Prep. Gen Acad. Voc. Ungraded. Man_Arts & Shop. **Expected outcome:** Return to local school (Avg length of stay: 2 yrs).
  Enr: 118.
  Est 1912. Nonprofit. **Spons:** Jewish Child Care Association.

PCS provides a combination of special education and clinical services for children with emotional and behavioral problems and their families. Services include prevocational training, behavior modification, psychotherapy, remedial speech and reading instruction, music and speech therapy. Counseling, home training and therapy are available for parents. The usual length of stay is two years.

P'TACH

Day — Coed Ages 6-18

Brooklyn, NY 11230. 1689 E 5th St.
Tel: 718-854-8600. Fax: 718-436-0357.
www.ptach.org   E-mail: info@ptach.org
Judah Weller, EdD, Educ Dir. **Chana Kugelman,** Adm.
  Conditions: Primary—ADHD APD Dx LD. **Sec**—Dg. **IQ 80-130.**
  Gen Acad. Gr 1-12. **Feat**—Judaic_Stud. **Expected outcome:** Graduation.
  Therapy: Lang Music Speech. **Psychotherapy:** Art. **Counseling:** Educ.
  Adm: Appl fee: $150. Appl due: Rolling. On-campus interview.
  Enr: 200. **Fac:** 75 (Full 35, Part 40). Spec ed 75.
  Tui '10-'11: Day $32,000-35,000/sch yr. **Aid:** School ($1,000,000).
  Est 1976. Nonprofit. Jewish.

A group of area parents and professionals founded Parents for Torah for All Children to fill a community need for Jewish private schooling for children with learning disabilities. P'TACH's individualized programming features resource rooms, supplemental classes for which children leave their regular classes for one to two hours daily to receive specialized help with basic skills. Staff employ a diagnostic/prescriptive approach that involves analysis, then recommendations for areas of remediation. In the resource rooms, boys and girls work on note-taking, organizational, test-taking, thinking and study skills, among others.

QUEENS CENTERS FOR PROGRESS

Day — Coed Ages 3-21

Jamaica, NY 11432. 82-25 164th St.
Tel: 718-374-0002. Fax: 718-380-3214.
www.queenscp.org   E-mail: info@queenscp.org
Nancy Glass, Dir. **Cindy Heller,** Adm.
     Conditions: Primary—Ap Apr CP DS IP LD MD ID Multi ON S SB TBI.
       Sec—ADHD Anx As Asp Au B/VI C CF CLP D Db D-B Dpx Dx ED Ep
       Hemo HI Lk MS NLD PDD SC TS. **Not accepted**—Psy SO Subst Sz.
     Gen Acad. Ungraded. **Expected outcome:** Graduation.
     Therapy: Hear Lang Occup Perceptual-Motor Phys Speech Visual.
       Psychotherapy: Fam Indiv Parent. **Counseling:** Educ.
     Adm: Appl fee: $0. Appl due: Year-round. On-campus interview.
     Enr: 124 (Cap: 124). **Fac:** 17. Spec ed 15. Lay 2.
     Tui '12-'13: Day $0/sch yr. **Summer prgm:** Day. Educ. Ther. 6 wks.
     Est 1954. Nonprofit.

     QCP's educational program features a preschool (beginning at age 3), as well as classes for children ages 5-21. When indicated by the student's Individualized Education Program, the facility also provides counseling services and occupational, physical, speech and visual therapy.

ROBERT LOUIS STEVENSON SCHOOL

Day — Coed Ages 13-18

New York, NY 10023. 24 W 74th St.
Tel: 212-787-6400. Fax: 212-873-1872.
www.stevenson-school.org   E-mail: dherron@stevenson-school.org
Douglas Herron, MA, Head.
     Conditions: Primary—ADHD Dc Dg Dx LD. **Sec**—AN Anx Bu ED Mood OCD
       ODD SP.
     Col Prep. Underachiever. Gr 8-12. **Feat**—Poetry Ecol Comp_Sci Robotics
       Econ Psych Sociol Philos Film Studio_Art Theater. **Expected outcome:**
       Graduation.
     Therapy: Speech. **Psychotherapy:** Indiv.
     Adm: Appl due: Rolling.
     Enr: 75. B 51. G 24. **Fac:** 14 (Full-time).
     Tui '10-'11: Day $47,000/sch yr. **Summer prgm:** Day. Educ. 4 wks.
     Plant val $12,000,000. Bldgs 1. Class rms 11. Comp/stud: 1:1
     Est 1908. Nonprofit.

     The Stevenson School accepts only bright underachievers, preparing them for high school graduation and college entrance and seeking to develop their organizational and study skills. The educational environment is designed to strengthen self-motivation, encouraging the fulfillment of each student's academic potential. Parental involvement is modified, and students are expected to complete homework assignments under school supervision and on their own initiative.

The school takes advantage of the cultural opportunities of New York City through both curricular and extracurricular activities.

ROCHESTER SCHOOL FOR THE DEAF

Bdg and Day — Coed Ages 3-21

Rochester, NY 14621. 1545 St Paul St.
Tel: 585-544-1240. TTY: 585-544-1240. Fax: 585-544-0383.
www.rsdeaf.org E-mail: info@rsdeaf.org
Harold Mowl, Jr., PhD, Supt. Paul Holmes, Adm.
   Conditions: Primary—AN D. **Sec**—ADHD Anx Ap Apr Ar Asp Au Bu C CD CLP CP Db D-B Dg Dpx DS Dx ED Ep Hemo HI IP ID LD Lk MD Mood MS Multi Nf NLD OCD ODD ON PDD Psy PTSD PW S SA SB SC SP Subst Sz TBI TS. **IQ 65-130. Not accepted**—B/VI.
   Col Prep. Gen Acad. Underachiever. Voc. Gr PS-PG. Shelt_Workshop. Support_Employ. **Feat**—ASL Computers Studio_Art Music. SAT/ACT prep. Interscholastic sports. **Expected outcome:** Graduation.
   Therapy: Hear Lang Occup Phys Speech. **Psychotherapy:** Group Indiv.
   Counseling: Educ.
   Adm: Appl fee: $0. Appl due: Rolling. On-campus interview.
   Enr: 140. Bdg 30. Day 110. B 79. G 61. **Fac:** 64.
   Aid: State 140 (100% of tui). **Summer prgm:** Day. Educ. Rec. Ther. Tui Bdg $0. Tui Day $0.
   Acres 6. Bldgs 7 (100% ADA). Dorms 2. Libs 2. Sci labs 2. Auds 1. Art studios 1. Music studios 1. Dance studios 1. Gyms 2. Fields 1. Courts 3. Pools 1. Comp labs 4. Laptop prgm Gr 6-PG.
   Est 1876. Nonprofit.

RSD provides a comprehensive educational program for deaf and hard-of-hearing children residing in the western and central portions of New York State. Courses of study are arranged as in public schools. Students may enter a vocational program that offers industrial and graphic arts, driver education, computer study, home economics and business science. The program of occupational and educational training provides off-campus work experience for high school juniors and seniors. Counseling is available.

Home-based early childhood programs accommodate children from birth to age 3 who are deaf or hard of hearing.

ST. FRANCIS DE SALES SCHOOL FOR THE DEAF

Day — Coed Ages 3-14

Brooklyn, NY 11225. 260 Eastern Pky.
Tel: 718-636-4573. Fax: 718-636-4577.
www.sfdesales.org E-mail: ewhelan@sfdesales.org
Maria Bartolillo, Dir. Eileen Whelan, Adm.
   Conditions: Primary—D.
   Gen Acad. Gr PS-8. **Feat**—Lib_Skills Computers Studio_Art.
   Therapy: Hear Lang Speech.

Enr: 106.
Est 1960. Nonprofit.

Serving profoundly deaf elementary and middle school children, St. Francis follows New York State curricular guidelines at all levels. The school's active learning approach features mediated learning lessons throughout the instructional day in all grades and subject areas. Early intervention services are in place for children from birth to age 3, while the preschool accommodates three- and four-year-olds.

Parental involvement is integral to the program, as St. Francis encourages them to help formulate the student's educational plan, to observe the child in class and to participate in parent education programming.

ST. JOSEPH'S SCHOOL FOR THE DEAF

Day — Coed Ages 3-14

Bronx, NY 10465. 1000 Hutchinson River Pky.
Tel: 718-828-9000. TTY: 718-828-1671. Fax: 718-792-6631.
www.sjsdny.org   E-mail: ncollins@sjsdny.org
Debra Arles, MSEd, Exec Dir. **Noreen Collins,** Adm.
   Conditions: Primary—APD D HI. **Sec**—ADHD Ap Ar Asp Au C CLP CP Db Dc Dg Dpx DS Dx ED Ep Hemo ID Lk NLD ON PDD S SB SC TS. **IQ 90-120.**
   Not accepted—D-B IP MD MS Nf OCD ODD Psy PTSD PW SA SO SP Subst Sz TBI.
   Gen Acad. Gr PS-8. **Expected outcome:** Graduation.
   Therapy: Hear Lang Occup Phys Speech. **Counseling:** Educ.
   Adm: Appl fee: $0. Appl due: Year-round. On-campus interview.
   Enr: 120 (Cap: 150). **Fac:** 25 (Full-time). Spec ed 25.
   Aid: State 120 (100% of tui). **Summer prgm:** Day. Educ. Tui Day $0. 6 wks.
   Bldgs 1. Class rms 25. Libs 1. Sci labs 1. Art studios 1. Dance studios 1. Gyms 1. Comp labs 1.
   Est 1869. Nonprofit.

This state-supported educational program for school-age children emphasizes communicational skills through an aural-oral approach. Children under age 3 take part in a parent-infant program that provides weekly mother-child participation, both individually and in small groups. Personal counseling is available. The school's summer session is open only to pupils enrolled in the school-year program.

ST. MARY'S SCHOOL FOR THE DEAF

Bdg — Coed Ages 5-21; Day — Coed 3-21

Buffalo, NY 14214. 2253 Main St.
Tel: 716-834-7200. TTY: 716-834-7200. Fax: 716-834-2720.
www.smsdk12.org   E-mail: timk@smsdk12.org
Timothy M. Kelly, Supt. **Richard Szafranek,** Adm.
   Conditions: Primary—D Dg. **Sec**—ADHD AN Anx Ap Apr Ar As Asp Au B/VI Bu CD CF CLP CP Dc DS Dx ED Ep Hemo IP ID LD MD Mood MS Nf

OCD ODD ON PDD S SA SB SC TBI. **IQ 50 and up. Not accepted**—SO
Subst.
Col Prep. Gen Acad. Voc. Gr PS-12. Culinary. Man_Arts & Shop. On-Job
Trng. Shelt_Workshop. Support_Employ. **Feat**—Computers Graphic_Arts
Studio_Art Drama Journ Home_Ec.
Therapy: Hear Lang Occup Perceptual-Motor Phys Play Rec Speech Visual.
Psychotherapy: Dance Indiv. **Counseling:** Educ Voc.
Enr: 143 (Cap: 257). Bdg 32. Day 111. B 91. G 52. **Fac:** 48 (Full-time). Spec
ed 48.
Aid: State 143 (100% of tui). **Summer prgm:** Bdg & Day. Educ. Rec. Ther. 6 wks.
Est 1853. Nonprofit.

Admitting children of all religious faiths, this school provides both residential and day programs for children with hearing losses. Standard academic curricula are followed, with emphasis on total communication. Language modes utilized at the school include speech, speech reading, gestures, sign language, finger spelling, reading, writing and residual hearing. Boys and girls in secondary-level programs receive vocational and commercial training including business subjects, home economics and industrial arts.

THE SCHOOL FOR ADAPTIVE & INTEGRATIVE LEARNING AT FERNCLIFF MANOR

Bdg — Coed Ages 3-21

Yonkers, NY 10710. 1154 Saw Mill River Rd.
Tel: 914-968-4854. Fax: 914-968-4857.
www.sailatferncliff.com
William Saich, Exec Dir. **Stephen Madey,** Educ Dir. **Sheila Chu,** Adm.
Conditions: Primary—DS ID. **Sec**—ADHD Ap As Au B/VI C CP D Db Dc Dg
Dx ED Ep IP MD Mood OCD ON Psy PTSD PW S SB SP Sz TBI. **IQ 0-69.**
Gen Acad. Ungraded.
Therapy: Hear Lang Music Occup Phys Rec Speech. **Psychotherapy:** Dance
Fam Indiv.
Enr: 53. B 28. G 25. **Fac:** 17.
Est 1935. Nonprofit.

Situated in a residential neighborhood, this specialized school offers year-round educational, habilitative, medical and residential services for children with multiple disabilities. Services include special education; occupational, physical and speech therapies; adaptive physical education; and psychological and social services. Personal computers and electronic adaptive devices facilitate the acquisition of academic and communicational skills, as well as the ability to control one's environment. Traditional approaches to fostering growth and development are also utilized.

SAIL at Ferncliff Manor encourages parents and family members to participate in the child's individualized program. Activities and social events provide children with recreational opportunities and also promote awareness in the community.

THE SCHOOL FOR LANGUAGE AND COMMUNICATION DEVELOPMENT

Day — Coed Ages 2-21

Glen Cove, NY 11542. 100 Glen Cove Ave.
Tel: 516-609-2000. Fax: 516-609-2014.
www.slcd.org   E-mail: info@slcd.org
  Nearby locations: 87-25 136th St, Richmond Hill 11418; 70-24 47th Ave, Woodside 11377.
Ellenmorris Tiegerman, PhD, Exec Dir. **Christine Radziewicz, Dir.**
  Helene Mermelstein, Adm.
  Conditions: Primary—ADHD Ap Apr Asp Au Dc Dg DS Dx ED LD ID ON PDD S. **Sec**—As CP D Ep HI OCD TBI. **IQ 59-115.**
  Gen Acad. Gr PS-12. **Feat**—Studio_Art Drama Music Dance.
  Therapy: Hear Lang Music Occup Perceptual-Motor Phys Play Rec Speech.
    Psychotherapy: Art Dance Group Indiv Parent. **Counseling:** Educ.
  Adm: Appl fee: $125. Appl due: Year-round. On-campus interview.
  Enr: 440 (Cap: 501). **Fac:** 56 (Full-time). Spec ed 56.
  Aid: State 440 (100% of tui).
  Est 1985. Nonprofit.

SLCD provides educational services for children with or without developmental special needs who have severe language and communication disorders. Services include education, clinical evaluations and therapy. In addition, the program provides full-day childcare and parent education classes. Parents may also learn techniques to facilitate language learning at home by watching the child during the day on a closed-circuit video system.

SLCD runs preschool, elementary school and middle school programs at the main campus in Glen Cove. A second middle school (grades 6-8) operates in Woodside, while the high school (grades 9-12) occupies quarters in Richmond Hills.

STEPHEN GAYNOR SCHOOL

Day — Coed Ages 3-14

New York, NY 10024. 148 W 90th St.
Tel: 212-787-7070. Fax: 212-787-3312.
www.stephengaynor.org   E-mail: jlong@stephengaynor.org
Scott Gaynor, PhD, Head. **Jackie Long,** Adm.
  Conditions: Primary—ADHD Dc Dg Dx LD. **IQ 89 and up.**
  Gen Acad. Ungraded. Man_Arts & Shop. **Feat**—Writing Computers Photog Studio_Art Drama Music Speech. **Expected outcome:** Return to local school.
  Therapy: Lang Occup.
  Adm: Appl fee: $150. Appl due: Rolling. On-campus interview.
  Enr: 199. **Fac:** 70 (Full-time).
  Tui '08-'09: Day $41,800/sch yr. **Aid:** School 20 ($195,900).
  Bldgs 1. Class rms 18. Libs 1. Sci labs 1. Art studios 2. Music studios 1. Gyms 1. Comp labs 1.
  Est 1962. Nonprofit.

The program addresses the needs of children of average to above-average intelligence with language-based learning differences. The curriculum, which emphasizes the mastery of basic subjects, employs a remedial approach that features multisensory teaching methods. Individual support supplements small-group instruction in ungraded classrooms. Teachers, speech and language therapists, reading and math specialists, and occupational therapists work together to return the student to a mainstream environment.

SUMMIT SCHOOL

Bdg and Day — Coed Ages 14-21

Upper Nyack, NY 10960. 339 N Broadway.
Tel: 845-358-7772. Fax: 845-358-5288.
www.summitnyack.com   E-mail: dsherwood@summitnyack.com
  Conditions: Primary—Asp ED OCD PDD Psy Sz. **Sec**—ADHD Dx LD. **IQ 75 and up.**
  Col Prep. Gen Acad. Voc. Gr 9-12. Man_Arts & Shop. **Feat**—Humanities Span Forensic_Sci Computers Econ Govt Psych Sociol Ceramics Fine_Arts Studio_Art Music Indus_Arts Health.
  Therapy: Speech. **Psychotherapy:** Fam Group Indiv Parent. **Counseling:** Educ Voc.
  Enr: 124. Bdg 109. Day 15. B 85. G 39.
  Aid: State 124 (100% of tui).
  Acres 9.
  Est 1974. Nonprofit.

Occupying a nine-acre campus overlooking the Hudson River 18 miles from New York City, Summit treats children who are learning disabled or emotionally disturbed. The program offers a therapeutic milieu, clinical intervention, academic remediation and psychotherapeutic treatment. The duration of enrollment varies.

THE SUMMIT SCHOOL

Day — Coed Ages 7-21

Jamaica, NY 11432. 187-30 Grand Central Pky.
Tel: 718-264-2931. Fax: 718-264-3030.
www.summitqueens.com   E-mail: nmorgenroth@summitqueens.com
  Nearby locations: 183-02 Union Tpke, Flushing 11366.
Richard Sitman, Exec Dir. **John Renner,** Dir. **Nancy Morgenroth,** Adm.
  Conditions: Primary—ADHD Anx APD Asp Dc Dg Dx LD NLD OCD PDD. **Sec**—AN Ap Apr Ar Au Bu CLP CP Db Dpx ED Ep HI Mood Multi Nf ODD PTSD PW S SC SP TBI TS. **IQ 90 and up. Not accepted**—B/VI C CD CF D D-B Hemo ID IP Lk MD MR MS ON Psy SA SB SO Subst Sz.
  Col Prep. Gen Acad. Gr 3-12. On-Job Trng. **Feat**—Marine_Bio/Sci Psych Studio_Art Music Health. Interscholastic sports. **Expected outcome:** Graduation.
  Therapy: Lang Occup Speech. **Psychotherapy:** Indiv. **Counseling:** Educ.
  Adm: Appl fee: $0. Appl due: Year-round. On-campus interview.

Enr: 276 (Cap: 276). B 203. G 73. **Fac:** 50 (Full-time). Spec ed 30. Lay 20.
Aid: State 270.
Est 1968. Nonprofit.

Summit, which serves students with specific learning disabilities, emotional challenges or both, enrolls boys and girls from all five New York City boroughs, as well as Nassau, Suffolk and Westchester counties. Most pupils are at or near grade level academically, but they typically have demonstrated uneven performance.

The school incorporates learning and organizational strategies into its academic program. The development of social skills and pragmatic language are also important elements of the program. Students in grades 9-12 attend a weekly community service class.

The lower school campus, serving grades 3-8, operates in Flushing.

VINCENT SMITH SCHOOL

Day — Coed Ages 9-18

Port Washington, NY 11050. 322 Port Washington Blvd.
Tel: 516-365-4900. Fax: 516-627-5648.
www.vincentsmithschool.org   E-mail: awishnew@vincentsmithschool.org
Arlene Wishnew, BA, MS, Head. **Christine V. Cralidis,** BA, MS, Prin.
  Conditions: Primary—ADHD Asp LD. **IQ 90 and up.**
  Col Prep. Gen Acad. Underachiever. Gr 4-12. **Feat**—Span Computers
    Studio_Art Band Chorus. Avg SAT: CR 560. M 440. W 450. Interscholastic
    sports. **Expected outcome:** Graduation.
  Therapy: Lang Occup Phys Speech Visual. **Psychotherapy:** Indiv.
  Adm: Appl fee: $100. Appl due: Rolling.
  Enr: 60. B 37. G 23. **Fac:** 17 (Full 15, Part 2).
  Tui '11-'12: Day $25,000-29,000/sch yr (+$750). **Aid:** School 15 ($200,000).
    Educ. 6 wks.
  Plant val $8,000,000. Acres 4. Bldgs 3. Class rms 20. Lib 5000 vols. Sci labs
    1. Auds 1. Art studios 1. Music studios 1. Gyms 1. Fields 1. Comp labs 1.
    Comp/stud: 1:7.
  Est 1924. Nonprofit.

Vincent Smith's highly structured program, known for its individualized approach to teaching reluctant learners and students with learning disabilities, emphasizes the development of reading, organizational and study skills. Suitable pupils may have attentional disorders, Asperger's syndrome, or expressive and receptive language issues. The school maintains a low student-teacher ratio, and tutoring, remedial reading services and writing skills classes are important aspects of the curriculum. In addition to traditional courses, boys and girls take compulsory classes in computers, art, music, health and physical education.

Boys and girls accumulate 30 hours of required community service prior to graduation.

WESTCHESTER EXCEPTIONAL CHILDREN'S SCHOOL

Day — Coed Ages 5-21

North Salem, NY 10560. 520 Rte 22.
Tel: 914-277-5533. Fax: 914-277-7219.
www.wecschool.org   E-mail: murphl@wecschool.org
Linda Zinn, Dir.
  Conditions: Primary—Asp Au DS ED PW TS. **Sec**—ADHD Ep ID LD SA SP TBI. **IQ 36-100.**
  Voc. Ungraded. Culinary. On-Job Trng. Shelt_Workshop. Interscholastic sports.
  Expected outcome: Return to local school (Avg length of stay: 3 yrs).
  Therapy: Hear Lang Occup Phys Speech. **Psychotherapy:** Fam Group Indiv Parent. **Counseling:** Voc.
  Enr: 80 (Cap: 80). B 55. G 25. **Fac:** 15 (Full-time). Spec ed 15.
  Est 1969. Nonprofit.

WEC follows a behavioral approach in providing year-round therapeutic education for children with emotional problems and preparing them for regular public schools or sheltered workshops. Individualized academics, therapy, prevocational work activities and functional living activities are part of the program. Time is allotted for enrichment activities such as French, horseback riding, Scouts and the school newspaper during the school day. The average length of stay is three years.

WINDWARD SCHOOL

Day — Coed Ages 6-15

White Plains, NY 10605. 13 Windward Ave.
Tel: 914-949-6968. Fax: 914-949-8220.
www.windwardny.org   E-mail: admissionsinquiry@windwardny.org
  Nearby locations: 40 W Red Oak Ln, White Plains 10604.
John J. Russell, EdD, Head. **Maureen A. Sweeney,** Adm.
  Conditions: Primary—Dx LD. **IQ 90 and up.**
  Gen Acad. Gr 1-9. **Feat**—Lib_Skills Studio_Art Music. Interscholastic sports.
  Expected outcome: Return to local school (Avg length of stay: 2-5 yrs).
  Adm: Appl fee: $50. Appl due: Rolling.
  Enr: 546. B 336. G 210. **Fac:** 150.
  Tui '11-'12: Day $44,700/sch yr (+$100). **Aid:** School ($2,500,000). **Summer prgm:** Day. Educ. Tui Day $2500. 4 wks.
  Endow $4,300,000. Plant val $25,000,000. Acres 17. Bldgs 5. Class rms 40. Lib 14,000 vols. Labs 4. Art studios 4. Gyms 2. Fields 3.
  Est 1926. Nonprofit.

Windward's language-based curriculum serves students of average to superior intelligence who have learning disabilities. Small-group basic skills remediation is supplemented by physical education, art, computer and library skills. Boys and girls attend daily math, science and social studies classes. The goal is to academically prepare the student for a return to the independent or public school of his or her choice.

The middle school (grades 5-9) occupies a separate campus on West Red Oak Lane.

WINSTON PREPARATORY SCHOOL
Day — Coed Ages 11-18

New York, NY 10011. 126 W 17th St.
Tel: 646-638-2705. Fax: 646-638-2706.
www.winstonprep.edu   E-mail: admissions@winstonprep.edu
Nearby locations: 57 W Rocks Rd, Norwalk CT 06851.
Scott Bezsylko, BS, MA, Exec Dir. **William DeHaven,** BA, MA, Head. **Kristin Wisemiller,** Adm.
Conditions: Primary—ADHD APD Asp Dc Dg Dpx Dx LD NLD S. **IQ 90 and up.**
Col Prep. Gen Acad. Gr 6-12. **Feat**—Filmmaking Photog Studio_Art. Avg SAT: CR 613. M 587. W 531. Interscholastic sports. **Expected outcome:** Return to local school.
Therapy: Lang Speech.
Adm: Appl fee: $70. Appl due: Rolling. On-campus interview.
Enr: 198. B 133. G 65. **Fac:** 61.
Tui '12-'13: Day $53,850/sch yr. **Aid:** School 47 ($500,000). Educ. Rec. 3-7 wks. Sci labs 2. Gyms 1. Comp labs 2.
Est 1981. Nonprofit.

Winston Prep provides a language-based curriculum with a multisensory approach for students of average to above-average intelligence who have learning differences such as dyslexia, nonverbal learning disabilities and executive functioning difficulties. The skills-based curriculum offers intensive instruction with a favorable student-teacher ratio in academics, organizational skills and study strategies. Each day, boys and girls participate in Focus, a one-to-one instructional period designed to be the diagnostic, instructional and mentoring basis of the program. Winston Prep's College Preview Program enables juniors and seniors to take college-level courses at New York University.

A second campus operates in Norwalk, CT.   **See Also Page 33**

NORTH CAROLINA

THE FLETCHER ACADEMY
Day — Coed Ages 6-20

Raleigh, NC 27609. 400 Cedarview Ct.
Tel: 919-782-5082. Fax: 919-782-5980.
www.thefletcheracademy.com   E-mail: tgregory@thefletcheracademy.com
Junell Blaylock, BA, MSEd, Head. **Tiffany Gregory,** Adm.
    Conditions: Primary—ADHD APD Dpx Dx LD Multi NLD. **Sec**—AN Anx Apr
    Ar Bu CLP CP Db Dc Dg Ep Hemo Lk MD Mood MS Nf OCD ON PDD
    PTSD PW S SA SB SC SP TBI TS. **IQ 90 and up. Not accepted**—Ap Asp
    B/VI C CD D D-B DS ED HI IP ODD Psy SO Subst Sz.
    Gen Acad. Gr 1-12. Culinary. On-Job Trng. **Feat**—Span Computers Studio_Art
    Journ. SAT/ACT prep. Interscholastic sports. **Expected outcome:** Graduation.
    Psychotherapy: Parent. **Counseling:** Educ.
    Adm: Appl fee: $50. Appl due: Year-round. On-campus interview.
    Enr: 110 (Cap: 125). B 85. G 25. **Fac:** 30 (Full 29, Part 1). Spec ed 30.
    Tui '12-'13: Day $21,194/sch yr (+$125). **Aid:** School. **Summer prgm:** Day.
    Educ. Rec. 5 wks.
    Acres 4. Bldgs 3 (100% ADA). Class rms 30. Libs 1. Sci labs 3. Lang labs 1.
    Art studios 1. Gyms 1. Fields 1. Comp labs 3.
    Est 1981. Nonprofit.

Students with learning disabilities and attentional disorders develop basic academic skills at the school by means of a multisensory, systematic approach. Contracts, contingent rewards and social reinforcement are used to increase motivation and self-esteem. Fletcher offers full-day programs, a summer program, hourly tutoring and a supervised study hall beginning in grade 6, as well as a program for individuals with mild educational handicaps.

Boys and girls accumulate 40 hours of required community service in grades 9-12.

THE JOHN CROSLAND SCHOOL
Day — Coed Ages 5-18

Charlotte, NC 28207. 1727 Providence Rd.
Tel: 704-365-5490. Fax: 704-365-3240.
www.johncroslandschool.org   E-mail: peley@johncroslandschool.org
Maria M. Leahy, MAEd, Head. **Portia M. Eley,** Adm.
    Conditions: Primary—ADHD APD Dc Dg Dpx Dx LD Multi NLD. **Sec**—Asp
    Au PDD S. **IQ 90-135. Not accepted**—CD ED Mood ODD Psy SO Sz.
    Col Prep. Gr K-12. **Feat**—Span Studio_Art Music. **Expected outcome:** Return
    to local school (Avg length of stay: 3-5 yrs).
    Counseling: Educ.
    Adm: Appl fee: $100. Appl due: Year-round. On-campus interview.
    Enr: 90 (Cap: 90). B 71. G 19. **Fac:** 15 (Full-time). Spec ed 15.

Tui '12-'13: Day $16,020-19,425/sch yr. **Aid:** School.
Acres 3. Bldgs 2. Libs 1. Art studios 1. Music studios 1. Fields 1. Comp labs 4.
Est 1978. Nonprofit.

This college preparatory school provides a full elementary and secondary course of studies for boys and girls with learning differences and attentional disorders. The curriculum, which encourages exploration and creative thinking, is structured to accommodate a range of learning styles. A multisensory approach to reading incorporates the Orton-Gillingham approach. Integrated technology plays an important role in the curriculum: Interactive whiteboards are present in each class, and the school maintains several computer labs. Crosland prepares students for a variety of options upon leaving the school. On average, pupils spend three to five years at the academy, although some remain until graduation.

Although Crosland does not conduct a formal summer program, students may enroll in hourly tutoring sessions.

MANUS ACADEMY

Day — Coed Ages 6-18

Charlotte, NC 28226. 6203 Carmel Rd.
Tel: 704-542-6471. Fax: 704-541-2858.
www.manusacademy.com
Lesley Taylor, MEd, Dir.
  Conditions: Primary—ADHD Anx APD Dc Dg Dpx Dx ED LD Mood Multi NLD OCD ODD PTSD SP TS. **Sec**—AN Ap Apr Ar Asp Au B/VI Bu C CF CLP CP Db Ep Hemo HI ID Lk MD MS Nf ON PDD Psy SA SB SC TBI. **IQ 70 and up. Not accepted**—CD D D-B IP SO Subst Sz.
  Col Prep. Gen Acad. Underachiever. Gr 4-12. **Feat**—Span Studio_Art Study_Skills. **Expected outcome:** Return to local school (Avg length of stay: 1-4 yrs).
  Therapy: Lang. **Psychotherapy:** Art. **Counseling:** Educ.
  Adm: Appl fee: $95. Appl due: Year-round. On-campus interview.
  Enr: 58 (Cap: 60). B 35. G 23. **Fac:** 22 (Full 10, Part 12). Spec ed 22.
  Tui '11-'12: Day $20,000/sch yr. Clinic $55 (Tutoring)/hr. **Aid:** State 2.
    Summer prgm: Day. Educ. Tui Day $80/day. 10 wks.
  Acres 1. Bldgs 1 (100% ADA). Libs 1. Sci labs 1. Fields 1. Courts 1.
  Est 1984. Inc.

The academy provides customized instruction, educational therapy, and diagnostic and consultative services for persons with learning disabilities, attentional disorders and other special needs. Manus conducts two distinct programs: a school for students in grades 4-12 and a tutoring center that serves pupils four days per week in the afternoons and evenings. Summer courses and tutoring are also available during the summer months. Social skills training, behavior management, parent coaching and teacher training are components of the program.

NOBLE ACADEMY
Day — Coed Ages 5-19

Greensboro, NC 27410. 3310 Horse Pen Creek Rd.
Tel: 336-282-7044. Fax: 336-282-2048.
www.nobleknights.org   E-mail: info@nobleknights.org
Linda Hale, Head. **Tim Montgomery,** Adm.
  Conditions: Primary—ADHD Dc Dg Dx LD. **Sec**—ED Mood OCD ON PTSD
  SP TS. **IQ 85 and up.**
  Col Prep. Gr K-12. **Feat**—British_Lit Span Anat & Physiol Environ_Sci Econ
  Film Drama Journ Speech. Interscholastic sports. **Expected outcome:**
  Return to local school (Avg length of stay: 4-5 yrs).
  Therapy: Play Rec. **Psychotherapy:** Dance. **Counseling:** Educ Nutrition Voc.
  Adm: Appl fee: $75. Appl due: Rolling. On-campus interview.
  Enr: 165 (Cap: 215). B 114. G 51.
  Tui '12-'13: Day $16,995-17,700/sch yr (+$1500). **Aid:** School. **Summer prgm:**
  Day. Educ. Tui Day $200-1500. 2-6 wks.
  Acres 19. Bldgs 5. Class rms 40. Libs 1. Sci labs 5. Auds 1. Art studios 2.
  Dance studios 1. Gyms 1. Fields 3. Courts 2. Pools 1.
  Est 1987. Nonprofit.

Noble enrolls students of average to above-average intelligence who have specific learning disabilities, attentional disorders or both. The individualized approach enables faculty to make appropriate accommodations in light of pupil needs. Among the accommodations provided are extended testing time, use of a computer for written work, use of charts and diagrams as a supplement to lecture, and access to special assistance in the form of a reader or a scribe.

THE PIEDMONT SCHOOL
Day — Coed Ages 5-14

High Point, NC 27265. 815 Old Mill Rd.
Tel: 336-883-0992. Fax: 336-883-4752.
www.thepiedmontschool.com   E-mail: info@thepiedmontschool.com
Kelli S. Saenz, BEd, JD, Int Dir.
  Conditions: Primary—ADHD APD Dc Dg Dpx Dx LD NLD. **IQ 85 and up.**
  Gen Acad. Gr K-8. **Feat**—Computers Studio_Art Drama Music. **Expected**
  outcome: Return to local school (Avg length of stay: 2-3 yrs).
  Adm: Appl due: Year-round. On-campus interview.
  Enr: 54 (Cap: 65). B 32. G 22. **Fac:** 10. Spec ed 10.
  Tui '12-'13: Day $9461-15,117/sch yr. Clinic $150 (Evaluation); $50 (Tutoring)/hr.
  Aid: School 24 ($100,000). **Summer prgm:** Day. Educ. Tui Day $1000-
  1800. 4 wks.
  Endow $500,000. Acres 15. Bldgs 1 (100% ADA). Libs 1. Sci labs 1. Auds 1.
  Fields 1. Courts 1. Comp labs 2.
  Est 1982. Nonprofit.

Students enrolled in the school program attend either full- or part-time. Participants receive remedial attention for basic academic skills and work to perform to academic potential at this school. The goal is to return the pupil to a regular school in two to three years. Individualized instruction and a student-teacher ratio of no more than 5:1 are provided for reading, writing, language and math instructions. Full-time students receive instruction in science, social studies, art, drama, physical education, computer studies and social skills in groups of no more than 10 children.

Piedmont also offers assessment and one-on-one tutoring services for students from grade 1 through college. Areas of concentration in the clinic are reading and comprehension, written language, math, study skills, homework assistance, and high-school-level math, literature and writing.

STONE MOUNTAIN SCHOOL

Bdg — Boys Ages 11-17

Black Mountain, NC 28711. 126 Camp Elliott Rd.
Tel: 828-669-8639, 888-631-5994. Fax: 828-669-2521.
www.stonemountainschool.com   E-mail: info@stonemountainschool.com
Louis Shagawat, BSW, MSW, Exec Dir. **Shannon Higgins,** Adm.
  Conditions: Primary—ADHD Anx Asp Dc Dg Dx ED LD Mood NLD ODD.
    Sec—OCD TBI. **IQ 85 and up. Not accepted**—Psy Subst.
  Gen Acad. Gr 5-12. **Feat**—Sci Soc_Stud. **Expected outcome:** Return to local
    school (Avg length of stay: 12-18 mos).
  Therapy: Hear Lang Milieu Speech. **Psychotherapy:** Dance Indiv Parent.
    Counseling: Educ.
  Enr: 50. Fac: 12 (Full 10, Part 2). Spec ed 4. Lay 8.
  Acres 100.
  Est 1990. Inc. **Spons:** Aspen Education Group.

Stone Mountain provides a structured academic and behavioral program in an outdoor environment for students who have exhibited learning disabilities, ADHD, or emotional or behavioral problems. SMS follows a nationally standardized curriculum, and course work is transferable to other private and public schools.

While earning academic credit, the boys learn life skills by participating in such activities as backpacking, swimming, canoeing, white-water rafting, primitive skills development, basic carpentry and campsite construction.

OHIO

ADRIEL SCHOOL

Bdg — Coed Ages 6-18

West Liberty, OH 43357. PO Box 188.
Tel: 937-465-0010. Fax: 937-465-8690.
www.adriel.org
Kay Wyse, BS, LSW, Pres. **Todd Hanes,** Prin.
Conditions: Primary—ADHD Anx CD ED ID OCD ODD PDD PTSD SA TBI.
Sec—LD. **IQ 55 and up.**
Gen Acad. Voc. Ungraded. On-Job Trng.
Psychotherapy: Fam Group Indiv.
Enr: 32. B 20. G 12.
Est 1896. Nonprofit. Mennonite.

Founded as the Mennonite Orphan's Home, the agency shifted its focus in 1957 toward serving children with learning, behavioral and emotional disorders. Adriel offers treatment for children with an array of adjustment and emotional problems and also works with the children's families to help them overcome difficulties that inhibit healthy functioning. Five area residential treatment centers provide therapy, spiritual opportunities and on-campus education.

ELEANOR GERSON SCHOOL PROGRAMS

Day — Coed Ages 11-21

Cleveland, OH 44102. 10427 Detroit Ave.
Tel: 216-694-7200. Fax: 216-521-2604.
www.applewoodcenters.org   E-mail: mfalls@applewoodcenters.org
Melanie K. Falls, Exec Dir.
Conditions: Primary—ADHD Anx Asp ED Mood PTSD SA SP. **Sec**—AN Bu OCD Psy Subst Sz TS.
Gen Acad. Gr 6-12. **Feat**—Studio_Art. **Expected outcome:** Return to local school (Avg length of stay: 2 yrs).
Counseling: Educ Voc.
Adm: Appl due: Rolling.
Enr: 50. B 25. G 25. **Fac:** 7 (Full 6, Part 1). Spec ed 4. Lay 3.
Tui '12-'13: Day $26,590-34,047/sch yr. **Aid:** State.
Est 1970. Nonprofit. **Spons:** Applewood Centers.

Eleanor Gerson offers an alternative middle and high school experience for adolescents of average intelligence who, for various personal, behavioral or relationship reasons, have not had success in standard educational settings. The program comprises two separate schools, Gerson West School (grades 6-9) and Gerson High School (grades 9-12). The schools emphasize education within a personal and therapeutic milieu to bring about positive growth that accounts for individual needs and abilities.

The school's downtown location gives students access to other education and cultural experiences, among them theater, ballet and other artistic performances.

JULIE BILLIART SCHOOL
Day — Coed Ages 5-14

Lyndhurst, OH 44124. 4982 Clubside Rd.
Tel: 216-381-1191. Fax: 216-381-2216.
www.juliebilliartschool.org   E-mail: jjohnston@jbschool.org
Sr. Agnesmarie LoPorto, MEd, Pres. **Jodi Johnston,** MEd, Prin.
  Conditions: Primary—ADHD Asp Dc Dg Dx LD. **Sec**—Anx CP NLD PW.
  IQ 80-130. Not accepted—Ap B/VI CD D D-B ED HI.
  Gen Acad. Gr K-8. **Feat**—Computers Relig Music. **Expected outcome:** Graduation.
  Therapy: Occup Speech. **Psychotherapy:** Art.
  Adm: Appl fee: $50. Appl due: Year-round. On-campus interview.
  Enr: 121 (Cap: 124). B 81. G 40. **Fac:** 18 (Full 17, Part 1).
  Tui '12-'13: Day $18,500/sch yr. **Aid:** School. State 117.
  Laptop prgm Gr 3-8.
  Est 1954. Nonprofit. Roman Catholic.

The school's program is designed for the high-functioning child with mild to moderate learning disabilities, for those who learn more slowly and for those who have problems in a regular classroom setting. The full scholastic program addresses the needs of each individual. Children with mild cerebral palsy may be accepted, but children with severe disabilities are not accepted.

LAWRENCE SCHOOL
Day — Coed Ages 5-18

Broadview Heights, OH 44147. 1551 E Wallings Rd.
Tel: 440-526-0003. Fax: 440-526-0595.
www.lawrenceschool.org   E-mail: admissions@lawrenceschool.org
  Nearby locations: 10036 Olde 8 Rd, Sagamore Hills 44067.
Lou Salza, BA, MEd, Head. **Douglas W. Hamilton,** Adm.
  Conditions: Primary—ADHD APD Dc Dg Dpx Dx LD NLD. **IQ 90-110.**
  Not accepted—Au CD DS ID MR ODD PDD.
  Col Prep. Gr K-12. AP courses (World_Hist). **Feat**—Creative_Writing Mythology ASL Span Astron Environ_Sci Forensic_Sci Geol Marine_Bio/Sci Comp_Sci Robotics Comp_Animation Civil_War Econ Law Psych Sociol Art_Hist Graphic_Arts Painting Studio_Art Video_Production Drama Chorus Music Finance Journ Speech Culinary_Arts. Avg SAT: CR/M 977. Interscholastic sports. **Expected outcome:** Graduation.
  Counseling: Educ.
  Adm: Appl fee: $100. Appl due: Rolling. On-campus interview.
  Enr: 289. **Fac:** 54 (Full 46, Part 8).
  Tui '12-'13: Day $16,900-20,750/sch yr (+$500-2000). **Aid:** School 95

($900,000). State. **Summer prgm:** Day. Educ. Rec. Tui Day $850-1300. 4 wks. Endow $2,047,000. Plant val $16,000,000. Acres 192. Bldgs 4 (100% ADA). Class rms 80. 2 Libs 7000 vols. Sci labs 4. Lang labs 1. Auds 1. Theaters 1. Art studios 2. Music studios 2. Dance studios 1. Gyms 3. Fields 3. Comp labs 5. Comp/stud: 1:1 Laptop prgm Gr 7-12. **Est 1969.** Nonprofit.

In addition to college preparatory academics, this state-chartered school provides remediation in the areas of academics and organizational and study skills for bright students with learning disabilities and attention deficits from approximately a dozen counties and 70 communities throughout Greater Cleveland and Akron. Lawrence employs ability grouping in a small-class setting to enable the student to progress at a suitable pace. The carefully sequenced curriculum places particular emphasis on language arts and mathematics, but also includes course work in social studies, science, art, music and physical education.

The lower school in Broadview Heights houses grades 1-6, while students in grades 7-12 attend the upper school in Sagamore Hills.

MARBURN ACADEMY
Day — Coed Ages 6-18

Columbus, OH 43229. 1860 Walden Dr.
Tel: 614-433-0822. Fax: 614-433-0812.
www.marburnacademy.org
E-mail: marburnadmission@marburnacademy.org
Earl B. Oremus, BA, MEd, Head. **Scott B. Burton,** Adm.
Conditions: Primary—ADHD Anx APD Dc Dg Dpx Dx ED LD NLD. **Sec**—Ap Apr Ar As Asp C CF CP Db Ep Hemo HI Lk Mood OCD PDD S SA SC SP TS. **IQ 90 and up. Not accepted**—AN Au B/VI Bu CD CLP D D-B DS ID IP MD MR MS Multi Nf ODD ON Psy PTSD PW SB SO Subst Sz TBI.
Col Prep. Voc. Underachiever. Gr 1-12. **Feat**—Span Computers Studio_Art Drama Music Study_Skills. Interscholastic sports. **Expected outcome:** Return to local school (Avg length of stay: 4 yrs).
Therapy: Lang Speech. **Counseling:** Educ Voc.
Adm: Appl fee: $100. Appl due: Rolling. On-campus interview.
Enr: 170. **Fac:** 27 (Full 25, Part 2).
Tui '11-'12: Day $18,900-20,900/sch yr (+$50). **Aid:** School 48 ($200,000). State. **Summer prgm:** Day. Educ. Tui Bdg $700-1800. 4 wks. Endow $50,000. Acres 10. Bldgs 1 (100% ADA). Class rms 13. Lib 5000 vols. Sci labs 1. Art studios 1. Music studios 1. Gyms 1. Fields 2. Comp labs 2. Comp/stud: 1:1 Laptop prgm Gr 9-12.
Est 1981. Nonprofit.

Enrolling pupils with learning disabilities from approximately 30 central Ohio communities, Marburn provides a full primary and secondary program that seeks to remediate students with academic problems in a college preparatory setting. The academy's typical student possesses average to superior intelligence and has previously unremediated problems caused by dyslexia, ADHD or another specific learning disability. The program addresses academic skills, social interaction and problem solving.

MARY IMMACULATE SCHOOL

Day — Coed Ages 6-14

Toledo, OH 43623. 3835 Secor Rd.
Tel: 419-474-1688. Fax: 419-479-3062.
www.maryimmaculatetoledo.org   E-mail: mi-info@mitoledo.org
Shelli A. Staudt, BE, MSEd, Prin.
  Conditions: Primary—ADHD APD Asp Dc Dg Dx LD. **Sec**—Anx As Au HI ID SP TS. **IQ 75 and up. Not accepted**—C ED Ep Hemo Lk NLD OCD ODD ON SC SO.
  Gen Acad. Gr 1-8. **Feat**—Computers Relig Studio_Art Music. **Expected outcome:** Return to local school (Avg length of stay: 5 yrs).
  Therapy: Music. **Psychotherapy:** Art Indiv. **Counseling:** Educ.
  Adm: Appl fee: $0. Appl due: Year-round. On-campus interview.
  Enr: 50 (Cap: 100). B 38. G 12. **Fac:** 10 (Full 5, Part 5). Spec ed 6. Lay 4.
  Tui '12-'13: Day $4600/sch yr (+$150). **Aid:** School 21 ($45,000). State 15.
  Est 1960. Nonprofit. Roman Catholic.

Sponsored by the Sisters of Notre Dame, Mary Immaculate provides general academic instruction for pupils with learning disabilities and other learning differences, among them Asperger's syndrome and ADHD. Good candidates for admission typically have difficulties learning in a typical classroom setting, but they have the ability to master the material.

NICHOLAS SCHOOL

Day — Coed Ages 5-14

Piqua, OH 45356. 1306 Garbry Rd.
Tel: 937-773-6979. Fax: 937-778-2561.
www.rcnd.org   E-mail: nicholasschool@woh.rr.com
Carla Bertke, Exec Dir. **Holly Felver,** Prin.
  Conditions: Primary—ADHD Ap Apr Asp Au CP Dc Dg DS Dx ED ID Multi NLD OCD ODD S TBI TS.
  Gen Acad. Ungraded. **Feat**—Studio_Art Music. **Expected outcome:** Return to local school (Avg length of stay: 2-3 yrs).
  Therapy: Perceptual-Motor Speech Visual.
  Enr: 27 (Cap: 35). **Fac:** 6 (Full-time). Spec ed 4. Lay 2.
  Summer prgm: Day. Educ. Ther. Tui Day $575. 4 wks.
  Est 1976. Nonprofit.

The school provides a comprehensive educational program of academic and perceptual-motor skills for children with learning disabilities, developmental disabilities or attentional disorders, as well as for those nondiagnosed children who have not succeeded in traditional settings. Class work consists of one-on-one and small-group instruction.

ST. RITA SCHOOL FOR THE DEAF

Bdg — Coed Ages 14-21; Day — Coed 6wks-21

Cincinnati, OH 45215. 1720 Glendale Milford Rd.
Tel: 513-771-7600. TTY: 513-771-7600. Fax: 513-326-8264.
www.srsdeaf.org   E-mail: gernst@srsdeaf.org
Gregory Ernst, Sr., MEd, Exec Dir. Rebecca Hardesty, Adm.
   Conditions: Primary—Ap APD Apr Au D HI NLD PDD S. Sec—ADHD Asp
      D-B Dg Dpx DS Dx ID LD Multi ON SA SP. Not accepted—AN Anx Ar Bu
      C CD CLP CP Db Dc ED Ep Hemo IP Lk MD Mood MS Nf OCD ODD Psy
      PTSD PW SB SC SO Subst Sz TBI TS.
   Col Prep. Gen Acad. Voc. Gr PS-12. On-Job Trng. Feat—Lat Computers
      Psych Relig Studio_Art Health. Interscholastic sports. Expected outcome:
      Graduation.
   Therapy: Hear Occup Phys Speech. Counseling: Educ Voc.
   Adm: Appl fee: $100. Appl due: Rolling. On-campus interview.
   Enr: 182 (Cap: 200). Fac: 32 (Full 22, Part 10). Spec ed 32.
   Tui '12-'13: Bdg $39,600/sch yr. Day $31,000/sch yr. Aid: School.
   Plant val $4,000,000. Acres 33. Bldgs 2. Dorms 2. Class rms 22. Libs 1. Sci
      labs 1. Auds 1. Art studios 1. Gyms 1. Fields 1. Comp labs 2.
   Est 1915. Nonprofit. Roman Catholic.

A residential school for deaf and hard-of-hearing children, St. Rita School uses total communication—a combination of the oral method of lip reading and the manual method of communicating through signed gestures and finger spelling—in educating its students.

Out-of-state and physically and educationally handicapped deaf children may enroll. SRSD administers entrance and placement tests measuring basic skills in reading, language and math to all applicants.

SPRINGER SCHOOL AND CENTER

Day — Coed Ages 6-14

Cincinnati, OH 45208. 2121 Madison Rd.
Tel: 513-871-6080. Fax: 513-871-6428.
www.springer-ld.org   E-mail: cmendoza@springer-ld.org
Shelly Weisbacher, MA, Exec Dir. Jamie Williamson, Prin. Carmen Mendoza,
   Adm.
   Conditions: Primary—Dc Dg Dx LD. Sec—ADHD. IQ 90 and up.
   Gen Acad. Gr 1-8. Feat—Lib_Skills Computers Studio_Art Music. Interscho-
      lastic sports. Expected outcome: Return to local school (Avg length of
      stay: 3-4 yrs).
   Therapy: Lang Perceptual-Motor Speech. Psychotherapy: Group Indiv.
   Adm: Appl due: Rolling. On-campus interview.
   Enr: 200.
   Tui '12-'13: Day $20,960/sch yr. Aid: School ($750,000). State 115. Summer
      prgm: Day. Educ. Rec. 4 wks.
   Laptop prgm Gr 7-8.
   Est 1971. Nonprofit.

Springer provides various services for individuals affected by learning disabilities. The school's comprehensive academic program, which serves elementary-age students, features small-group instruction and diagnostic teaching. Pupils develop the skills and strategies necessary for success in traditional school settings. Individualized student programs may include one or more of the following elements: language therapy, psychotherapy and motor skills training. Springer provides each seventh and eighth grader with a laptop computer for school and home use.

The center provides information and offers referral services and programs for parents, teachers and students.

OKLAHOMA

TOWN & COUNTRY SCHOOL
Day — Coed Ages 6-18

Tulsa, OK 74145. 8906 E 34th St.
Tel: 918-296-3113. Fax: 918-298-8175.
www.tandcschool.org   E-mail: tstone@tandcschool.org
Loretta Keller, Int Head. **Tonya Stone,** Adm.
Conditions: Primary—ADHD Asp Dc Dg Dx LD TS. **IQ 90 and up.**
Col Prep. Gen Acad. Gr 1-12. **Feat**—Humanities Environ_Sci Computers
Studio_Art Drama Music. SAT/ACT prep. **Expected outcome:** Graduation.
Therapy: Lang Occup Speech. **Psychotherapy:** Parent. **Counseling:** Educ
Voc.
Adm: Appl fee: $25. Appl due: Year-round.
Enr: 155. **Fac:** 35 (Full 32, Part 3).
Tui '12-'13: Day $9950-11,100/sch yr (+$200-300). **Aid:** School.
Est 1961. Nonprofit.

The school aids children with learning disabilities, attentional disorders and developmental delays. Town & Country employs an individualized approach and a flexible curriculum that lessens scholastic stress and allows students to think, read, write, communicate and perform more effectively. To gain admittance, pupils must have a primary diagnosis of a learning disability.

OREGON

THE ACADEMY AT SISTERS

Bdg — Girls Ages 13-18

Bend, OR 97708. PO Box 5986.
Tel: 541-389-2748, 800-910-0412. Fax: 541-389-2897.
www.academyatsisters.org E-mail: cstrowd@academyatsisters.org
Stephanie Alvstad, BA, Exec Dir. **Rick Buening,** BSW, MAT, Educ Dir.
Chesley Strowd, Adm.
Conditions: Primary—CD ED LD Mood ODD Subst.
Gen Acad. Ungraded. **Feat**—Anat & Physiol Debate Journ Speech. **Expected outcome:** Return to local school (Avg length of stay: 14-18 mos).
Psychotherapy: Equine Indiv.
Adm: Appl due: Year-round.
Enr: 50 (Cap: 50). **Fac:** 5.
Tui '12-'13: Bdg $5900/mo (+$1500/yr).
Est 1994.

The academy provides academic, behavioral and emotional services for troubled, at-risk adolescent girls. Typical students have run away from home, chosen poor peer relationships, have boundary issues, have a history of poor academic performance or truancy, have substance-abuse problems, continually put themselves in dangerous situations and are considered to be beyond their parents' control.

The school's individualized approach utilizes cognitive behavior therapy to effect behavioral change. Educational services address the needs of pupils with various learning styles, from those with mild learning disabilities to high achievers. Recreational pursuits make use of the academy's wilderness location: Downhill and cross-country skiing, snowboarding, rock climbing, rafting, canoeing and camping supplement traditional music, art and athletic offerings.

Girls with active drug or alcohol issues and those on medication must be stabilized prior to admittance.

BRIDGES ACADEMY

Bdg — Boys Ages 13-18

Bend, OR 97701. 67030 Gist Rd.
Tel: 541-318-9345, 888-283-7362. Fax: 541-383-4108.
www.bridgesboysacademy.com E-mail: info@bridgesboysacademy.com
Joan McOmber, BS, MS, LMFT, Exec Dir. **Kelley Jones,** BS, Prgm Dir.
Conditions: Primary—ADHD Anx Asp CD ED Mood OCD ODD PDD SP Subst. **Sec**—Db Dg Dx LD NLD.
Col Prep. Gen Acad. Gr 9-12. **Feat**—British_Lit Creative_Writing Poetry Span Anthro Econ Asian_Stud Film Public_Speak Home_Ec. ESL.
Psychotherapy: Fam Group Indiv Parent. **Counseling:** Educ.
Adm: Appl fee: $0. Appl due: Year-round.

Enr: 20 (Cap: 24). **Fac:** 3 (Full 2, Part 1). Spec ed 1. Lay 2.
Tui '12-'13: Bdg $5600/mo (+$2000/yr). **Aid:** School.
Acres 18. Bldgs 5 (90% ADA). Dorms 1. Dorm rms 15. Class rms 3. Libs 1. Sci
labs 1. Art studios 1. Music studios 1. Fields 1. Comp labs 1.
Est 1997. Inc.

Bridges program for temperamentally challenged boys is based on four specific components: small population size, individually paced education, family involvement and a single-sex student population. The minimum length of enrollment is one year, with some boys requiring additional time to achieve their program goals.

Bridges conducts a year-round, self-paced middle and high school program that promotes credit recovery and transferable credits. Students who remain until graduation may earn a diploma. In addition to academics, the academy offers individual, group and family counseling; experiential learning opportunities; and community living options. Required community service is also part of the program.

OPEN MEADOW ALTERNATIVE SCHOOLS
Day — Coed Ages 11-18

Portland, OR 97217. 7621 N Wabash Ave.
Tel: 503-978-1935. Fax: 503-978-1989.
www.openmeadow.org   E-mail: contact@openmeadow.org
  Nearby locations: 7602 N Emerald Ave, Portland 97217; 7633 N Wabash
  Ave, Portland 97217; 7654 N Crawford St, Portland 97203.
Andrew Mason, BA, MSW, Exec Dir.
  Conditions: Primary—ADHD Asp Dx ED LD.
  Col Prep. Gen Acad. Gr 6-12. On-Job Trng. **Expected outcome:** Return to
  local school (Avg length of stay: 2 mos to 4 yrs).
  Counseling: Educ Voc.
  Adm: Appl fee: $0. On-campus interview.
  Enr: 180. B 90. G 90.
  Tui '12-'13: Day $0/sch yr.
  Est 1971. Nonprofit.

Open Meadow emphasizes peer counseling and group interaction. Students share in decisions regarding school rules, personal and group goals, class offerings and course content. Courses such as youth and the law, horticulture and creative writing supplement the basic educational program. The duration of enrollment ranges from two months to four years.

THOMAS A. EDISON HIGH SCHOOL
Day — Coed Ages 14-18

Portland, OR 97225. 9020 SW Beaverton Hillsdale Hwy.
Tel: 503-297-2336. Fax: 503-297-2527.
www.taedisonhs.org
Patrick J. Maguire, BA, MA, Dir.
  Conditions: Primary—ADHD Asp Dc Dg Dx LD NLD TS. **Sec**—ED. **IQ 90-110.**

Gen Acad. Gr 9-12. Interscholastic sports. **Expected outcome:** Graduation.
Therapy: Speech. **Psychotherapy:** Group Indiv. **Counseling:** Educ Voc.
Adm: Appl fee: $50. Appl due: Apr. On-campus interview.
Enr: 80 (Cap: 80). **Fac:** 20.
Tui '12-'13: Day $19,550/sch yr. **Aid:** School. **Summer prgm:** Day. Educ. Tui
    Day $865. 5 wks.
Est 1973. Nonprofit.

Edison offers an individualized high school program for adolescents who, due to learning disabilities or difficulties, have been unable to succeed in a traditional school setting. The curriculum focuses on reading and study skills, language arts, math, social studies, science and health. Classes are small and a noncompetitive grading system is used. Many pupils graduate from Edison, although some conclude their high school studies elsewhere.

PENNSYLVANIA

ACLD TILLOTSON SCHOOL
Day — Coed Ages 7-21

Pittsburgh, PA 15227. 4900 Girard Rd.
Tel: 412-881-2268. Fax: 412-881-2263.
www.acldonline.org   E-mail: info@acldonline.org
Kathleen Donahoe, PhD, Exec Dir.
  Conditions: Primary—ADHD Asp Au Dc Dg Dx LD NLD ON PDD. Sec—Anx
    Ap Apr Ar As C CF CLP CP Db Dpx Ep HI ID Nf OCD ODD PTSD S SB SP
    TBI TS. IQ 80-110. Not accepted—CD ED.
  Gen Acad. Gr 1-12. Feat—Computers Studio_Art Music. Expected outcome:
    Return to local school (Avg length of stay: 5-6 yrs).
  Therapy: Lang Occup Phys Speech. Counseling: Educ Voc.
  Adm: Appl fee: $0. Appl due: Rolling. On-campus interview.
  Enr: 83. B 51. G 32. Fac: 22 (Full 21, Part 1). Spec ed 16. Lay 6.
  Tui '12-'13: Day $44,295/sch yr. Aid: State 83. Summer prgm: Day. Educ. Tui
    Day $1300. 4 wks.
  Plant val $7,300,000. Acres 10. Bldgs 1 (100% ADA). Class rms 14. Libs 1.
    Auds 1. Art studios 1. Music studios 1. Gyms 1. Fields 1. Comp labs 1.
  Est 1972. Nonprofit.

ACLD Tillotson School provides a comprehensive educational and social transition program for boys and girls with moderate to severe neurological impairments and severe specific learning disabilities that may involve a complex combination of disorders. The school maintains small classes to facilitate individualized attention to student needs. ACLD's educational program is a composite and adaptation of a system of programs: learning support (with a concentration on language development, reading and learning strategies); life skills support and transition services; emotional support and social skills training; and specific types of physical support. Services are delivered in a highly structured and therapeutic setting.

Length of stay averages five to six years. Pupils who remain at the school through grade 12 and successfully complete their IEP earn a certified high school diploma.

ALLIED SERVICES
DEPAUL SCHOOL
Day — Coed Ages 7-14

Scranton, PA 18508. 475 Morgan Hwy.
Tel: 570-341-4398. Fax: 570-341-4396.
www.allied-services.org
Suzanne R. Rickard, Prin.
  Conditions: Primary—ADHD Dx. Sec—Dg. IQ 100 and up.
    Not accepted—DS ID MR.
  Gen Acad. Ungraded. Feat—Computers Studio_Art Music.

Expected outcome: Return to local school (Avg length of stay: 2-3 yrs).
Therapy: Hear Lang Speech.
Adm: Appl fee: $0. Appl due: Year-round. On-campus interview.
Enr: 45 (Cap: 60). B 28. G 17. **Fac:** 7 (Full 6, Part 1).
Tui '10-'11: Day $12,900/sch yr. **Aid:** School. **Summer prgm:** Day. Educ. 4 wks.
Class rms 8. Libs 1.
Est 1980. Nonprofit.

The dePaul School provides elementary education for dyslexic students of average to above-average intelligence. Candidates for admission should have no primary emotional problems and should not have been classified as behaviorally disturbed or mentally retarded. Course work, which is designed to help students gain independence in their learning, emphasizes organizational, study, test-taking, note-taking and textbook skills.

Parental involvement as a means of reinforcement is an integral part of the program. The usual length of enrollment is two to three years.

BENCHMARK SCHOOL

Day — Coed Ages 6-14

Media, PA 19063. 2107 N Providence Rd.
Tel: 610-565-3741. Fax: 610-565-3872.
www.benchmarkschool.org
E-mail: benchmarkinfo@benchmarkschool.org
Robert W. Gaskins, BA, MS, PhD, Head. **Adam Lemisch,** Adm.
Conditions: Primary—ADHD APD Dc Dg Dpx Dx LD. **IQ 90 and up.**
Not accepted—Au DS TBI.
Gen Acad. Underachiever. Gr 1-8. **Feat**—Lat Studio_Art Music. Interscholastic sports. **Expected outcome:** Return to local school.
Therapy: Speech. **Counseling:** Educ.
Adm: Appl fee: $125. Appl due: Rolling. On-campus interview.
Enr: 155. **Fac:** 76 (Full-time).
Tui '12-'13: Day $28,000/sch yr (+$300-550). **Aid:** School 47 ($665,000).
Educ. Rec. Tui Day $1120-3140. 5 wks.
Endow $6,634,000. Plant val $10,336,000. Acres 23. Bldgs 3 (100% ADA).
Class rms 25. Libs 2. Sci labs 4. Auds 1. Theaters 1. Art studios 1. Music studios 1. Gyms 1. Fields 2. Courts 1. Pools 1.
Est 1970. Nonprofit.

Benchmark serves bright underachievers, providing a complete curriculum of social studies, math, science, art, music, physical education and health, in addition to reading and language arts. Instruction in all subjects is individualized according to the student's needs. The program includes professional guidance in helping students to overcome social and emotional problems that may accompany academic underachievement. The successful return of each student to mainstream education is a school goal.

BUXMONT ACADEMY

Bdg and Day — Coed Ages 12-18

Pipersville, PA 18947. PO Box 283.
Tel: 215-348-8881. Fax: 215-348-1563.
www.csfbuxmont.org   E-mail: rickpforter@csfbuxmont.org
Craig Adamson, BA, MA, PhD, Exec Dir. **Rick Pforter,** Adm.
> **Conditions: Primary**—ADHD Dc Dg ED Mood OCD ODD PTSD SA SP
> Subst. **Sec**—AN Bu Dx ID SC SO.
> **Gen Acad.** Gr 6-12. **Feat**—Computers Photog Studio_Art Music.
> **Counseling:** Educ.
> **Adm:** Appl due: Year-round.
> **Enr:** 808. Bdg 78. Day 730. B 403. G 405. **Fac:** 41 (Full 5, Part 36). Spec ed 5.
> Lay 36.
> **Tui '12-'13:** Bdg $200-220/day. Day $110-120/day.
> **Est 1977.** Nonprofit.

In conjunction with Community Service Foundation, Buxmont offers special education residential and day services for students with social and emotional disturbances in grades 6-12. The residential program consists of 16 homes in Bucks and Montgomery counties, each of which accommodates six boys or six girls. Residents attend one of eight licensed special education schools. Candidates for this program have mental health or substance abuse issues; exhibit aggressive, impulsive or ungovernable behavior; have family problems or have suffered physical, emotional or sexual abuse; resist or refuse school attendance; or are pregnant.

The day program accepts boys and girls who have been referred by the juvenile justice system, children's and youth agencies, drug and alcohol commissions, and eastern Pennsylvania school districts. Buxmont formulates Individualized Education Plans and enrolls pupils in an academic program that leads to a high school diploma. Typical day students are truant or have been suspended or expelled from a previous school; exhibit aggressive, impulsive or disruptive behavior; have learning difficulties; have mental health or self-esteem issues; have had problems with the law; abuse drugs or alcohol; or have family problems or have encountered physical, emotional or sexual abuse.

CAMPHILL SPECIAL SCHOOL

Bdg and Day — Coed Ages 5-21

Glenmoore, PA 19343. 1784 Fairview Rd.
Tel: 610-469-9236. Fax: 610-469-9758.
www.camphillspecialschool.org
> **E-mail: information@camphillspecialschool.org**
`Bernard Wolf,` BA, Dir.
> **Conditions: Primary**—Au DS ID PDD. **Sec**—ADHD Ap Asp CP Dx ED Ep LD
> ON PW S TBI. **IQ 20-75.**
> **Gen Acad.** Gr K-12. Culinary. Hort. Man_Arts & Shop. **Feat**—Poetry Ger
> Photog. **Expected outcome:** Graduation.
> **Therapy:** Lang Massage Music Occup Phys Speech. **Psychotherapy:** Art
> Dance.

Adm: Appl fee: $0. Appl due: Year-round. On-campus interview.
Enr: 88 (Cap: 90). Bdg 58. Day 30. B 50. G 38. **Fac:** 12 (Full-time). Spec ed
  10. Lay 2.
Tui '11-'12: Bdg $69,000/sch yr. Day $37,000/sch yr. **Aid:** School 15
  ($400,000). State 80. **Summer prgm:** Bdg & Day. Educ. Tui Bdg $6900. Tui
  Day $3700. 4 wks.
Endow $1,000,000. Plant val $6,000,000. Acres 80. Bldgs 20. Dorm rms 25.
  Class rms 12. Libs 1. Sci labs 1. Auds 1. Theaters 1. Art studios 1. Music
  studios 1. Dance studios 1. Pools 1. Stables 1.
Est 1954. Nonprofit.

Accepting profoundly retarded trainable and educable children with intellectual disabilities, Camphill also provides care for those with Down syndrome, brain injury, autism, prepsychosis and multiple handicaps. The program includes special education classes, arts, crafts, music, drama and individual therapy and exercises. Results of periodic evaluations determine whether or not a child continues in the program.

In addition to developmentally appropriate cognitive training for each child, Camphill places emphasis on social, artistic and practical skills. Teachers utilize a curriculum adapted from Waldorf education, with its focus on experiential learning through the fine and practical arts.

CARSON VALLEY CHILDREN'S AID

Bdg — Boys Ages 9-18, Girls 12-18; Day — Coed 6-18

Flourtown, PA 19031. 1419 Bethlehem Pike.
Tel: 215-233-1960. Fax: 215-233-2386.
www.carsonvalley.org   E-mail: info@cvca-pa.org
Roberta L. Trometta, BS, JD, CEO.
  Conditions: Primary—ADHD ED LD Mood ODD. **Sec**—Sz.
  Gen Acad. Voc. Gr 1-12. Culinary. Man_Arts & Shop. **Expected outcome:**
    Return to local school.
  Therapy: Music Speech. **Psychotherapy:** Art Dance Fam Group Indiv Parent.
    Counseling: Educ.
Enr: 200.
Aid: State 200 (100% of tui).
Est 1917. Nonprofit.

Carson Valley provides children and adolescents with severe emotional disturbances or behavioral problems with residential treatment and therapy, as well as educational, parental and personal counseling. Neither fire setters, children with severe drug or alcohol dependencies, nor severely to profoundly retarded youths are accepted. Average length of stay in the residential treatment program is 14 months; placement in the school program is also fairly short in duration.

CLELIAN HEIGHTS SCHOOL FOR EXCEPTIONAL CHILDREN
Bdg and Day — Coed Ages 5-21

Greensburg, PA 15601. 135 Clelian Heights Ln.
Tel: 724-837-8120. Fax: 724-837-6480.
www.clelianheights.org   E-mail: clelian@aol.com
Sr. Ritamary Schulz, ASCJ, Exec Dir. **Sr. Charlene Celli, ASCJ,** MSEd, Prin.
Conditions: Primary—DS ID. **Sec**—ADHD Au CP Dc Ep Mood OCD ODD
  ON PDD TBI TS. **IQ 30-70.**
Gen Acad. Voc. Ungraded. Man_Arts & Shop. On-Job Trng. Shelt_Workshop.
  Feat—Sci Computers Soc_Stud Studio_Art Music.
Therapy: Aqua Hear Lang Music Occup Phys Rec Speech. **Psychotherapy:**
  Art Equine. **Counseling:** Voc.
Adm: Appl due: Year-round.
Enr: 90.
Summer prgm: Bdg & Day. Educ. Rec. 4 wks.
Est 1961. Nonprofit. Roman Catholic.

Clelian Heights offers individualized programs of language arts, math, science and self-help skills. Art and music courses are also available. In addition, the school conducts physical education in the areas of gymnastics, calisthenics, swimming, perceptual-motor training and team sports.

Supplementing the educational program are workshops in woodworking, grooming arts, needlecraft, greenhouse, ceramics and domestic arts. The school provides vocational training in the form of custodial work, groundskeeping, food preparation, small-parts assembly, childcare, domestic and commercial laundry, and dishwashing. Field trips and dances are an additional feature of Clelian Heights' program.

COMMUNITY COUNTRY DAY SCHOOL
Day — Coed Ages 6-20

Erie, PA 16506. 5800 Old Zuck Rd.
Tel: 814-833-7933. Fax: 814-835-2250.
www.ccdserie.com   E-mail: cshaffer@ccdserie.com
Aaron Collins, Exec Dir. **Karen Kitza,** Prin. **Carrie Shaffer,** Adm.
  Conditions: Primary—ADHD AN Anx Ap APD Apr Ar Asp Au B/VI C CD CLP
  CP D D-B Db Dg Dpx Dx ED HI Hemo IP MD Mood Lk MS Multi Nf OCD
  ODD PTSD SA SB SC Subst TS. **Sec**—Ep ID LD. **IQ 75 and up.**
  Not accepted—Psy PW SO SP Sz TBI.
Gen Acad. Gr 1-12. On-Job Trng. SAT/ACT prep. **Expected outcome:** Return
  to local school (Avg length of stay: 1 yr).
Therapy: Milieu Rec Speech. **Psychotherapy:** Art Fam Group Indiv.
  Counseling: Educ Nutrition Voc.
Enr: 90. B 50. G 40. **Fac:** 10 (Full-time). Spec ed 1. Lay 9.
Tui '12-'13: Day $50/mo. Clinic $18/hr. **Aid:** School.
Est 1968. Nonprofit.

The school features personal attention in a structured environment. Each student receives individual instruction in standard courses, and counseling is available. The usual duration of treatment is one year. Fees are determined along a sliding scale.

THE CONCEPT SCHOOL

Day — Coed Ages 11-18

Westtown, PA 19395. 1120 E Street Rd, PO Box 54.
Tel: 610-399-1135. Fax: 610-399-0767.
www.theconceptschool.org
James Symonds, Dir.
   Conditions: Primary—LD. IQ 90 and up.
   Col Prep. Underachiever. Gr 6-12. **Feat—**Span Anat Environ_Sci Health.
   Expected outcome: Graduation.
   Adm: Appl fee: $75. Appl due: Rolling. On-campus interview.
   Fac: 11 (Full-time).
   Tui '12-'13: Day $18,750/sch yr (+$1075).
   Est 1972. Nonprofit.

TCS enrolls boys and girls of average to above-average intelligence who have not fared well in a large-class environment but who have the potential for college placement. Subject matter incorporates various methodologies, and staff make classroom accommodations for learning-style differences. A multisensory teaching approach takes the pupil's learning profile into account and allows the school to determine the most effective manner to present material. Enrichment and remediation are available as needed.

CREFELD SCHOOL

Day — Coed Ages 12-18

Philadelphia, PA 19118. 8836 Crefeld St.
Tel: 215-242-5545. Fax: 215-242-8869.
www.crefeld.org   E-mail: info@crefeld.org
George Zeleznik, BS, MA, Head. **Stacey Cunitz,** Adm.
   Conditions: Primary—ADHD LD. IQ 90 and up.
   Col Prep. Underachiever. Gr 7-12. **Feat—**Span Environ_Sci Forensic_Sci
      Computers Psych Drawing Sculpt Bookbinding Glass_Blowing Acting
      Music Dance Debate. Mid 50% SAT: CR 490-640. M 470-580. W 470-590.
      Interscholastic sports. **Expected outcome:** Graduation.
   Adm: Appl fee: $75. Appl due: Rolling. On-campus interview.
   Enr: 96. B 60. G 36. **Fac:** 20 (Full 16, Part 4).
   Tui '12-'13: Day $24,000-27,050/sch yr (+$300). **Aid:** School 43 ($400,000).
      Summer prgm: Day. Educ. Rec. Tui Day $800/4-wk ses. 8 wks.
   Plant val $2,500,000. Acres 4. Bldgs 2. Class rms 21. Libs 1. Sci labs 1. Lang
      labs 1. Auds 1. Theaters 1. Art studios 3. Music studios 1. Dance studios 1.
      Gyms 1. Fields 1. Basketball courts 1. Comp labs 2. Comp/stud: 1:3.
   Est 1970. Nonprofit.

Guided by the principles of the Coalition of Essential Schools and research on multiple intelligences and learning styles, this progressive school follows a flexible and collaborative approach to learning. Crefeld serves able students, some of whom have learning differences, and it accommodates differences in learning style through differentiated instruction. When necessary, the school works closely with both the student's parents and outside professionals to coordinate efforts and formulate strategic plans.

Various electives, with an emphasis on the arts, complement the academic program. All students satisfy a two-hour weekly community service requirement during the school day.

DELAWARE VALLEY FRIENDS SCHOOL

Day — Coed Ages 11-19

Paoli, PA 19301. 19 E Central Ave.
Tel: 610-640-4150. Fax: 610-296-9970.
www.dvfs.org   E-mail: admissions@dvfs.org
Pritchard Garrett, BA, Kalamazoo College, MEd, Harvard Univ, Head.
  Mary Ellen Trent, Adm.
  Conditions: Primary—ADHD Dc Dg Dx LD. **IQ 100 and up.**
  Col Prep. Gr 6-12. **Feat**—Span Asian_Stud Photog Studio_Art Music. Mid 50% SAT: CR 440-550. M 370-490. W 420-560. ACT: Mid 50% 16-25. Interscholastic sports. **Expected outcome:** Graduation.
  Counseling: Educ.
  Adm: Appl fee: $100. Appl due: Rolling.
  Enr: 176. B 102. G 74. **Fac:** 39 (Full 34, Part 5).
  Tui '12-'13: Day $36,300-37,400/sch yr. **Aid:** School 48 ($667,600). **Summer prgm:** Day. Educ. Tui Day $2900. 5 wks.
  Endow $4,286,000. Plant val $10,300,000. Acres 8. Bldgs 1 (100% ADA). Class rms 46. Lib 5000 vols. Sci labs 4. Auds 1. Art studios 4. Gyms 1. Fields 2. Comp labs 2. Comp/stud: 1:1 Laptop prgm Gr 6-12.
  Est 1986. Nonprofit. Religious Society of Friends.

Enrolling intelligent students with learning disabilities, DVFS features language arts learning skills laboratories that provide small-group remedial and developmental assistance. All students take part in a daily reading and writing lab, and the school conducts an adaptive Outward Bound-type program that includes courses in rock climbing, backpacking, bicycle touring, ropes and hiking. Seniors participate in a compulsory, off-campus work-study internship, and each pupil is required to perform community service.

THE DELTA SCHOOL

Day — Coed Ages 5-21

Philadelphia, PA 19154. 3380 Byberry Rd.
Tel: 215-637-8235. Fax: 215-612-0469.
www.deltaschool.us
  Nearby locations: 3515 Woodhaven Rd, Philadelphia 19154.
Stanley M. Stein, CEO. **Cynthia Stein,** Adm.
  Conditions: Primary—Dx ED Ep LD ID.

Gen Acad. Ungraded. Man_Arts & Shop.
Therapy: Lang Occup Speech. **Psychotherapy:** Group Indiv.
Adm: Appl due: Year-round.
Enr: 150. B 134. G 16.
Aid: State 150 (100% of tui).
Est 1958. Nonprofit.

The school provides intensive education for individuals with learning disabilities caused by emotional problems and neurological dysfunctions. A primary focus is placed on building a foundation for learning skills. The secondary program prepares adolescents to return to a traditional academic setting. Psychological and vocational counseling is offered, and community work and work-study programs are available.

DEPAUL SCHOOL FOR HEARING AND SPEECH
Day — Coed Ages 3-14

Pittsburgh, PA 15206. 6202 Alder St.
Tel: 412-924-1012. TTY: 412-924-1012. Fax: 412-924-1036.
www.speakmiracles.org   E-mail: depaulschool@depaulinst.com
Ruth Auld, EdD, Exec Dir. **Mary Jo Maynard,** MA, MEd, Prin.
  Conditions: Primary—D HI S. **Sec**—ADHD Apr C CP LD ON. **IQ 90-119.**
  Gen Acad. Gr PS-8. **Feat**—Studio_Art Music Health.
  Therapy: Hear Lang Occup Phys Speech. **Counseling:** Educ.
  Enr: 72. B 45. G 27. **Fac:** 25 (Full 24, Part 1). Spec ed 14. Lay 11.
  Aid: State 72 (100% of tui). **Summer prgm:** Day. Educ. Tui Day $0. 4 wks.
  Est 1908. Nonprofit. Roman Catholic.

DePaul provides oral and aural education for children with severe to profound hearing loss through the use of the auditory/oral method of communication. The school also offers on-site and outreach services in the child's home, as well as on campus.

FRIENDSHIP ACADEMY
Day — Coed Ages 6-21

Pittsburgh, PA 15206. 255 S Negley Ave.
Tel: 412-365-3800. Fax: 412-361-6775.
www.thewatsoninstitute.org   E-mail: mboylan@thewatsoninstitute-fa.org
Mary Beth Boylen, PhD, Clin Dir. **Lauri Kragness,** MEd, Educ Dir.
  Jennifer Johnson, Intake.
  Conditions: Primary—ADHD Anx Asp Au CD ED Mood OCD ODD PDD Psy PTSD. **Sec**—Dc Dg Dx SA Sz TS. **IQ 82 and up.**
  Gen Acad. Voc. Gr 1-12. Culinary. Man_Arts & Shop. On-Job Trng. **Expected outcome:** Return to local school (Avg length of stay: 2-3 yrs).
  Therapy: Lang Milieu Music Occup Play Speech. **Psychotherapy:** Dance Fam Group Indiv Parent. **Counseling:** Educ Nutrition.
  Adm: Appl fee: $0. Appl due: Year-round. On-campus interview.
  Enr: 152. B 115. G 37. **Fac:** 34 (Full-time). Spec ed 26. Lay 8.

Tui '12-'13: Day $234/day. **Summer prgm:** Day. Educ. Ther. 4 wks.
Bldgs 100% ADA. Class rms 15. Libs 1. Sci labs 1. Art studios 1. Music studios
1. Gyms 1. Comp labs 1.
Est 1966. Nonprofit. **Spons:** Watson Institute.

The academy provides comprehensive, family-oriented social, educational and behavioral health services for children with severe emotional disturbances. The elementary program stresses appropriate work habits to enable the child to return to or enter community schools. A psychotherapeutic, rehabilitative secondary program for adolescents emphasizes skills relevant to employment or mainstreaming to public schools.

Vocational evaluation and counseling are available. Treatment typically lasts two to three years.

GREEN TREE SCHOOL
Day — Coed Ages 3-21

Philadelphia, PA 19144. 146 W Walnut Ln, PO Box 25639.
Tel: 215-843-4528. Fax: 215-843-2688.
www.greentreeschool.org   E-mail: admin@greentreeschool.org
Bill Goldschmidt, BA, MEd, Int Exec Dir. **Keish Smith,** Adm.
Conditions: Primary—Asp Au ED PDD. **Sec**—ADHD. **IQ 70-119.**
Gen Acad. Underachiever. Voc. Ungraded. Culinary. Hort. Man_Arts & Shop.
   Interscholastic sports. **Expected outcome:** Return to local school (Avg
   length of stay: 3-5 yrs).
Therapy: Lang Music Occup Phys Speech. **Psychotherapy:** Dance Group
   Indiv.
Adm: Appl fee: $0. Appl due: Year-round. On-campus interview.
Enr: 82 (Cap: 173). B 66. G 16. **Fac:** 40 (Full-time). Spec ed 23. Lay 17.
Aid: State 82 (100% of tui). **Summer prgm:** Day. Educ. Tui Day $0. 6 wks.
Est 1957. Nonprofit.

Green Tree provides a therapeutic and academic program for children and youths who have been diagnosed with serious emotional disturbances, neurological impairments or both. Many have displayed several behavioral problems that have prevented them from succeeding in traditional settings. In addition to receiving instruction in basic academics, students participate in movement therapy and physical education.

Twice a year, staff members comprehensively evaluate a student's progress and restructure the program accordingly. Parental participation is encouraged at all levels. The usual length of stay at Green Tree is three to five years, with pupils then proceeding to a regular public school, a more advanced special school, a vocational facility or college.

HILL TOP PREPARATORY SCHOOL
Day — Coed Ages 10-18

Rosemont, PA 19010. 737 S Ithan Ave.
Tel: 610-527-3230. Fax: 610-527-7683.
www.hilltopprep.org   E-mail: mfitzpatrick@hilltopprep.org

Thomas W. Needham, BA, MEd, Head. **Meredith Reaves Fitzpatrick,** Adm.
Conditions: Primary—ADHD Asp Dc Dg LD. **Sec**—Anx Dx SP TS. **IQ 90 and up. Not accepted**—Au CD ED ID Mood MR ODD Psy SO Subst Sz.
Col Prep. Gr 5-12. **Feat**—Span Psych Ceramics Film Photog Studio_Art Fiber_Arts Drama Public_Speak Woodworking. Interscholastic sports.
Expected outcome: Graduation.
Psychotherapy: Group Indiv. **Counseling:** Educ.
Adm: Appl fee: $75. Appl due: Rolling.
Enr: 82. B 67. G 15. **Fac:** 30 (Full 28, Part 2).
Tui '12-'13: Day $38,050/sch yr. **Aid:** School 21 ($127,000). State. **Summer prgm:** Day. Educ. Rec. Tui Day $2000-3600. 3-6 wks.
Acres 25. Bldgs 4. Class rms 20. Libs 1. Sci labs 1. Photog labs 1. Art studios 1. Gyms 1. Fields 1. Courts 1. Pools 1. Comp labs 4. Laptop prgm Gr 6-12.
Est 1971. Nonprofit.

For students of average and above-average intelligence who have learning disabilities or attention deficit disorder, the specially designed program utilizes individualized instruction to prepare students for college and employment. Reality-oriented group counseling sessions are integral to the program.

THE HILLSIDE SCHOOL

Day — Coed Ages 5-13

Macungie, PA 18062. 2697 Brookside Rd.
Tel: 610-967-3701. Fax: 610-965-7683.
www.hillsideschool.org E-mail: office@hillsideschool.org
David Mendlewski, BA, MSEd, Head. **Jacqueline Wynocker,** Adm.
Conditions: Primary—Dc Dg Dx LD. **Sec**—ADHD Apr Dpx ED HI S SP.
IQ 100 and up. Not accepted—Asp Au B/VI D D-B ID MR ODD PDD Psy SO Subst Sz TBI.
Gen Acad. Gr K-6. **Feat**—Studio_Art Music. **Expected outcome:** Return to local school (Avg length of stay: 3 yrs).
Therapy: Lang Speech. **Counseling:** Educ.
Adm: Appl fee: $100. Appl due: Year-round. On-campus interview.
Enr: 117 (Cap: 128). **Fac:** 20 (Full 15, Part 5).
Tui '12-'13: Day $19,005/sch yr. **Aid:** School 50 ($360,000). **Summer prgm:** Day. Educ. Rec. 2 wks.
Est 1983. Nonprofit.

Hillside offers a carefully structured educational program for children of average to above-average intelligence who have learning disabilities. The student is placed in an individualized program of remedial, developmental and accelerated approaches. The child's social and emotional development is also emphasized. Parents participate in conferences with staff members.

HMS SCHOOL FOR CHILDREN WITH CEREBRAL PALSY

Bdg and Day — Coed Ages 2-21

Philadelphia, PA 19104. 4400 Baltimore Ave.
Tel: 215-222-2566. Fax: 215-222-1889.
www.hmsschool.org   E-mail: dgallagher@hmsschool.org
Diane L. Gallagher, MEd, PhD, Exec Dir. **Christina Coia,** Educ Dir.
Peter McGinness, Adm.
Conditions: Primary—CP Multi ON TBI. **Sec**—Ap As B/VI D Ep ID LD S.
Gen Acad. Ungraded. **Feat**—Studio_Art. **Expected outcome:** Return to local
   school (Avg length of stay: 6-8 yrs).
Therapy: Hear Lang Music Occup Phys Rec Speech. **Psychotherapy:** Dance.
Counseling: Nutrition.
Adm: Appl due: Year-round.
Enr: 58. Bdg 16. Day 42. B 34. G 24. **Fac:** 21 (Full 19, Part 2). Spec ed 10. Lay 11.
Aid: State 58 (100% of tui).
Est 1882. Nonprofit.

Originally named Home of the Merciful Saviour for Crippled Children, HMS School is
an educational and habilitation center for children with severe disabilities stemming from
cerebral palsy or traumatic brain injury. The school's emphasis is on assistive technology
(including power mobility and computer-assisted instruction), the development of communication systems for nonspeaking children, and special education and intensive therapy.
Nursing services and medical support are available on a 24-hour basis.

Parents incur no financial charges when state and local education agencies agree to this
approved private school placement. The average length of stay is six to eight school years.

THE JANUS SCHOOL

Day — Coed Ages 6-19

Mount Joy, PA 17552. 205 Lefever Rd.
Tel: 717-653-0025. Fax: 717-653-0696.
www.thejanusschool.org   E-mail: info@thejanusschool.org
Janet Gillespie, BS, MA, Head. **Robin Payne,** Adm.
Conditions: Primary—ADHD Asp Dx LD.
Gen Acad. Gr 1-12. **Feat**—Sci Soc_Stud Study_Skills. **Expected outcome:**
   Return to local school (Avg length of stay: 3 yrs).
Therapy: Lang Occup Speech.
Adm: Appl fee: $75.
Enr: 80.
Tui '12-'13: Day $25,860-26,360/sch yr.
Est 1991. Nonprofit.

Janus offers an intensive remedial academic program for students diagnosed with a specific learning disability. Pupils typically take part in the program for an average of three
years before transitioning back into their local school systems.

MAIN LINE ACADEMY

Day — Coed Ages 5-21

Bala Cynwyd, PA 19004. 124 Bryn Mawr Ave.
Tel: 610-617-0383. Fax: 610-660-8416.
www.mainlineacademy.com
June Brown, MA, EdD, Exec Dir.
Conditions: Primary—ADHD Dc Dg Dx LD ID.
Gen Acad. Ungraded. Feat—Studio_Art.
Adm: Appl due: Year-round.
Enr: 20. Fac: 7 (Full 5, Part 2). Spec ed 5. Lay 2.
Tui '10-'11: Day $24,000/sch yr.
Est 1982.

This small school enrolls boys and girls with learning differences and attentional disorders.

MILL CREEK SCHOOL

Day — Coed Ages 12-20

Philadelphia, PA 19139. 111 N 49th St.
Tel: 215-471-4900. Fax: 215-471-9639.
www.millcreekschool.org   E-mail: arthur.friedman@uphs.upenn.edu
Arthur Friedman, MA, Dir.
Conditions: Primary—ADHD Anx Asp Dc Dg Dx ED Mood OCD PTSD SA
SP. IQ 90 and up.
Col Prep. Gen Acad. Gr 7-12. Feat—Visual_Arts Music. Expected outcome:
Return to local school (Avg length of stay: 2½ yrs).
Psychotherapy: Fam Group. Counseling: Educ.
Adm: On-campus interview.
Enr: 60 (Cap: 60). B 30. G 30. Fac: 8 (Full-time). Spec ed 8.
Aid: State 60 (100% of tui). Summer prgm: Day. Educ. 2½ wks.
Est 1971. Nonprofit. Spons: University of Pennsylvania Health System.

Mill Creek School, part of a total treatment milieu called the Adolescent Treatment Center of the Institute of Pennsylvania Hospital, treats adolescents with emotional disturbances. Offering self-contained classes and a licensed secondary education program, the humanistic approach is designed to return students to a more typical school setting.

Parental involvement is emphasized, and outpatient services are available through the Institute of Pennsylvania Hospital. The average duration of enrollment is two and a half years. More than half of the graduating seniors continue on to college or postsecondary training.

THE OAKLAND SCHOOL

Day — Coed Ages 13-18

Pittsburgh, PA 15213. 362 McKee Pl.

Tel: 412-621-7878. Fax: 412-621-7881.
www.theoaklandschool.org   E-mail: oschool@stargate.net
Jack King, BS, MEd, Dir. **Jan Stein**, Adm.
  Conditions: Primary—LD. **IQ 90 and up. Not accepted**—CD Multi ODD ON
    Psy PW S SO Sz TBI.
  Col Prep. Gen Acad. Underachiever. Gr 8-12. AP courses (Eng Studio_Art).
    Feat—Humanities Fr Ger Span Environ_Sci Comp_Sci Psych Art_Hist Film
    Theater Music Communications. Avg SAT: CR 556. M 550. W 502. ESL.
    SAT/ACT prep. **Expected outcome:** Graduation.
  Adm: Appl fee: $100. Appl due: Year-round. On-campus interview.
  Enr: 40 (Cap: 70). B 21. G 19. **Fac:** 9 (Full 8, Part 1).
  Tui '11-'12: Day $9700/sch yr (+$300-400). **Aid:** School 4. State 3.
  Bldgs 1. Class rms 8. Art studios 1. Fields 2. Basketball courts 1. Tennis courts 1.
  Est 1982. Nonprofit.

Located in the city's Oakland neighborhood, the school draws students from Allegheny, Beaver, Butler, Washington and Westmoreland counties. In a small-class setting, Oakland accommodates a varied population that includes special-needs pupils, as well as traditional learners in the average to gifted range of intelligence. Communications, arts, foreign languages and computer classes complement course work in the standard subjects. Specific programs serve underachieving students.

Boys and girls accumulate 45 hours of required community service prior to graduation.

OUR LADY OF CONFIDENCE DAY SCHOOL

Day — Coed Ages 4½-21

Willow Grove, PA 19090. 314 N Easton Rd.
Tel: 215-657-9311. Fax: 215-657-9312.
www.ourladyofconfidence.org   E-mail: apconf01@nni.com
Sr. Judith Moeller, IHM, BS, MA, Prin.
  Conditions: Primary—ID TBI. **Sec**—ADHD. **IQ 0-70.**
  Voc. Ungraded. Culinary. Man_Arts & Shop.
  Therapy: Hear Lang Music Occup Phys Speech Visual. **Psychotherapy:** Indiv.
  Adm: Appl due: Year-round. On-campus interview.
  Enr: 90. **Fac:** 13 (Full 8, Part 5). Spec ed 13.
  Est 1954. Nonprofit. Roman Catholic.

The emphasis of this school is on growth in the areas of spiritual, physical, academic, social and vocational development. Independent living skills training is provided. Children with intellectual disabilities must be at either the trainable or the educable level to be eligible for enrollment.

THE PATHWAY SCHOOL

Day — Coed Ages 5-21

Norristown, PA 19403. 162 Egypt Rd.
Tel: 610-277-0660. Fax: 610-539-1973.

www.pathwayschool.org   E-mail: dphifer@pathwayschool.org
David M. Maola, JD, MBA, Pres. **Diana M. Phifer,** Adm.
Conditions: Primary—Anx APD Asp Au Dc Dx LD Mood ID NLD ON PDD TS. **Sec**—ADHD ED OCD ODD PTSD S TBI. **IQ 50-120.**
Not accepted—AN Bu CD Psy SA SO Subst Sz.
Col Prep. Gen Acad. Voc. Ungraded. Man_Arts & Shop. On-Job Trng. Support_Employ. **Expected outcome:** Return to local school (Avg length of stay: 2 yrs).
Therapy: Lang Music Occup Speech. **Psychotherapy:** Group Indiv.
Adm: Appl due: Year-round.
Enr: 132 (Cap: 160). B 104. G 28.
Tui '12-'13: Day $45,425-49,950/sch yr. **Aid:** State 131. Educ. Rec. Ther. Tui Day $6990-8550. 6 wks.
Acres 13. Bldgs 13. Class rms 25. Libs 1. Gyms 1. Fields 1. Comp labs 2.
Est 1961. Nonprofit.

Located on a suburban campus near Valley Forge Park, Pathway provides habilitative services for children who have varying degrees of learning and behavioral problems. A total team approach that includes the cooperative participation of parents provides an individualized program of educational, social and emotional involvement.

Pathway also offers career education and individually prescribed speech, language, reading and math programs, in addition to off-campus work experience.

PENNSYLVANIA SCHOOL FOR THE DEAF

Day — Coed Ages 3-21

Philadelphia, PA 19144. 100 W School House Ln.
Tel: 215-951-4700. TTY: 215-951-4703. Fax: 215-951-4708.
www.psd.org   E-mail: info@psd.org
Marja Brandon, BA, EdM, Int Head. **Gail Bober,** Adm.
Conditions: Primary—D HI. **Sec**—ADHD Anx Apr Ar Asp Au B/VI C CD CF CLP CP Db D-B Dc Dg Dpx DS Dx ED Ep Hemo IP ID LD Lk Mood MS OCD ON PDD SA SB SC. **Not accepted**—ODD SO.
Gen Acad. Voc. Gr PS-12. **Feat**—ASL Environ_Sci Civics Econ Govt Studio_Art Drama. SAT/ACT prep. **Expected outcome:** Graduation.
Therapy: Hear Lang Occup Phys Play Speech. **Psychotherapy:** Dance Group Indiv. **Counseling:** Educ Voc.
Adm: Appl fee: $0. Appl due: Rolling. On-campus interview.
Enr: 220 (Cap: 250). B 105. G 115. **Fac:** 48 (Full-time). Spec ed 45. Lay 3.
Aid: State 220 (100% of tui). **Summer prgm:** Day. Educ. Rec. Tui Day $0. 5 wks.
Endow $15,000,000. Plant val $10,000,000. Acres 8. Bldgs 10. Sci labs 3. Art studios 1. Gyms 1. Fields 1. Comp labs 5.
Est 1820. Nonprofit.

Located on an eight-acre campus in Germantown, PSD offers academic programs beginning with three-year-old preschool and extending through high school to deaf and hard-of-hearing students. In addition, the school operates an early intervention program for infants and toddlers and their families, as well as a bilingual play group for two-year-olds. Language accessibility is integral to PSD's learning process, and counseling and behavioral supports are available as needed. An on-campus community resource center provides assistance with educational transition and job training for deaf individuals of high school age and older.

PHELPS SCHOOL

Bdg and Day — Boys Ages 12-18

Malvern, PA 19355. 583 Sugartown Rd.
Tel: 610-644-1754. Fax: 610-644-6679.
www.thephelpsschool.org   E-mail: admis@thephelpsschool.org
Michael J. Reardon, Head. **Ira Miles,** Adm.
  Conditions: Primary—ADHD Dc Dg Dx LD. **Sec**—S. **IQ 80-125.**
  Col Prep. Underachiever. Gr 7-PG. Man_Arts & Shop. AP courses (Calc US_
  Hist). **Feat**—British_Lit Span Stats Environ_Sci Comp_Sci Geog Govt Psych
  Sociol Ethics Sculpt Public_Speak Culinary_Arts Health Study_Skills. ESL.
  Interscholastic sports. **Expected outcome:** Graduation.
  Therapy: Speech. **Psychotherapy:** Indiv.
  Adm: Appl fee: $50. Appl due: Rolling. On-campus interview.
  Enr: 120. **Fac:** 28 (Full-time).
  Tui '12-'13: Bdg $41,500/sch yr (+$500-860). Day $22,500/sch yr (+$500-860).
  Endow $643,000. Plant val $12,000,000. Acres 70. Bldgs 18. Dorms 8. Class
  rms 8. Lib 6200 vols. Sci labs 1. Auds 1. Art studios 1. Gyms 1. Fields 4.
  Courts 4. Pools 1. Riding rings 2. Stables 2. Comp labs 1.
  Est 1946. Nonprofit.

Phelps offers an intensive diagnostic, remedial and guidance program to boys who are underachieving or who have a specific learning disability such as dyslexia or attention deficit disorder. Phelps features small classes and an academic support program. Other program opportunities are English as a Second Language, industrial arts, oceanography and driver education.

All students participate in an afternoon activity. Options include various sports, as well as arts and crafts, wood shop, photography, drama and computers.

THE QUAKER SCHOOL AT HORSHAM

Day — Coed Ages 5-15

Horsham, PA 19044. 250 Meetinghouse Rd.
Tel: 215-674-2875. Fax: 215-674-9913.
www.quakerschool.org   E-mail: info@quakerschool.org
Ruth Joray, MS, Head. **Mia Glenn,** Adm.
  Conditions: Primary—ADHD APD Asp Dg Dx LD Multi NLD PDD. **Sec**—Anx
  Ap Apr Au Dc Dpx ED OCD PTSD. **IQ 85-120. Not accepted**—CD ID MR
  ODD ON Psy SO Subst Sz TBI.
  Gen Acad. Gr K-9. **Feat**—Computers Ceramics Studio_Art Woodworking.
    Expected outcome: Return to local school (Avg length of stay: 4 yrs).
  Therapy: Occup Speech. **Psychotherapy:** Group. ·
  Adm: Appl fee: $100. Appl due: Rolling. On-campus interview.

Enr: 64 (Cap: 80). B 54. G 10. **Fac:** 15 (Full 14, Part 1). Spec ed 15.
Tui '12-'13: Day $28,655-34,625/sch yr. **Aid:** School 30 ($200,000). **Summer prgm:** Day. Educ. Rec. 5 wks.
Laptop prgm Gr 9.
Est 1982. Nonprofit. Religious Society of Friends.

TQS offers a varied academic program to children with different learning styles of average or above-average intelligence. A teacher and a teacher assistant work with a group of no more than eight children. Speech and occupational therapy supplement the educational program, and the average length of stay is four years. Students of all faiths may enroll.

ROYER-GREAVES SCHOOL FOR BLIND
Bdg and Day — Coed Ages 5-21

Paoli, PA 19301. 118 S Valley Rd.
Tel: 610-644-1810. Fax: 610-644-8164.
www.royer-greaves.org   E-mail: info@royer-greaves.org
Joseph T. Coleman, BS, MEd, EdD, Exec Dir. **Vicky Mayer,** Adm.
  Conditions: Primary—B/VI D. **Sec**—ADHD Au CP Db DS ED Ep HI ID LD ON TBI. **IQ 0-70. Not accepted**—AN Anx Bu CD SO Subst Sz.
  Voc. Gr K-12. Shelt_Workshop. **Expected outcome:** Graduation.
  Therapy: Hear Lang Music Occup Phys Speech. **Psychotherapy:** Indiv.
  Adm: Appl fee: $0. Appl due: Year-round. On-campus interview.
  Enr: 28 (Cap: 28). Bdg 20. Day 8. B 12. G 16. **Fac:** 4 (Full 3, Part 1). Spec ed 2. Lay 2.
  Summer prgm: Bdg & Day. Educ. Rec. 5 wks.
  Acres 13. Bldgs 7 (100% ADA). Dorms 1. Dorm rms 14. Class rms 3. Music studios 1. Gyms 1. Pools 1.
  Est 1921. Nonprofit.

Multihandicapped visually impaired students receive education and training at this residential school, which is located on a country estate. Community life and academics are combined in an individualized program. Royer-Greaves places particular emphasis on helping students attain the greatest degree of independence possible.

ST. ANTHONY SCHOOL PROGRAMS
Day — Coed Ages 5-21

Wexford, PA 15090. 2000 Corporate Dr, Ste 580.
Tel: 724-940-9020. Fax: 724-940-9064.
www.stanthonyschoolprograms.com
  E-mail: lgeorge@stanthonyschoolprograms.com
Lisa George, BA, MA, Educ Dir.
  Conditions: Primary—Asp Au DS ID Multi PDD PW. **Sec**—ADHD Ap Apr Ar C CF CLP CP Db ED Ep Hemo Lk MD Mood MS Nf OCD ODD PTSD S SB SC TBI TS. **IQ 0-75. Not accepted**—APD Dg Dpx Dx LD NLD ON Psy SO SP Sz.

Gen Acad. Voc. Ungraded. On-Job Trng. **Expected outcome:** Graduation. **Therapy:** Occup Perceptual-Motor Speech. **Psychotherapy:** Indiv. **Counseling:** Voc.
Adm: Appl fee: $100. Appl due: Year-round. On-campus interview. **Enr:** 100. B 70. G 30. **Fac:** 7 (Full-time). Spec ed 7.
Tui '12-'13: Day $5600-8200/sch yr. **Aid:** School. State. **Summer prgm:** Day. Rec. 4 wks.
Est 1953. Nonprofit. Roman Catholic.

Children, adolescents and young adults with autism, Down syndrome and other developmental disabilities who live within the six counties of the Diocese of Pittsburgh may enroll in this Catholic school. Programming addresses the student's academic, social and vocation needs. In addition to spending part of their day in a regular classroom setting, boys and girls receive additional instruction in the areas of general and religious education, daily living and motor skills. Older pupils also participate in vocational training.

ST. JOSEPH CENTER FOR SPECIAL LEARNING

Day — Coed Ages 4-21

Pottsville, PA 17901. 2075 W Norwegian St.
Tel: 570-622-4638. Fax: 570-622-3420.
www.stjosephctr.com   E-mail: stjosephcenter@comcast.net
Julia Leibensperger, BS, MS, Prin.
   Conditions: Primary—ADHD Ap Apr Ar As Asp Au C CD CP Dc Dg DS Dx ED Ep IP LD MD ID MS Nf OCD ON PDD PW SB Sz TBI TS. **IQ 0-78.**
Gen Acad. Ungraded. **Feat**—Studio_Art Music.
Therapy: Occup Phys Speech.
Enr: 18. **Fac:** 3. Spec ed 3.
Est 1955. Nonprofit. Roman Catholic.

Sponsored by the Diocese of Allentown for children, adolescents and young adults with intellectual disabilities and other developmental disabilities in Schuylkill County, this school provides academic instruction and educational activities nine months per year.

The curriculum consists of educational, developmental and spiritual elements. Serving to enhance the basic program are the following offerings: adaptive physical education, speech and language therapy, medical services, psychological evaluations, vocational services and nursing services. SJC also provides instruction in such practical skills areas as computer literacy, cooking and music.

SAINT KATHERINE DAY SCHOOL

Day — Coed Ages 4½-21

Wynnewood, PA 19096. 930 Bowman Ave.
Tel: 610-667-3958. Fax: 610-667-3625.
www.stkatherinedayschool.org   E-mail: skdsprincipal@yahoo.com
   Nearby locations: 211 Matsonford Rd, Radnor 19087.
Margaret Devaney, MS, Prin.

Conditions: Primary—ID. **Sec**—ADHD Dx LD ON. **IQ 45-70.**
Voc. Ungraded. Culinary. On-Job Trng.
Therapy: Music Occup Phys Speech. **Psychotherapy:** Indiv Parent.
    Counseling: Voc.
Enr: 140. **Fac:** 11. Spec ed 11.
Est 1953. Inc. Roman Catholic.

SKDS offers education and vocational training to youth with mental retardation. Speech, physical and occupational therapy complement the academic program. Counseling is also available for parents. High school course work takes place at Archbishop John Carroll High School in Radnor.

SAINT LUCY DAY SCHOOL FOR CHILDREN WITH VISUAL IMPAIRMENTS ARCHBISHOP RYAN ACADEMY FOR THE DEAF

Day — Coed Ages 3-14

Philadelphia, PA 19124. 4251 L St.
Tel: 215-289-4220. Fax: 215-289-4229.
www.slds.org   E-mail: aplucy01@nni.com
Sr. M. Margaret Fleming, IHM, MEd, Prin.
    Conditions: Primary—B/VI D. **Sec**—LD. **IQ 80 and up.**
    Gen Acad. Gr PS-8.
    Therapy: Lang Occup Speech. **Psychotherapy:** Art.
    Enr: 31. B 20. G 11.
    Tui.'12-'13: Day $3150-5800/sch yr. **Aid:** State 6.
    Est 1955. Nonprofit. Roman Catholic.

After initially operating independently, Saint Lucy Day School and Archbishop Ryan Academy for the Deaf effected a merger in 2006. The resulting institution serves children with both visual and hearing impairments. SLDS/ARAD provides intense instruction in regular and special curricular areas for school-age children, with part-time mainstreaming employed at nearby Holy Innocents School in grades 1-8. Parental guidance and support are part of the program.

Early intervention services are available to infants and toddlers.

STRATFORD FRIENDS SCHOOL

Day — Coed Ages 5-14

Newtown Square, PA 19073. 2 Bishop Hollow Rd.
Tel: 610-355-9580. Fax: 610-355-9585.
www.stratfordfriends.org   E-mail: gvare@stratfordfriends.org
Timothy P. Madigan, BA, MEd, PhD, Head. **Gretchen S. Vare,** Adm.
    Conditions: Primary—Dx LD. **Sec**—ADHD Dc Dg. **IQ 100 and up.**
    Not accepted—ID MR.
    Gen Acad. Gr K-8. **Feat**—Studio_Art Music Speech Woodworking. **Expected**
    outcome: Graduation.

Therapy: Music Speech.
Adm: Appl fee: $75. Appl due: Rolling. On-campus interview.
Enr: 78. B 52. G 26. **Fac:** 19 (Full 17, Part 2).
Tui '12-'13: Day $33,960/sch yr (+$50). **Aid:** School 26 ($330,000). **Summer prgm:** Day. Educ. Rec. Tui Day $1700-2200. 5 wks.
Endow $700,000. Plant val $6,000,000. Acres 7. Bldgs 1. Class rms 14. Libs 1. Sci labs 1. Art studios 1. Music studios 1. Fields 2. Laptop prgm Gr 7-8.
Est 1976. Nonprofit. Religious Society of Friends.

Stratford Friends enrolls children of average to above-average intelligence who have language-based learning differences. The multisensory program includes speech, math and reading instruction. The reading program utilizes the Orton-Gillingham approach. An extended-day option is available.

THE VANGUARD SCHOOL

Day — Coed Ages 4-21

Paoli, PA 19301. 1777 N Valley Rd, PO Box 730.
Tel: 610-296-6700. Fax: 610-640-0132.
www.vanguardschool-pa.org   E-mail: info@vanguardschool-pa.org
Timothy Lanshe, MEd, Educ Dir. **Peggy Osborne,** Adm.
   Conditions: Primary—Asp Au ED ON PDD S TBI. **Sec**—ADHD Anx Ap As Dc Dg Dx Ep LD Mood OCD PTSD PW SP TS. **IQ 60 and up.**
   Col Prep. Gen Acad. Voc. Gr PS-12. Culinary. Hort. Man_Arts & Shop. On-Job Trng. Shelt_Workshop. **Feat**—Lib_Skills Computers Studio_Art Indus_Arts Home_Ec.
   Therapy: Lang Music Occup Perceptual-Motor Phys Play Rec Speech.
   Psychotherapy: Indiv. **Counseling:** Educ Voc.
   Adm: Appl due: Rolling.
   Enr: 250 (Cap: 225). **Fac:** 49. Spec ed 30. Lay 19.
   Summer prgm: Day. Educ. Rec. Ther. 5 wks.
   Acres 53.
   Est 1959. Nonprofit.

Consisting of lower, middle and upper schools, Vanguard occupies a 53-acre campus. The educational program serves students with serious emotional and learning adjustment problems and stresses language development, affective-cognitive learning and vocational experience. As part of its counseling program, the school conducts PACE, a series of structured group activities designed to promote behavior change and self-esteem improvement. Vanguard shares its campus with Crossroads School.

Clinical services available through Vanguard include individual and group therapy, evaluations, and psycho-educational and skills training. Sending school districts generally cover tuition costs.

WESLEY SPECTRUM ACADEMY
Day — Coed Ages 9-21

Pittsburgh, PA 15241. 243 Johnston Rd.
Tel: 412-833-6444. Fax: 412-308-0168.
www.wesleyspectrum.org   E-mail: atownsend@wesleyspectrum.org
Amy Townsend, MEd, Dir. Melissa Garvin, Adm.
Conditions: Primary—ADHD AN Anx Bu Dx ED Mood OCD PTSD SP Subst. IQ 90-130.
Col Prep. Gen Acad. Ungraded. Feat—Fr Span Computers. Expected outcome: Graduation.
Adm: On-campus interview.
Enr: 140 (Cap: 156). Fac: 16 (Full-time). Spec ed 9. Lay 7.
Tui '10-'11: Day $23,000/sch yr.
Est 1965. Nonprofit. Spons: Wesley Spectrum Services.

The academy provides an educational alternative for students who require more individualized attention and emotional support than is normally available in public school. Offering both full- and part-time programs, Wesley utilizes a full academic curriculum to develop self-esteem, personal responsibility, mutual respect and social adjustment. The individualized curriculum accommodates students' particular needs and abilities.

WESTERN PENNSYLVANIA SCHOOL FOR BLIND CHILDREN
Bdg and Day — Coed Ages 3-21

Pittsburgh, PA 15213. 201 N Bellefield Ave.
Tel: 412-621-0100, 800-444-1897. Fax: 412-621-4067.
www.wpsbc.org   E-mail: salovayd@wpsbc.org
Todd S. Reeves, Exec Dir. Donna M. Salovay, Adm.
Conditions: Primary—Apr Ar As Asp Au B/VI CLP CP Ep IP MD MS Nf S SB TBI. Sec—C Db D-B HI ID ON PDD. Not accepted—D.
Gen Acad. Gr PS-12. Expected outcome: Graduation.
Therapy: Hydro Lang Occup Phys Speech. Psychotherapy: Fam Indiv.
Counseling: Voc.
Adm: Appl fee: $0. Appl due: Year-round. On-campus interview.
Enr: 175.
Tui '12-'13: Bdg $0/day. Day $0/day. Summer prgm: Bdg & Day. Educ. Ther. Tui Bdg $4200. Tui Day $2600. 2 wks.
Est 1887. Inc.

An independently operated residential school for legally blind students from the 33 counties of western Pennsylvania, this school stresses functional skills. Integrated and clinical therapies augment the educational focus. Most students have severe disabilities accompanying their visual impairment. Three-quarters of the student body remain until graduation. The facility is completely adapted for both the physically handicapped and the blind. Residential facilities serve those from outlying districts.

The school also provides early intervention services and outreach services for visually impaired pupils who may or may not have additional special needs. Some preschool-aged children have the single disability of blindness; the early training that they receive may enable them to complete their education at a public school.

All programs and services are available at no charge.

WESTERN PENNSYLVANIA SCHOOL FOR THE DEAF

Bdg and Day — Coed Ages 3-21

Pittsburgh, PA 15218. 300 E Swissvale Ave.
Tel: 412-371-7000, 800-624-3323. TTY: 800-624-3323. Fax: 412-244-4223.
www.wpsd.org   E-mail: dfell@wpsd.org
Donald E. Rhoten, MS, MEd, Supt. **Marybeth Lauderdale,** MAEd, EdS, Dir.
Deborah Fell, Adm.
   Conditions: Primary—D. **Sec**—ID ON. **IQ 40 and up.**
   Col Prep. Gen Acad. Gr PS-12. Man_Arts & Shop. On-Job Trng. **Feat**—Sci
      Computers.
   Therapy: Hear Lang Occup Phys Speech. **Psychotherapy:** Art Group Indiv.
      Counseling: Educ Voc.
   Enr: 197. **Fac:** 65 (Full 62, Part 3). Spec ed 53. Lay 12.
   Aid: State 197 (100% of tui). **Summer prgm:** Bdg & Day. Educ. Rec. 1 wk.
      Acres 21.
   Est 1869. Nonprofit.

WPSD serves hearing-impaired individuals who are residents of Pennsylvania. In addition to its academic program, the school provides a complete after-school program that includes sports, clubs and activities for students of all ages; support services; a learning center featuring a mini-max theater; and a TV studio and video production department where students use digital technology to produce videos and daily news programs.

A training program for teachers and a parent-teacher association are integral parts of the program for the education of the deaf.

WORDSWORTH ACADEMY

Day — Coed Ages 5-21

Fort Washington, PA 19034. 2101 Pennsylvania Ave.
Tel: 215-643-5400, 800-769-0088. Fax: 215-643-0595.
www.wordsworth.org   E-mail: info@wordsworth.org
Linda Williams, Exec Dir.
   Conditions: Primary—ADHD Asp Au CD ED LD Mood ODD PTSD. **Sec**—AN
      Anx As Bu C CF CP Db Dc Dg Dx Ep Hemo ID Lk NLD OCD ON Psy PW
      SA SC SO SP Subst Sz TBI TS. **IQ 90-130. Not accepted**—Ap D D-B DS
      HI.
   Gen Acad. Voc. Gr K-12. Culinary. Hort. Man_Arts & Shop. On-Job Trng.
   Therapy: Lang Music Rec Speech. **Psychotherapy:** Art Fam Group Indiv.
      Counseling: Educ Voc.
   Adm: Appl due: Year-round. On-campus interview.
   Enr: 216 (Cap: 264).
   Summer prgm: Day. Educ. Rec. Ther. 6 wks.

Est 1952. Nonprofit.

Formerly The Matthews School, this remedial school serves children who have had serious difficulty—especially with reading—in an ordinary school setting. Instruction in all subjects, geared to building reading and math skills, begins at the student's present level of achievement.

Psychotherapy, speech and vision therapy, family therapy, counseling and diagnostic services are available. Clinical services are recommended on an individual basis as needed. The academy also conducts a remedial summer school and a recreational summer camp program.

RHODE ISLAND

HAMILTON SCHOOL AT WHEELER

Day — Coed Ages 6-14

Providence, RI 02906. 216 Hope St.
Tel: 401-421-8100. Fax: 401-751-7674.
www.wheelerschool.org   E-mail: annadistefano@wheelerschool.org
Jonathan Green, MEd, Dir. **Jeanette Epstein,** Adm.
  Conditions: Primary—ADHD Dc Dg Dx LD. **Sec**—ID TS. **IQ 90 and up.**
  Gen Acad. Gr 1-8. **Feat**—Lib_Skills Studio_Art Music. Interscholastic sports.
  Expected outcome: Return to local school (Avg length of stay: 2+ yrs).
  Therapy: Lang Occup Speech.
  Adm: Appl fee: $60. Appl due: Feb. On-campus interview.
  Enr: 68 (Cap: 70). B 47. G 21. **Fac:** 13 (Full-time).
  Tui '12-'13: Day $40,355/sch yr. **Aid:** School. **Summer prgm:** Day. Educ. Tui
    Day $285-1500. 1-5 wks.
  Est 1988. Nonprofit. **Spons:** Wheeler School.

Located on the campus of The Wheeler School, Hamilton enrolls elementary students with language-based learning differences. Staff teach compensatory strategies as children develop fundamental academic skills.

HARMONY HILL SCHOOL

Bdg and Day — Boys Ages 8-18

Chepachet, RI 02814. 63 Harmony Hill Rd.
Tel: 401-949-0690. Fax: 401-949-2060.
www.harmonyhillschool.org   E-mail: admissions@hhs.org
Eric James, MA, Pres. **Cynthia McDermott,** Educ Dir. **Donald Jackson,** Adm.
  Conditions: Primary—ADHD Asp CD ED LD Mood ODD SO SP TS. **Sec**—
    Anx As Dc Dg Dx Ep ID MS OCD ON PDD Psy PTSD S. **IQ 70 and up.**
  Gen Acad. Gr 2-12. On-Job Trng. **Feat**—Studio_Art Music Woodworking
    Health. **Expected outcome:** Return to local school (Avg length of stay: 12-
    18 mos).
  Therapy: Lang Milieu Music Phys Play Rec Speech. **Psychotherapy:** Art Fam
    Group Indiv Parent.
  Adm: Appl due: Year-round. On-campus interview.
  Enr: 89. Bdg 62. Day 27. **Fac:** 11. Spec ed 11.
  Summer prgm: Bdg & Day. Educ. Rec. Ther. 7 wks.
  Acres 120.
  Est 1976. Nonprofit.

Harmony Hill provides residential, community and day treatment programs for boys with behavioral disorders and learning disabilities who cannot receive treatment within the local educational system or through community-based mental health programs. The school's objective is to successfully return students to their communities.

Programming consists of education, group activities, and peer and counselor support systems. Special offerings include a diagnostic program for a limited number of individuals with moderate to severe behavioral disorders and, for an additional fee, a program for sex offenders. Length of treatment typically falls between 12 and 18 months.

SOUTH CAROLINA

CAMPERDOWN ACADEMY
Day — Coed Ages 5-14

Greenville, SC 29615. 501 Howell Rd.
Tel: 864-244-8899. Fax: 864-244-8936.
www.camperdown.org   E-mail: pgolus@camperdown.org
Dan Blanch, Head. **Courtney Stefanick**, Adm.
  Conditions: Primary—ADHD APD Dc Dg Dpx Dx LD NLD. **Sec**—HI. **IQ 100**
    and up. Not accepted—Au CD SO Subst Sz TBI TS.
  Gen Acad. Gr 1-8. Man_Arts & Shop. **Feat**—Studio_Art Drama. Interscholas-
    tic sports. **Expected outcome:** Return to local school (Avg length of stay:
    3-4 yrs).
  Therapy: Lang.
  Adm: Appl fee: $75. Appl due: Year-round. On-campus interview.
  Enr: 71 (Cap: 100). B 47. G 24. **Fac:** 20 (Full 19, Part 1).
  Tui '12-'13: Day $15,750-19,250/sch yr. **Aid:** School 21 ($75,000). **Summer**
    prgm: Day. Educ. Tui Day $2000. 4 wks.
  Libs 1. Sci labs 2. Fields 2. Courts 1. Comp labs 4.
  Est 1986. Nonprofit.

This elementary and middle school provides a multisensory program for children of average to above-average intelligence who have specific learning disabilities. Teachers help students learn through whichever visual, auditory, kinesthetic or tactile channels are appropriate. The academy stresses accountability, self-discipline and the development of management skills that enable children to cope with their learning differences. Camperdown enrolls pupils from Greenville, Greenwood, Oconee, Pickens, Spartanburg and Union counties.

CHEROKEE CREEK BOYS SCHOOL
Bdg — Boys Ages 11-15

Westminster, SC 29693. 198 Cooper Rd.
Tel: 864-647-1885. Fax: 866-399-1869.
www.cherokeecreek.net   E-mail: info@cherokeecreek.net
David LePere, MEd, Exec Dir. **Shaler Black Cooper**, Adm.
  Conditions: Primary—ADHD Asp CD Dc Dg Dx ED Mood NLD OCD SA SP
    TS. **IQ 88 and up. Not accepted**—Db DS SO Sz.
  Gen Acad. Gr 5-9. **Feat**—Span Environ_Sci. **Expected outcome:** Return to
    local school (Avg length of stay: 15-24 mos).
  Therapy: Lang Milieu Perceptual-Motor Phys Play Rec. **Psychotherapy:** Equine
    Fam Group Indiv Parent. **Counseling:** Educ.
  Adm: Appl due: Year-round.
  Enr: 26 (Cap: 32). **Fac:** 5 (Full 3, Part 2). Spec ed 3. Lay 2.
  Tui '12-'13: Bdg $6200/mo. **Aid:** School. State.

Est 2003.

Boys of middle school age who are struggling emotionally, personally or socially receive treatment at Cherokee Creek. The program offers opportunities for academic success, personal growth, social responsibility, physical challenge, and moral and spiritual exploration.

GLENFOREST SCHOOL

Day — Coed Ages 6-18

West Columbia, SC 29169. 1041 Harbor Dr.
Tel: 803-796-7622. Fax: 803-796-1603.
www.glenforest.org   E-mail: admin@glenforest.org
Chris Winkler, Head. **Shayna Simoneaux,** Adm.

Conditions: Primary—ADHD AN Anx Ap APD Ar Asp Au B/VI Bu C CLP CP Db Dc Dg DS Dpx Dx Ep HI Hemo LD MD Mood Lk MS Multi Nf OCD S SA SC SP. **Sec**—ED ID ON PTSD Subst TBI TS. **IQ 90 and up. Not accepted**—CD D D-B ODD Psy SB SO Sz.

Col Prep. Gen Acad. Underachiever. Voc. Gr 1-12. Man_Arts & Shop. On-Job Trng. **Feat**—Span Fine_Arts Theater. SAT/ACT prep. Interscholastic sports. **Expected outcome:** Return to local school (Avg length of stay: 2+ yrs).

Therapy: Lang Occup Perceptual-Motor Phys Play Speech. **Counseling:** Educ Nutrition Voc.

Adm: Appl fee: $150. Appl due: Year-round. On-campus interview.

Enr: 64 (Cap: 130). B 50. G 14. **Fac:** 18 (Full 16, Part 2). Spec ed 1. Lay 17.

Tui '12-'13: Day $19,250-23,600/sch yr. **Aid:** School 25 ($100,000). State.

Summer prgm: Day. Educ. Rec. Ther. 6 wks.

Endow $50,000. Plant val $5,000,000. Acres 32. Bldgs 2 (100% ADA). Class rms 15. Lib 5000 vols. Sci labs 2. Lang labs 2. Auds 1. Theaters 1. Art studios 2. Music studios 1. Dance studios 1. Gyms 1. Fields 2. Courts 1. Comp labs 2.

Est 1983. Nonprofit.

Glenforest's programs are designed for students of average to above-average intelligence who have a learning disability or an attentional disorder, as well as those who have not achieved to potential in traditional classroom settings. The school uses such educational methods as direct instruction, multisensory teaching, computerized teaching and the Orton-Gillingham method.

HIDDEN TREASURE CHRISTIAN SCHOOL

Day — Coed Ages 5-21

Taylors, SC 29687. 500 W Lee Rd.
Tel: 864-235-6848. Fax: 864-233-6366.
www.hiddentreasure.org   E-mail: info@hiddentreasure.org
John J. McCormick, BS, MS, MA, EdD, Admin.

Conditions: Primary—ADHD Anx Ap APD Apr As Asp Au CD CP Dc Dg DS Dx ED Ep LD ID MS Nf OCD ODD ON PDD PW S SB TBI TS. **Sec**—B/VI C D Db. **IQ 40-120. Not accepted**—SO Subst Sz.
Col Prep. Gen Acad. Gr K-12. On-Job Trng. Shelt_Workshop. **Feat**—Span Fine_Arts Speech. **Expected outcome:** Return to local school (Avg length of stay: 5-6 yrs).
Therapy: Music Occup Speech. **Counseling:** Educ Voc.
Enr: 65 (Cap: 120). **Fac:** 14 (Full 13, Part 1). Spec ed 14.
Tui '08-'09: Day $15,000/sch yr. **Aid:** School.
Est 1981. Nonprofit. Baptist.

Hidden Treasure serves children with a range of special needs, among them physical, mental and learning disabilities, attention deficit disorder, autism, cerebral palsy and aphasia. In addition to special education services, the school offers the following programs: vocational training, physical therapy, occupational therapy, speech therapy, infant stimulation, and creative and nurturing skills.

PINE GROVE

Bdg and Day — Coed Ages 5-18

Elgin, SC 29045. 1500 Chestnut Rd, PO Box 100.
Tel: 803-438-3011, 855-746-3476. Fax: 803-438-8611.
www.pinegroveinc.com   E-mail: donnam@pinegroveinc.com
David S. Perhach, MSW, LCSW, Pres. **Donna J. Moen,** Adm.
Conditions: Primary—Au ED ID TBI.
Gen Acad. Ungraded.
Therapy: Lang Music Occup Speech. **Psychotherapy:** Art Group Indiv.
Adm: Appl due: Year-round.
Enr: 23.
Acres 32.
Est 1970. Inc.

Located on 32 acres of wooded land, Pine Grove treats children with autism and developmental disabilities, accompanied by significant behavioral problems, communication deficits and poor social judgment. Emphasizing behavior modification and communication development, the school conducts an intensive academic program. Parents are offered behavior modification training and must participate in the child's program.

SANDHILLS SCHOOL

Day — Coed Ages 6-18

Columbia, SC 29209. 1500 Hallbrook Dr.
Tel: 803-695-1400. Fax: 803-695-1214.
www.sandhillsschool.org   E-mail: info@sandhillsschool.org
Anne M. Vickers, Head. **Erika Senneseth,** Adm.
Conditions: Primary—ADHD Dc Dg Dx LD. **IQ 100 and up.**
Gen Acad. Gr 1-12. **Feat**—Computers Studio_Art. **Expected outcome:** Return

to local school (Avg length of stay: 2-3 yrs).
Therapy: Lang Speech. **Psychotherapy:** Indiv. **Counseling:** Educ.
Adm: Appl fee: $75. Appl due: Year-round. On-campus interview.
Enr: 55. **Fac:** 15 (Full 14, Part 1). Spec ed 15.
Tui '12-'13: Day $20,095/sch yr (+$0-325). **Aid:** School. **Summer prgm:** Day.
Educ. Tui Day $2100. 5 wks.
Acres 22. Bldgs 1 (100% ADA). Libs 1. Sci labs 1. Art studios 1.
Est 1970. Nonprofit.

Sandhills offers a curriculum of individualized instruction to students with dyslexia, attention deficit disorder and other learning disabilities. Each child attends a session of one-on-one language development instruction daily. Extracurricular activities include soccer, softball and basketball teams; interest clubs; and a student council.

One-on-one educational therapy is available during after-school hours for students not enrolled in the school full-time. The five-week summer school, which consists of small-group and individual instruction, is open to students from other schools.

TRIDENT ACADEMY

Day — Coed Ages 5-19

Mount Pleasant, SC 29464. 1455 Wakendaw Rd.
Tel: 843-884-3494. Fax: 843-884-1483.
www.tridentacademy.com   E-mail: admissions@tridentacademy.com
Sandi Clerici, BA, MS, Int Head. **Corbin Bettencourt,** Adm.
Conditions: Primary—ADHD APD Dc Dg Dpx Dx LD NLD. **IQ 90 and up.**
Col Prep. Gen Acad. Gr K-12. **Feat**—Span Speech. Interscholastic sports.
Expected outcome: Graduation.
Therapy: Lang. **Counseling:** Educ.
Adm: Appl fee: $150. Appl due: Rolling. On-campus interview.
Enr: 100. B 74. G 26. **Fac:** 30 (Full-time). Spec ed 30.
Tui '12-'13: Day $24,310/sch yr (+$1220-1370). **Aid:** School 21 ($250,000).
Summer prgm: Day. Educ. Tui Day $2250. 5 wks.
Endow $600,000. Plant val $3,500,000. Acres 11. Bldgs 2. Libs 1. Sci labs 3.
Art studios 1. Music studios 1. Gyms 1. Fields 1. Comp labs 3.
Est 1972. Nonprofit.

This college preparatory school serves children with language-based learning disabilities who possess average to above-average intelligence. Diagnosis of a learning disability is required for admission. The academy utilizes a multisensory teaching approach within a structured, individualized environment. Students in grades 10-12 perform required community service.

TENNESSEE

ADVENT HOME LEARNING CENTER

Bdg — Boys Ages 12-18

Calhoun, TN 37309. 900 County Rd 950.
Tel: 423-336-5052. Fax: 423-336-8224.
www.adventhome.org   E-mail: info@adventhome.org
Blondel E. Senior, PhD, Exec Dir.
   Conditions: Primary—ADHD Anx Asp Au CD ED LD Mood OCD ODD. **IQ 90 and up.**
   Gen Acad. Gr 6-12. On-Job Trng. **Expected outcome:** Return to local school (Avg length of stay: 18 mos).
   Psychotherapy: Fam Group Indiv. **Counseling:** Educ.
   Adm: Appl due: Rolling.
   Enr: 32 (Cap: 32). **Fac:** 5 (Full-time). Spec ed 5.
   Tui '10-'11: Bdg $37,200/yr.
   Acres 225. Dorms 2. Dorm rms 8. Class rms 6. Libs 1. Sci labs 1.
   Est 1985. Nonprofit. Seventh-day Adventist.

Advent Home provides a year-round alternative to school suspension and dismissal, accepting students who do not function well in the traditional classroom and need more tutoring and remedial support than is available in a traditional classroom. To aid families, Advent Home also conducts weekend parent training sessions.

BEACON SCHOOL

Bdg and Day — Coed Ages 5-18

Greeneville, TN 37744. PO Box 188.
Tel: 423-787-8708. Fax: 423-639-7171.
www.holstonhome.org   E-mail: fredadavis@holstonhome.org
Arthur S. Masker, BS, MS, Pres.
   Conditions: Primary—ADHD Asp Au CD CP DS Dx ED LD Mood ID MS OCD ON PDD Psy PTSD PW S SP Sz TBI TS. **Sec**—AN Anx Ap Apr As Bu C Db Dc Dg Ep IP MD Nf SB. **IQ 25 and up.**
   Col Prep. Gen Acad. Voc. Gr K-12. On-Job Trng. **Feat**—Soc_Stud. **Expected outcome:** Return to local school (Avg length of stay: 4-6 mos).
   Therapy: Lang Milieu Occup Perceptual-Motor Phys Play Rec Speech.
   Psychotherapy: Dance Fam Group Indiv Parent. **Counseling:** Educ Voc.
   Enr: 99. Bdg 63. Day 36. B 87. G 12. **Fac:** 12 (Full 11, Part 1). Spec ed 9. Lay 3.
   Est 1895. Nonprofit. United Methodist. **Spons:** Holston United Methodist Home for Children.

Students at the school begin their educational experience with a needs assessment. The pupil then progresses through one-on-one and small-group opportunities in the classroom, in counseling, in spiritual guidance and in recreational activities. Beacon aims to successfully return every child to a public school or a less intensive day program.

BENTON HALL ACADEMY
Day — Coed Ages 8-19

Franklin, TN 37069. 2422 Bethlehem Loop Rd.
Tel: 615-791-6467. Fax: 615-791-6522.
www.bentonhallacademy.org   E-mail: r.hodges@bentonhallacademy.org
Veronica Paradis, BA, MS, Int Head.
　　Conditions: Primary—ADHD Anx As Asp CP Db DS Dx ED Ep Mood OCD TS. **Sec**—Au ID ON SP. **IQ 75 and up. Not accepted**—D-B SO.
　　Col Prep. Gen Acad. Gr 3-12. **Feat**—Span Ecol Comp_Sci Econ Govt Performing_Arts Visual_Arts. ACT: Avg 27. **Expected outcome:** Graduation.
　　Therapy: Lang Occup Phys Speech. **Psychotherapy:** Art Group.
　　Counseling: Educ Voc.
　　Adm: Appl fee: $49. Appl due: Year-round. On-campus interview.
　　Enr: 75 (Cap: 130). B 55. G 20. **Fac:** 10 (Full-time). Spec ed 4. Lay 6.
　　Tui '11-'12: Day $12,225-12,875/sch yr (+$150). **Aid:** School 10 ($50,000).
　　Summer prgm: Day. 6 wks.
　　Est 1977. Nonprofit.

Enrolling boys and girls with various special needs, Benton Hall offers a highly individualized program designed to accommodate particular learning styles. In addition to academics, the school addresses the social, behavioral and emotional development of the student. Seniors satisfy a 15-hour community service requirement.

THE BODINE SCHOOL
Day — Coed Ages 6-14

Germantown, TN 38139. 2432 Yester Oaks Dr.
Tel: 901-754-1800. Fax: 901-751-8595.
www.bodineschool.org   E-mail: communications@bodineschool.org
Josh J. Clark, BS, MA, Head. **Rene Friemoth Lee,** Adm.
　　Conditions: Primary—Dx LD. **Sec**—ADHD. **IQ 95 and up.**
　　Gen Acad. Gr 1-8. **Feat**—Lib_Skills Computers Studio_Art Drama Music.
　　Expected outcome: Return to local school (Avg length of stay: 3-5 yrs).
　　Therapy: Lang Speech. **Counseling:** Educ.
　　Adm: Appl fee: $100. Appl due: Rolling.
　　Enr: 75. **Fac:** 17.
　　Summer prgm: Day. Educ. Ther. 3½ wks.
　　Est 1972. Nonprofit.

The school offers elementary and middle programs for children with dyslexia. The goal of both programs is to remediate language-based learning disabilities to the degree that students are able to return to traditional educational institutions. Using specialized teaching methods, Bodine develops an Individualized Education Program for each pupil that encourages the student to progress at a suitable pace.

The full curriculum includes math, social studies and science, as well as computer, physical education, library and art. As a complement to academics, students gain exposure to a range of cultural experiences through art classes, field trips, and interaction with visiting artists and speakers. Leadership skills—which boys and girls develop through participation in community service, student government and community activities—are integral to the program.

CURREY INGRAM ACADEMY

Day — Coed Ages 5-18

Brentwood, TN 37027. 6544 Murray Ln.
Tel: 615-507-3242, 877-507-3242. Fax: 615-507-3170.
www.curreyingram.org   E-mail: cindy.burch@curreyingram.org
Kathleen G. Rayburn, BS, MA, Head. Amber Cathey, Adm.
Conditions: Primary—ADHD Dc Dg Dx LD. IQ 90 and up.
Col Prep. Gr K-12. Feat—Creative_Writing Span Calc Environ_Sci Econ Govt Ethics Studio_Art Theater Music Music_Theory Dance Finance Health ACT_Prep. SAT/ACT prep. Interscholastic sports.
Therapy: Lang. Counseling: Educ.
Adm: Appl fee: $250. Appl due: Rolling. On-campus interview.
Enr: 300. Fac: 91 (Full 76, Part 15).
Tui '12-'13: Day $33,070-36,690/sch yr (+$300). Aid: School 119 ($1,200,000). Educ. Rec. 4 wks.
Endow $2,885,000. Plant val $19,688,000. Acres 83. Bldgs 10. Class rms 65. Libs 2. Sci labs 5. Art studios 2. Music studios 2. Gyms 2. Fields 3. Stables 1. Comp labs 2. Comp/stud: 1:1 Laptop prgm Gr K-12.
Est 1968.

Currey Ingram provides an individualized elementary and secondary program for students of average to above-average intelligence who have learning differences. The school's college preparatory program assists pupils in developing effective learning strategies. In a setting that encourages active participation in the learning process, course work balances the acquisition of knowledge and skills with the meeting of individual and group needs. Children in kindergarten and grade 1 each receive an iPad for school use, while a one-to-one laptop program serves those in grades 2-12.

THE KING'S DAUGHTERS' SCHOOL
AND THE CENTER FOR AUTISM

Bdg — Coed Ages 7-22; Day — Coed 7-30

Columbia, TN 38401. 412 W 9th St.
Tel: 931-388-3810. Fax: 931-388-0405.
www.tkds.org   E-mail: info@tkds.org
David Craig, Exec Dir. Shauna Bryant, Adm.
Conditions: Primary—APD Asp Au DS ID NLD PDD PW TBI. Sec—ADHD

Ap Apr CD CLP CP ED Ep HI LD Mood OCD ODD S SB TS. **IQ 40-82.**
Not accepted—AN B/VI D-B.
Gen Acad. Underachiever. Voc. Ungraded. On-Job Trng. Shelt_Workshop.
Support_Employ. **Expected outcome:** Return to local school (Avg length of
stay: 3+ yrs).
Therapy: Hear Lang Occup Phys Rec Speech. **Psychotherapy:** Group Indiv.
Counseling: Educ Voc.
Adm: Appl fee: $0. Appl due: Year-round.
Enr: 103 (Cap: 107). Bdg 98. Day 5. B 69. G 34. **Fac:** 35. Spec ed 11. Lay 24.
Tui '12-'13: Bdg $5000-10,000/mo (+$50/mo). Day $1200-2500/mo (+$50/
mo). **Summer prgm:** Bdg & Day. Educ. Rec. 8 wks.
Acres 5. Libs 1. Sci labs 1. Lang labs 1. Gyms 2. Pools 2. Comp labs 3.
Est 1955. Nonprofit.

The school serves individuals with various developmental disabilities, and students
may have a dual diagnosis. The Total Lifestyles Program, the core program of TKDS, is a
year-round boarding school that emphasizes education and independence. Under 24-hour
supervision, pupils follow specialized plans that are tailored to their academic and social
needs and abilities. Independent living skills training, vocational/employment opportunities, leisure and recreational activities, behavioral analysis and modification, social/adap-
tive behavior training and cognitive behavior therapy are all elements of the program.

For individuals over the age of 22, TKDS maintains the Young Adult Academy. The
academy provides participants with vocational and independent living skills training.
Courses, which are designed to have a collegiate feel, include banking, current events,
health and nutrition, and home maintenance. Active community involvement is an important aspect of the program.

MEMPHIS ORAL SCHOOL FOR THE DEAF

Day — Coed Ages 2-6

Germantown, TN 38138. 7901 Poplar Ave.
Tel: 901-758-2228. Fax: 901-531-6735.
www.mosdkids.org   E-mail: tschwartz@mosdkids.org
Teresa Patterson Schwartz, BA, Exec Dir.
Conditions: Primary—D HI. **IQ 90 and up.**
Gen Acad. Gr PS. **Expected outcome:** Return to local school (Avg length of
stay: 4 yrs).
Therapy: Hear Lang Speech.
Adm: Appl due: Year-round. On-campus interview.
Enr: 28 (Cap: 32). **Fac:** 10 (Full-time).
Est 1959. Nonprofit.

MOSD provides auditory-oral education, family training, speech and language therapy,
audiology services and specialized instruction for young children with hearing impairments. Children participate daily in age-appropriate activities designed to hasten the development of speech and language skills, and also to help them develop cognitive skills prior
to their entry into kindergarten.

Tuition fees are determined along a sliding scale according to family income.

VANDERBILT UNIVERSITY
SUSAN GRAY SCHOOL

Day — Coed Ages 3-5

Nashville, TN 37203. 230 Appleton Pl, Peabody Box 329.
Tel: 615-322-8200. Fax: 615-322-8201.
http://peabody.vanderbilt.edu/admin-offices/sgs
 E-mail: kiersten.kinder@vanderbilt.edu
Kiersten Kinder, Dir.
 Conditions: Primary—Ap Asp Au B/VI CP D DS Ep IP ID ON PDD SB TBI.
Gen Acad. Gr PS.
Therapy: Occup Phys Speech.
Enr: 135 (Cap: 135). **Fac:** 20 (Full-time). Spec ed 12. Lay 8.
Tui '12-'13: Day $775/mo.
Est 1968. Nonprofit.

Part of Peabody College and the Vanderbilt Kennedy Center for Research on Human Development, SGS provides educational services for preschool-age children with special needs. Early intervention is available for at-risk infants and toddlers.

Susan Gray School also provides a setting for training future teachers and researchers, and for demonstrating educational models serving young children with special needs. In addition, the school supports research on developmental disabilities and related aspects of human development.

TEXAS

THE BRIARWOOD SCHOOL
Day — Coed Ages 5-21

Houston, TX 77077. 12207 Whittington Dr.
Tel: 281-493-1070. Fax: 281-493-1343.
www.briarwoodschool.org   E-mail: info@briarwoodschool.org
Yvonne Streit Shudde, BA, Exec Dir. **Carole C. Wills,** BBA, Head. **Priscilla Mitchell,** Adm.
Conditions: Primary—ADHD LD. IQ 100 and up.
Col Prep. Gen Acad. Voc. Gr K-12. On-Job Trng. **Feat**—Studio_Art Drama Bus.
Therapy: Lang Occup Speech. **Psychotherapy:** Fam Parent. **Counseling:** Educ Voc.
Adm: Appl fee: $100. Appl due: Rolling. On-campus interview.
Enr: 300. B 200. G 100.
Tui '11-'12: Day $17,960-18,270/sch yr (+$400-1450). **Aid:** School. **Summer prgm:** Day. Rec. Tui Day $435. 3 wks.
Est 1967. Nonprofit.

Originally founded for children with learning problems, the school now provides instruction for both children with learning differences and those with developmental delays. Briarwood conducts two programs for children of average to above-average intelligence who have learning difficulties: the lower school serves elementary pupils in grades K-6, while the middle/upper school accepts the same population in grades 7-12. The curriculum at the middle/upper school level provides a college preparatory program for students who are planning to continue their education after high school, as well as a basic educational program for those who are better suited to an alternative curriculum.

The special school operates with an 8:1 pupil-teacher ratio. Designed for the child with developmental delays, the program serves individuals ages 5-21 and includes art, visual and auditory perception, gross-motor training, recreation, vocational training and language development.

THE CENTER FOR HEARING AND SPEECH
MELINDA WEBB SCHOOL
Day — Coed Ages 1½-6

Houston, TX 77019. 3636 W Dallas St.
Tel: 713-523-3633. TTY: 713-874-1173. Fax: 713-523-8399.
www.centerhearingandspeech.org
   E-mail: info@centerhearingandspeech.org
Renee S. Davis, Exec Dir. **Pam Black,** BS, Educ Dir.
Conditions: Primary—D HI. Sec—S.
Gen Acad. Gr PS. **Feat**—Computers Studio_Art Music. **Expected outcome:** Graduation.

Therapy: Hear Lang Music Occup Play Speech. **Psychotherapy:** Art. **Counseling:** Educ.
Adm: Appl due: Rolling.
Enr: 30. **Fac:** 9 (Full-time). Spec ed 6. Lay 3.
Tui '12-'13: Clinic $119-11,880/sch yr.
Est 1947. Nonprofit.

Melinda Webb School provides specialized instruction designed to accelerate spoken language development in young children whose primary deficit is either hearing impairment or deafness. Full-day programming includes audition, speech, language, academics, computer lab, art, music and movement. Speech therapists conduct weekly speech-language therapy sessions, and boys and girls also have access to on-site audiological services and support. Before- and after-school daycare is available.

THE CRISMAN SCHOOL

Day — Coed Ages 5-14

Longview, TX 75605. 2455 N Eastman Rd.
Tel: 903-758-9741. Fax: 903-758-9767.
www.crismanschool.org   E-mail: lblanks@crismanschool.org
Laura Lea Blanks, EdD, Dir.
   Conditions: Primary—ADHD APD Asp Au Dc Dg Dpx Dx LD NLD PDD S.
   Sec—Ep. **IQ 85 and up.**
   Gen Acad. Gr K-8. Interscholastic sports. **Expected outcome:** Return to local school.
   Therapy: Lang Perceptual-Motor Speech. **Psychotherapy:** Equine.
   Counseling: Educ Voc.
   Adm: Appl fee: $50. Appl due: Year-round. On-campus interview.
   Enr: 50. B 35. G 15. **Fac:** 12 (Full 6, Part 6).
   Tui '12-'13: Day $7740-8000/sch yr (+$325). **Aid:** School. **Summer prgm:** Day. Educ. 3 wks.
   Acres 7. Bldgs 2 (100% ADA). Class rms 8. Libs 1. Sci labs 1. Auds 1. Art studios 1. Music studios 1. Gyms 1. Fields 1. Courts 1. Comp labs 1.
   Est 1970. Nonprofit.

Crisman provides students with learning differences with specialized courses, small classes, flexible schedules, frequent evaluations of progress, multisensory activities and the opportunity to receive instruction for each subject at the level on which they function. The school's staff remains flexible in the choice of methods, materials and placement for each child. Pupils in all grades attend classes in art, computer and physical education, as well as foundational academic courses. Each subject area emphasizes strong reading and writing skills at all grade levels.

Middle school students may take part in an interscholastic sports program. Other extracurricular activities include drama and yearbook.

DALLAS ACADEMY

Day — Coed Ages 5-18

Dallas, TX 75218. 950 Tiffany Way.
Tel: 214-324-1481. Fax: 214-327-8537.
www.dallas-academy.com   E-mail: jrichardson@dallas-academy.com
Jim Richardson, MS, Head.
  Conditions: Primary—ADHD Ap APD Asp Dc Dg Dx LD. **IQ 90 and up.**
  Col Prep. Gen Acad. Gr 1-12. **Feat**—Span Graphic_Arts Photog Studio_Art
    Theater Music. SAT/ACT prep. Interscholastic sports. **Expected outcome:**
    Graduation.
  Therapy: Lang Music. **Psychotherapy:** Art. **Counseling:** Educ.
  Adm: Appl fee: $0. Appl due: Year-round. On-campus interview.
  Enr: 175 (Cap: 200). B 116. G 59. **Fac:** 28 (Full 26, Part 2). Spec ed 28.
  Tui '12-'13: Day $11,000-17,500/sch yr (+$700). **Aid:** School 40. **Summer
    prgm:** Day. Educ. Ther. Tui Day $800. 4 wks.
  Acres 2. Bldgs 1 (100% ADA). Class rms 30. Lib 10,000 vols. Sci labs 3. Lang
    labs 1. Auds 1. Theaters 1. Art studios 3. Music studios 1. Dance studios 1.
    Gyms 1. Fields 4. Comp labs 5.
  Est 1965. Nonprofit.

The academy's program addresses the needs of young people who have such learning differences as dyslexia; dysgraphia; ADHD; and reading, writing and math disorders. It offers both an elementary division and a four-year high school program that leads to a diploma. The course of studies balances traditional school activities with specialized training in reading, writing, spelling and math.

High school students perform four hours of required community service per semester.

EL PASO BRIDGES ACADEMY

Day — Coed Ages 6-14

El Paso, TX 79902. 901 Arizona Ave.
Tel: 915-532-6647. Fax: 915-532-8767.
www.bridgesacademy.org   E-mail: ikeys@bridgesacademy.org
Irma Alva Keys, BS, Dir.
  Conditions: Primary—ADHD Asp Dc Dg Dx LD PDD S. **Sec**—AN Anx Apr
    Ar As Au CD CF CLP CP Db ED Ep ID MD Mood MS Nf OCD ODD SB SP
    TBI TS. **IQ 80-130. Not accepted**—B/VI Bu C D DS IP ON Psy PW SA SO
    Subst Sz.
  Gen Acad. Gr 1-9. **Feat**—Studio_Art Music Ballet. **Expected outcome:** Return
    to local school (Avg length of stay: 3 yrs).
  Therapy: Lang Music Perceptual-Motor Speech. **Psychotherapy:** Art.
    Counseling: Educ.
  Enr: 66 (Cap: 72). B 48. G 18. **Fac:** 18 (Full 14, Part 4).
  Tui '12-'13: Day $7600-10,600/sch yr (+$400). **Aid:** State.
  Est 1979. Nonprofit.

The academy serves learning-disabled children in all academic areas, including specialized therapeutic instruction. Teachers have received training in such methods as Alphabet

Phonics, Wilson Reading and Winston Grammar. The school encourages families, teachers, counselors and physicians to work together to provide students with a tailored learning program.

THE FAIRHILL SCHOOL
Day — Coed Ages 6-18

Dallas, TX 75248. 16150 Preston Rd.
Tel: 972-233-1026. Fax: 972-233-8205.
www.fairhill.org   E-mail: fairhill@fairhill.org
Jane Sego, MEd, Exec Dir. **Melinda Cameron & Carla Stanford,** Adms.
   Conditions: Primary—ADHD APD Dc Dg Dx LD. **IQ 90 and up.**
   Col Prep. Gr 1-12. **Feat**—Span Comp_Sci Econ Govt Psych Performing_Arts Studio_Art Band Journ Speech. **Expected outcome:** Return to local school (Avg length of stay: 4-5 yrs).
   Psychotherapy: Indiv Parent. **Counseling:** Educ.
   Adm: Appl fee: $100. Appl due: Year-round. On-campus interview.
   Enr: 245 (Cap: 250). **Fac:** 32 (Full-time). Spec ed 30. Lay 2.
   Tui '12-'13: Day $15,000-15,500/sch yr (+$250). **Aid:** School. **Summer prgm:** Day. Educ. Rec. Tui Day $1000. 4 wks.
   Acres 16. Bldgs 2. Sci labs 4. Lang labs 1. Art studios 1. Music studios 1. Gyms 1. Fields 1. Courts 1. Comp labs 2.
   Est 1971. Nonprofit.

Fairhill enrolls students of average and above intelligence who have been diagnosed with a learning difference. While some pupils complete their high school education and graduate from Fairhill, many others make the transition to a public or private school after recognizing the nature of their learning style and developing appropriate study and organizational skills.

High school students satisfy the following community service requirements: 15 hours in grade 9, 20 hours in grade 10, 25 hours in grade 11 and 30 hours in grade 12.

GATEWAY SCHOOL
Day — Coed Ages 10-19

Arlington, TX 76012. 2570 NW Green Oaks Blvd.
Tel: 817-226-6222. Fax: 817-226-6225.
www.gatewayschool.com   E-mail: info@gatewayschool.com
Harriet R. Walber, Exec Dir.
   Conditions: Primary—ADHD APD Asp Dc Dg Dpx Dx LD NLD OCD ODD. **IQ 90 and up.**
   Col Prep. Gen Acad. Gr 5-12. **Feat**—Comp_Sci TX_Hist Studio_Art Drama Speech. **Expected outcome:** Return to local school.
   Counseling: Educ.
   Adm: Appl fee: $150. Appl due: Rolling.
   Enr: 30. **Fac:** 5 (Full 4, Part 1).
   Tui '12-'13: Day $14,200/sch yr (+$650).

Acres 7. Bldgs 100% ADA. Class rms 13. Libs 1. Sci labs 1. Art studios 1. Music studios 1. Comp labs 1.
Est 1981. Nonprofit.

Gateway offers pupils of average to above-average intelligence with learning differences an alternative education. A low student-teacher ratio provides allows for individualized attention. The school helps students develop alternative learning strategies so that they can successfully return to their local schools. High schoolers perform 18 hours of required community service each year.

HILL SCHOOL
Day — Coed Ages 6-18

Fort Worth, TX 76133. 4817 Odessa Ave.
Tel: 817-923-9482. Fax: 817-923-4894.
www.hillschool.org   E-mail: hillschool@hillschool.org
   Nearby locations: 204 N Dooley St, Grapevine 76051.
Audrey Boda-Davis, MBA, Exec Dir. **Judy M. King,** Adm.
   Conditions: Primary—ADHD AN APD Asp CP Dc Dg Dx LD OCD SB. **IQ 90 and up.**
   Gen Acad. Gr 1-12. **Feat**—ASL Span Comp_Sci Econ Govt Psych Photog Theater. SAT/ACT prep. **Expected outcome:** Graduation.
   Therapy: Lang Play Speech. **Psychotherapy:** Group. **Counseling:** Educ.
   Adm: Appl fee: $75. Appl due: Rolling.
   Enr: 225. B 165. G 60. **Fac:** 60 (Full 45, Part 15).
   Tui '12-'13: Day $14,300-15,600/sch yr. **Aid:** School.
   Est 1973. Nonprofit.

The school enrolls children of average and above-average intelligence who have learning disabilities. Focusing on academic skills, self-esteem, study skills, self-discipline and social skills, the program seeks to instill a sense of responsibility in the student while also enhancing his or her self-concept. Daily instruction stresses the acquisition of communicative, problem-solving and reasoning skills, as well as self-sufficiency. Boys and girls satisfy a 70-hour community service requirement prior to graduation.
A branch of the school, Hill School Grapevine Campus, serves students in grades 1-8.

HOUSTON LEARNING ACADEMY
Day — Coed Ages 14-18

Houston, TX 77069. 13029 Champions Dr, Ste B-1.
Tel: 281-537-6433.
www.hlahighschools.com
   Nearby locations: 3964 Bluebonnet Dr, Stafford 77477.
   Conditions: Primary—LD. **Sec**—ADHD Dx ED. **IQ 95-126.**
   Col Prep. Gen Acad. Gr 9-12. **Feat**—Span.
   Therapy: Lang Speech. **Psychotherapy:** Indiv.
   Enr: 60. B 40. G 20. **Fac:** 18.

Summer prgm: Day. 1½ wks.
Est 1983. Inc. **Spons:** Nobel Learning Communities.

At two campuses in the Houston area, HLA offers small, structured classes to students of average or above-average ability who have had performance problems in traditional secondary schools. In addition to a college preparatory track, the school maintains a general academic program for those who are not planning to attend college. A career counselor assists pupils with college planning, job placement and career preparation.

In addition to the main Houston location, the academy maintains a campus in Stafford (281-240-6060).

INCLUDING KIDS

Day — Coed Ages 3-18

Humble, TX 77346. 5364 FM 1960 E.
Tel: 281-852-0501. Fax: 281-852-0502.
www.includingkids.org   E-mail: admissions@includingkids.org
Jennifer C. Dantzler, BCBA, MSEd, Exec Dir. Tammy Smith, Adm.
   Conditions: Primary—Apr Asp Au CD ED PDD. **Sec**—ADHD Ap DS ID LD
      OCD ODD TBI. **Not accepted**—SO.
   Gen Acad. Ungraded.
   Therapy: Lang.
   Adm: Appl fee: $0. Appl due: Rolling.
   Enr: 38. **Fac:** 23 (Full-time). Spec ed 3. Lay 20.
   Tui '10-'11: Day $4500/mo. **Aid:** School ($50,000).
   Est 2003. Nonprofit.

Following the principles of Applied Behavior Analysis, the program provides full-time, one-on-one instruction for children with autism and related disorders. An Individualized Education Plan is the foundation for the child's program, and a behavior analyst (or assistant behavior analyst) oversees each program. When students are ready, the center includes them in typical classroom settings, and time spent in these settings increases as appropriate. Social skills training is part of programming.

The facility maintains separate sites for younger and older children: Younger boys and girls devote most of their time to one-on-one instruction, while also partaking in group activities; older students split the day between one-on-one programming and group activities.

Training for parents with developmental delays addresses teaching, behavior management and child advocacy. Including Kids delivers services to parents through one-on-one training, workshops and consultations. In addition to its full-time program, Including Kids offers part-time social skills groups, community outreach and after-school tutoring.

KENLEY SCHOOL

Day — Coed Ages 6-14

Abilene, TX 79605. 1434 Matador St.
Tel: 325-698-3220. Fax: 325-692-7387.

www.kenleyschool.org   E-mail: kenley@suddenlinkmail.com
Marianne Kwiecinski, BAEd, MEd, Dir.
  Conditions: Primary—ADHD Ap APD Asp Au C Db Dc Dg Dpx Dx Ep Hemo
  LD Lk Multi NLD ON SC TBI TS. **Sec**—HI OCD SA SP. **IQ 80 and up. Not
  accepted**—CD D D-B DS ID Mood MR ODD Psy PTSD PW SO Subst Sz.
  Gen Acad. Gr 1-8. **Feat**—Studio_Art Drama Music Study_Skills. **Expected
  outcome:** Return to local school.
  Therapy: Lang Rec Speech. **Psychotherapy:** Art.
  Adm: Appl fee: $0. Appl due: Year-round. On-campus interview.
  Enr: 60 (Cap: 60). B 40. G 20. **Fac:** 10 (Full 5, Part 5). Spec ed 2. Lay 8.
  Tui '11-'12: Day $4600/sch yr (+$150). **Aid:** School. **Summer prgm:** Day.
  Educ. 4 wks.
  Endow $2,000,000. Plant val $262,000. Bldgs 2 (50% ADA). Class rms 5. Lib
  3000 vols. Art studios 1. Fields 1. Courts 1. Comp labs 1.
  Est 1971. Nonprofit.

Conducting a curriculum similar to that found in public elementary schools, Kenley
enrolls children who typically have language-based learning disabilities and thus have special learning needs in the areas of reading, spelling, and written and oral language. Upon
entry to the school, students take a battery of diagnostic tests. Kenley staff then develop a
learning profile for each pupil that enables instructors to address specific learning styles
and academic needs.

Each class completes an annual community service project.

KEY SCHOOL

Day — Coed Ages 6-18

Fort Worth, TX 76119. 3947 E Loop 820 S.
Tel: 817-446-3738. Fax: 817-496-3299.
www.thekeyschool.com   E-mail: administration@thekeyschool.com
Mary Ann Key, MLA, Dir.
  Conditions: Primary—ADHD APD Asp Dc Dg Dx Ep LD TBI. **Sec**—D S.
  IQ 90-120.
  Gen Acad. Underachiever. Gr 1-12. **Feat**—Span Computers Study_Skills.
  Expected outcome: Return to local school (Avg length of stay: 2 yrs).
  Therapy: Hear Lang Speech.
  Adm: Appl due: Year-round. On-campus interview.
  Enr: 105. B 72. G 33. **Fac:** 50 (Full 40, Part 10).
  Tui '11-'12: Day $17,500/sch yr (+$850). **Aid:** School. **Summer prgm:** Day.
  Educ. Tui Day $360-820/crse. 4 wks.
  Est 1966. Nonprofit.

This alternative school offers full elementary and secondary programs that address the
student's developmental, enrichment and remedial needs. Boys and girls further develop
their basic language and math skills to build a foundation for academic success. Summer
courses, which encompass a variety of subject areas, are available. The usual length of stay
at the school is two years, although some pupils remain until graduation.

THE MONARCH SCHOOL
Day — Coed Ages 3-30

Houston, TX 77080. 2815 Rosefield Dr.
Tel: 713-479-0800. Fax: 713-464-7499.
www.monarchschool.org E-mail: admissions@monarchschool.org
Deborah Hall, PhD, Head. **Audrey Omenson,** Adm.
 Conditions: Primary—ADHD Anx Ap APD Asp Au Dc Dg Dpx Dx LD Mood NLD OCD ODD ON PDD PW S TS. **Sec**—AN Apr As Bu CD CP Db ED Ep ID MS PTSD SA SP TBI. **IQ 55 and up. Not accepted**—SO Subst.
 Col Prep. Gen Acad. Underachiever. Voc. Gr PS-12. Culinary. Hort. On-Job Trng. Support_Employ. AP courses (Span Calc Bio US_Hist US_Govt & Pol). **Feat**—British_Lit Shakespeare Stats Environ_Sci Econ Studio_Art Drama Debate Journ Woodworking. SAT/ACT prep. **Expected outcome:** Return to local school (Avg length of stay: 3+ yrs).
 Therapy: Aqua Lang Milieu Music Occup Perceptual-Motor Phys Play Rec Speech. **Psychotherapy:** Art Dance Fam Group Indiv Parent.
 Counseling: Educ Nutrition Voc.
 Adm: Appl fee: $550. Appl due: Year-round. On-campus interview.
 Enr: 112 (Cap: 250). B 86. G 26. **Fac:** 31 (Full-time). Spec ed 31.
 Tui '12-'13: Day $24,000-52,000/sch yr (+$550). **Aid:** School 30 ($180,000). State 1. **Summer prgm:** Res & Day. Educ. Rec. Ther. Tui Bdg $4300-6200. Tui Day $2300-4200. 6 wks.
 Acres 11. Bldgs 1.
 Est 1997. Nonprofit.

Monarch provides a therapeutic learning environment for children with such neurological differences as ADD, learning disabilities, pervasive developmental disorder, Asperger's syndrome, Tourette's syndrome, seizure disorder and bipolar disorder. Teachers and psychologists work together with the student and his or her parents on emotional and behavioral self-regulation, as well as relationship and communicational skills. Academics span from the elementary grades through high school. Music therapy incurs an additional hourly fee.

NOTRE DAME SCHOOL
Day — Coed Ages 8-23

Dallas, TX 75204. 2018 Allen St.
Tel: 214-720-3911. Fax: 214-720-3913.
www.notredameschool.org   E-mail: tfrancis@notredameschool.org
Theresa Francis, MEd, Prin.
 Conditions: Primary—DS ID Multi PDD. **IQ 40-70.**
 Voc. Ungraded. On-Job Trng. Support_Employ. **Feat**—Computers Relig Music.
 Expected outcome: Graduation.
 Therapy: Lang Music Occup Speech. **Counseling:** Voc.
 Adm: Appl due: Rolling. On-campus interview.
 Enr: 150. B 85. G 65. **Fac:** 21 (Full 18, Part 3). Spec ed 21.
 Tui '12-'13: Day $7000/sch yr. **Aid:** School 45 ($160,000).

Bldgs 95% ADA. Class rms 25. Libs 1. Music studios 1. Gyms 1. Comp labs 1.
Est 1963. Nonprofit. Roman Catholic.

Notre Dame provides students with intellectual disabilities with a curriculum that emphasizes mathematics, reading, spelling and writing. Music, religion and physical education classes are part of the program at all levels, while independent living skills, job skills and career exploration are important elements in the upper school. Christian values and attitudes prevail.

Area youth volunteers work and interact with the students in their classrooms on a regular basis. Notre Dame pupils engage in regularly scheduled activities with nonhandicapped peers.

THE PARISH SCHOOL
Day — Coed Ages 1½-11

Houston, TX 77043. 11001 Hammerly Blvd.
Tel: 713-467-4696. Fax: 713-467-8341.
www.parishschool.org   E-mail: bmedina@parishschool.org
Margaret Noecker, BS, MEd, Head. **Nancy Bewley,** BS, MAT, CCC-SLP, Prin.
  Brooke Medina, Adm.
  Conditions: Primary—Ap APD Apr Asp Au Dpx Dx LD NLD S TBI.
    Sec—ADHD Anx Ar C CLP CP Db Dc Dg ED Ep Hemo IP Lk MD MS Nf
    OCD ON PW SB SC SP TS. **IQ 90 and up.**
  Gen Acad. Gr PS-5. **Feat**—Computers Study_Skills. **Expected outcome:** Return
    to local school (Avg length of stay: 2-3 yrs).
  Therapy: Lang Occup Perceptual-Motor Play Rec Speech.
    Psychotherapy: Fam Group Indiv Parent.
  Adm: Appl fee: $50. Appl due: Year-round. On-campus interview.
  Enr: 132 (Cap: 146). B 95. G 37. **Fac:** 21 (Full-time). Spec ed 21.
  Tui '10-'11: Day $20,000-22,500/sch yr (+$400). Clinic $110-150 (Therapy)/hr.
    Aid: School. **Summer prgm:** Bdg & Day. Educ. Rec. Ther. Tui Bdg $1500/
    wk. Tui Day $250/wk. 4 wks.
  Acres 17. Bldgs 7 (100% ADA). Class rms 16. Libs 1. Art studios 1. Music stu-
    dios 1. Fields 1. Comp labs 1.
  Est 1983. Nonprofit.

The school provides Individualized Education Plans for children with average or above-average abilities who have poor social interaction skills or minimal delays in language or fine- or gross-motor skills. In addition to the primary conditions served, Parish can accommodate pupils with pervasive developmental disorder, apraxia and coordination disorders. The program promotes the development of language, speech and thinking skills, and the school encourages family involvement. Length of enrollment averages two to three years.

RIVER CITY CHRISTIAN SCHOOL
Day — Coed Ages 5-19

San Antonio, TX 78216. 5810 Blanco Rd.

Tel: 210-384-0297. Fax: 210-384-0446.
www.rivercitychristianschool.com   E-mail: rccs1@sbcglobal.net
Ezzard G. Castillo, MEd, MA, Head. **Barbara Moore,** Adm.
Conditions: Primary—ADHD AN Anx Ap APD As Asp Au C CP Dc Dg Dx
   ED Ep LD Mood MS OCD ON PDD PTSD S SP TBI TS. **Sec**—Apr B/VI Bu
   CD D Db ID MD Nf PW. **IQ 75 and up.**
Col Prep. Gen Acad. Voc. Gr K-12. On-Job Trng. **Expected outcome:** Return
   to local school (Avg length of stay: 2-4 yrs).
Therapy: Lang Music Occup Perceptual-Motor Play Speech.
   Psychotherapy: Dance. **Counseling:** Educ.
Adm: Appl fee: $25. On-campus interview.
Enr: 112. B 73. G 39. **Fac:** 14 (Full 11, Part 3). Spec ed 14.
Tui '11-'12: Day $7500/sch yr (+$555-640). **Summer prgm:** Day. Educ. Ther.
   Tui Day $150-450. 1-2 wks.
Est 1990. Nonprofit. Nondenom Christian.

The school serves students who have been diagnosed with a learning disability. Upon leaving River City, many students successfully return to a mainstream educational environment. A transitional program for children with autism is also offered. Speech and occupational therapies are available.

SHELTON SCHOOL AND EVALUATION CENTER
Day — Coed Ages 3-18

Dallas, TX 75248. 15720 Hillcrest Rd.
Tel: 972-774-1772. Fax: 972-991-3977.
www.shelton.org   E-mail: wdeppe@shelton.org
Suzanne Stell, BS, MEd, Exec Dir. **Linda Kneese,** MEd, Head.
Diann Slaton, Adm.
Conditions: Primary—ADHD Dc Dg Dx LD. **Sec**—Anx Ap Apr As D Db OCD
   TS. **IQ 90 and up.**
Gen Acad. Gr PS-12. **Feat**—ASL Lat Span Computers Econ Govt Psych
   Ethics Studio_Art Theater_Arts Music Speech. **Expected outcome:** Graduation.
Therapy: Hear Lang Phys Speech. **Psychotherapy:** Fam Group Indiv.
   Counseling: Educ.
Adm: Appl fee: $50. Appl due: Rolling.
Enr: 853. B 536. G 317. **Fac:** 151 (Full 149, Part 2).
Tui '12-'13: Day $19,050-20,660/sch yr (+$655-2800). **Summer prgm:** Day.
   Educ. Rec. Ther. 6 wks.
Endow $5,004,000. Plant val $18,000,000. Acres 8. Bldgs 4 (100% ADA).
   Class rms 93. 2 Libs 23,575 vols. Sci labs 5. Lang labs 1. Auds 1. Theaters
   2. Art studios 3. Music studios 2. Dance studios 1. Gyms 1. Fields 2. Courts
   2. Playgrounds 2. Comp labs 3. Laptop prgm Gr 7-12.
Est 1976. Nonprofit.

The school offers learning-disabled children specialized training through multisensory instruction. Highly structured, small classes provide ongoing work in study skills. Supplementary offerings include perceptual-motor training, physical education and intramural athletic competition, computer classes and a variety of extracurricular activities. Students in grades 7-12 lease laptop computers from the school for classroom work and homework assignments.

Shelton's Evaluation Center conducts comprehensive tests designed to assess academic levels, intellectual ability, perceptual-motor development, language skill usage and coping techniques. The center specializes in the diagnosis and the treatment of dyslexia and attention deficit disorder, with and without hyperactivity. Interpretation of results and educational and therapeutic recommendations are imparted to parents in a teaching conference.

SUNSHINE COTTAGE SCHOOL FOR DEAF CHILDREN
Day — Coed Ages 3-19

San Antonio, TX 78212. 603 E Hildebrand Ave.
Tel: 210-824-0579. Fax: 210-826-0436.
www.sunshinecottage.org   E-mail: info@sunshinecottage.org
Carolyn Walthall, MEd, Exec Dir. **Nancy Henderson,** EdD, Prin.
  Conditions: Primary—D. **IQ 90 and up.**
  Gen Acad. Gr PS-12. **Feat**—Lib_Skills Studio_Art Music.
  Therapy: Hear Lang Speech. **Psychotherapy:** Parent. **Counseling:** Educ.
  Adm: Appl due: Rolling.
  Enr: 149. B 81. G 68. **Fac:** 31 (Full 29, Part 2). Spec ed 27. Lay 4.
  Tui '12-'13: Day $6003/sch yr (+$75).
  Est 1947. Nonprofit.

The educational program for hearing-impaired children at the Sunshine Cottage School employs the oral-auditory method. Students ranging from infant to high school age receive hearing and speech-language therapies. Audiological management and cochlear implant habilitation are among the training programs offered.

TEXAS CHRISTIAN UNIVERSITY STARPOINT SCHOOL
Day — Coed Ages 6-12

Fort Worth, TX 76129. 2805 Stadium Dr, TCU Box 297410.
Tel: 817-257-7141. Fax: 817-257-7168.
www.starpoint.tcu.edu   E-mail: starpoint@tcu.edu
Marilyn Tolbert, BS, MEd, EdD, Dir.
  Conditions: Primary—Dx LD. **Sec**—ADHD Dc Dg NLD. **IQ 90-118.**
  Gen Acad. Ungraded. **Feat**—Computers Studio_Art Music. **Expected outcome:** Return to local school (Avg length of stay: 2+ yrs).
  Therapy: Lang Occup Speech. **Psychotherapy:** Group Parent. **Counseling:** Educ.
  Adm: Appl fee: $50. Appl due: Mar. On-campus interview.
  Enr: 61. B 37. G 24. **Fac:** 8 (Full-time). Spec ed 8.
  Tui '12-'13: Day $12,400/sch yr (+$250). **Aid:** School ($40,000).
  Est 1966. Nonprofit.

TCU faculty members and supervised teacher-trainees provide learning-disabled students with a full academic day program, conducted through TCU's School of Education. The curriculum includes the traditional subjects, and Starpoint places particular emphasis on the acquisition of organizational and study skills. The school's program also includes educational and parental counseling.

THE WESTVIEW SCHOOL

Day — Coed Ages 2-14

Houston, TX 77043. 1900 Kersten Dr.
Tel: 713-973-1900. Fax: 713-973-1970.
www.westviewschool.org   E-mail: info@westviewschool.org
Donna Marshall, Head.
   Conditions: Primary—Ap APD Apr Asp Au NLD PDD S. **Sec**—ADHD Anx CLP CP Db Dc Dg Dpx Dx ED Ep ID LD Nf OCD ON PTSD PW SA SB SP TS. **Not accepted**—AN Ar B/VI Bu C CD CF D D-B HI IP MD Mood MS Multi ODD Psy SO Subst Sz TBI.
   Gen Acad. Ungraded. **Feat**—Computers Studio_Art Drama Music. **Expected outcome:** Return to local school.
   Therapy: Lang Occup Speech.
   Adm: Appl fee: $0. Appl due: Year-round. On-campus interview.
   Enr: 135. B 111. G 24. **Fac:** 31. Spec ed 31.
   Tui '12-'13: Day $14,328-19,635/sch yr. Clinic $120 (Therapy)/hr.
      Aid: School 20 ($220,000). **Summer prgm:** Day. Educ. Ther. 6 wks.
   Acres 7. Bldgs 2. Libs 2. Sci labs 1. Lang labs 1. Auds 1. Theaters 1. Art studios 1. Music studios 2. Gyms 2. Fields 1. Tracks 2. Playgrounds 2. Comp labs 2.
   Est 1981. Nonprofit.

Westview provides a structured learning environment for children with high-function autism spectrum disorders or other communicational or social impairments. The school maintains a full academic curriculum while also working with students to ameliorate social and communication difficulties. Speech/language and occupational therapy are available on site.

THE WINSTON SCHOOL

Day — Coed Ages 6-19

Dallas, TX 75229. 5707 Royal Ln.
Tel: 214-691-6950. Fax: 214-691-1509.
www.winston-school.org   E-mail: info@winston-school.org
Polly A. Peterson, BSW, MSW, PhD, Head. **Sara Collins,** Adm.
   Conditions: Primary—ADHD APD Dc Dg Dx LD NLD.
   Col Prep. Gr 1-12. **Feat**—Lat Span Engineering Ceramics Fine_Arts Studio_Art Drama Music. Avg SAT: CR 547. M 510. W 530. ACT: Avg 24.5. Interscholastic sports. **Expected outcome:** Graduation.
   Adm: Appl fee: $195. Appl due: Rolling. On-campus interview.

Enr: 200. B 137. G 63. **Fac:** 34 (Full 32, Part 2). Spec ed 1. Lay 33.
Tui '12-'13: Day $19,061-24,218/sch yr (+$1440-2990). **Aid:** School 43
($415,075). **Summer prgm:** Day. Educ. Rec. Tui Day $1400. 5 wks.
Endow $5,000,000. Plant val $7,000,000. Acres 6. Bldgs 4 (100% ADA). Class
rms 24. Lib 6000 vols. Sci labs 3. Lang labs 1. Art studios 2. Music studios
1. Gyms 1. Fields 1. Comp labs 3. Comp/stud: 1:1.5 (1:1 Laptop prgm Gr
7-12).
Est 1975. Nonprofit.

Winston's individualized program utilizes various assessment processes and teaching
methods to address the specific cognitive needs of boys and girls who have learning differences. After the student is assessed at the school's testing and evaluation center, teachers
formulate an educational plan based upon the results. Cocurricular programs in the visual
and performing arts, athletics, compulsory community service projects, student government and solar science are integral aspects of school life.

THE WINSTON SCHOOL SAN ANTONIO

Day — Coed Ages 5-19

San Antonio, TX 78229. 8565 Ewing Halsell Dr.
Tel: 210-615-6544. Fax: 210-615-6627.
www.winston-sa.org   E-mail: web@winston-sa.org
Charles J. Karulak, MS, EdD, Head. **Julie A. Saboe,** Adm.
  Conditions: Primary—ADHD Dc Dg Dx LD. **IQ 90 and up.**
  Not accepted—CD DS ED ID MR ODD PDD Psy SO Sz.
  Col Prep. Gr K-12. **Feat**—Span Anat & Physiol Comp_Sci Econ Govt
  Graphic_Arts Studio_Art Drama Music Jazz_Band Journ Speech Health.
  SAT/ACT prep. Interscholastic sports. **Expected outcome:** Graduation.
  Psychotherapy: Parent. **Counseling:** Educ.
  Adm: Appl fee: $100. Appl due: Year-round. On-campus interview.
  Enr: 199. B 143. G 56. **Fac:** 29 (Full 28, Part 1). Spec ed 15. Lay 14.
  Tui '12-'13: Day $16,500/sch yr. **Aid:** School 54 ($325,000). **Summer prgm:**
  Day. Educ. Rec. Sports. Tui Day $450-950. 4 wks.
  Acres 16. Bldgs 2 (100% ADA). Class rms 30. Libs 1. Sci labs 3. Art studios 1.
  Music studios 1. Gyms 1. Fields 2. Courts 1. Comp labs 3.
  Est 1985. Nonprofit.

WSSA conducts diagnostic and educational programs for the treatment of learning disabilities. Students follow individualized programs suited to their personal learning styles.
Afternoon study hall is available five days per week in the lower school, four days weekly
in the middle school. Computer-aided instruction, sports and extracurricular activities are
notable features of the program. During the high school years, boys and girls compile 20
hours of required community service annually.

UTAH

CEDAR RIDGE ACADEMY

Bdg — Coed Ages 13-18

Roosevelt, UT 84066. Rte 1, Box 1477.
Tel: 435-353-4498, 866-471-6629. Fax: 435-353-4898.
www.cedaridge.net   E-mail: admissions@cedaridge.net
Wes Nielson, MS, Dir. **Steve Miller,** Adm.
Conditions: Primary—ADHD Anx ED Mood OCD ODD PTSD SA. **Sec**—AN As Bu LD SP Subst TS. **IQ 90 and up. Not accepted**—B/VI C D Db DS Hemo ID MR PDD SC Sz.
Col Prep. Gr 8-12. **Feat**—ACT_Prep. **Expected outcome:** Return to local school (Avg length of stay: 16-18 mos).
Therapy: Milieu Rec. **Psychotherapy:** Art Dance Fam Group Hypno Indiv. **Counseling:** Educ Voc.
Adm: Appl due: Year-round.
Enr: 60. B 41. G 19. **Fac:** 14 (Full 6, Part 8). Lay 14.
Acres 130.
Est 1996.

Located on a 130-acre site in the foothills of the Uintah Mountains, this therapeutic boarding school serves students who have mild to moderate emotional disorders. At the academy, individual therapy sessions are scheduled weekly, while a group therapy session is held each day. Family workshops, experiential activities, karate training and outdoor recreation are among the therapeutic options.

Students enrolled at Cedar Ridge take compulsory courses in the core subjects of math, English, science and social studies. In addition, boys and girls receive individualized college counseling and career guidance. ACT test preparation is available to grade-eligible pupils.

DISCOVERY ACADEMY

Bdg — Coed Ages 13-17

Provo, UT 84601. 105 N 500 W.
Tel: 801-374-2121. Fax: 801-373-4451.
www.discoveryacademy.com
Brent Hall, LMFT, Exec Dir. **Lanny Adamson,** MEd, Head.
Triston Morgan, Adm.
Conditions: Primary—ADHD Dx LD ID Subst. **Sec**—Asp ED OCD ODD ON PTSD. **IQ 95 and up.**
Col Prep. Gen Acad. Gr 6-12. On-Job Trng. **Feat**—Span. ACT: Avg 22. SAT/ACT prep. **Expected outcome:** Return to local school (Avg length of stay: 18 mos).
Therapy: Occup Speech. **Psychotherapy:** Art Equine Fam Group Indiv Parent. **Counseling:** Educ.

Adm: Appl due: Year-round.
Enr: 82 (Cap: 82). B 50. G 32. **Fac:** 10 (Full-time). Spec ed 1. Lay 9.
Tui '12-'13: Bdg $6400/mo (+$1450/yr).
Est 1989. Inc. **Spons:** RedCliff Ascent.

The academy combines residential treatment with a competency-based tutorial program that allows underachieving, often troubled adolescents to progress at an appropriate pace. Individuals with severe physical, emotional and intellectual handicaps are not accepted, and pupils spend a minimum of one year at Discovery.

HERITAGE SCHOOL

Bdg — Coed Ages 12-18

Provo, UT 84604. 5600 N Heritage School Dr.
Tel: 801-226-4600, 800-433-9413. Fax: 801-226-4641.
www.heritagertc.org   E-mail: susie.fell@heritagertc.org
Glen R. Zaugg, CEO. **Susie Fell,** Adm.
  Conditions: Primary—ADHD Anx CD ED Mood ODD Psy PTSD SA SP
    Subst Sz. **Sec**—Ap Apr Ar As Asp CF CLP Db Dc Dg Dx Ep LD OCD PW
    S TS. **IQ 70 and up. Not accepted**—AN Au B/VI Bu C CP D D-B DS Hemo
    HI ID IP MD MR MS Nf SB SC SO TBI.
  Gen Acad. Gr 7-12. **Feat**—Fr Span. **Expected outcome:** Return to local
    school (Avg length of stay: 14 mos).
  Therapy: Lang Milieu Rec Speech. **Psychotherapy:** Equine Fam Group Indiv
    Parent. **Counseling:** Educ Substance_Abuse.
  Adm: Appl fee: $0. Appl due: Year-round.
  Enr: 160 (Cap: 170).
  Tui '11-'12: Bdg $363/day. **Aid:** State 100.
  Acres 19. Perf arts ctrs 1. Fields 2. Basketball courts 2. Volleyball courts 1.
    Pools 1. Climbing walls 1.
  Est 1984. Nonprofit.

Providing year-round residential services for adolescents in need of a structured educational and psychotherapeutic environment, Heritage employs a multidisciplinary team approach to help residents replace inappropriate patterns of behavior. Staff formulate individual academic programs, and all students attend school regularly. Progress evaluations occur weekly. Special arrangements for gifted and learning-disabled residents are available. The program also features counseling, therapy and substance abuse recovery groups.

LOGAN RIVER ACADEMY

Bdg — Coed Ages 13-17

Logan, UT 84321. 1683 S Hwy 89-91.
Tel: 435-755-8400. Fax: 435-755-8540.
www.loganriver.com   E-mail: information@loganriver.com
Larry Carter, MHA, Exec Dir. **Kirk Farmer,** MS, Educ Dir.
  Conditions: Primary—ADHD AN Anx APD Asp Dg Dpx Dx ED LD Mood

NLD OCD ODD PTSD SA SP Subst TBI TS. **Sec**—Bu HI ON. **IQ 80 and up. Not accepted**—Au C CD Db Ep Hemo Lk Psy SC SO Sz.
Col Prep. Gen Acad. Underachiever. Gr 8-12. **Feat**—Span Computers Health. ACT: Avg 22. SAT/ACT prep. Interscholastic sports. **Expected outcome:** Graduation.
Therapy: Milieu. **Psychotherapy:** Equine Fam Group Indiv. **Counseling:** Educ.
Adm: Appl fee: $0. Appl due: Year-round.
Enr: 90 (Cap: 90). B 54. G 36. **Fac:** 10. Spec ed 3. Lay 7.
Tui '10-'11: Bdg $7500/mo. **Aid:** School. State.
Acres 12. Bldgs 100% ADA. Dorms 10. Dorm rms 40. Class rms 11. Libs 1. Sci labs 1. Art studios 1. Gyms 1. Fields 2. Courts 1. Riding rings 1. Stables 1. **Est 2000.**

Enrolling boys and girls who have had difficulties at home, in the community and at school, Logan River provides year-round services for students with learning disabilities, emotional special needs or substance abuse issues. The multidisciplinary program balances education, therapy and a structured residential environment. Middle school and high school course work satisfies state core requirements and includes independent study and online class options.

Residential staff model appropriate behavior and provide direct assistance for students. Pupils engage in three main types of recreational activities: adventure learning pursuits; diversionary/incentive activities, which are awarded for progress and achievement; and organized sports and routine fitness activities.

MAPLE LAKE ACADEMY

Bdg — Girls Ages 13-18

Payson, UT 84651. PO Box 175.
Tel: 801-798-7700. Fax: 801-798-7739.
www.maplelakeacademy.com   E-mail: info@maplelakeacademy.com
Nichol Holwege, BS, Prgm Dir. **Wendy LeFevre,** BS, Educ Dir.
Patti Hollenbeck-Dial, Adm.
Conditions: Primary—ADHD Anx Asp Au Dc Dg Dx ED LD Mood NLD OCD ODD PTSD SP Subst TS. **Sec**—Ar As CLP Ep ON SA. **IQ 80 and up. Not accepted**—AN Bu CD Psy SO Sz.
Gen Acad. Ungraded. Support_Employ. **Feat**—Computers Drama. **Expected outcome:** Return to local school (Avg length of stay: 10-12 mos).
Therapy: Milieu Play Rec Speech. **Psychotherapy:** Art Equine Fam Group Indiv Parent. **Counseling:** Educ Nutrition Voc Substance_Abuse.
Enr: 12 (Cap: 12). **Fac:** 4 (Full 1, Part 3). Spec ed 2. Lay 2.
Est 2003. Inc.

The academy conducts a year-round program for girls with verbal and nonverbal learning differences that may contribute to emotional or behavioral problems. Asperger's syndrome and high-functioning autism may also be primary conditions that the student faces. Individually formulated educational plans address specific needs and offer interventions and strategies that deal with visual/perceptual, auditory processing, spatial awareness, conceptual, memory and social skills deficits, as well as emotional and psychological issues.

Clinical services form an important part of school life. Each week, girls receive 20 hours of therapeutic interventions. Individual therapy focuses on specific LD and emotional issues, while weekly family therapy addresses both those issues and relevant family dynamics and skill building in communication and relationships. Girls typically spend 10 to 12 months at the academy.

PROVO CANYON SCHOOL

Bdg — Coed Ages 8-18

Provo, UT 84604. 4501 N University Ave.
Tel: 801-227-2000, 800-848-9819. Fax: 801-227-2095.
www.provocanyon.com   E-mail: pcsinfo@provocanyon.com
  Nearby locations: 1350 E 750 N, Orem 84097.
  Conditions: Primary—Anx Asp ED LD OCD PTSD Subst. **Sec**—ADHD Mood. **IQ 80 and up.**
  Col Prep. Gen Acad. Voc. Gr 3-12. Man_Arts & Shop. On-Job Trng.
    Feat—British_Lit Creative_Writing Fr Ger Span Calc Zoology Programming Web_Design Econ Govt Ceramics Sculpt Studio_Art Bus Communications Marketing Indus_Arts. **Expected outcome:** Graduation.
  Therapy: Rec. **Psychotherapy:** Fam Group Indiv.
  Enr: 242 (Cap: 242). B 132. G 110. **Fac:** 28.
  Acres 15. Bldgs 3. Dorms 8. Class rms 22. Libs 2. Sci labs 1. Auds 1. Art studios 2. Gyms 2. Fields 2. Courts 2. Pools 1. Comp labs 2.
  Est 1971.

On two campuses, Provo Canyon serves boys and girls who are experiencing academic difficulties or behavioral problems. The school offers an individualized academic program featuring both remedial and accelerated emphasis; individual, group, family and milieu therapy; and supervised recreational experiences. The school offers single-gender treatment for boys on the main Provo campus. On the Orem campus, a coeducational program for pupils ages 8-12 leads into an all-girls setting for students ages 12-17.

SEPS LEARNING CENTER

Day — Coed Ages 4-18

Salt Lake City, UT 84106. 604 E Wilmington Ave.
Tel: 801-467-2122. Fax: 801-467-2148.
www.sepslc.com   E-mail: ava.eva.seps@sepslc.com
AvaJane Pickering, PhD, Exec Dir.
  Conditions: Primary—ADHD Anx Ap APD Apr Dc Dg Dx ED Ep LD TBI TS. **Sec**—As Asp Au B/VI C CP D Db Mood OCD PTSD S SB SP. **IQ 85 and up.**
  Col Prep. Gen Acad. Gr PS-12. **Feat**—Studio_Art Health.
  Therapy: Lang Play Rec Speech. **Psychotherapy:** Fam.
  Enr: 114. B 79. G 35. **Fac:** 28 (Full 5, Part 23). Spec ed 28.
  Summer prgm: Day. Educ. Rec. Ther.
  Est 1974. Inc.

SEPS offers academic remediation for pupils with learning disabilities, attentional disorders, and hyperactivity. Individualized programs address the needs of each student and feature one-on-one instruction. Special services include life skills and adaptive behaviors training; scientific learning and language therapy; mathematics, foreign language conversation and writing workshops; and workshops designed to assist parents of special-needs children.

SORENSON'S RANCH SCHOOL

Bdg — Coed Ages 12-18

Koosharem, UT 84744. 410 N 100 E, PO Box 440219.
Tel: 435-638-7318, 888-830-4802. Fax: 435-638-7582.
www.sorensonsranch.com   E-mail: admissions@sorensonsranch.com
Shane Sorenson, MA, Dir. **Layne Bagley,** Adm.
Conditions: Primary—Ap APD Asp CD Dg Dpx Dx ED LD Mood ID Multi NLD OCD ODD PDD PTSD S SA SP Subst. **Sec**—AN Anx As Bu Db Dc Ep HI TS. **Not accepted**—Au B/VI C D D-B DS Hemo Lk ON Psy PW SC SO Sz TBI.
Col Prep. Gen Acad. Voc. Gr 7-12. Hort. Man_Arts & Shop. **Feat**—Comp_Sci Drawing Studio_Art Guitar Woodworking Health. **Expected outcome:** Return to local school (Avg length of stay: 1 yr).
Therapy: Milieu Play Rec. **Psychotherapy:** Equine Fam Group Indiv.
Counseling: Educ.
Adm: Appl due: Year-round.
Enr: 70 (Cap: 80). **Fac:** 8. Spec ed 1. Lay 7.
Tui '10-'11: Bdg $66,000/yr. **Aid:** State. **Summer prgm:** Bdg. Educ. Rec. Ther. Tui Bdg $5500. 4 wks.
Est 1982. Nonprofit.

Sorenson's serves students with a history of problems with parents, substance abuse, low or nonexistent self-esteem, learning differences, running away, school dropping out or expulsion, or extreme mental stress. Utilizing professional counseling, group counseling and staff-student relationships, the school aims to help young people function successfully both at home and in society. Parental involvement is preferred but not compulsory.

The school's maintains wilderness and work programs to teach students the importance of loyalty, respect, self-esteem, personal management, respect for property, cleanliness and trustworthiness.

Sorenson's also serves as a licensed residential treatment facility that includes drug and alcohol treatment. Staff develop an individualized treatment plan for each child. Group counseling sessions and intensive one-on-one time with Sorenson staff members is part of treatment.

VERMONT

THE AUSTINE SCHOOL AND VERMONT CENTER FOR THE DEAF AND HARD OF HEARING

Bdg and Day — Coed Ages 3-21

Brattleboro, VT 05301. 60 Austine Dr.
Tel: 802-258-9500. TTY: 802-258-9500. Fax: 802-258-9574.
www.vcdhh.org E-mail: bcarter@vcdhh.org
Bert Carter, MA, Pres. Janet Dickinson, Dir. Peggy Lee, Adm.
  Conditions: Primary—D D-B HI. Sec—ADHD Anx Ap Apr Ar Asp Au B/VI C
    CD CLP CP Db Dc Dg Dpx DS Dx ED Ep LD MD Mood MS Multi Nf NLD
    OCD ODD ON PDD PTSD S SB SP TBI TS. IQ 70 and up.
  Col Prep. Gen Acad. Underachiever. Voc. Gr K-12. Man_Arts & Shop. On-
    Job Trng. Feat—Computers Studio_Art. SAT/ACT prep. Interscholastic
    sports.
  Therapy: Hear Lang Massage Occup Phys Play Rec Speech.
    Psychotherapy: Group Indiv Parent. Counseling: Educ Voc.
  Adm: Appl due: Year-round.
  Enr: 63 (Cap: 80). Bdg 29. Day 34. B 40. G 23. Fac: 22 (Full 20, Part 2).
  Tui '10-'11: Bdg $90,162/sch yr. Day $47,330/sch yr. Aid: State. Summer
    prgm: Bdg & Day. Educ. Rec. Ther. 6 wks.
  Endow $2,000,000. Plant val $4,000,000. Acres 175. Bldgs 7.
  Est 1904. Nonprofit.

Located on a 175-acre campus, the school offers academic, prevocational and vocational programs for students who are deaf or hard of hearing. Counseling is available and
the length of enrollment varies. Students have the opportunity to take mainstream classes
at a local public school. Many pupils go on to attend similar postsecondary educational
schools.

BENNINGTON SCHOOL

Bdg — Coed Ages 8-21

Bennington, VT 05201. 192 Fairview St.
Tel: 802-447-1557, 800-639-3156. Fax: 802-447-3234.
www.benningtonschoolinc.org
  E-mail: admissions@benningtonschoolinc.org
Lisa Smith, Adm.
  Conditions: Primary—ADHD CD Dx ED LD OCD. IQ 65 and up.
  Gen Acad. Voc. Ungraded. Man_Arts & Shop. Feat—Computers Studio_Art.
    Interscholastic sports. Expected outcome: Return to local school (Avg
    length of stay: 12-18 mos).
  Therapy: Lang Occup Phys Speech. Psychotherapy: Group Indiv.
    Counseling: Educ.
  Enr: 115. B 75. G 40.

Est 1980. Inc.

The school provides year-round educational instruction, behavior management and clinical services within a therapeutic milieu. Vocational, educational and personal counseling are also offered. Students generally enroll for 12 to 18 months.

THE GREENWOOD SCHOOL

Bdg and Day — Boys Ages 11-17

Putney, VT 05346. 14 Greenwood Ln.
Tel: 802-387-4545. Fax: 802-387-5396.
www.greenwood.org   E-mail: admissions@greenwood.org
Stewart Miller, Head. **Melanie Miller,** Adm.
  Conditions: Primary—ADHD Anx APD Dc Dg Dpx Dx LD NLD PDD S SP.
  Sec—Asp. **IQ 80-130. Not accepted**—Au CD ED ODD SO.
  Gen Acad. Gr 6-11. Man_Arts & Shop. **Feat**—Computers Studio_Art Music
  Speech Metal_Shop Woodworking. ESL. Interscholastic sports. **Expected
  outcome:** Return to local school (Avg length of stay: 2-4 yrs).
  Therapy: Lang Occup Speech. **Psychotherapy:** Indiv.
  Adm: Appl fee: $75. Appl due: Rolling. On-campus interview.
  Enr: 47. Bdg 42. Day 5. **Fac:** 29 (Full 20, Part 9).
  Tui '12-'13: Bdg $65,870/sch yr (+$2000). Day $50,400/sch yr (+$300).
    Aid: School 14 ($464,610). State 3.
  Endow $840,000. Plant val $3,226,000. Acres 100. Bldgs 17 (100% ADA).
  Dorms 1. Dorm rms 18. Class rms 19. Lib 5500 vols. Art studios 1. Music
  studios 1. Gyms 1. Fields 1. Comp/stud: 1:1 Laptop prgm Gr 6-11.
  Est 1978. Nonprofit.

Greenwood's program is designed to help boys of average to above-average intelligence overcome such learning differences as dyslexia, attentional disorders and executive functioning deficits. Instruction combines individualized remedial programming with enrichment. The school presents course work in the traditional subject areas in a manner that enables students to practice literary skills and organizational strategies across the curriculum; the residential life skills program further reinforces these strategies outside the classroom. Support services include occupational therapy, social pragmatics and speech therapy.

Greenwood's 100-acre, forested campus provides boys with athletic and recreational opportunities in soccer, baseball, downhill and cross-country skiing, rock climbing, ice skating, fishing, canoeing, mountain biking and skateboarding, among others.

ROCK POINT SCHOOL

Bdg and Day — Coed Ages 14-18

Burlington, VT 05408. 1 Rock Point Rd.
Tel: 802-863-1104. Fax: 802-863-6628.
www.rockpoint.org   E-mail: ledson@rockpoint.org
Camillo J. Spirito, BA, MEd, Head. **Hillary Kramer,** Adm.

Conditions: Primary—ADHD LD NLD. **IQ 90 and up.**
Col Prep. Gen Acad. Underachiever. Gr 9-PG. **Feat**—20th-Century_Lit
Photog Studio_Art Theater. Mid 50% SAT: CR 560. M 500. W 500.
Expected outcome: Graduation.
Adm: Appl fee: $50. Appl due: Rolling. On-campus interview.
Enr: 40. B 17. G 23. **Fac:** 8 (Full 5, Part 3).
Tui '12-'13: Bdg $53,550/sch yr (+$500). Day $26,000/sch yr. **Aid:** School 9
($140,000).
Endow $1,600,000. Plant val $5,300,000. Acres 150. Bldgs 2. Dorms 2. Dorm
rms 29. Class rms 6. Lib 3000 vols. Sci labs 1. Art studios 2. Fields 1.
Courts 1. Comp labs 1. Comp/stud: 1:2.5.
Est 1928. Nonprofit. Episcopal.

Rock Point conducts a high school program for pupils of average to above-average intelligence who stand to benefit from the structure and personal contact available in a small-school environment. The school places particular emphasis on the arts and community service. A senior seminar assists students with college placement and applications.

The 150-acre campus is situated on a peninsula in Lake Champlain, about one mile from the center of the city. Rock Point stresses accountability and work within the school community: Students attend frequently scheduled school meetings and meet with an advisor for 40 minutes once a week. Prominent evening and weekend offerings include trips to Montreal, Canada, and Boston, MA, as well as an off-campus outdoor program that features hiking, camping, cross-country skiing, snowboarding, and local music an sporting event attendance.

ST. JOHNSBURY ACADEMY

Bdg — Coed Ages 14-19; Day — Coed 14-18

St Johnsbury, VT 05819. 1000 Main St, PO Box 906.
Tel: 802-751-2130. Fax: 802-748-5463.
www.stjohnsburyacademy.org   E-mail: hilltoppers@stjacademy.org
Thomas W. Lovett, BS, AM, Head. **Mary Ann Gessner,** Adm.
Conditions: Primary—LD. **Sec**—ADHD AN Anx Ap Apr Ar Asp Au B/VI Bu C
CD CF D Db D-B Dc Dg Dpx Dx ED Ep Hemo HI ID Lk MD Mood MS Multi
Nf NLD OCD ODD ON PDD PTSD S SA SB SC SP Subst TBI TS. **IQ 90
and up.**
Col Prep. Underachiever. Gr 9-PG. Culinary. AP courses (Eng Fr Japan Span
Calc Stats Comp_Sci Bio Chem Environ_Sci Physics Eur_Hist US_Hist
Psych US_Govt & Pol Studio_Art Music_Theory). **Feat**—Creative_Writing
Chin Lat Anat & Physiol Astron Forensic_Sci Genetics Robotics Web_Design
Philos Photog Acting Theater Dance Accounting Journ Drafting Nutrition. Avg
SAT: CR 516. M 550. Interscholastic sports. **Expected outcome:** Return to
local school (Avg length of stay: 1-4 yrs).
Psychotherapy: Indiv. **Counseling:** Educ Voc.
Adm: Appl fee: $20. Appl due: Rolling. On-campus interview.
Enr: 889. Bdg 248. Day 641. **Fac:** 115 (Full-time). Spec ed 11. Lay 104.
Tui '12-'13: Bdg $44,700/sch yr. Day $14,570/sch yr. **Aid:** School 39
($782,900).
Endow $14,000,000. Plant val $60,000,000. Acres 142. Bldgs 28. Dorms 9.

Dorm rms 91. Class rms 85. Lib 20,000 vols. Sci labs 7. Lang labs 2. Auds 1. Theaters 2. Music studios 2. Dance studios 1. Gyms 2. Fields 6. Courts 4. Field houses 1. Pools 1. Comp labs 5. Comp/stud: 1:3. **Est 1842.** Nonprofit.

A comprehensive high school, the academy offers courses for students of all levels of ability, including remedial education and Advanced Placement work. In all academic courses, students are grouped according to ability. Graduates go on to attend colleges throughout the US and Canada.

The academy also maintains a technical education department that offers courses in electricity/electronics, construction trades, drafting, forestry and culinary arts, each in a two-year sequence. All of these programs incorporate hands-on experiences in real-world projects; the construction trades class annually builds a house.

SHELDON ACADEMY

Day — Coed Ages 6-18

Rutland, VT 05701. 88 Park St.
Tel: 802-775-2395. Fax: 802-773-9656.
www.vac-rutland.com   E-mail: mgolub@vac-rutland.com
Mitch Golub, Educ Dir.
    Conditions: Primary—Asp Au PDD. **Sec**—ADHD Anx Ap Ar CD Dc Dg Dx ED ID LD Mood OCD ODD ON Psy PTSD S TS. **IQ 70 and up.**
    Gen Acad. Gr 1-12. Culinary. **Feat**—Studio_Art. **Expected outcome:** Return to local school (Avg length of stay: 1+ yr).
    Therapy: Lang. **Psychotherapy:** Fam Indiv. **Counseling:** Educ Voc.
    Enr: 50. B 46. G 4.
    Summer prgm: Day. Rec. Ther. 6 wks.
    Est 1937. Nonprofit. **Spons:** Vermont Achievement Center.

Children with autism, Asperger's syndrome and pervasive developmental disorder receive treatment at Sheldon, which is a program of Vermont Achievement Center. The program focuses on treatment, family support and academic skills. Staff members tailor individual and group therapy, counseling and behavioral training to the student's specific needs.

During the high school years, students ages 13-18 who are interested in developing the skills and acquiring the knowledge necessary for a career in food preparation or food services may enroll in a culinary arts program. Boys and girls learn to follow recipes, and instruction also addresses basic cooking techniques, kitchen safety and new ingredients.

VIRGINIA

BLUE RIDGE AUTISM AND ACHIEVEMENT CENTER
Day — Coed Ages 2-22

Roanoke, VA 24019. 312 Whitwell Dr.
Tel: 540-366-7399. Fax: 540-366-5523.
www.achievementcenter.org   E-mail: braac.roanoke@gmail.com
Angela Leonard, BA, Exec Dir. **Tammie Woody,** Adm.
  Conditions: Primary—ADHD Asp Au Dx LD. **Sec**—ON. **IQ 85 and up.**
  Gen Acad. Gr PS-8. **Feat**—Computers Studio_Art Music. **Expected outcome:**
    Return to local school (Avg length of stay: 2-3 yrs).
  Therapy: Lang Occup Phys Speech.
  Adm: Appl fee: $50. Appl due: Year-round. On-campus interview.
  Enr: 63 (Cap: 66). B 43. G 20. **Fac:** 57 (Full 54, Part 3). Spec ed 7. Lay 50.
  Tui '12-'13: Day $11,500-55,000/sch yr. **Aid:** School 8. State 40. **Summer**
    prgm: Day. Educ. Tui Day $1200-4000. 6 wks.
  Est 1975. Nonprofit.

The center utilizes a multisensory approach to learning disabilities and related emotional problems. The educational program, serving preschool through grade 8, emphasizes language arts, reading and math. Other aspects of the program include recreational therapy, educational counseling, music, social studies, science and social development. The overall program seeks to rebuild the student's self-esteem and self-concept.

A year-round tutoring program serves both children and adults, while the center's half-day summer session accepts boys and girls not enrolled in the regular program.

CHARTERHOUSE SCHOOL
Bdg and Day — Coed Ages 11-18

Richmond, VA 23230. 3900 W Broad St.
Tel: 804-239-1080. Fax: 804-521-7957.
www.charterhouseschool.org   E-mail: info@chs4u.org
Brendan A. Folmar, BA, MEd, Prin.
  Conditions: Primary—ADHD Asp CD Dx ED LD ID OCD. **Sec**—As Ep Psy.
    IQ 70 and up.
  Gen Acad. Voc. Gr 6-12. Culinary. Man_Arts & Shop. **Feat**—Computers
    Studio_Art Music Health. **Expected outcome:** Return to local school (Avg
    length of stay: 6-10 mos).
  Psychotherapy: Group Indiv.
  Adm: Appl due: Year-round. On-campus interview.
  Enr: 87 (Cap: 95).
  Tui '12-'13: Bdg $320/day. Day $174/day. **Aid:** School. State 85. **Summer**
    prgm: Res & Day. Educ. Ther. 7 wk.
  Est 1979. Nonprofit. United Methodist. **Spons:** United Methodist Family
    Services.

Charterhouse offers individualized education to adolescents with severe problems who require a more restrictive environment than usual. The middle and high school curricula include a broad range of courses in the traditional disciplines, as well as in horticulture and computer technology. Independent study options are also available. Boys and girls may participate in career and technical education programs.

THE DISCOVERY SCHOOL OF VIRGINIA

Bdg — Coed Ages 11-17

Dillwyn, VA 23936. PO Box 1160.
Tel: 434-983-5616. Fax: 434-983-5617.
www.discoveryschool.org   E-mail: dsadmissions@yahoo.com
Chris Yates, Dir. **Don Williams,** Adm.
   Conditions: Primary—ADHD Anx APD CD ED LD Mood NLD ODD SP Subst. **Sec**—AN Ap Asp Bu CLP Dc Dg Dpx Dx HI Multi OCD PDD PTSD S SA TS. **IQ 80 and up. Not accepted**—Apr Ar Au B/VI C CP D Db D-B DS Ep Hemo ID IP Lk MD MR MS Nf ON Psy SB SC SO Sz TBI.
   Col Prep. Gen Acad. Underachiever. Voc. Gr 6-12. On-Job Trng.
   Feat—Indus_Arts Home_Ec. **Expected outcome:** Return to local school (Avg length of stay: 14-16 mos).
   Therapy: Milieu Rec. **Psychotherapy:** Group. **Counseling:** Educ.
   Adm: Appl fee: $0. Appl due: Year-round.
   Enr: 60 (Cap: 82). **Fac:** 10 (Full 9, Part 1). Spec ed 3. Lay 7.
   Tui '11-'12: Bdg $165/day (+$40/mo).
   Acres 450. Class rms 12. Libs 2. Fields 6.
   Est 1998. Inc.

Maintaining separate campuses for boys and girls, Discovery School enrolls students who have various emotional, behavioral and learning problems. Eligible pupils have at least an average IQ and the physical capacity to engage in the school's outdoor living program. While boys and girls are typically considered immature for their age, they are able to function in a group setting and they are capable of developing mutually supportive relationships. Candidates for enrollment have experienced ongoing frustration or failure in traditional—and perhaps in other nontraditional—school settings. This lack of success may stem from specific learning disabilities, attentional disorders, hyperactivity, lack of motivation, poor study skills, behavioral problems or emotional issues.

Academics for each student commence with enrollment in an experiential program designed to help the individual work on emotional/behavioral goals while also preparing for formal academic instruction. Once pupils make sufficient progress in reaching their goals, they begin attending individualized formal classes that offer flexibility in pacing and rigor.

Residential activities are integral to the program. Each small, gender-segregated group lives on a campsite with two adult group leaders. All residents follow a daily routine, with each week's work and recreational activities determined by a group vote. The community schedules group meetings to organize the group, resolve interpersonal issues and evaluate the group's performance after each activity.

GRAFTON SCHOOL

Bdg and Day — Coed Ages 3-21

Winchester, VA 22604. PO Box 2500.
Tel: 540-542-0200, 888-955-5205. Fax: 540-542-1722.
www.grafton.org   E-mail: admissions@grafton.org
  Nearby locations: PO Box 112, Berryville 22611; 407 Elm St, Winchester
  22601; 801 Children's Center Rd SW, Leesburg 20175; 4100 Price Club
  Blvd, Midlothian 23112.
James G. Gaynor II, PhD, Pres.
  Conditions: Primary—ADHD Anx Asp Au CD Dx ED LD Mood ID PDD Psy.
  Sec—As B/VI CP D Ep IP MD MS OCD ON S SB Sz TBI. **IQ 25-130.**
  Gen Acad. Voc. Ungraded. On-Job Trng. **Expected outcome:** Return to local
  school (Avg length of stay: 2 yrs).
  Therapy: Lang Occup Speech. **Psychotherapy:** Fam Group Indiv Parent.
  Counseling: Educ Voc.
  Adm: Appl due: Rolling. On-campus interview.
  Enr: 277. Bdg 240. Day 37.
  Est 1958. Nonprofit.

Originally established to provide a homelike situation for children with learning differences, Grafton now also serves individuals with emotional disturbances, mental retardation, autism and behavioral disorders. The behaviorally oriented treatment process assists individuals with educational, prevocational and independent living skills to ease the transition back into the community. The school serves boys and girls at four Virginia locations.

LITTLE KESWICK SCHOOL

Bdg — Boys Ages 10-17

Keswick, VA 22947. 500 Little Keswick Ln, PO Box 24.
Tel: 434-295-0457. Fax: 434-977-1892.
www.littlekeswickschool.net   E-mail: lksinfo@littlekeswickschool.net
Marc J. Columbus, MEd, Head. **Terry Columbus,** MEd, Dir.
  Conditions: Primary—ADHD Anx APD Asp Dc Dg Dpx Dx ED LD Mood
  Multi NLD OCD ODD ON PDD PTSD SP TS. **Sec**—Ep S. **IQ 80 and up.**
  Underachiever. Ungraded. Man_Arts & Shop. **Feat**—Studio_Art Music Wood-
  working. Interscholastic sports. **Expected outcome:** Return to local school
  (Avg length of stay: 2 yrs).
  Therapy: Lang Occup Speech. **Psychotherapy:** Art Fam Group Indiv.
  Adm: Appl fee: $350. Appl due: Rolling. On-campus interview.
  Enr: 34. **Fac:** 7 (Full-time). Spec ed 7.
  Tui '12-'13: Bdg $103,131/yr. **Summer prgm:** Bdg. Educ. Rec. Ther. Tui Bdg
  $9850. 5 wks.
  Acres 30. Bldgs 11. Dorms 4. Class rms 5. Libs 1. Art studios 1. Gyms 1.
  Fields 2. Pools 1. Riding rings 1. Stables 1. Comp labs 1.
  Est 1963. Inc.

This therapeutic, special-education boarding school serves boys of below-average to superior intelligence who have one or more of the following: learning problems, emotional disorders or behavioral disorders. While highly structured, the program operates in a small, open setting. LKS also offers specialized academics; an independent living program; individual and family counseling; and speech and language, occupational and art therapies. All students must attend the school's five-week summer session.

MORRISON SCHOOL

Day — Coed Ages 6-18

Bristol, VA 24202. 139 Terrace Dr.
Tel: 276-669-2823. Fax: 276-669-2823.
www.morrisonschool.org   E-mail: morrisonschool@bvunet.net
Sharon Morrison, EdD, Dir.
   Conditions: Primary—ADHD APD Asp Dc Dg Dx NLD. **IQ 90-130.**
   Col Prep. Gen Acad. Underachiever. Gr 1-12. SAT/ACT prep. **Expected outcome:** Return to local school (Avg length of stay: 2-3 yrs).
   Psychotherapy: Group Indiv Parent. **Counseling:** Educ.
   Adm: Appl fee: $50. Appl due: Year-round. On-campus interview.
   Enr: 30. B 20. G 10. **Fac:** 5 (Full 3, Part 2). Spec ed 4. Lay 1.
   Tui '10-'11: Day $7500-8800/sch yr. **Aid:** School. State. **Summer prgm:** Day. Educ. Tui Day $700. 5 wks.
   Acres 2. Bldgs 1. Class rms 9. Libs 1. Fields 1.
   Est 1977. Nonprofit. **Spons:** Foundation for Educational and Developmental Opportunity.

Among Morrison's services for students with learning differences are full- and part-time day school, preschool, after-school tutoring, summer school, psycho-educational testing and child management consultation. Emphasis is placed on correction of or compensation for the disability, with the goal of returning the pupil to a traditional school environment as soon as possible.

THE NEW COMMUNITY SCHOOL

Day — Coed Ages 11-18

Richmond, VA 23227. 4211 Hermitage Rd.
Tel: 804-266-2494. Fax: 804-264-3281.
www.tncs.org   E-mail: info@tncs.org
Nancy L. Foy, BA, MEd, Head. **Gita Morris,** Adm.
   Conditions: Primary—Dc Dg Dx LD. **Sec**—ADHD. **IQ 87 and up.**
   Col Prep. Gr 6-12. **Feat**—Creative_Writing Stats Govt Ethics Fine_Arts Photog Drama Health SAT_Prep. Avg SAT: CR 520. M 470. W 510. Interscholastic sports. **Expected outcome:** Return to local school (Avg length of stay: 2-3 yrs).
   Therapy: Lang. **Counseling:** Educ.
   Adm: Appl fee: $75. Appl due: Rolling.
   Enr: 90. B 58. G 32. **Fac:** 30 (Full 27, Part 3).
   Tui '12-'13: Day $25,360-26,600/sch yr. **Aid:** School 25 ($315,650). **Summer prgm:** Day. Educ. Tui Day $225-900. 4 wks.

Endow $3,080,000. Plant val $3,094,000. Acres 9. Bldgs 12 (80% ADA). Class rms 22. Libs 1. Sci labs 4. Art studios 1. Gyms 1. Fields 1. Comp labs 5. Comp/stud: 1:2. **Est 1974.** Nonprofit.

Providing college preparation for students with dyslexia, TNCS offers a highly structured, individualized educational environment that allows pupils to work at an appropriate intellectual level while developing language skills that help compensate for their learning difficulties. The curriculum includes both remediation of language skills and sufficient academic challenge for students of average to above-average intelligence. Once the pupil's reading, writing and spelling skills are commensurate with his or her intelligence level, the school may recommend transfer to a less-specialized setting.

Continuous faculty training and professional development are emphasized with weekly in-service programs conducted by outside consultants and school staff. In addition, a teacher-training internship for university graduate students is available.

NEW VISTAS SCHOOL

Day — Coed Ages 5-19

Lynchburg, VA 24501. 520 Eldon St.
Tel: 434-846-0301. Fax: 434-528-1004.
www.newvistasschool.org   E-mail: cmorgan@newvistasschool.org
Charlotte G. Morgan, MEd, MFA, Head. **Lisa Thomas,** Adm.
   Conditions: Primary—ADHD APD Dc Dg Dx LD Multi NLD. **Sec**—Anx Ap Apr Ar Asp Au CP Db ED Ep Mood OCD PDD PTSD S SA SP Subst TBI TS. **IQ 90 and up. Not accepted**—AN B/VI Bu C CD CLP D D-B DS Dpx Hemo HI ID IP Lk MD MR MS Nf ODD ON Psy PW SB SC SO Sz.
   Col Prep. Gen Acad. Gr K-12. Man_Arts & Shop. On-Job Trng. **Feat**—Environ_Sci Govt Studio_Art Drama Health. SAT/ACT prep.
   Therapy: Lang Speech. **Psychotherapy:** Group. **Counseling:** Educ.
   Adm: Appl fee: $150. Appl due: Rolling.
   Enr: 49 (Cap: 60). B 28. G 21. **Fac:** 14.
   Summer prgm: Day. Educ. 8 wks.
   Est 1986. Nonprofit.

Serving pupils who have not previously had successful school experiences, the school's small-class and tutorial program features multisensory activities designed to meet particular learning styles. Structured, individually designed programs enable students to develop social skills and strengthen self-concepts while also improving their learning skills. Other services of the school include after-school and summer tutorial programs, psychological evaluations, educational assessments, transitional support, and individual, group and family counseling.

OAKLAND SCHOOL

Bdg and Day — Coed Ages 6-14

Keswick, VA 22947. Boyd Tavern.

Tel: 434-293-9059. Fax: 434-296-8930.
www.oaklandschool.net   E-mail: information@oaklandschool.net
Carol Williams, BA, MEd, Dir. Jamie Cato, Adm.
Conditions: Primary—Dx LD. Sec—ADHD Dc Dg Dpx ED NLD. IQ 90-130.
Gen Acad. Gr 1-9. Feat—Computers Study_Skills. Interscholastic sports.
Expected outcome: Return to local school (Avg length of stay: 2-4 yrs).
Therapy: Lang Speech. Psychotherapy: Group Indiv.
Adm: Appl fee: $0. Appl due: Rolling. On-campus interview.
Enr: 42. Bdg 19. Day 23. Fac: 14 (Full-time).
Tui '12-'13: Bdg $46,500/sch yr (+$500). Day $27,500/sch yr (+$100).
    Aid: School 10 ($75,000). Summer prgm: Res & Day. Educ. Rec. Tui Bdg
    $8200. Tui Day $4700. 6 wks.
Acres 450. Bldgs 25. Dorms 5. Dorm rms 33. Class rms 15. Libs 1. Gyms 1.
    Athletic ctrs 2. Fields 2. Tennis courts 2. Pools 1. Riding rings 1. Stables 1.
    Comp labs 2. Comp/stud: 1:2.
Est 1950. Nonprofit.

Accepting children of average to above-average ability with dyslexia and other learning disabilities, Oakland provides a year-round academic curriculum stressing basic skills in one-on-one and small-class settings. The school specializes in the teaching of reading, math, written language and study skills.

The school also offers a full recreational program, team sports, daily physical education and horseback riding. Those receiving ninth grade credits perform 20 hours of required community service per semester. Most students return to a traditional educational setting after two to four years.

OAKWOOD SCHOOL

Day — Coed Ages 5-14

Annandale, VA 22003. 7210 Braddock Rd.
Tel: 703-941-5788. Fax: 703-941-4186.
www.oakwoodschool.com   E-mail: mjedlicka@oakwoodschool.com
Robert C. McIntyre, BA, MA, Head. Muriel A. Jedlicka, Adm.
    Conditions: Primary—ADHD APD Dc Dg Dpx Dx LD.
    Gen Acad. Gr K-8. Feat—Computers Studio_Art. Expected outcome: Return
    to local school (Avg length of stay: 2-5 yrs).
Therapy: Lang Occup Speech.
Adm: Appl fee: $50. Appl due: Rolling. On-campus interview.
Enr: 106. B 79. G 27. Fac: 31 (Full 30, Part 1). Spec ed 25. Lay 6.
Tui '12-'13: Day $29,900/sch yr (+$150-300). Aid: School 11 ($120,000).
    Summer prgm: Day. Educ. Rec. Tui Day $650/wk. 4 wks.
Plant val $3,000,000. Acres 5. Bldgs 2. Class rms 15. Libs 1. Sci labs 1. Art
    studios 1. Music studios 1. Gyms 1. Fields 1. Comp labs 1.
Est 1971. Nonprofit.

Serving pupils with mild to moderate learning differences, Oakwood conducts a program that includes adaptive physical education, individualized education planning, speech-language and occupational therapies, and psycho-educational evaluations. Offered in a small-class setting, the school's individualized program follows a multisensory approach.

Therapy is available on an as-needed basis, and staff members use ongoing assessments of student progress to monitor program effectiveness. Most boys and girls return to a traditional educational setting after two to five years.

RIVERSIDE SCHOOL
Day — Coed Ages 5-14

Richmond, VA 23235. 2110 McRae Rd.
Tel: 804-320-3465. Fax: 804-320-6146.
www.riversideschool.org   E-mail: info@riversideschool.org
Julie D. Wingfield, MS, Head.
  Conditions: Primary—As C Db Dx LD. **Sec**—ADHD. **IQ 100 and up.**
  Gen Acad. Gr K-8. **Feat**—Study_Skills. **Expected outcome:** Return to local school (Avg length of stay: 3 yrs).
  Therapy: Occup Speech. **Psychotherapy:** Indiv. **Counseling:** Educ.
  Adm: Appl fee: $100. Appl due: Year-round.
  Enr: 70 (Cap: 75).
  Tui '12-'13: Day $21,150/sch yr. **Aid:** School. **Summer prgm:** Day. Educ. 9 wks.
  Est 1970. Nonprofit.

Riverside modifies its educational program to meet the needs of the dyslexic student body. Teachers administer comprehensive tests at the beginning and the end of each school year, and students attend 45-minute individual tutoring sessions four times per week. Riverside attempts to develop pupils' maturity and academic competence levels enough to successfully return them to mainstream schools. The usual duration of treatment is three years.

ST. JOSEPH'S VILLA
DOOLEY SCHOOL
Day — Coed Ages 5-21

Richmond, VA 23227. 8000 Brook Rd.
Tel: 804-553-3200, 800-273-6553. Fax: 804-553-3259.
www.neverstopbelieving.org   E-mail: hporter@sjvmail.net
Dana Hawes, Educ Dir. **Hattie Porter,** Adm.
  Conditions: Primary—Asp Au ED LD ID. **Not accepted**—SO Subst.
  Col Prep. Gen Acad. Voc. Gr K-12. On-Job Trng.
  Therapy: Speech. **Psychotherapy:** Fam Group Indiv. **Counseling:** Educ Voc.
  Adm: Appl due: Year-round.
  Enr: 90. B 70. G 20.
  Tui '12-'13: Day $175-250/day.
  Acres 82. Bldgs 14. Class rms 25. Auds 1. Gyms 1.
  Est 1970. Nonprofit.

The Dooley School's program educates youth who have a diagnosed learning disability, an emotional disturbance or a behavioral disorder. Educable pupils with intellectual disabilities are also accepted. Educational and therapeutic plans are designed to remediate disabilities and return the child to a regular classroom setting, as well as to teach appropriate social and personal behaviors.

A separate classroom serves middle and high school children with Asperger's syndrome, and the Sarah Dooley Center for Autism provides integrated speech services for students with autism spectrum disorders. The Dooley Center for Alternative Education enrolls boys and girls who have been suspended or expelled from their previous schools.

The sending school district typically pays all tuition costs.

TIMBER RIDGE SCHOOL

Bdg and Day — Boys Ages 10-22

Winchester, VA 22604. PO Box 3160.
Tel: 540-888-3456, 877-877-3004. Fax: 540-888-4511.
www.timber-ridge-school.org   E-mail: phillips@trschool.org
John Lamanna, Exec Dir. **Jennie L. Johnson,** MA, MS, Educ Dir. **Jeff Phillips,** Adm.
Conditions: Primary—ADHD ED. **Sec**—CD Dx LD. **IQ 85-120.**
Gen Acad. Voc. Gr 6-12. Man_Arts & Shop. On-Job Trng.
Therapy: Speech. **Psychotherapy:** Fam Group Indiv Parent.
Adm: Appl due: Year-round. On-campus interview.
Enr: 96 (Cap: 96). Bdg 96.
Tui '12-'13: Bdg $257-414/day. Day $174/day.
Bldgs 2. Dorms 7. Gyms 1. Fields 2. Tennis courts 2.
Est 1969. Nonprofit.

Timber Ridge places emphasis on the treatment of emotional disorders and the remediation of learning disabilities. Regular classroom teachers are supported by a staff psychologist, consulting psychiatrists, learning disabilities specialists, residential counselors and vocational instructors. Suitable candidates for admission typically will have displayed emotional disturbance, social maladjustment or behavioral disorders, and they will also have exhibited inappropriate behavior, short attention span, hyperactivity, delinquency, authority conflicts, poor peer and family relationships, and low frustration threshold.

VIRGINIA HOME FOR BOYS AND GIRLS
THE JOHN G. WOOD SCHOOL

Bdg and Day — Coed Ages 12-18

Richmond, VA 23294. 8716 W Broad St.
Tel: 804-270-6566. Fax: 804-935-7675.
www.boysandgirlshome.org   E-mail: dglenn@boysandgirlshome.org
Claiborne Mason, Pres. **Monica R. Manns,** BA, MEd, Prin. **Claudia Webb,** Adm.
Conditions: Primary—Anx Asp CD ED LD Mood ID Multi OCD ODD PDD S Subst. **Sec**—ADHD Apr Ar CLP CP D Db Dc Dg Dx HI ON SA SC TBI TS. **IQ 50-125. Not accepted**—Au B/VI D-B IP MD MS.
Gen Acad. Voc. Gr 6-12. On-Job Trng. **Feat**—Computers Law Graphic_Arts Studio_Art. Interscholastic sports. **Expected outcome:** Return to local school (Avg length of stay: 1 yr).

Therapy: Music Speech. **Psychotherapy:** Art Fam Group Indiv.
Adm: On-campus interview.
Enr: 29 (Cap: 40). **Fac:** 7 (Full-time). Spec ed 2. Lay 5.
Tui '12-'13: Bdg $320/day. Day $160/day. **Summer prgm:** Day. Educ. Rec. Tui
  Day $600. 2 wks.
Est 1846. Nonprofit.

The John G. Wood School offers academic and transitional services to students with a history of behavioral, social/emotional and learning difficulties. Boys and girls may exhibit poor motivation, poor impulse control, short attention span and withdrawn behaviors. The curriculum, which meets state standards, comprises a broad range of middle and high school courses in the traditional subject areas. Independent study opportunities and GED preparation are also available. Students have access to both individual and group therapy throughout the week.

WASHINGTON

HAMLIN ROBINSON SCHOOL
Day — Coed Ages 6-14

Seattle, WA 98122. 1700 E Union St.
Tel: 206-763-1167. Fax: 206-763-7149.
www.hamlinrobinson.org   E-mail: info@hamlinrobinson.org
Joan Beauregard, Head. **Stacy Turner,** Adm.
Conditions: Primary—APD Dc Dg Dx LD. **Sec**—ADHD Anx Dpx.
Gen Acad. Gr 1-8. **Feat**—Lib_Skills Computers Studio_Art Music. **Expected outcome:** Return to local school.
Therapy: Lang Speech.
Adm: Appl fee: $100. Appl due: Year-round. On-campus interview.
Enr: 170 (Cap: 175). **Fac:** 15 (Full 14, Part 1). Spec ed 1. Lay 14.
Tui '12-'13: Day $17,500-19,100/sch yr. **Aid:** School. **Summer prgm:** Day. Educ. Tui Day $135-800. 1-4 wks.
Est 1983. Nonprofit.

The school offers remediation and education to students of average to superior intelligence with dyslexia and related language difficulties. The program focuses on both the educational and the emotional needs of pupils to build self-esteem and self-confidence. While stress is placed heavily on a multisensory approach to language arts, the school also presents a full curriculum with an emphasis on creative arts.

Additional offerings at Hamlin Robinson include adult services, teacher training, and individual speech and language therapy.

MORNINGSIDE ACADEMY
Day — Coed Ages 7-17

Seattle, WA 98109. 201 Westlake Ave N.
Tel: 206-709-9500. Fax: 206-709-4611.
www.morningsideacademy.org   E-mail: info@morningsideacademy.org
Kent Johnson, PhD, Exec Dir. **Joanne Robbins,** PhD, Prin. **Dawn Oliver,** Adm.
Conditions: Primary—ADHD APD Dc Dg Dx LD. **IQ 90-119.**
   Not accepted—CD ODD Psy SO Sz.
Gen Acad. Underachiever. Gr 1-9. **Feat**—Study_Skills. **Expected outcome:** Return to local school (Avg length of stay: 2-3 yrs).
Adm: Appl fee: $0. Appl due: Year-round. On-campus interview.
Enr: 90.
Tui '12-'13: Day $21,900/sch yr. **Aid:** School 10. Educ. Tui Day $2680. 4 wks.
Est 1980. Nonprofit.

Offering elementary and middle school programs, the academy enrolls students who have not performed to potential in traditional school settings. Entering pupils, who typically score in the first or second quartile on standardized achievement tests in reading, language and math, may have diagnosed learning disabilities or attentional disorders. Some boys and girls have fallen behind their classmates despite no diagnosed learning difference.

Morningside utilizes extensive assessments and research-based methods while teaching children to practice compensatory learning strategies. Instructors construct behavioral repertoires to correct skill deficits in the fundamental academic areas, inadequate learning skills (in such areas as goal setting, listening, noticing, reasoning, thinking, studying and organizing) and deficient performance skills.

The month-long summer session features morning and afternoon reading, language, writing and math programming.

NORTHWEST SCHOOL FOR HEARING-IMPAIRED CHILDREN

Day — Coed Ages 3-14

Seattle, WA 98103. PO Box 31325.
Tel: 206-364-4605. Fax: 206-367-3014.
www.northwestschool.com   E-mail: adminnws@comcast.net
Judy Ottren Callahan, Co-Dir. **Karen Appelman,** Co-Dir.
   Conditions: Primary—D.
   Gen Acad. Gr PS-8.
   Therapy: Hear Lang Speech.
   Enr: 54. B 30. G 24.
   Est 1982. Nonprofit.

NWSFHIC uses teaching techniques resulting in communication that is delivered in complete English sentences and seeks the achievement of academic success and growth in self-esteem. School subjects such as math, reading, science, social studies, music and writing are offered. Speech, lip reading and auditory training are also provided. Class sizes are small to ensure a good learning environment.

In most cases, the sending school district pays tuition expenses.

ST. CHRISTOPHER ACADEMY

Day — Coed Ages 14-19

Seattle, WA 98116. 4141 41st Ave SW.
Tel: 206-246-9751. Fax: 253-639-3466.
www.stchristopheracademy.com
   E-mail: jevne@stchristopheracademy.com
Darlene Jevne, MA, Dir.
   Conditions: Primary—ADHD Anx APD Dg Dpx Dx LD NLD. **Sec**—Ap Apr Ar
   CLP Db Hemo Lk Multi ON SC. **IQ 80 and up. Not accepted**—AN Asp Au
   B/VI Bu C CD CF CP D D-B Dc DS ED Ep HI ID IP MD Mood MR MS Nf
   OCD ODD PDD Psy PTSD PW SA SB SO SP Subst Sz TBI TS.
   Col Prep. Gen Acad. Underachiever. Gr 9-12. Man_Arts & Shop. **Feat**—ASL
   Fr Span. ESL. SAT/ACT prep. Interscholastic sports. **Expected outcome:**
   Graduation.
   Therapy: Lang. **Psychotherapy:** Indiv. **Counseling:** Educ.
   Adm: Appl fee: $50. Appl due: Year-round. On-campus interview.

Enr: 15 (Cap: 30). **Fac:** 4 (Full-time). Spec ed 4.
Tui '12-'13: Day $18,600/sch yr. **Aid:** School.
Laptop prgm Gr 9-12.
Est 1982. Inc.

The academy offers a full academic curriculum for students with attention deficit disorder and learning disabilities. The program includes art and computer course work, as well as electives and interscholastic sports. St. Christopher issues a laptop to each pupil for school use. All boys and girls perform 10 hours of required community service per semester. Diagnostic services and counseling are available at all grade levels.

WISCONSIN

EAU CLAIRE ACADEMY
Bdg — Coed Ages 10-18

Eau Claire, WI 54702. 550 N Dewey St, PO Box 1168.
Tel: 715-834-6681. Fax: 715-834-9954.
www.clinicarecorp.com/eau-claire   E-mail: admissions@clinicarecorp.com
   Conditions: Primary—ADHD CD ED Mood OCD SO Subst Sz. **Sec**—AN As
   Ep ON Psy. **IQ 75 and up.**
   Gen Acad. Voc. Ungraded. Culinary. Man_Arts & Shop. On-Job Trng.
   Feat—Computers Studio_Art Music Health. **Expected outcome:** Return to
   local school (Avg length of stay: 1 yr or less).
   Psychotherapy: Fam Group Indiv.
   Enr: 135 (Cap: 135).
   Est 1967. Inc. **Spons:** Clinicare Corporation.

ECA provides psychotherapy, special education, group living and recreation for severely emotionally and behaviorally disturbed children. An individually designed educational program uses psycho-educational and behavior modification methods of teaching.

A developmental program accommodates students who cannot tolerate a full academic day. Counseling and psychotherapy are integral parts of treatment. Length of stay usually does not exceed one year.

ST. COLETTA DAY SCHOOL OF MILWAUKEE
Day — Coed Ages 8-16

Milwaukee, WI 53208. 1740 N 55th St.
Tel: 414-453-1850.
www.scdsmke.org   E-mail: scdsmke@gmail.com
William A. Koehn, Admin.
   Conditions: Primary—ADHD Asp Au DS Dx LD ID PDD. **IQ 50-75.**
   Gen Acad. Ungraded. **Feat**—Studio_Art Music.
   Enr: 7 (Cap: 12). B 3. G 4. **Fac:** 2 (Full-time). Spec ed 1. Lay 1.
   Est 1956. Nonprofit.

Children with mild to moderate intellectual disabilities from the Milwaukee area receive ungraded academic instruction at this school, which limits enrollment to 12 students. Boys and girls along the autism spectrum may also enroll, at the school's discretion. Programming stresses social and attitudinal development, as well as life skills training. The sequential development educational program includes reading, math and language arts.

SCDS seeks pupils with sufficient self-care skills and the potential for academic achievement.

WALBRIDGE SCHOOL

Day — Coed Ages 5-18

Madison, WI 53717. 7035 Old Sauk Rd.
Tel: 608-833-1338. Fax: 608-833-2197.
www.walbridgeschool.com   E-mail: info@walbridgeschool.com
Nancy Donahue, MEd, Dir. **Amanda Talbert,** Adm.
   Conditions: Primary—ADHD Anx Dc Dg Dx ED LD. **Sec**—OCD PTSD SP.
   IQ 80-135.
   Col Prep. Gen Acad. Gr K-12. **Feat**—Computers Studio_Art Music Health
   Study_Skills. **Expected outcome:** Graduation.
   Adm: Appl fee: $150. Appl due: Year-round. On-campus interview.
   Enr: 26 (Cap: 36). B 15. G 11. **Fac:** 8 (Full 3, Part 5). Spec ed 4. Lay 4.
   Tui '12-'13: Day $13,200/sch yr. **Aid:** School. State 1. **Summer prgm:** Day.
   Educ. Arts. Tui Day $375. 4 wks.
   Libs 1. Art studios 1. Music studios 1. Gyms 1.
   Est 1986. Nonprofit.

Walbridge offers an alternative, full-day elementary and middle school program that emphasizes multisensory teaching and individualization to address learning differences. Specialized and personalized instruction accommodates students with such learning disabilities as dyslexia and ADHD, as well as other barriers that have hindered learning in more traditional settings. After operating for decades as an elementary school, Walbridge added a high school diploma program in 2012 that combines classroom experiences in core academic and elective areas with online courses.

To better serve the student body, teachers have received training in a variety of reading methods. Social skills training is part of the curriculum.

WYALUSING ACADEMY

Bdg — Coed Ages 10-18

Prairie du Chien, WI 53821. 601 S Beaumont Rd, PO Box 269.
Tel: 608-326-6481. Fax: 608-326-6166.
www.clinicarecorp.com/wyalusing   E-mail: rjreilly@clinicarecorp.com
Rad J. Reilly, Adm.
   Conditions: Primary—ADHD Asp CD ED LD OCD ODD PDD PTSD SA SO.
   Sec—AN Anx Ap As Bu Db Dx ID Mood Nf ON Psy S Sz TBI TS. **IQ 45-100.**
   Gen Acad. Voc. Ungraded. Man_Arts & Shop. On-Job Trng. **Feat**—Computers
   Bus. **Expected outcome:** Return to local school (Avg length of stay: 8 mos).
   Therapy: Lang Rec Speech. **Psychotherapy:** Fam Group Indiv.
   Enr: 81. B 56. G 25. **Fac:** 19 (Full-time). Spec ed 5. Lay 14.
   Est 1969. Inc. **Spons:** Clinicare Corporation.

Wyalusing serves dependent, neglected, delinquent and emotionally disturbed youths. Psychiatric consultations are available as needed, and residents may receive speech therapy for an additional fee. On-grounds vocational and academic educational opportunities include auto mechanics, landscaping, building trades, food service, cosmetology, art, family consumer education, independent living skills and business education.

Treatment lasts roughly eight months. The academy does not accept fire setters or those with unmedicated psychoses or schizophrenia.

ASSOCIATIONS AND ORGANIZATIONS

The following are organizations in the United States directly or indirectly concerned with the welfare of special-needs children.

ACCREDITING ORGANIZATIONS

AMERICAN CAMP ASSOCIATION
5000 State Rd 67 N, Martinsville, IN 46151. Tel: 765-342-8456.
Toll-free: 800-428-2267. Fax: 765-342-2065. E-mail: psmith@acacamps.org.
Web: www.acacamps.org.
Accrediting organization helps camps provide safe, appropriate camping environments for all children, including those with special needs or learning disabilities.

CARF INTERNATIONAL
6951 E Southpoint Rd, Tucson, AZ 85756. Tel: 520-325-1044.
Toll-free: 888-281-6531. TTY: 888-281-6531. Fax: 520-318-1129.
Web: www.carf.org.
Reviews and accredits facilities specializing in medical rehabilitation, programs for the aging, child and family services, behavioral health, employment and community services.

ADVOCACY ORGANIZATIONS

GENERAL

ADVOCATES IN ACTION
PO Box 41528, Providence, RI 02940. Toll-free: 877-532-5543.
Fax: 877-471-4180. E-mail: aina@advocatesinaction.org.
Web: www.advocatesinaction.org.
Advocates for people with disabilities through meetings, networking, presentations and publications.

ALLIANCE FOR TECHNOLOGY ACCESS
1119 Old Humboldt Rd, Jackson, TN 38305. Tel: 731-554-5282.
Toll-free: 800-914-3017. TTY: 731-554-5284. Fax: 731-554-5283.
E-mail: atainfo@ataccess.org. Web: www.ataccess.org.
Provides children and adults with disabilities information and support for standard, assistive and information technologies.

THE AMERICAN ASSOCIATION OF PEOPLE WITH DISABILITIES
2013 H St, 5th Fl, Washington, DC 20006. Tel: 202-457-0046.
Toll-free: 800-840-8844. TTY: 202-457-0046. Fax: 866-536-4461.
Web: www.aapd.com.
Works with other disability organizations to ensure economic self-sufficiency
and political empowerment for Americans with disabilities.

AMERICAN COUNCIL ON RURAL SPECIAL EDUCATION
West Virginia Univ, 509 Allen Hall, PO Box 6122, Morgantown, WV 26506.
Tel: 304-293-3450. E-mail: acres-sped@mail.wvu.edu.
Web: http://acres-sped.org.
Promotes education and services for individuals with special needs living in
rural America.

AMERICAN EPILEPSY SOCIETY
342 N Main St, West Hartford, CT 06117. Tel: 860-586-7505.
Fax: 860-586-7550. E-mail: ctubby@aesnet.org. Web: www.aesnet.org.
Works to improve the quality of life of those with epilepsy through communication, research and education.

ASSOCIATION FOR CHILDHOOD EDUCATION INTERNATIONAL
1101 16th St NW, Ste 300, Washington, DC 20036. Tel: 202-372-9986.
Toll-free: 800-423-3563. E-mail: headquarters@acei.org. Web: www.acei.org.
Promotes the optimal education and development of children from birth to early
adolescence.

THE ASSOCIATION FOR THE EDUCATION
OF GIFTED UNDERACHIEVING STUDENTS
6 Wildwood St, Burlington, NJ 01803. E-mail: aegusquestions@gmail.com.
Web: www.aegus1.org.
Association for gifted underachievers serves as a clearinghouse for relevant
research, supports program development, and works to develop increased awareness among educators, policymakers and the general public.

ASSOCIATION OF UNIVERSITY CENTERS ON DISABILITIES
1100 Wayne Ave, Ste 1000, Silver Spring, MD 20910. Tel: 301-588-8252.
Fax: 301-588-2842. E-mail: aucdinfo@aucd.org. Web: www.aucd.org.
Seeks to advance policy and practice for people with developmental and other
disabilities, their families and their communities through research, education and
service activities.

CARL AND RUTH SHAPIRO FAMILY NATIONAL CENTER
FOR ACCESSIBLE MEDIA
1 Guest St, Boston, MA 02135. Tel: 617-300-3400. TTY: 617-300-2489.
Fax: 617-300-1035. E-mail: ncam@wgbh.org. Web: http://ncam.wgbh.org.
Works to expand access to present and future media and technologies for people
with disabilities.

CENTER ON HUMAN POLICY, LAW, AND DISABILITY STUDIES
Syracuse Univ, School of Education, 805 S Crouse Ave, 101 Hoople Bldg,
Syracuse, NY 13244. Tel: 315-443-3851. TTY: 315-443-4355.
Fax: 315-443-4338. E-mail: staylo01@syr.edu.
Web: http://disabilitystudies.syr.edu.
Policy, research and advocacy organization seeking equal rights for people with
disabilities.

CONNECTICUT PARENT ADVOCACY CENTER
338 Main St, Niantic, CT 06357. Tel: 860-739-3089. Toll-free: 800-445-2722.
TTY: 860-739-7460. E-mail: cpac@cpacinc.org. Web: www.cpacinc.org.
Offers information and support to parents of children with various disabilities
and chronic illnesses.

COUNCIL OF PARENT ATTORNEYS AND ADVOCATES
PO Box 6767, Towson, MD 21285. Tel: 410-372-0208. Fax: 410-372-0209.
Web: www.copaa.net.
Organization of attorneys, advocates, parents and professionals works to protect
special-education rights and improve education for children with disabilities.

DISABILITY LAW CENTER
11 Beacon St, Ste 925, Boston, MA 02108. Tel: 617-723-8455.
Toll-free: 800-872-9992. TTY: 617-227-9464. Fax: 617-723-9125.
E-mail: mail@dlc-ma.org. Web: www.dlc-ma.org.
Provides legal advocacy on disability issues that promote the rights of people
with disabilities to participate fully and equally in social and economic life.

DISABILITY RIGHTS CENTER OF KANSAS
635 SW Harrison St, Ste 100, Topeka, KS 66603. Tel: 785-273-9661.
Toll-free: 877-776-1541. TTY: 877-335-3725. Fax: 785-273-9414.
E-mail: info@drckansas.org. Web: www.drckansas.org.
Advocates for the rights of people with disabilities in Kansas, providing legal
representation, information and referrals.

DISABILITY RIGHTS CENTER OF MAINE
24 Stone St, Ste 204, Augusta, ME 04330. Tel: 207-626-2774.
Toll-free: 800-452-1948. TTY: 207-626-2774. Fax: 207-621-1419.
E-mail: advocate@drcme.org. Web: www.drcme.org.
Provides information, training, referrals and legal representation for Maine residents with disabilities.

DISABILITY RIGHTS EDUCATION AND DEFENSE FUND
3075 Adeline St, Ste 210, Berkeley, CA 94703. Tel: 510-644-2555.
TTY: 510-644-2555. Fax: 510-841-8645. E-mail: info@dredf.org.
Web: www.dredf.org.
Provides legal representation, public advocacy, training and education for individuals with disabilities.

DISABILITY RIGHTS IOWA
400 E Court Ave, Ste 300, Des Moines, IA 50309. Tel: 515-278-2502.
Toll-free: 800-779-2502. TTY: 515-278-0571. Fax: 515-278-0539.
E-mail: info@disabilityrightsiowa.org. Web: www.disabilityrightsiowa.org.
Advocates for people with disabilities in such areas as education, employment,
housing and treatment.

DISABILITY RIGHTS WASHINGTON
315 5th Ave S, Ste 850, Seattle, WA 98104. Tel: 206-324-1521.
TTY: 206-957-0728. Fax: 206-957-0729. E-mail: info@dr-wa.org.
Web: www.disabilityrightswa.org.
Disseminates disability rights information and provides referrals, community
education and training, as well as legal services for disability discrimination.

DISABILITY RIGHTS WISCONSIN
131 W Wilson St, Ste 700, Madison, WI 53703. Tel: 608-267-0214.
Toll-free: 800-928-8778. TTY: 888-758-6049. Fax: 608-267-0368.
Web: www.disabilityrightswi.org.
Provides protection and advocacy for people with disabilities.

EQUIP FOR EQUALITY
20 N Michigan Ave, Ste 300, Chicago, IL 60602. Tel: 312-341-0022.
Toll-free: 800-537-2632. TTY: 800-610-2779. Fax: 312-541-7544.
E-mail: contactus@equipforequality.org. Web: www.equipforequality.org.
Provides self-advocacy assistance, legal services and disability rights education
for children and adults with physical and mental disabilities.

FAMILY VOICES
3701 San Mateo Blvd NE, Ste 103, Albuquerque, NM 87110.
Tel: 505-872-4774. Toll-free: 888-835-5669. Fax: 505-872-4780.
E-mail: lkeene@familyvoices.org. Web: www.familyvoices.org.
Provides information, education and advocacy for children with special health-
care needs.

GENETIC ALLIANCE
4301 Connecticut Ave NW, Ste 404, Washington, DC 20008. Tel: 202-966-5557.
Fax: 202-966-8553. E-mail: info@geneticalliance.org.
Web: www.geneticalliance.org.
Promotes collaboration among genetic research, advocacy, community and gov-
ernment organizations through funding, technical assistance and resources.

GEORGIA ADVOCACY OFFICE
150 E Ponce de Leon Ave, Ste 430, Decatur, GA 30030. Tel: 404-885-1234.
Toll-free: 800-537-2329. TTY: 800-537-2329. Fax: 404-378-0031.
Web: www.thegao.org.
Advocacy services for individuals from Georgia who have mental illness or
other disabilities.

INSTITUTE FOR COMMUNITY INCLUSION
c/o Univ of Massachusetts-Boston, 100 Morrissey Blvd, Boston, MA 02125.
Tel: 617-287-4300. TTY: 617-287-4350. Fax: 617-287-4352.
E-mail: ici@umb.edu. Web: www.communityinclusion.org.
Offers training, clinical and employment services; conducts research; and provides assistance for organizations that are advocating for people with disabilities.

THE INSTITUTES FOR THE ACHIEVEMENT OF HUMAN POTENTIAL
8801 Stenton Ave, Wyndmoor, PA 19038. Tel: 215-233-2050.
Toll-free: 800-736-4663. Fax: 215-233-9312. E-mail: help@iahp.org.
Web: www.iahp.org.
Provides information and designs educational programs for parents of children with brain injuries and learning disorders; offers early-learning programs for all children.

JBI INTERNATIONAL
110 E 30th St, New York, NY 10016. Tel: 212-889-2525.
Toll-free: 800-433-1531. Fax: 212-689-3692. E-mail: admin@jbilibrary.org.
Web: www.jbilibrary.org.
Addresses the cultural needs of individuals with visual impairments, blindness, physical handicaps and reading disabilities of all ages and backgrounds.

KENTUCKY EDUCATION RIGHTS CENTER
1323 Moores Mill Rd, Midway, KY 40347. Tel: 859-983-9222.
E-mail: kerc@edrights.com. Web: www.edrights.com.
Advocacy group serves families with special-needs children who have school-related problems.

THE LEGAL CENTER FOR PEOPLE WITH DISABILITIES AND OLDER PEOPLE
455 Sherman St, Ste 130, Denver, CO 80203. Tel: 303-722-0300.
Toll-free: 800-288-1376. TTY: 303-722-3619. Fax: 303-722-0720.
E-mail: tlcmail@thelegalcenter.org. Web: www.thelegalcenter.org.
Works to protect the human, civil and legal rights of people with disabilities and older people through legal representation and advocacy.

MARYLAND DISABILITY LAW CENTER
1500 Union Ave, Ste 2000, Baltimore, MD 21211. Tel: 410-727-6352.
Toll-free: 800-233-7201. TTY: 410-235-5387. Fax: 410-727-6389.
E-mail: virginiak@mdlclaw.org. Web: www.mdlclaw.org.
Provides legal representation, technical assistance, information and referrals for people with disabilities.

**MASSACHUSETTS ASSOCIATION OF SPECIAL EDUCATION
PARENT ADVISORY COUNCILS**
529 Main St, Fl 1M, Ste 1102, Boston, MA 02129. Tel: 617-236-7210.
TTY: 617-236-7210. Fax: 617-241-0330. E-mail: info@masspac.org.
Web: www.masspac.org.
Statewide network of parents, school councils, professionals and agencies that
supports appropriate education for special-needs students.

MOBILITY INTERNATIONAL USA
132 E Broadway, Ste 343, Eugene, OR 97401. Tel: 541-343-1284.
TTY: 541-343-1284. Fax: 541-343-6812. Web: www.miusa.org.
Works to empower people with disabilities to achieve human rights through
international exchange and development.

NATIONAL ASSOCIATION FOR CHILD DEVELOPMENT
549 25th St, Ogden, UT 84401. Tel: 801-621-8606. Fax: 801-621-8389.
Web: www.nacd.org.
Works with parents to provide neuro-developmental assessments and formulate
individualized learning programs for children with various special needs.

**NATIONAL ASSOCIATION OF PRIVATE
SPECIAL EDUCATION CENTERS**
601 Pennsylvania Ave, Ste 900, South Bldg, Washington, DC 20004.
Tel: 202-434-8225. Fax: 202-434-8224. E-mail: napsec@aol.com.
Web: www.napsec.org.
Promotes quality programs for individuals with disabilities and their families
and advocates for access to alternative placements and services.

**NATIONAL CENTER FOR EDUCATION
IN MATERNAL AND CHILD HEALTH**
Georgetown Univ, Box 571272, Washington, DC 20057. Tel: 202-784-9770.
Fax: 202-784-9777. E-mail: mchgroup@georgetown.edu.
Web: www.ncemch.org.
Develops and disseminates child health and development information, launches
national health initiatives, and maintains a virtual library of publications and
databases.

NATIONAL ORGANIZATION FOR RARE DISORDERS
55 Kenosia Ave, Danbury, CT 06810. Tel: 203-744-0100. TTY: 203-797-9590.
Fax: 203-798-2291. Web: www.rarediseases.org.
Promotes the treatment and the cure of rare diseases through education, advocacy, research and services.

NATIONAL ORGANIZATION ON DISABILITY
77 Water St, Ste 204, New York, NY 10005. Tel: 646-505-1191.

Fax: 646-505-1184. E-mail: info@nod.org. Web: www.nod.org.
Raises awareness of disabilities through programs and information.

PACER CENTER
8161 Normandale Blvd, Minneapolis, MN 55437. Tel: 952-838-9000.
Toll-free: 888-248-0822. TTY: 952-838-0190. Fax: 952-838-0199.
E-mail: pacer@pacer.org. Web: www.pacer.org.
Works to expand opportunities and improve the quality of life of children and
young adults with disabilities.

PEAK PARENT CENTER
611 N Weber St, Ste 200, Colorado Springs, CO 80903. Tel: 719-531-9400.
Toll-free: 800-284-0251. Fax: 719-531-9452. E-mail: info@peakparent.org.
Web: www.peakparent.org.
Provides resources, information and technical assistance for families having
children with disabilities.

PENNSYLVANIA HEALTH LAW PROJECT
123 Chestnut St, Ste 400, Philadelphia, PA 19106. Tel: 215-625-3990.
Fax: 215-625-3879. E-mail: staff@phlp.org. Web: www.phlp.org.
Provides free legal services to lower-income consumers, seniors, and persons
with disabilities who are having trouble accessing publicly funded healthcare
coverage or services.

PROFESSIONAL ASSOCIATION OF
THERAPEUTIC HORSEMANSHIP INTERNATIONAL
PO Box 33150, Denver, CO 80233. Tel: 303-452-1212. Toll-free: 800-369-7433.
Fax: 303-252-4610. E-mail: pathintl@pathintl.org. Web: www.pathintl.org.
Membership organization that fosters safe, professional, ethical and therapeutic
equine activities through education, standard setting and research.

SINERGIA
2082 Lexington Ave, 4th Fl, New York, NY 10035. Tel: 212-643-2840.
Toll-free: 866-867-9665. Fax: 212-643-2871.
E-mail: information@sinergiany.org. Web: www.sinergiany.org.
Provides service coordination, information and support for families of children
with disabilities.

TASH
1001 Connecticut Ave NW, Ste 235, Washington, DC 20036. Tel: 202-540-9020.
Fax: 202-540-9019. E-mail: info@tash.org. Web: www.tash.org.
Promotes the equality and inclusion of people with disabilities through research,
education and advocacy.

UNIVERSITY LEGAL SERVICES
220 I St NE, Ste 130, Washington, DC 20002. Tel: 202-547-0198.
Fax: 202-547-2662. Web: www.uls-dc.org.
Provides information, referrals, education, legal counsel and technical assistance
for individuals with disabilities.

WISCONSIN FAMILY TIES
16 N Carroll St, Ste 230, Madison, WI 53703. Tel: 608-267-6888.
Toll-free: 800-422-7145. Fax: 608-267-6801. E-mail: info@wifamilyties.org.
Web: www.wifamilyties.org.
Provides advocacy, support groups, education, information and referrals for
families of children and adolescents who have emotional, behavioral or mental
disorders.

AUTISM

AUTISM RESEARCH INSTITUTE
4182 Adams Ave, San Diego, CA 92116. Tel: 619-281-7165.
Toll-free: 866-366-3361. Fax: 619-563-6840. Web: www.autism.com.
Conducts research and disseminates information on the causes of autism and
on methods of preventing, diagnosing and treating autism and other childhood
behavioral disorders.

AUTISM SPEAKS
1 E 33rd St, 4th Fl, New York, NY 10016. Tel: 212-252-8584.
Toll-free: 888-288-4762. Fax: 212-252-8676.
E-mail: contactus@autismspeaks.org. Web: www.autismspeaks.org.
Supports research and raises awareness of autism and autistic spectrum disor-
ders.

THE DOUG FLUTIE, JR. FOUNDATION FOR AUTISM
PO Box 767, Framingham, MA 01701. Tel: 508-270-8855.
Toll-free: 866-328-8476. Fax: 508-270-6868.
E-mail: info@dougflutiejrfoundation.org. Web: www.dougflutiejrfoundation.org.
Funds education and research into autism, aids disadvantaged families of chil-
dren with autism, and serves as a clearinghouse for autism programs and ser-
vices.

FAMILIES FOR EARLY AUTISM TREATMENT
PO Box 255722, Sacramento, CA 95865. Tel: 916-303-7405.
Fax: 916-303-7405. E-mail: feat@feat.org. Web: www.feat.org.
Organization of parents, educators and other professionals that provides educa-
tion, support and advocacy for children with autism spectrum disorders.

BLINDNESS

AMERICAN COUNCIL OF THE BLIND
2200 Wilson Blvd, Ste 650, Arlington, VA 22201. Tel: 202-467-5081.
Toll-free: 800-424-8666. Fax: 703-465-5085. E-mail: info@acb.org.
Web: www.acb.org.
Provides information, referrals, scholarships, advocacy and a monthly magazine
for the blind and the visually impaired.

AMERICAN FOUNDATION FOR THE BLIND
2 Penn Plz, Ste 1102, New York, NY 10121. Tel: 212-502-7600.
Fax: 888-545-8331. E-mail: afbinfo@afb.net. Web: www.afb.org.
Provides resources, training and technology access for the blind and the visually
impaired.

ASSOCIATED SERVICES FOR THE BLIND AND VISUALLY IMPAIRED
919 Walnut St, Philadelphia, PA 19107. Tel: 215-627-0600. Fax: 215-922-0692.
E-mail: asbinfo@asb.org. Web: www.asb.org.
Provides rehabilitation, technological and media access services for the blind
and the visually impaired.

BRAILLE INSTITUTE
741 N Vermont Ave, Los Angeles, CA 90029. Tel: 323-663-1111.
Fax: 323-663-0867. Web: www.brailleinstitute.org.
In addition to producing braille publications, provides counseling, community
outreach, courses and career services for the blind and visually impaired.

CHRISTIAN RECORD SERVICES FOR THE BLIND
PO Box 6097, Lincoln, NE 68506. Tel: 402-488-0981. Fax: 402-488-7582.
E-mail: info@christianrecord.org. Web: www.christianrecord.org.
Publishes a variety of Bibles, books and periodicals in braille, large print and
audio, while also operating camps for the blind and the visually impaired.

THE DEAFBLIND CHILDREN'S FUND
PO Box 11234, Spring, TX 77391. Toll-free: 877-332-3254.
E-mail: deafblindchildren@yahoo.com. Web: www.deafblindchildren.org.
Services, intervention and relief care for families with deaf-blind and deaf-blind
multihandicapped children.

THE FOUNDATION FIGHTING BLINDNESS
7168 Columbia Gateway Dr, Ste 100, Columbia, MD 21046. Tel: 410-423-0600.
Toll-free: 800-683-5555. TTY: 410-363-7139. E-mail: info@blindness.org.
Web: www.blindness.org.
Funds and supports research into preventions, treatments and cures for people
affected by retinitis pigmentosa, macular degeneration, Usher syndrome and
other degenerative retinal diseases.

GUIDE DOGS OF AMERICA
13445 Glenoaks Blvd, Sylmar, CA 91342. Tel: 818-362-5834.
Fax: 818-362-6870. E-mail: mail@guidedogsofamerica.org.
Web: www.guidedogsofamerica.org.
Provides guide dogs for people who are blind or visually impaired.

HELEN KELLER INTERNATIONAL
352 Park Ave S, 12th Fl, New York, NY 10010. Tel: 212-532-0544.
Fax: 212-532-6014. E-mail: info@hki.org. Web: www.hki.org.
Works to eradicate preventable blindless and combat poor nutrition in 22 coun-
tries.

JUNIOR BLIND OF AMERICA
5300 Angeles Vista Blvd, Los Angeles, CA 90043. Tel: 323-295-4555.
Toll-free: 800-352-2290. Fax: 323-296-0424. E-mail: info@juniorblind.org.
Web: www.juniorblind.org.
Provides a variety of education, recreation, training and rehabilitation programs
for children who are blind or visually impaired.

LEARNING ALLY
20 Roszel Rd, Princeton, NJ 08540. Toll-free: 800-221-4792.
Fax: 609-987-8116. E-mail: custserv@learningally.org.
Web: www.learningally.org.
Maintains an educational library of 75,000 digitally recorded textbooks and literature titles for people who cannot read standard print due to blindness, visual
impairment, dyslexia or another learning disability.

LIGHTHOUSE INTERNATIONAL
111 E 59th St, New York, NY 10022. Tel: 212-821-9200.
Toll-free: 800-829-0500. TTY: 212-821-9713. Fax: 212-821-9707.
E-mail: info@lighthouse.org. Web: www.lighthouse.org.
Provides rehabilitation services, professional education, research and advocacy
for people who are blind or partially sighted.

**NATIONAL ASSOCIATION FOR PARENTS OF CHILDREN WITH
VISUAL IMPAIRMENTS**
PO Box 317, Watertown, MA 02471. Tel: 617-972-7441.
Toll-free: 800-562-6265. Fax: 617-972-7444. E-mail: napvi@perkins.org.
Web: www.napvi.org.

Enables parents to find information and resources for their visually impaired children. Also provides leadership, support and training services.

NATIONAL BRAILLE PRESS
88 St Stephen St, Boston, MA 02115. Tel: 617-266-6160.
Toll-free: 888-965-8965. Fax: 617-437-0456. E-mail: contact@nbp.org.
Web: www.nbp.org.
Promotes the literacy of blind children through braille publications.

NATIONAL CONSORTIUM ON DEAF-BLINDNESS
345 N Monmouth Ave, Monmouth, OR 97361. Toll-free: 800-864-9376.
TTY: 800-864-7013. Fax: 503-838-8150. E-mail: info@nationaldb.org.
Web: www.nationaldb.org.
Coordinates and disseminates information on deaf-blindness to parents, teachers and others.

NATIONAL FEDERATION OF THE BLIND
200 E Wells St, Baltimore, MD 21230. Tel: 410-659-9314. Fax: 410-685-5653.
E-mail: pmaurer@nfb.org. Web: www.nfb.org.
Provides advocacy, education, research and technology services for the blind.

NATIONAL INDUSTRIES FOR THE BLIND
1310 Braddock Pl, Alexandria, VA 22314. Tel: 703-310-0500.
E-mail: communications@nib.org. Web: www.nib.org.
Provides training, employment and rehabilitative services for the blind.

PREVENT BLINDNESS AMERICA
211 W Wacker Dr, Ste 1700, Chicago, IL 60606. Tel: 847-843-2020.
Toll-free: 800-331-2020. Fax: 847-843-8458.
E-mail: info@preventblindness.org. Web: www.preventblindness.org.
Provides training, research, screenings and advocacy in an effort to save sight and prevent blindness.

EMOTIONAL DISTURBANCES

AMERICAN ACADEMY OF CHILD AND ADOLESCENT PSYCHIATRY
3615 Wisconsin Ave NW, Washington, DC 20016. Tel: 202-966-7300.
Fax: 202-966-2891. E-mail: ehughes@aacap.org. Web: www.aacap.org.
Promotes understanding of mental illness by distributing information, supporting training and research programs, lobbying elected officials and continuing medical education.

MENTAL HEALTH AMERICA
2001 N Beauregard St, 6th Fl, Alexandria, VA 22311. Tel: 703-684-7722.
Toll-free: 800-969-6642. Fax: 703-684-5968.
E-mail: info@mentalhealthamerica.net. Web: www.mentalhealthamerica.net.
Educates the public about mental health issues, increases access to effective care, promotes research, and provides support for individuals with mental health or substance-abuse problems.

NATIONAL ALLIANCE ON MENTAL ILLNESS
3803 N Fairfax Dr, Ste 100, Arlington, VA 22203. Tel: 703-524-7600.
Toll-free: 800-950-6264. Fax: 703-524-9094. E-mail: danac@nami.org.
Web: www.nami.org.
Works to eradicate mental illness and improve the quality of life of people with mental illnesses through research, education, advocacy and support.

NATIONAL ASSOCIATION OF ANOREXIA NERVOSA
AND ASSOCIATED DISORDERS
PO Box 640, Naperville, IL 60566. Tel: 630-577-1333.
E-mail: anadhelp@anad.org. Web: www.anad.org.
Provides resources and support groups for individuals with eating disorders, promotes research into prevention and treatment, and educates healthcare professionals and the general public.

NATIONAL FEDERATION OF FAMILIES
FOR CHILDREN'S MENTAL HEALTH
9605 Medical Center Dr, Ste 280, Rockville, MA 20850. Tel: 240-403-1901.
Fax: 240-403-1909. E-mail: ffcmh@ffcmh.com. Web: www.ffcmh.org.
Provides national advocacy for children and youth with emotional, behavioral and mental health challenges, and offers leadership and technical assistance to family-run organizations.

PRADER-WILLI SYNDROME ASSOCIATION
8588 Potter Park Dr, Ste 500, Sarasota, FL 34238. Tel: 941-312-0400.
Toll-free: 800-926-4797. Fax: 941-312-0142. E-mail: pwsausa@pwsausa.org.
Web: www.pwsausa.org.
Provides information, education and support services for individuals with Prader-Willi syndrome through research, conferences and publications.

INTELLECTUAL DISABILITIES

ALABAMA COUNCIL FOR DEVELOPMENTAL DISABILITIES
RSA Union Bldg, 100 N Union St, PO Box 301410, Montgomery, AL 36130.
Tel: 334-242-3973. Toll-free: 800-232-2158. Fax: 334-242-0797.
E-mail: debra.florea@mh.alabama.gov. Web: www.acdd.org.
Advocates for Alabama residents who have developmental disabilities.

THE ARC
1825 K St, Ste 1200, Washington, DC 20006. Tel: 202-534-3700.
Toll-free: 800-433-5255. Fax: 202-534-3731. E-mail: info@thearc.org.
Web: www.thearc.org.
Aims to improve support systems, connect families, motivate communities and
influence public policy.

MILE HIGH DOWN SYNDROME ASSOCIATION
3515 S Tamarac Dr, Ste 320, Denver, CO 80237. Tel: 303-797-1699.
Fax: 303-756-6144. E-mail: info@mhdsa.org. Web: www.mhdsa.org.
Provides education, resources and support for individuals with Down syndrome
and their families.

NATIONAL ASSOCIATION FOR DOWN SYNDROME
PO Box 206, Wilmette, IL 60091. Tel: 630-325-9112. E-mail: info@nads.org.
Web: www.nads.org.
Provides direct support, products and publications, conferences and information
for individuals with Down syndrome.

NATIONAL ASSOCIATION FOR THE DUALLY DIAGNOSED
132 Fair St, Kingston, NY 12401. Tel: 845-331-4336. Toll-free: 800-331-5362.
Fax: 845-331-4569. E-mail: info@thenadd.org. Web: www.thenadd.org.
Membership association serving professionals, care providers and families seeks
to promote understanding of and services for individuals with development disabilities and mental health needs.

NATIONAL ASSOCIATION OF STATE DIRECTORS OF
DEVELOPMENTAL DISABILITIES SERVICES
113 Oronoco St, Alexandria, VA 22314. Tel: 703-683-4202. Fax: 703-683-8773.
E-mail: nthaler@nasddds.org. Web: www.nasddds.org.
Assists state agencies in developing effective, efficient services for people with
developmental disabilities.

NATIONAL DOWN SYNDROME CONGRESS
30 Mansell Ct, Ste 108, Roswell, GA 30076. Tel: 770-604-9500.
Toll-free: 800-232-6372. Fax: 770-604-9898. E-mail: info@ndsccenter.org.
Web: www.ndsccenter.org.
Provides information, advocacy and support concerning all aspects of life for
individuals with Down syndrome.

NATIONAL DOWN SYNDROME SOCIETY
666 Broadway, 8th Fl, New York, NY 10012. Tel: 212-460-9330.
Toll-free: 800-221-4602. Fax: 212-979-2873. E-mail: info@ndss.org.
Web: www.ndss.org.
Benefits individuals with Down syndrome and their families through education,
research and advocacy.

PARCA
800 Airport Blvd, Ste 320, Burlingame, CA 94010. Tel: 650-312-0730.
Fax: 650-312-0737. E-mail: parca@parca.org. Web: www.parca.org.
Provides programs, family services and advocacy for children and adults with developmental disabilities.

SHARING DOWN SYNDROME ARIZONA
745 N Gilbert Rd, Ste 124, PMB 273, Gilbert, AZ 85234. Tel: 480-926-6500.
Fax: 480-926-6145. E-mail: gina@sharingds.org. Web: www.sharingds.org.
Educates parents of children with Down syndrome through meetings, speakers, hospital visits and a newsletter.

LEARNING DISABILITIES

ATTENTION DEFICIT DISORDER RESOURCES
223 Tacoma Ave S, Ste 100, Tacoma, WA 98402. Tel: 253-759-5085.
Fax: 253-572-3700. E-mail: office@addresources.org.
Web: www.addresources.org.
Helps individuals with attentional disorders achieve to potential through education, support and networking opportunities.

CHILDREN AND ADULTS WITH
ATTENTION DEFICIT/HYPERACTIVITY DISORDER
8181 Professional Pl, Ste 150, Landover, MD 20785. Tel: 301-306-7070.
Fax: 301-306-7090. Web: www.chadd.org.
Membership organization serves individuals with ADHD and their families by providing information, conducting conferences and advocating for policies.

COUNCIL FOR LEARNING DISABILITIES
11184 Antioch Rd, Box 405, Overland Park, KS 66210. Tel: 913-491-1011.
Fax: 913-491-1012. E-mail: cldinfo@cldinternational.org.
Web: www.cldinternational.org.
Membership organization promotes effective teaching and research to enhance the education and the development of individuals with learning disabilities.

INTERNATIONAL DYSLEXIA ASSOCIATION
40 York Rd, 4th Fl, Baltimore, MD 21204. Tel: 410-296-0232.
Fax: 410-321-5069. E-mail: info@interdys.org. Web: www.interdys.org.
Provides information and referrals, research, advocacy and services for professionals in the field of dyslexia.

LEARNING DISABILITIES ASSOCIATION OF AMERICA
4156 Library Rd, Pittsburgh, PA 15234. Tel: 412-341-1515.
Toll-free: 888-300-6710. Fax: 412-344-0224. E-mail: info@ldaamerica.org.
Web: www.ldaamerica.org.

Provides information, referrals and support to people with learning disabilities. Also holds an annual conference on learning disabilities research.

NATIONAL CENTER FOR LEARNING DISABILITIES
381 Park Ave S, Ste 1401, New York, NY 10016. Tel: 212-545-7510.
Toll-free: 888-575-7373. Fax: 212-545-9665. E-mail: ncld@ncld.org.
Web: www.ncld.org.
Provides information for parents, professionals and individuals with learning disabilities, promotes research and programs, and advocates for educational rights.

ORTHO/NEURO IMPAIRMENTS

ALABAMA HEAD INJURY FOUNDATION
3100 Lorna Rd, Ste 200, Hoover, AL 35216. Tel: 205-823-3818.
Fax: 205-823-4544. E-mail: ahif1@bellsouth.net. Web: www.ahif.org.
Provides information, referrals, support groups and programs for people with traumatic brain injuries.

THE BALANCED MIND FOUNDATION
566 W Lake St, Suite 430, Chicago, IL 60661. Tel: 847-492-8510.
Fax: 847-492-8520. E-mail: info@thebalancedmind.org.
Web: www.thebalancedmind.org.
Provides guidance for parents who are raising children with mood disorders.

BIRTH DEFECT RESEARCH FOR CHILDREN
800 Celebration Ave, Ste 225, Celebration, FL 34747. Tel: 407-566-8304.
E-mail: staff@birthdefects.org. Web: www.birthdefects.org.
Provides information and support for expectant parents and parents of children with birth defects.

BRAIN INJURY ASSOCIATION OF AMERICA
1608 Spring Hill Rd, Ste 110, Vienna, VA 22182. Tel: 703-761-0750.
Toll-free: 800-444-6443. Fax: 703-761-0755. E-mail: info@biausa.org.
Web: www.biausa.org.
Provides information, research, education and advocacy services for those affected by brain injuries.

COMMUNICATION INDEPENDENCE FOR THE NEUROLOGICALLY IMPAIRED
PO Box 263, Manorville, NY 11949. Tel: 631-878-0642. Fax: 631-878-8333.
E-mail: cini@cini.org. Web: www.cini.org.
Disseminates information about communication devices and assistive technologies to people with ALS (Lou Gehrig's disease).

EASTER SEALS
233 S Wacker Dr, Ste 2400, Chicago, IL 60606. Tel: 312-726-6200.
Toll-free: 800-221-6827. TTY: 312-726-4258. Fax: 312-726-1494.
Web: www.easter-seals.org.
Offers various services, among them camps, therapy, rehabilitation and job train-
ing, to people with disabilities.

EPILEPSY FOUNDATION OF AMERICA
8301 Professional Pl, Landover, MD 20785. Tel: 301-459-3700.
Toll-free: 800-332-1000. Fax: 301-577-2684. E-mail: contactus@efa.org.
Web: www.epilepsyfoundation.org.
Works to prevent, control and cure epilepsy through research, education, advocacy and services, and to ensure that people with seizures are able to participate
in all life experiences.

LOWE SYNDROME ASSOCIATION
PO Box 864346, Plano, TX 75086. Tel: 972-733-1338.
Web: www.lowesyndrome.org.
Provides information and supports research on Lowe syndrome.

THE MAGIC FOUNDATION
6645 W North Ave, Oak Park, IL 60302. Tel: 708-383-0808.
Toll-free: 800-362-4423. Fax: 708-383-0899.
E-mail: dianne@magicfoundation.org. Web: www.magicfoundation.org.
Provides support services for the families of children afflicted with various
chronic and critical disorders, syndromes and diseases that affect a child's
growth.

MUSCULAR DYSTROPHY ASSOCIATION
3300 E Sunrise Dr, Tucson, AZ 85718. Tel: 520-529-2000.
Toll-free: 800-572-1717. Fax: 520-529-5300. E-mail: mda@mdausa.org.
Web: www.mda.org.
Combats muscular dystrophy, ALS and related neuromuscular diseases through
research, comprehensive medical and support services, and professional and
public health education.

NATIONAL ATAXIA FOUNDATION
2600 Fernbrook Ln, Ste 119, Minneapolis, MN 55447. Tel: 763-553-0020.
Fax: 763-553-0167. E-mail: naf@ataxia.org. Web: www.ataxia.org.
Works to improve the lives of people affected by ataxia through support, education and research.

NATIONAL HEMOPHILIA FOUNDATION
116 W 32nd St, 11th Fl, New York, NY 10001. Tel: 212-328-3700.
Fax: 212-328-3777. E-mail: egoody@hemophilia.org.
Web: www.hemophilia.org.

Works to find treatments and cures for bleeding and clotting disorders through research funding, education, advocacy and research.

NATIONAL MULTIPLE SCLEROSIS SOCIETY
733 3rd Ave, 3rd Fl, New York, NY 10017. Tel: 212-986-3240.
Toll-free: 800-344-4867. Fax: 212-986-7981. E-mail: info@msnyc.org.
Web: www.nationalmssociety.org.
Supports multiple sclerosis research, offers services to individuals with the disease, provides professional education and furthers advocacy efforts.

NATIONAL ORGANIZATION ON FETAL ALCOHOL SYNDROME
1200 Eton Ct NW, 3rd Fl, Washington, DC 20007. Tel: 202-785-4585.
Toll-free: 800-666-6327. Fax: 202-466-6456. E-mail: information@nofas.org.
Web: www.nofas.org.
Increases public awareness of fetal alcohol spectrum disorders, develops prevention and education programs, and provides information and referrals to people suffering from FASD and their families.

NATIONAL SPINAL CORD INJURY ASSOCIATION
75-20 Astoria Blvd, Jackson Heights, NY 11370. Tel: 718-803-3782.
Web: www.spinalcord.org.
Provides a support network for individuals with spinal cord injuries and raises awareness through education and publications.

NATIONAL TAY-SACHS AND ALLIED DISEASES ASSOCIATION
2001 Beacon St, Ste 204, Boston, MA 02135. Toll-free: 800-906-8723.
Fax: 617-277-0134. E-mail: info@ntsad.org. Web: www.ntsad.org.
Dedicated to the treatment and prevention of Tay-Sachs and other genetic diseases through family support, research, screenings, education and advocacy.

OSTEOGENESIS IMPERFECTA FOUNDATION
804 W Diamond Ave, Ste 210, Gaithersburg, MD 20878. Tel: 301-947-0083.
Toll-free: 800-981-2663. Fax: 301-947-0456. E-mail: bonelink@oif.org.
Web: www.oif.org.
Hosts support groups for people with osteogenesis imperfecta, funds research and educational programs, and raises awareness of the disease.

REHABILITATION INTERNATIONAL
25 E 21st St, 4th Fl, New York, NY 10010. Tel: 212-420-1500.
Fax: 212-505-0871. E-mail: ri@riglobal.org. Web: www.riglobal.org.
Global network of people with disabilities, government organizations, service providers, researchers and advocates works to improve rehabilitation and other services for the disabled.

SPINA BIFIDA ASSOCIATION OF AMERICA
4590 MacArthur Blvd NW, Ste 250, Washington, DC 20007. Tel: 202-944-3285.
Toll-free: 800-621-3141. Fax: 202-944-3295. E-mail: sbaa@sbaa.org.
Web: www.sbaa.org.
A network of chapters working to improve the lives of children with spina bifida
through education, advocacy, research and services.

TOURETTE SYNDROME ASSOCIATION
42-40 Bell Blvd, Bayside, NY 11361. Tel: 718-224-2999. Fax: 718-279-9596.
E-mail: ts@tsa-usa.org. Web: www.tsa-usa.org.
Offers referrals and resources to people with Tourette's syndrome, while also
raising awareness through education and publications.

TUBEROUS SCLEROSIS ALLIANCE
801 Roeder Rd, Ste 750, Silver Spring, MD 20910. Tel: 301-562-9890.
Toll-free: 800-225-6872. Fax: 301-562-9870. E-mail: info@tsalliance.org.
Web: www.tsalliance.org.
Provides information and advocacy and works toward finding a cure for tuber-
ous sclerosis while improving the lives of those affected.

UNITED CEREBRAL PALSY ASSOCIATIONS
1825 K St NW, Ste 600, Washington, DC 20006. Tel: 202-776-0406.
Toll-free: 800-872-5827. Fax: 202-776-0414. E-mail: info@ucp.org.
Web: www.ucp.org.
Advocates for people with cerebral palsy and other disabilities through research,
education and support services.

WILLIAMS SYNDROME ASSOCIATION
570 Kirts Blvd, Ste 223, Troy, MI 48084. Tel: 248-244-2229.
Toll-free: 800-806-1871. Fax: 248-244-2230.
E-mail: info@williams-syndrome.org. Web: www.williams-syndrome.org.
Supports research, develops educational materials, and holds conferences and
events pertaining to Williams syndrome.

SPEECH AND HEARING DISORDERS

ALEXANDER GRAHAM BELL ASSOCIATION
FOR THE DEAF AND HARD OF HEARING
3417 Volta Pl NW, Washington, DC 20007. Tel: 202-337-5220.
TTY: 202-337-5221. Fax: 202-337-8314. E-mail: info@agbell.org.
Web: www.agbell.org.
A support network and advocacy group that provides publications, outreach,
training, scholarships and financial aid for people with hearing loss.

AMERICAN HEARING RESEARCH FOUNDATION
8 S Michigan Ave, Ste 1205, Chicago, IL 60603. Tel: 312-726-9670.
Fax: 312-726-9695. Web: www.american-hearing.org.
Funds research and educates the public about hearing loss.

AMERICAN SOCIETY FOR DEAF CHILDREN
800 Florida Ave NE, Ste 2047, Washington, DC 20002. Toll-free: 800-942-2732.
Fax: 410-795-0965. E-mail: asdc@deafchildren.org.
Web: www.deafchildren.org.
Supports and educates families of deaf and hard-of-hearing children and advocates for appropriate programs and services.

CLEFT PALATE FOUNDATION
1504 E Franklin St, Ste 102, Chapel Hill, NC 27514. Tel: 919-933-9044.
Toll-free: 800-243-5338. Fax: 919-933-9604. E-mail: info@cleftline.org.
Web: www.cleftline.org.
Provides information, research grants and resources for people with craniofacial deformities.

CONFERENCE OF EDUCATIONAL ADMINISTRATORS OF SCHOOLS AND PROGRAMS FOR THE DEAF
PO Box 1778, St Augustine, FL 32085. Tel: 904-810-5200. Fax: 904-810-5525.
E-mail: nationaloffice@ceasd.org. Web: www.ceasd.org.
Offers accreditation and supports the development of schools and programs for the deaf and the hard of hearing.

HEARING HEALTH FOUNDATION
363 7th Ave, 10th Fl, New York, NY 10001. Tel: 212-257-6140.
Toll-free: 866-454-3924. TTY: 888-435-6104. Fax: 212-257-6139.
E-mail: info@hearinghealthfoundation.org.
Web: www.hearinghealthfoundation.org.
Awards funding for basic and clinical research in hearing and balance science.

HEARING LOSS ASSOCIATION OF AMERICA
7910 Woodmont Ave, Ste 1200, Bethesda, MD 20814. Tel: 301-657-2248.
Fax: 301-913-9413. Web: www.hearingloss.org.
Provides deaf and hard-of-hearing people with tools for self-help, educates the public and advocates for communication access.

INTERNATIONAL ASSOCIATION OF LARYNGECTOMEES
925B Peachtree St NE, Ste 316, Atlanta, GA 30309. Toll-free: 866-425-3678.
E-mail: ialed@theial.com. Web: www.theial.com.
Supports the rehabilitation of laryngectomees through the exchange of ideas and the dissemination of information to member clubs and the public.

NATIONAL ASSOCIATION OF THE DEAF
8630 Fenton St, Ste 820, Silver Spring, MD 20910. Tel: 301-587-1788.
TTY: 301-587-1789. Fax: 301-587-1791. Web: www.nad.org.
Advocates for the deaf and the hard of hearing on such issues as accessibility,
education, employment, healthcare, rehabilitation, technology, communications
and transportation.

**NATIONAL INSTITUTE ON DEAFNESS
AND OTHER COMMUNICATION DISORDERS**
31 Center Dr, MSC 2320, Bethesda, MD 20892. Tel: 301-496-7243.
Fax: 301-402-0018. E-mail: nidcdinfo@nidcd.nih.gov.
Web: www.nidcd.nih.gov.
Conducts and supports research in the processes of hearing, balance, smell, taste,
voice, speech and language.

STUTTERING FOUNDATION OF AMERICA
1805 Moriah Woods Blvd, Ste 3, Memphis, TN 38117. Tel: 901-761-0343.
Toll-free: 800-992-9392. Fax: 901-761-0484. E-mail: info@stutteringhelp.org.
Web: www.stutteringhelp.org.
Provides resources, services and support for individuals who stutter.

TELECOMMUNICATIONS FOR THE DEAF
8630 Fenton St, Ste 121, Silver Spring, MD 20910. Tel: 301-563-9112.
TTY: 301-589-3006. Fax: 301-589-3797. E-mail: info@tdiforaccess.org.
Web: www.tdiforaccess.org.
Advocates for equal access to telecommunications for people who are deaf, hard
of hearing or deaf-blind.

PROFESSIONAL ASSOCIATIONS

**AMERICAN ACADEMY FOR CEREBRAL PALSY AND
DEVELOPMENTAL MEDICINE**
555 E Wells St, Ste 1100, Milwaukee, WI 53202. Tel: 414-918-3014.
Fax: 414-276-2146. E-mail: info@aacpdm.org. Web: www.aacpdm.org.
Works to promote education and research into cerebral palsy and other develop-
mental disorders.

AMERICAN ACADEMY OF OPHTHALMOLOGY
PO Box 7424, San Francisco, CA 94120. Tel: 415-561-8500.
Fax: 415-561-8533. E-mail: comm@aao.org. Web: www.aao.org.
Association of ophthalmologists that provides education, information and advo-
cacy services.

AMERICAN ACADEMY OF PEDIATRICS
141 NW Point Blvd, Elk Grove Village, IL 60007. Tel: 847-434-4000.
Toll-free: 800-433-9016. Fax: 847-434-8000. Web: www.aap.org.
Organization of primary-care pediatricians, pediatric medical subspecialists and pediatric surgical specialists conducts research and promotes continuing education through courses, seminars and publications.

AMERICAN ACADEMY OF PHYSICAL MEDICINE AND REHABILITATION
9700 W Bryn Mawr Ave, Ste 200, Rosemont, IL 60018. Tel: 847-737-6000.
Fax: 847-737-6001. E-mail: info@aapmr.org. Web: www.aapmr.org.
Membership association for physical medicine and rehabilitation physicians.

AMERICAN ASSOCIATION OF CHILDREN'S RESIDENTIAL CENTERS
11700 W Lake Park Dr, Milwaukee, WI 53224. Toll-free: 877-332-2272.
Fax: 877-362-2272. E-mail: info@aacrc-dc.org. Web: www.aacrc-dc.org.
Conducts clinical conferences, provides continuing education opportunities and encourages research on therapeutic living environments for children and adolescents with behavioral health disorders.

AMERICAN COUNSELING ASSOCIATION
5999 Stevenson Ave, Alexandria, VA 22304. Tel: 703-823-9800.
Toll-free: 800-347-6647. Fax: 703-823-0252. E-mail: cneiman@counseling.org.
Web: www.counseling.org.
Offers leadership training, publications, continuing education opportunities and advocacy services to counseling professionals.

AMERICAN DANCE THERAPY ASSOCIATION
10632 Little Patuxent Pky, Ste 108, Columbia, MD 21044. Tel: 410-997-4040.
Fax: 410-997-4048. Web: www.adta.org.
Promotes high standards of professional education and competence in the field of dance (or movement) therapy.

AMERICAN MUSIC THERAPY ASSOCIATION
8455 Colesville Rd, Ste 1000, Silver Spring, MD 20910. Tel: 301-589-3300.
Fax: 301-589-5175. Web: www.musictherapy.org.
Works to advance education, training, professional standards, credentials and research in support of the music therapy profession.

AMERICAN OCCUPATIONAL THERAPY ASSOCIATION
4720 Montgomery Ln, Ste 200, Bethesda, MD 20814. Tel: 301-652-2682.
TTY: 800-377-8555. Fax: 301-652-7711. Web: www.aota.org.
Professional organization of occupational therapy practitioners, assistants and students.

AMERICAN ORTHOPSYCHIATRIC ASSOCIATION
c/o Clemson University, IFNL, 225 S Pleasantburg Dr, Ste B-11, Greenville, SC 29607. Tel: 864-250-4622. Fax: 864-250-4668.
E-mail: orthocontact@aoatoday.com. Web: www.amerortho.org.
Provides opportunities for collaborative study, research and information exchange among individuals engaged in preventive, treatment and advocacy approaches to mental health.

AMERICAN PSYCHOLOGICAL ASSOCIATION
750 1st St NE, Washington, DC 20002. Tel: 202-336-5500.
Toll-free: 800-374-2721. TTY: 202-336-6123. Fax: 202-336-5997.
Web: www.apa.org.
Establishes standards of psychological ethics and conduct, promotes research and education, and disseminates information through meetings, reports and publications.

AMERICAN PUBLIC HUMAN SERVICES ASSOCIATION
1133 19th St NW, Ste 400, Washington, DC 20036. Tel: 202-682-0100.
Fax: 202-204-0071. E-mail: memberservice@aphsa.org. Web: www.aphsa.org.
Organization of state and local public human service agencies that develops and promotes policies to improve public health.

AMERICAN SCHOOL HEALTH ASSOCIATION
4340 East West Hwy, Ste 403, Bethesda, MD 20814. Tel: 301-652-8072.
Fax: 301-652-8077. E-mail: info@ashaweb.org. Web: www.ashaweb.org.
Promotes collaboration, development, advocacy and research for health professionals who work at schools.

AMERICAN SOCIETY FOR ADOLESCENT PSYCHIATRY
PO Box 570218, Dallas, TX 75357. Tel: 972-613-0985.
E-mail: adpsych@aol.com. Web: www.adolpsych.org.
Membership organization dedicated to education development and advocacy for adolescent psychiatry professionals.

AMERICAN SPEECH-LANGUAGE-HEARING ASSOCIATION
2200 Research Blvd, Rockville, MD 20850. Tel: 301-296-5700.
Toll-free: 800-638-8255. TTY: 301-296-5650. Fax: 301-296-8580.
Web: www.asha.org.
A professional, scientific and credentialing organization for speech, language and hearing professionals that also advocates for people with communicational disorders.

AMERICAN THERAPEUTIC RECREATION ASSOCIATION
629 N Main St, Hattiesburg, MS 39401. Tel: 601-450-2872. Fax: 601-582-3354.
E-mail: national@atra-online.com. Web: www.atra-online.com.
A national membership organization for recreational therapists focusing on professional practices, advocacy, networking and education.

ASSOCIATION FOR EDUCATION AND REHABILITATION OF THE BLIND AND VISUALLY IMPAIRED

1703 N Beauregard St, Ste 440, Alexandria, VA 22311. Tel: 703-671-4500.
Fax: 703-671-6391. E-mail: aer@aerbvi.org. Web: www.aerbvi.org.
Supports professionals working in all phases of education and rehabilitation of
the blind and the visually impaired through continuing education, scholarships,
publications and advocacy.

CLOSING THE GAP

526 Main St, PO Box 68, Henderson, MN 56044. Tel: 507-248-3294.
Fax: 507-248-3810. E-mail: info@closingthegap.com.
Web: www.closingthegap.com.
Promotes the use of computer technology for people with special needs.

COUNCIL FOR EXCEPTIONAL CHILDREN

2900 Crystal Dr, Ste 1000, Arlington, VA 22202. Tel: 703-620-3660.
Toll-free: 888-232-7733. TTY: 866-915-5000. Fax: 703-264-9494.
E-mail: service@cec.sped.org. Web: www.cec.sped.org.
Lobbies for government policies, sets professional standards, promotes continuing
education and advocates for special-needs and gifted students.

COUNCIL OF ADMINISTRATORS OF SPECIAL EDUCATION

101 Katelyn Cir, Ste E, Warner Robins, GA 31088. Tel: 478-333-6892.
Fax: 478-333-2453. E-mail: lpurcell@casecec.org. Web: www.casecec.org.
Provides leadership and support for special educators by shaping policies and
practices that impact the quality of education.

COUNCIL OF AMERICAN INSTRUCTORS OF THE DEAF

PO Box 377, Bedford, TX 76095. Tel: 817-354-8414. TTY: 817-354-8414.
E-mail: caid@swbell.net. Web: www.caid.org.
Serves teachers, administrators, educational interpreters, residential personnel
and other professionals involved in the education of the deaf.

NATIONAL ASSOCIATION OF COUNCILS ON DEVELOPMENTAL DISABILITIES

1825 K St NW, Ste 600, Washington, DC 20006. Tel: 202-506-5813.
Fax: 202-506-5846. E-mail: info@nacdd.org. Web: www.nacdd.org.
Provides support and assistance for member councils in advocating for people
with disabilities.

NATIONAL ASSOCIATION OF SPECIAL EDUCATION TEACHERS

1250 Connecticut Ave NW, Ste 200, Washington, DC 20036.
Toll-free: 800-754-4421. Fax: 800-424-0371. E-mail: info@naset.org.
Web: www.naset.org.
Membership organization for special education teachers conducts conferences,
offers career services and releases publications.

NATIONAL BRAILLE ASSOCIATION
95 Allens Creek Rd, Bldg 1, Ste 202, Rochester, NY 14618. Tel: 585-427-8260.
Fax: 585-427-0263. Web: www.nationalbraille.org.
Provides continuing education for those who prepare braille, and disseminates braille materials to the blind and the visually impaired.

NATIONAL EDUCATION ASSOCIATION
1201 16th St NW, Washington, DC 20036. Tel: 202-833-4000.
Fax: 202-822-7974. Web: www.nea.org.
Employee organization works to advance public education from preschool through university graduate programs.

REGISTRY OF INTERPRETERS FOR THE DEAF
333 Commerce St, Alexandria, VA 22314. Tel: 703-838-0030.
TTY: 703-838-0459. Fax: 703-838-0454. E-mail: cmckenna@rid.org.
Web: www.rid.org.
Provides training, certification and ethical standards for professional interpreters who work with the deaf and the hard of hearing.

SOCIETY FOR ADOLESCENT HEALTH AND MEDICINE
111 Deer Lake Rd, Ste 100, Deerfield, IL 60015. Tel: 847-753-5226.
Fax: 847-480-9282. E-mail: info@adolescenthealth.org.
Web: www.adolescenthealth.org.
Raises awareness of adolescent health issues through education, research, advocacy and clinical services.

RECREATIONAL ORGANIZATIONS

AMERICAN ASSOCIATION OF ADAPTED SPORTS PROGRAMS
PO Box 451047, Atlanta, GA 31145. Tel: 404-294-0070. Fax: 404-294-5758.
E-mail: sports@adaptedsports.org. Web: www.adaptedsports.org.
Builds interscholastic sports leagues for students with disabilities. Develops training and certificate programs for coaches, officials and coordinators.

NATIONAL ARTS AND DISABILITY CENTER
Tarjan Ctr, 11075 Santa Monica Blvd, Ste 200, Los Angeles, CA 90025.
Tel: 310-825-5054. Fax: 310-794-1143. E-mail: bstoffmacher@mednet.ucla.edu.
Web: www.semel.ucla.edu/nadc.
An information and training center that promotes the inclusion of people with disabilities in the arts community through artist showcases, publications, research and technical assistance.

NATIONAL DISABILITY SPORTS ALLIANCE
25 W Independence Way, Kingston, RI 02881. Tel: 401-792-7130.
Fax: 401-792-7132. E-mail: info@ndsaonline.org.
Web: www.nationaldisabilitysportsalliance.webs.com.
Formulates rules, implements policies, coordinates national championships and disseminates information on various sports for athletes with cerebral palsy, traumatic brain injuries and other disabilities.

SPECIAL OLYMPICS
1133 19th St NW, Washington, DC 20036. Tel: 202-628-3630.
Toll-free: 800-700-8585. Fax: 202-824-0200. E-mail: info@specialolympics.org.
Web: www.specialolympics.org.
Offers year-round training and athletic competition in a variety of sports for children and adults with intellectual disabilities.

UNITED STATES ASSOCIATION FOR BLIND ATHLETES
1 Olympic Plz, Colorado Springs, CO 80909. Tel: 719-866-3224.
Fax: 719-866-3400. E-mail: msimpson@usaba.org. Web: www.usaba.org.
Works to increase sports programming for people with visual impairments through support for athletes and coaches, sports camps and event management.

USA DEAF SPORTS FEDERATION
PO Box 910338, Lexington, KY 40591. Tel: 605-367-5760.
TTY: 605-367-5761. Fax: 605-782-8441. E-mail: homeoffice@usdeafsports.org.
Web: www.usdeafsports.org.
Coordinates annual athletic competitions for deaf and hard-of-hearing athletes.

VSA: THE INTERNATIONAL ORGANIZATION ON ARTS AND DISABILITY
John F Kennedy Center for the Performing Arts, 2700 F St NW, Washington, DC 20566. Tel: 202-467-4600. Toll-free: 800-444-1324.
E-mail: vsainfo@kennedy-center.org.
Web: www.kennedy-center.org/education/vsa.
Administers arts education programs for people with disabilities and supports artists with disabilities.

WHEELCHAIR & AMBULATORY SPORTS, USA
PO Box 5266, Kendall Park, NJ 08824. Tel: 732-266-2634. Fax: 732-355-6500.
Web: www.wsusa.org.
Organizes wheelchair athletic competitions and provides other services for wheelchair athletes.

INDEX
OF PROGRAMS

INDEX OF PROGRAMS

Schools are referenced by page number. Boldface page numbers refer to the optional Featured Schools section of schools that subscribe for space. Cross-references to Featured Schools also appear at the end of the free descriptive listings of subscribing schools.

362 **Guide to Private Special Education**

Yes, send me the most recent editions of:

Title	Price	Qty	Total
The Handbook of Private Schools (Hardcover)	$99.00		
Guide to Private Special Education (Paperback)	$32.00		
Guide to Summer Programs (Paperback)	$27.00		
Guide to Summer Programs (Hardcover)	$45.00		

Order Amount	Shipping	
$1-$50	$6.95	Subtotal
$51-$200	$15.95	US shipping (*see rates at left*)
$201-$300	$19.95	**TOTAL**
$300+	6% of total	

☐ Check or money order enclosed (payable on a US bank)

☐ Bill me (organizations only)

☐ Visa   ☐ MasterCard

Card # _____ Exp. Date _____

3-digit Security Code _____

Card Holder_____

Signature _____

Charge on your statement will read "ALY*ALLOYEDUCATION"

First Name   Last Name

Company Name

Street Address (no P.O. Boxes, please)

City   State   Zip

Country   Postal Code

E-mail _____

Daytime phone _____ GPSE13

PORTER SARGENT HANDBOOKS
A division of Carnegie Communications
2 LAN Dr   Ste 100   Westford, MA 01886   USA
Tel: 978-842-2812   Fax: 978-692-2304
info@portersargent.com   www.portersargent.com